©Disney

Anneke van Doorninck

To
Anneka
with Best Wishes
and good Reading

Jan. '0?

THE EMIL AND KATHLEEN SICK LECTURE-BOOK SERIES
IN WESTERN HISTORY AND BIOGRAPHY

THE EMIL AND KATHLEEN SICK LECTURE-BOOK SERIES
IN WESTERN HISTORY AND BIOGRAPHY

Under the provisions of a Fund established by the children of Mr. and Mrs. Emil Sick, whose deep interest in the history and culture of the American West was inspired by their own experience in the region, distinguished scholars are brought to the University of Washington to deliver public lectures based on original research in the fields of Western history and biography. The terms of the gift also provide for the publication by the University of Washington Press of the books resulting from the research upon which the lectures are based. This book is the sixth volume in the series.

The Great Columbia Plain: A Historical Geography, 1805–1910,
by Donald W. Meinig

Mills and Markets: A History of the Pacific Coast Lumber Industry to 1900,
by Thomas R. Cox

Radical Heritage: Labor, Socialism, and Reform in Washington and British Columbia, 1885–1917, by Carlos A. Schwantes

The Battle for Butte: Mining and Politics on the Northern Frontier, 1864–1906,
by Michael P. Malone

The Forging of a Black Community: Seattle's Central District, from 1870 through the Civil Rights Era, by Quintard Taylor

Warren G. Magnuson and the Shaping of Twentieth-Century America,
by Shelby Scates

Warren G. Magnuson

and the Shaping of

Twentieth-Century America

Shelby Scates

UNIVERSITY OF WASHINGTON PRESS

Seattle and London

Library of Congress Cataloging-in-Publication Data

Scates, Shelby.
     Warren G. Magnuson and the shaping of twentieth-century America /
Shelby Scates.
        p.   cm.—(Emil and Kathleen Sick lecture-book series in
western history and biography)
     Includes index.
     ISBN 0-295-97631-4 (acid-free paper)
     1. Magnuson, Warren Grant, 1905–1989.   2. Legislators—United
States—Biography.   3. United States. Congress. Senate—Biography.
4. United States—Politics and government—20th century.   I. Title.
II. Series
E840.8.M343S33   1997
328.73'092
[B]—DC21   97-24392
                                                                CIP

The paper used in this publication meets the minimum requirements of American National Standards for Information Sciences—Permanence of Paper for
Printed Library Materials, ANSI A39.48-1984.

To Jermaine Magnuson and the "Bumblebees"—

keepers of the flame, transmitters of the lamp

Contents

Preface

To the casual observer, Senator Warren Magnuson dropped a lot of false leads about his character and competency in the last twenty years of his forty-nine-year political career. From a distance, he looked too lackadaisical, even lazy, certainly uninspiring. Yet his bills kept passing into laws reshaping American society and the Pacific Northwest landscape. Journalists watching the legislator from close range saw another Magnuson, a master at work on his art. I was one such, and this gap in perceptions enhanced a question about the man: how (and why) did he get so good (or so bad)? This biography derives from that question.

Modest to a degree almost unknown in politicians of the late television age, Magnuson didn't make a lot of noise about either himself or his work. To the end he resisted requests for a detailed recounting of his life and times, although he did give a lengthy report on his friendship and working relations with Lyndon Johnson to the Johnson Library at the University of Texas.

Instead, the man had to be found in his papers at the University of Washington Library and through newspapers and books in the Washington State Library in Olympia, and finally through interviews with his friends and associates: in sum, through research. Wherewithal for this came from a grant by the Burlington Northern Foundation for which the author is grateful. I trust future generations will share this gratitude. Don Ellegood, the wise and delightful director emeritus of the University of Washington Press, pushed the project and kept the writer inspired. More help and encouragement came from University of Washington professors emeritus Tom Pressly and Brewster Denny and from Stimson Bullitt, himself the writer of a classic study of modern American politics and a piercing autobiography. Professors Pressly and Richard Kirkendall of the University of Washington and George Packard of the Johns Hopkins School of International Studies were gracious and thorough critics of the book's early draft, sparing the reader more errors of fact and emphasis than the author dares admit. Karyl Winn and Gary Lundell of the UW Library archives and Gayle Palmer and Vince Kueter of the Washington State Library were more than helpful in my pursuit of books and papers. They were tolerant of an overly impatient interloper in the world of academia. Arlene Seidel, clerk of the Senate Commerce Committee, generously shared time, office space, and committee records. Joe Ortiz of Twentieth Century-Fox International directed an innocent pilgrim toward an understanding of Hollywood's all-powerful studio bosses, now passé.

Mrs. Nancy Hevly, my longtime colleague on the *Seattle Post-Intelligencer*, was merely invaluable to this project as an editor and fellow fact-miner in the volumes of Magnuson papers scrupulously catalogued and stored in the archives of the UW Library.

In the last analysis, however, only the writer remains accountable to the reader for the facts and judgments of this biography.

Shelby Scates, Seattle, November 1996

Warren G. Magnuson
and the Shaping of
Twentieth-Century America

CHAPTER 1

Seattle, May 24, 1989

The funeral mourners went down from the grand Episcopalian cathedral in Seattle to the northeast side of Capitol Hill, where the wake was arranged in a large mansion smelling of May blossoms. They came to this second celebration to tell "Maggie" stories.

"Maggie," Warren Grant Magnuson, the individual most responsible for the shape and prosperity of the Pacific Northwest, was dead after eighty-four years of joy, hard living, and legislation that also helped define twentieth-century America by increasing civil rights, mandating corporate accountability, and funding medical research. The mighty and the lowly, not a godly mix, had filled St. Mark's great hall to witness his last parade in a coffin borne by ten pallbearers, "Bumblebees," members of Senator Magnuson's staff in the last decades of his fifty-year political career.[1] No other legislator from west of the Mississippi in this century, save perhaps a mentor, Sam Rayburn, or his friend President Lyndon Johnson, could match his achievements. The difference from these great legislators, the consumer crusader Ralph Nader has noted dryly, was that Magnuson did not boast of his achievements.[2] He let his record speak for itself and that record, like his name, carried heft.

The funeral had been a sober church ceremony for one accustomed to a cup and a laugh, until the Reverend Lowell E. Knutson, a Lutheran minister, said that "Maggie will get few words of praise for religious piety." Muted laughter interrupted. Maggie was not a man for prayer breakfasts, even less for hypocrisy.

Magnuson had taken care of the little guys, the working stiffs, yet never failed the big guys of the downtown Rainier and University Clubs, if it served the broader interests of the people. He was a liberal determined to endure, a democrat confident that capitalism could flourish, given government help, and thus best serve the country.

Dorothy Bullitt, widow of Alexander Scott Bullitt, sat upright, stone-faced, during the funeral service that marked the end of a political alliance that began with Magnuson's career in 1928. The balance of a generation that propagated the New Deal, along with their private interests, was dead and gone: Scott Bullitt, Saul Haas, Homer T. Bone, Joseph Drumheller, William O. Douglas, Howard MacGowan, Bill Edris,

3

Joe Gottstein, Harry Truman, Lyndon Johnson, Sam Rayburn, Nick Bez, Henry M. Jackson, William Stern, Croil Hunter.

Tom Foley, an aide to Senator Jackson before gaining his own seat in Congress from Spokane, left a leadership crisis in Washington, D.C., to deliver the main eulogy. He would return to the Capitol and within days become Speaker of the House of Representatives in place of the resigned Jim Wright of Texas. But Foley would not leave until after the wake. He had his share of stories to tell.

They spoke in the church in celebration of Magnuson's achievements: Senators Daniel Inouye, Mark Hatfield, Ted Stevens, Brock Adams, and Congressman Norm Dicks, himself a Bumblebee before moving to a seat in Congress. There wasn't time, and enough memory, to tell all of Magnuson's accomplishments. These ranged from primitive versions of Social Security and unemployment compensation, engineered through Washington's state legislature in 1933 in advance of Franklin Roosevelt's New Deal measures, to his passage of bills to protect consumers and marine mammals and to finance medical research. Almost forgotten was his irreplaceable legislative skill in the passage of President Kennedy's civil rights legislation, which altered the nation's conception and practice of property rights in order to expand human rights. It was not mentioned.

How does one describe the work of an artist, even one humble and familiar as "Maggie"? We admire and marvel when we watch a natural, a Babe Ruth at baseball or a Horowitz at Chopin. If they are popular, we weave stories around them and make legends of them.

Like Magnuson, F. Scott Fitzgerald's tragic American Jay Gatsby emerged from rather uncertain origins in sere North Dakota to chase the dreams that come with the great American promise of a classless, mobile society. Gatsby failed. At the end, says Fitzgerald's fictional narrator, "He had come a long way and his dream must have seemed so close that he could hardly fail to grasp it. He did not know that it was already behind him, somewhere back in the vast obscurity . . . where the dark fields of the Republic rolled on under the night."[3]

What the eulogies in St. Mark's, and the stories at his wake, suggested was that Magnuson's dreams came true. The dark fields of North Dakota, and the Jazz Age of America's 1920s, were prelude to the magnificent achievements in American politics—acts that employed democratic legislative power to increase the health and welfare of average Americans. Such was Magnuson's striving. Gatsby's aim, his "green light" in Fitzgerald's metaphor, was social status to overcome the poverty of his origins. He was for a few months, and then in his mind forever, "an Oggsford man." Attainment of the beautiful, careless woman, Daisy

Buchanan, was the crystallization of Gatsby's dream, the promise of the green light.

Magnuson had more accessible goals: the pleasure of poker and Hollywood starlets, his paintings, the dining room of Seattle's Olympic Hotel or Vito's Restaurant on First Hill, the swift trains devouring the plains he had left behind between Washington, D.C., Seattle, and Los Angeles. He would never seek, probably could not have attained, admission to Seattle's University Club, the peak of social acceptance in the city's downtown establishment. He could laugh at the irony of a club whose members, titans of business and finance, he had helped enrich. Power did not inflame or corrupt Maggie. It did serve as a tool for his dreams of altruism and his extravagant personal appetites. Gatsby's escape from North Dakota and his vehicle to pursue the American dream was bootlegging. Magnuson made extra money as a congressman through deals that would in the 1990s be condemned as conflicts of interest—but not so in his time. Neither the fictional Gatsby nor the flesh and blood Maggie was venal. They had bigger, more dangerous, dreams. Gatsby's failed him. Magnuson, most fortunate in the timing of his career, succeeded. He was a magnificent American.

At the end of the wake at the home of Betty Salter, widow of John Salter, the astute aide to Henry Jackson, Magnuson was as much a legend as a reality, beloved but for new generations somewhat remote. The Maggie stories, a genre of their own, bridged the living and the legend. If not revealing the real Magnuson, they reflected the kindly man the narrators had known. The stories gave common ground for this tribal celebration of Washington State politics. Twice told, thrice told, no matter. Many were even factual. They came from mourner after mourner crowded inside the Salter mansion overlooking Portage Bay. Maggie would have loved it.

Wine flowed along with talk. Finally, the crowd overflowed into a garden on the side of the hill. Congressmen Foley and Adams; the senator's brilliant administrative assistants Stan Barer and Jerry Grinstein; the scholar Brewster Denny, descendant of Seattle's first, nonaboriginal, family; Ancil Payne, the television executive; the skilled state legislators August Mardesich, Robert Schaefer, and John L. O'Brien; a few newsmen. It takes a pro to know a pro. They retold his malapropisms: "Joe Cauliflower" for President Johnson's aide Joe Califano; "Average Bundy" for the excessively pompous U.S. Olympics Committee chairman, Avery Brundage. From the lips of a whimsical Magnuson came "Dag Hammerschlog" for U.N. Secretary-General Dag Hammarskjöld, and simply "Poopidoo" for the imperious French President Georges Pompidou. Wilbur Mills, the powerful House Ways and Means Committee chairman, came out like the other Wright brother, "Orville." Magnuson may have learned this wordplay as a youth from a Norwegian janitor with whom he had "convinsations" at his uncle's cafe-bar in Moorhead, Minnesota.

Taking a left-handed poke at zealous environmentalists as they shot down Boeing's Supersonic Transport, Magnuson intoned: "We can't all live at Walden's pond. . . . Even Walden only lived there two years."

He knew better. His early writings are models of syntax, grammar, and, of all things, spelling. He also knew the delight he afforded by dumbing down. He knew, like a congressional contemporary, Mo Udall, and a model, Abe Lincoln, the value of a good story. Gerald Hoeck told one from Maggie's days as the King County (Seattle) prosecutor, about a murder trial with a reluctant witness, a Native American from Alaska:

"When she refused to speak, I kept asking her if she hadn't been subpoenaed as a witness and brought to Seattle by a deputy sheriff," said Maggie. "The woman wouldn't answer until, finally, ordered to do so by the judge she admitted, 'Yes, that sheriff subpoenaed me twice, once in Juneau and once on the boat to Seattle.'"

William Prochnau, a former *Seattle Times* reporter and Magnuson aide, remembered Maggie's recollections on the Latin American military. Straight-faced he said, "all their generals with their medals—you'd think they went through seventeen war engagements. I got a medal from Costa Rica once years ago. I was down there talking about a second canal. Geeze, they hung it on me. . . . It was so goddamed heavy that I had to bend over."

Another reporter related Magnuson's unscientific description of a proposal by the Boeing Company to place solar cells in space to convert sun rays into energy. Maggie said energy would be transmitted "by running a long light-cord back to earth."

Some remembered the time an old pal and classmate from the University of Washington asked Magnuson's administrative aide, Irv Hoff, for the senator's help on a project. When told by Hoff that his pal was desperate, Maggie replied, "Irv, don't you know my friend is a congenial liar." And Magnuson's withering description of the arrogant Admiral Lewis Strauss: "The only man I ever saw who could strut while sitting in a chair."[4] Strauss subsequently failed to win Senate confirmation as President Eisenhower's secretary of commerce.

There were Maggie's political maxims: "If you have the votes you don't need the speeches; if you need the speeches you don't have the votes"—that one an echo of the mighty Texan Sam Rayburn. "Never hold a grudge; that man you hate today may be a vote you need tomorrow." Pure Magnuson.

All but a few of these celebrants could recite verbatim the exaggerated tribute from President John Kennedy on how, in a most off-handed manner, the senator created Grand Coulee Dam.

In fact, he was smarter than this pretense. They all knew it was Maggie's way of softly carrying his power. So too his gruff manner that barely masked a man of kindness and complexity. A hard drinker, and a consummate horseplayer, the legislator also liked poetry and ballet. He was an amateur painter of surprising skill.

The best, if inadvertent, description of Magnuson the politician came several years before these funny stories and formal eulogies, in Stimson Bullitt's classic work *To Be a Politician*. Bullitt, son of Dorothy Bullitt and Magnuson's earliest mentor, Scott Bullitt, wrote:

> To enjoy politics one must enjoy people; it helps if one likes them as well. . . .
> He [a politician] must be with them, and a friendly relationship makes it easier
> for him to satisfy and please. He meets and works with every kind. He is
> enabled to associate with the best, and compelled by duty and circumstance
> to spend time with some of the worst. . . .
> A politician should feel at home in both the abstract and the concrete. . . .
> [His] inclinations should be balanced between people and ideas. . . . One who
> puts too much emphasis on issues forgets his fellow citizens, each of them,
> whose welfare is the object of his work. Free from the facts of human needs,
> here and now, he risks becoming dogmatic. . . .
> A superior politician combines two contrasting qualities: In the details of
> his work he is flexible, yet the outlines of his personality are definite. The
> flexibility is necessary to do justice under the democratic process, and also to
> permit him to survive in politics. His nature must be well enough defined for
> him to know who he is, so that his policies may cohere. Few great public men
> have differed from this pattern.[5]

Ancil Payne noted that while Maggie's moral rudder may have wobbled at times, his course stayed true: he aimed to do good for average Americans. Whatever else, this he did. But he did it without boasting and fanfare, a rare trait for any human, much less one accountable to constituents at election time. Turn-of-the-century America takes for granted the right of equal access for all citizens to public accommodations. Only a few scholars and old politicians could recall that the man most responsible for this radical change in our time was Warren Magnuson. He wouldn't blow his own horn.

Leaving the common celebration of this extraordinary politician, a few may have wondered at the incomplete measure of Magnuson the man in contrast to the legislator and the myth. "There were several Magnusons," said Hoeck, the advertising executive. He had helped the senator through reelection campaigns in 1950 and again in 1956 when the opponent, a sanctimonious, nondrinking Christian, Arthur Langlie, bequeathed a decidedly different portrait of Senator Magnuson.

Langlie, a three-term Republican governor of the state, launched a crusade against the "morally bankrupt" incumbent whose career had been "absolutely Hollywoodian, with guys and dolls and gangsters, an unsuccessful marriage and all the other elements of a cheap film production."[6] In fact, Magnuson had enjoyed what he did, and had done what he enjoyed.

Langlie carried but one rural county in his bid for Magnuson's Senate seat. He did raise questions never really answered. Yet he could join mourners in knowing we'd never again see the likes of Magnuson in our Congress. Television and the devaluation of congressional seniority would have wrecked Magnuson's style: vote-getting by work in the rills, creeks, and tributaries, the backwaters of Congress, that determine the course of mainstream policy. His career was shaped by the unique political culture of his adoptive state and the times of an American in the twentieth century. The wake at the house on the side of Capitol Hill in Seattle celebrated an institution, a legislator whose accomplishments showed a touch of genius. But who was the man?

CHAPTER 2

Fargo/Moorhead

Moorhead, Minnesota, harsh, windswept, sits astride the Red River, where it rolls toward Canada a few hundred miles to the north. Opposite Moorhead is Fargo, North Dakota, a metropolis of sorts (population 53,000) in this underpopulated nether region of the American Midwest. It's a minute away by bridge traffic. The land around these towns is as black and rich as the Volga steppes, relic of an Ice Age lake. Their saloons, banks, and modest commerce are a product of this good earth and James J. Hill's Great Northern Railroad, which brought in European homesteaders and merchants and carried back to the East their wheat, potatoes, flax, and cattle. The Seventh and Eighth U.S. Cavalry units pacified intransigent aborigines, Dakota Indians, and their great leader Crazy Horse. There was a lot of mutual slaughter between the intruders and the owners, but never any question about the outcome late in the nineteenth century, given the cavalry's discipline and carbines.

Fargo/Moorhead, as the twin towns are combined, is a far ways from the industry of Seattle, the power of Washington, D.C., and the glitter of Hollywood. There are three colleges within one hundred blocks of each other and a Fargo/Moorhead symphony orchestra, a fact not much known beyond these parts. Fargo hosts the annual Dakota Square Dance Convention, and, lately, the "Wunnerful Welk Weekend," featuring in 1994 two former "champagne ladies" from the popular Lawrence Welk orchestra of the 1950s and 1960s. The aim is to raise money for the Lawrence Welk Music Scholarship fund at North Dakota State University.

Fargo and Moorhead are the kind of church-going, tree-lined small places that made America great because they inspired their more gifted offspring to get out, go forth, and prosper. One such was Sinclair Lewis, the novelist from nearby Sauk Centre ("Gopher Prairie"), a few miles down the Red River Valley on the road to St. Paul. Another, Warren Magnuson.

Magnuson's birthday, it is said, was April 12, 1905. "It is said" in the absence of birth data. The best hard evidence lies sealed in the Clay County, Minnesota, courthouse where next of kin deem it should remain unexamined. It is the record of Magnuson's adoption by William Grant and Emma Anderson Magnuson. They were Minnesota-born offspring of Scandinavian immigrants, as were many Moorhead residents. They named him Warren Grant Magnuson. It is not likely that he ever knew his natural parents, a gnawing fact that may have driven the young man's ambition to move on into bigger, more important worlds—Seattle, Washington, D.C., Manhattan, Hollywood—places and styles far distant from his origins.

Several published reports say his natural parents died when the infant was "less than a month old" and that he was subsequently placed in the Florence Crittenden Home in Fargo. Remaining records of the home, now in custody of the Lutheran Social Service Center in Fargo, give no indication of a male child resembling Magnuson in the period of April 1905. That is not conclusive, however. Records of that period, even if they survived, were at best haphazard.

In 1936, during his first run for election to Congress, Magnuson wrote the Florence Crittenden Home requesting an "authentic birth certificate to establish the fact I was born in this country." There's no subsequent acknowledgment that he received such a document.

A more plausible account of Magnuson's birth comes from his first cousin, Maude Elaine Knudtson, a sprightly octogenarian who lives in a well-kept home on Twelfth Street in Moorhead. Elaine, a former schoolteacher and admirer of her famed cousin, says he was born in the Northwest Hospital in Moorhead to a friend of his adoptive mother, Emma. The natural mother was from Kathryn, North Dakota, perhaps a farm girl turned café waitress. The babe was taken into the Magnuson household three days later, and baptized in Bethesda Lutheran Church (Swedish) by the Reverend J. O. Nyvall on December 10, 1905. His confirmation came years later in the Norwegian Lutheran Church.

Northwest Hospital became St. Asgar Hospital, run by an order of Roman Catholic nuns in Moorhead. St. Asgar then merged into the Heartlands Hospital in Fargo. What remains of its records from April 1905 gives no indication of the birth of a male infant in that period. But there is no certainty that all records have survived ninety years and two hospital mergers.

What makes Elaine Knudtson's explanation most plausible, apart from the absence of contrary records, is the witness of Carol Parker Cahill, one of Magnuson's great loves, a sometime companion to his adoptive mother, Emma.

"One day we sat on the porch of her new home on Bainbridge Island, Washington, where Warren had moved her," said Mrs. Cahill, a onetime nightclub singer and Hollywood movie player under contract to Paramount Pictures. "Emma said 'there's something I want to show you.' It was, she said, a letter from Warren's real mother in Minneapolis. Emma apparently remained in touch with her. She may have also told me 'don't tell Warren.' I don't think Warren ever knew his natural parents. Emma would have told me if the girl was a maid in the Magnuson household, as some stories have it. She was, said Emma, a farm girl turned waitress in another town. She never named the other town."[1]

The former starlet, a resident of Ajijic, Mexico, said she disliked Emma Magnuson, "a really tough person—you don't meet many people that tough anymore. She could make anybody a slave. Maybe it came from running a saloon." The Magnusons owned and operated the Nickleplate bar in Moorhead. Six feet tall, broad-shouldered, with black hair and green eyes, Emma had the physique to run the saloon by herself.

Magnuson, however, adored and protected his mother, caring for her when she was ill and, finally in 1941, bringing her to shelter in a home he purchased across Puget Sound from Seattle on Bainbridge Island. He publicly acknowledged that he was an orphan during his first campaign for Congress from the First District (Seattle) in 1936. It was a rebuttal to what he called "gossip on the street."

"There is the story that I don't even know my own name," wrote Magnuson in this prepared speech. He was setting a pattern of addressing campaign slurs head-on. "It happens to be true. I am an orphan. . . . That I received the care and attention of loving and kindly hands in my childhood is a source of constant thankfulness." The rest of his script was crossed out. It said, "Whatever I am now or hope to be I owe to the dear people who made a home for me as though I were their own."[2]

In contrast to his adoration of Emma, Magnuson had a cool disdain for his adoptive father, William. In the 1930s, Magnuson would formally turn aside desperate appeals for money from William, who signed his letters "Your Dad." The Nickleplate burned in 1921. William left Emma then and drifted westward through Missoula, Montana, to Portland, Oregon, working as a carpenter, railroad hand, and, finally, in Portland's wartime shipyards. He would die in Portland, a virtual pauper, largely ignored by Warren.

"Dear Son Warren," wrote William from Portland in 1934. "Wrote some time ago and want to hear from you so bad, but no answer. Say Warren if you could help in any other way I wish you could help me get something to do. Enything I don't car watt [sic] it is. . . . As ever, Dady. Please answer."

Warren's reply a few months later: "Dear Bill, I have been very neglectful in answering your letters. . . . I've been so busy. I am feeling well and
keeping an eagle eye open [for a job]. . . . With kindest regards, Warren
G. Magnuson."[3]

There's a curious parallel to Magnuson in Abraham Lincoln's love of
his stepmother and cool treatment of his father. Called to the bedside of
his dying father in January 1851, Lincoln turns aside, writing that he is
too busy with his work, and, besides, "my own wife is sick abed (I suppose
it is not dangerous). I sincerely hope Father may yet recover his health,
but in all events tell him to remember to call upon our great, good, and
merciful Maker."

In January 1860, shortly before his inauguration as president, Lincoln
rode all night in the caboose of a train to visit the ailing Sally Lincoln.
He told companions that she was the best friend he ever had. He spent
the next day in Farmington, Illinois, hugging her, holding her hand,
and talking about the times of their lives. Lincoln said how happy her
presence had made their household. She was, says his biographer Stephen
Oates, the only member of the Lincoln family that he loved.[4]

Elaine Knudtson and Lois Magnuson, Warren's cousin-in-law, give a
glowing picture of the Magnuson household in Moorhead, one that belies
stories that the youngster struggled in material poverty—stories that have
been suggested by Magnuson himself.

"It was a quality household," says Elaine Knudtson. The two-story
white frame house at 214 Second Avenue, Moorhead, had the solid,
square architectural style that would fit any middle-class American neighborhood in the Midwest. The living and dining rooms were spacious
and neatly tended. The parlor featured a baby grand piano and a fine
set of china for chocolate. Four bedrooms upstairs would accommodate
boarders after the saloon burned in 1921 and William divorced Emma
to move west. A few blocks away was the river where young Magnuson
went to improve his baseball skills by chucking rocks.

Even then, Warren was uncommonly handsome and spirited. He
worked part-time in his uncle's grocery store, where he and his cousin
Elaine often would play. Once Magnuson flashed a hooked knife used
for cutting bananas in a mock attack on Elaine. She tossed up a hand
so abruptly that it hit the knife. There was a deep cut, a lot of blood.
"Warren was distraught, really scared. Mother—the house next door was
our home—staunched the blood and Warren recovered. I've always had
the scar as a reminder of our play together."

Although Magnuson would later tell of a bleak childhood, the old-
timers in Moorhead describe an orderly, pleasant middle-class environ-

ment. They suggest a dislike for William Magnuson and no regrets that the saloon-keep left town. They admired Emma, who lavished Warren and his "Sis," Clara, with toys and good food. "They had everything they ever wanted as children," says Elaine.

Not quite everything, according to Gertrude Hansman, a member of Warren's high school class. Young Magnuson wanted his adoptive parents to tell him the identity of his natural parents and their fates.

"Emma refused, according to what she told my mother," says Mrs. Hansman. "Emma said she told her son only that his mother was an unfortunate woman who gave him up. Warren never found out. I don't think he ever felt really happy in that family. He was frustrated, not knowing his real mother, and I think this frustration was part of his very determined ambition."

Unable to bear children of her own, Emma did not stop with Warren. A year after his adoption she sought to adopt another infant named Clara, offspring of a woman known to Elaine Knudtson. But the mother balked. Emma turned to another "unfortunate," adopting her girl, and naming her Clara. Magnuson called her "Sis" and cared for her throughout the years much as he cared for Emma, despite Clara's apparent deep envy of his success.

"Clara was a very different sort, not very studious," said Elaine. "I don't think she finished high school." Sixteen years old, and pregnant by Lloyd Junkin, as she would later claim, Clara wed the man in 1924. They lived with Emma for nine years, then divorced in 1937. Clara claimed Lloyd, a bootlegger, used her to run his illegal whiskey past federal revenue officers.[5]

By contrast, Warren became a high school ball of fire, possibly in compensation for frustration at home. His few remaining classmates almost sing in concert in their description of the teenager: handsome, likable, nice, excellent student, crack athlete, but self-conscious about his height—five feet, nine inches—the favorite of all the girls, an enduring pattern in the man's life.

"He never studied at school, but he was the smartest guy in the class," said Oliver "Lars" Sondrall, like Magnuson, Moorhead High School class of 1923. "Oh, I was just proud to be in the same class with somebody so smart and athletic. Sorry that none of it rubbed off. He got his name 'Maggie' playing quarterback for the Moorhead football team, the 'Spuds.' Then it became 'Gritty Maggie' when he injured his ankle and wouldn't come out of the game. He just kept playing. His mother, Emma, was a big, strong Norwegian woman, but she never had to whip Warren. He never had to be disciplined. But he wasn't a teacher's pet—he just knew everything."

As an afterthought, Sondrall says Magnuson must have done a lot of studying at home out of sight of his classmates. He, Lois, and Elaine remembered Magnuson's love of Emma's klob, a Norwegian dumpling made of flour, potatoes, and pork or herring. "You always knew when Warren was coming home to visit," said Elaine. "You could smell Emma's klob on the kitchen stove."

His classmates' portrait of the young man as something like radio hero Jack Armstrong, "the all-American boy," makes all the more puzzling an entry on his transcript from Moorhead High School. After his name it reads "Date of Birth: 4-12-05—Japan." There is no factual explanation for the entry of his birthplace as Japan, a land at that time as far removed from Moorhead as the moon would be today. Perhaps it was bitter whimsy, Magnuson's oblique way of saying he really didn't know where he came from.

Chio-Kio, the 1923 high school yearbook, gives more of the portrait of the young all-American, no allusion at all to "Japan" and scant hint of the exceptional student described by Sondrall. Magnuson was treasurer of his senior class, captain of the baseball team, three-year letterman in football "displaying college form." He also sang in the glee club and played roles in high school operettas—Scary in "Love Pirates of Hawaii," and Everett Evans in the melodrama "Clever Match-Makers." He was a member of the high school's Wig and Mask Club. The caption beneath his senior class picture says, "I fell in love again today."

"Oh, he was likable all right and handsome," said Gertrude Hansman. "But he knew how to get ahead and he always wanted to be on top even if it meant cutting a corner. He was talented and very ambitious. Sometimes he would start things and leave it to others to finish. This happened with the operettas. I now think that from the start, politics was really his calling."

It was a rite of passage in the small towns and farms of an earlier American era for lads, regardless of station, to hold part-time employment. Work was next to religion in the American ethic. In addition to helping in his uncle's grocery, young Magnuson delivered the *Fargo Courier News*, and worked as a messenger for Western Union. As much as anything else in his boyhood, Western Union wired his fate. It frequently led him into the lobby of the Dakota National Bank, where its managers and owners, Alex Stern and his son William, kept office—out front, the better to greet farmers, merchants, idlers, messengers. Warren became almost like a fourth son to Alex Stern, and a surrogate younger brother to William Stern, his lifelong friend and sometime banker. The Stern-Magnuson relationship would later yield some confusion about Maggie's origins.

There is no accounting for Warren Magnuson without the influence of Alex and Bill Stern, the elder a Jewish immigrant born in Giessen, Germany, in 1857. Alex came west on James J. Hill's Iron Horse to Fargo, Dakota Territory. The Eighth Cavalry had yet to vanquish the Dakota tribes. Stern opened a clothing store, and later the Dakota National Bank.

When he died in 1934, Alex bequeathed his store to his son Sam Stern, the bank to Bill. Edward, another son, went to New York to work as a stockbroker. Bill attended Harvard College, served in the Army Quartermaster Corps in World War I, and was a member of the postwar committee that founded the American Legion. He was a Republican, in fact "Mr. Republican" in North Dakota, a bachelor who, like Magnuson, loved women and liquor. Slender, and homely, Bill Stern, Fargo's most influential and prominent banker, on occasion had the tongue of an angry mule skinner. Once in Manhattan's swank Stork Club, a young woman companion got so shaken with his foul language, she stalked past Sherman Billingsley, the Stork's keeper, and out the door, leaving the banker with his memories and mixed drink.

Bill Stern was fifteen years older than Magnuson and would aid the young man's passage from Fargo/Moorhead to Seattle, sponsor his role in the early formation of Northwest Airlines, and, possibly, promote the connection between the young congressman and the Minneapolis milling giant, Archer Daniels Midland. He would become, as Magnuson matured, more boon companion than big brother, Magnuson's entree to the wider world of American business and politics. While Magnuson was, literally, from the other side of the river, he was neither literally nor metaphorically from the other side of the tracks. It was a young place. Class lines between the son of a saloon-keeper and the heir to a new fortune had yet to harden. American egalitarianism was in its flower.

Their close relationship later led to speculation that Magnuson was reared by "Jewish bankers." George Dixon, the former Hearst columnist, reported Bill Stern "raised Maggie" but "Maggie got away from him and became a Democrat."[6] Maggie never got away from Bill Stern. They were friends until Stern's death in 1964. In the early 1950s, Stern, Magnuson, and Seattle hotel magnate Bill Edris sometimes shared a three-bedroom home in Palm Springs, California, a handsome hillside retreat owned by Edris and later sold to Magnuson.

"Bill liked to help everybody," says Ed Stern, elegant owner of present-day Fargo's finest clothing store, but not related to the Alex Stern family. "No doubt he helped Warren from very early on."

Magnuson told the *Fargo Forum*, "I was in the bank a lot with the newspapers and Western Union messages." Senator Magnuson flew to Stern's sickbed in 1963 straight from a meeting with former President Harry Truman. The *Forum* quoted Magnuson as saying, "President Truman told me to tell that old goat [Stern] to get well."

Another old hometown friend, Frank Van Osdel, a retired lawyer, knew Magnuson as his fraternity brother at the University of North Dakota in Grand Forks for one semester in 1923. He remembers, "a great party guy, a hard drinker, very handsome, not too tall, a real go-getter. You could see that he was going to be a politician—outgoing, gregarious, an opportunist—he went with the labor unions when he went out to Seattle. He wasn't exactly a preacher, but he was a good man."

Van Osdel, ninety, is certain that Bill Stern helped young Magnuson, as well as other Fargo/Moorhead youth. Stern apparently had absolute control over the Dakota National Bank. He never suffered from lack of money, and he shared his wealth.

"He helped Warren at North Dakota University and then helped him go west to Seattle. No question," says Van Osdel. "Bill and Croil Hunter, another Fargo friend, helped start Northwest Airlines. It was a hometown thing, so we all had a stake in it—Warren too. I'd say politicians are but a few who don't cut corners."

Come summertime and Magnuson, like most teenagers around Fargo/Moorhead, worked on adjacent wheat farms, a normal routine for that time and place. Lacking self-propelled combines and heavy tractors, such farming was labor intensive. It was also superb conditioning for a promising football player.

In the spring of 1924, Magnuson transferred from the University of North Dakota to North Dakota Agricultural College (now North Dakota State) in Fargo to be closer to Emma. His only mention in the *Bison*, the college yearbook, is as a letterman on the freshman football team at quarterback. He would leave Fargo for Seattle, where he enrolled in the University of Washington, October 2, 1925.[7]

There's no remaining witness to his flight from the upper Midwest to his new life in the Pacific Northwest, a young region of unlimited promise. "Going West" is an American trait as old as the nation, all the more so for the young, energetic, talented and—probably in the case of Magnuson—disaffected. No doubt he knew of the University of

Washington law school and the city's seaport and may have yearned, as many flatlanders are wont, to go to sea.

He was not, as some, including Maggie himself, have said, recruited from Fargo by Coach Enoch Bagshaw to play on the University of Washington football team. Peggins Sutter, his first wife, says that whatever else prompted his move, there was a girl. He followed a high school sweetheart, one Loretta Welsh, who had moved with her family to Seattle. They were in love.

Certainly the migration was an early display of his unusual ability to look ahead and segregate possibility from fantasy; a journey of hope, as much as an escape from an unsatisfying home life. He claimed he hoboed his way west on freight trains, a common, even glamorous practice of adventuresome youth at that time, according to Ed Stern. Van Osdel speculates that he may have purchased a Model T Ford jalopy with money from Bill Stern and driven to Seattle.

Whatever the means of transport, every account suggests a young man driven by ambition, fueled with enormous energy, and determined to make his mark; an orphan who did not know his real name aiming to make one for himself.

CHAPTER 3

Seattle, 1925

The young Magnuson picked up his life as a frat house playboy, begun in North Dakota, when he reached the Theta Chi fraternity at the University of Washington in Seattle, October 2, 1925. Otherwise he had made a radical change, moving from a farm world to an emerging industrial society, albeit one based on natural resources, mainly timber, fish, and, soon-to-come, water-generated electricity. Bill Boeing's aircraft factory had yet to take off from its humble home in a bright red, barn-shaped building alongside the Duwamish River.

Only dreamers—and Magnuson was one such—foresaw the day when his adopted city would be the transportation gateway, and commercial center for a chart-busting, transpacific trade, one rivaling older cities down the coast.

Described by one early lover as "absolutely charming, absolutely beautiful—golden hair, broad shoulders that tapered down to slim hips"[1]— Magnuson would take to Seattle's beauty and commerce and the state's volatile politics with the same relish he displayed for his mother's Norwegian dumplings. He was twenty years old, sixteen years younger than the state itself. He had moved from the political equivalent of a sandbox into a house of mirrors; from the orderly, Calvinist Midwest to a cauldron of social and economic ideologies, a state like none other in the union. It was the right fit for a youth with the ambitions and complexity of young Magnuson.

Seattle had a booming waterfront around Elliott Bay, a deep harbor sheltered from the wild Pacific by the Olympic Mountains. China silk trade moved from Pier 91 beneath Magnolia Bluff to Shanghai. South, from piers jutting out of downtown, the Port of Seattle held a near monopoly on trade to Alaska. Much of this moved through the Skinner family's Alaska Steamship Company at Pier 42. There were timber barons with a touch of old money, shipyards that prospered from World War I, big banks, big merchants, and swell nightlife—saloons and whorehouses. This was the Roaring Twenties. The national prohibition on legal liquor drove people to drink and gave emotional shape to much of the state's political conflict. Grasping all of this must have intoxicated the lad from Moorhead as much as any Theta Chi party on Saturday night.

The good times and relative prosperity may have masked from new-comers the underlying social reality of this place. Eastern swells did not sail around the Horn to settle Washington, as, indeed, some did come to Oregon on the south side of the Columbia River. Its demographic texture was studded with misfits coming up from Oregon Territory, just as many of Virginia's eighteenth-century malcontents crossed the Appalachians to settle Kentucky and Tennessee. A surprising number migrated to Washington Territory from the South. The nation's Civil War became a source of violent argument in the capitals of Salem, Oregon, and Olympia, Washington. Confederate sympathizers killed a resolution in support of the Union in Washington's 1862 Territorial Legislature. President Lincoln expressed his dismay, followed by an abrupt reduction of federal funds to the territory. Unionists turned it around in 1863 with a resolution in support of the Union, influenced as much by the shortfall in federal aid as by the tide of battle.[2] To the dismay of the righteous and God-fearing, seeds of nonconformist social action came with these early settlers.

The first great leap from farming and fishing toward an urban-industrial society such as Magnuson would discover came with the railroads, the Northern Pacific to Tacoma on south Puget Sound in 1883, a steel link as significant as completion of the Union Pacific to California sixteen years earlier. James J. Hill's Great Northern conquered Stevens Pass in the Cascades with its iron path to reach Seattle ten years later, 1893. The railroad companies sold the glories of the region even as they bought its politicians in Olympia. Timber companies, whose influence remained dominant, learned their wicked ways around Olympia and Washington, D.C., from the old masters, railroad lobbyists. But sell the railroads did. In 1883, the Northern Pacific had 831 sales agents in Britain and 123 elsewhere in Europe. Their sales literature boasted of the Northwest's "vast and inexhaustible resources"—and so, until recently, it has seemed. They plugged its "ideal climate, hot springs, abundant water" and "cool nights conducive to sound slumber."

They brought immigrants from Italy to mine coal in the western Cascade foothills and to clear old-growth cedar from forests of the Olympic Peninsula. There were Chinese around Tacoma and Seattle, muscle that had laid the ties and steel. But of foreigners coming to Washington, a plurality was Scandinavian. They gathered, mainly, around Puget Sound, where the woods, water, hills, and climate reminded them of home. Italians, Asians, American southerners, and Adriatic Slavs left their mark in shaping the new state, but no migrant group so much as those from Norway, Sweden, and Denmark. They planted and cultivated a new social ethic.

By 1910, at least 100,000 Scandinavians were settled around Puget Sound, about 25,000 having come directly from the old countries. Others were "second stage" Scandinavians from Minnesota, Illinois, the Dakotas, and Iowa. One newcomer wrote to his home folks, "It reminds me of my home in Norway. I don't feel as if I'm in a strange land."[3]

They encouraged others to come. A familiar pattern for these immigrants was to work in a sawmill, save their earnings, and buy a small farm, a "stump ranch," around the Sound or in the Cascade foothills. Migrants from Appalachia to the foothills brought a talent for distilling moonshine whiskey and a taste for its consumption and sale. One early settler from Carolina told his grandson, "This here was right nice country until all them Swedes come up and started farming and messed it up."[4]

Scandinavians were a decisive factor in Washington politics until the late twentieth century, a fact never lost on two sons of the old countries, Senators Henry Jackson and Warren Magnuson, even though they were generations removed.

Scattered among the misfits, laborers, capitalists, moonshiners, and farmers came another kind of adventurer, Utopians, social idealists looking to make an alternative to the industrial society they abhorred. They were surely spurred by the great depression of the late nineteenth century, an illustration of capitalism's inhumanity. They established small communal societies with names like "Harmony," "Freeland," and "Equality," and, as Ed Pelton, a founder of "Equality" announced, they were the "advance guard of a mighty host." They withered and vanished as the state's economy expanded, leaving behind a hard streak of egalitarianism at the core of Northwest politics.

"For some reason, the West Coast has a strange attraction for people of impractical and romantic turns of mind," sighed one Chicago newspaper columnist. Harsher critics labeled the communes as hotbeds of free love. In fact, they attracted confirmed socialists, as well as pioneer seekers of a better life, whose mating habits were the same as Americans elsewhere. Their economic life, however, was different, more akin to the Israeli kibbutzim of the 1950s than the rampant capitalism of Seattle in the gold rush of the 1890s, which they disdained. The people of "Equality" cleared a forest along Puget Sound in Skagit County and practiced a rigorous, probably excessive, democracy. Departments were established for housing, laundry, agriculture, fishing, and forestry; department heads were nominated by their laborers and elected by the colony's general assembly. Founded in 1897, "Equality" had a population of 300 by 1899, its members living in single rooms of rough apartments. Bachelors slept in a dormitory. Work was hard, pay 5 cents an hour in colony script, but housing, laundry, and medical care were free. Colonists paid $2 a week for food, which they ate in a communal mess hall. The fare was plain but hearty. Religion was left strictly to the individual. Most members were probably agnostic. As on the collective farms of Stalinist Russia, there was a killing disparity between industrious and slothful workers and a critical lack of skilled workmen. "Equality" fell into dissension within a few years and finally dissolved in 1907.[5] The "mighty host" forecast by Ed Pelton never arrived. But the great ghost of these communes, the ballot proposal for a socialist state, Initiative 119, came again in Washington in the 1930s and played a haunting role in the early political career of young Warren Magnuson.

Outside the borders of "Harmony," "Equality," and "Freeland" the state was a rough stew of political conflict from its inception. Farmer-labor revulsion against railroad and bank monopolies reached its formal political expression in a big-shouldered Populist movement during the burst of industrial growth that followed the Civil War. Populists elected a governor, John Rogers, and majorities in the state House and Senate in 1897. On paper, anyway, they controlled the state capitol.

A native of Brunswick, Maine, Rogers embodied the core of Populist principles: democratic and humanitarian. These principles he preached as a journalist. One biographer calls Rogers a "secular theologian." For a time in the 1850s he worked at the commissary on a relative's plantation near Terry, Mississippi. He avoided service in the Civil War, then founded a newspaper, the *Kansas Commoner,* in Newton, Kansas. He followed his son west to Washington, promptly emerging as a leading figure in the fusion of urban and rural populists.

Elected governor with the Northwest landslide of William Jennings Bryan, Rogers rode a streetcar to the capitol for his inauguration as governor, rather than travel in a carriage with a military escort. He wore a red flannel shirt, cowhide boots, and $2 pants. Once installed in the office, he walked from the state capitol to his home at Fifteenth and Franklin for lunch each day. Mrs. Rogers did the housework without the help of servants. "The individual is everything," Rogers said. "Only non-conformists are truly great." Wary of capitalism, he was disdainful of its opposite, socialism, since it would "erode individual rights and responsibilities." His inaugural address called for "labor to get its just share of wealth," for "the voice of the people is the voice of God." His legislative program included taxes to provide funding for the state's common schools, highways, and help for the infirm and orphans. He went on to seek "regulations for control of the corporate bodies whose avarice leads them to disregard the interests of the individual." His aim was "to improve the quality of people's lives."[6]

Despite Populist majorities in the legislature, Rogers was a short-term failure as governor. They were all too green in the ways and wiles of process, too much in dispute among themselves, to pass legislation of much significance. In the last analysis, they were too divided between their urban and rural factions. At best the Populists were a fusion of progressive Republicans and Democrats. They did, however, lay down underlying principles for succeeding generations of state politicians. There is scant ideological distance from John Rogers of 1897 to Governor Mike Lowry in 1994. This was Warren Magnuson's inheritance. This was the mainstream of Washington politics for a century to come, regardless of the party in power in Olympia.

Populists had a more immediate impact, however, laying the foundation for subsequent "progressive" political reforms, the people's right to direct legislation through referendum and initiative, and the selection of party nominees by direct primary election. These are still mainstays of Northwest politics—severe blows against the power of political parties decades before the invention of television.

Those enduring institutional reforms were copied later by other states. Urban Populists also left Washington with an economic and political polarity by advocating and backing public ownership of electric power. If racism marked the southern populism of "Pitchfork" Ben Tillman, J. K. Vardaman, and Theodore Bilbo, public power was the dominant institutional manifestation of populism in the Northwest. This public-private power struggle has yet to be duplicated in its endurance and intensity elsewhere in the union. "Socialism!" those favoring investor-owned utilities have shouted ever since, although not so much at first. The initial public power company, Tacoma City Light, founded in 1893, provided consumers the cheapest power rates in the nation. It was an ideal expression of populist values—a cheap public commodity stripped of private profit.

Their rural counterparts, angry at the railroads that made the state then gouged back their profit, stressed the need to regulate railroads and other utilities. These goals would drive the young politician Magnuson three decades later.

Public power had no better or more eloquent advocate than Homer T. Bone, the Indiana-born son of a Union soldier. A Tacoma lawyer turned legislator, and later a U.S. senator, Bone helped defeat a 1922 referendum, pushed by private power, to restrict the expansion of city-owned utilities into areas served by the private power companies. In essence, the fight over the right to expand public utilities became the preeminent theme of Washington politics for the next six decades.

"Cheap power harnessed by the great cities of Puget Sound, Seattle and Tacoma, will make them centers of industry," said Bone when the public-private power fight crystallized in 1922. "Kept under the thumb of Stone and Webster [a prominent private utilities holding company] it means profits for Boston, corruption for our state and local governments and high power rates that cripple the future of the Pacific Northwest."[7]

Millions of words have flowed over this subject, but none ever improved on Bone's statement defining the public power cause. He would remain a force in Northwest politics until the 1940s. His major political effort for at least a decade was adoption of the "Bone bill" giving municipal utilities power of eminent domain to acquire power systems owned by private companies.

Bone, like Alexander Scott Bullitt, would become a major influence in the political life of Warren Magnuson. Early on he described himself as a "constructive Socialist." Peers said he had a natural empathy with the underdog; that he was a rebel against a society based on wealth. Perhaps it's a paradox that the three dominant influences on the young Magnuson's politics were Bullitt, a Kentucky aristocrat, son of a Confederate soldier; Bone, a self-made socialist, son of a Union soldier; and Saul Haas, son of a Jewish ghetto dweller on New York's Lower East Side. But, given the young man's complexity, perhaps not.

For all of its sound and fury, and critical economic importance, the public-private power battles were models of civility compared with confrontations between labor and capital. Workers, many of them immigrants carrying the internationalist "one big union" idea of the European social philosopher Georges Sorel, were stiffening against the exploitation by primitive capitalists in the late nineteenth century. Their pocket battles would flare in the woods, streets, and waterfronts until the mid-twentieth century, when they settled into the civil processes of the state legislature.

Labor's shock troops were members of the Industrial Workers of the World, "Wobblies," intellectual offspring of philosopher Sorel, mainly woods workers, itinerants. They created the physical pressure for the reform of wages and working conditions in the early 1900s—pressure that endured even after Wobbly massacres during gun battles on the Everett waterfront and the main street of Centralia. Nothing excites peaceful reform so much as the threat of socialism, the aim of these "romantic rebels."

William O. Douglas, future U.S. Supreme Court justice from Yakima, carried a Wobbly card if only as a security measure while hoboing around the country. For the same reason, as well as sentiment, so did Warren Magnuson. They bore an early Wobbly imprint on the need for improved economic equality, if not for "one big union."

Farmers beefed against the railroads for price gouging, no doubt with justification. The rail barons of St. Paul and New York did not build their roads west on behalf of Christian charity.

World War I, with its emphasis on centralized authority and national loyalty, was a prime factor in the undoing of the Wobblies as, later, World War II would be for the Communist Party in the Northwest. So was the prosperity the Great War brought to the Northwest. It was Seattle's second great boom, this one even greater than the commercial fall-out from the discovery of gold in the Klondike in 1897. Bank deposits in the state jumped from $193 million to $425 million in the years between 1915 and 1920. Seattle's shipyards roared with hammers and rivets wielded by 40,000 wartime workers who could refresh themselves with Happy-Peppy Beer from the local Hemrich brewery. Its stock soared.

Cutting the slack in postwar job orders, Ford placed an auto assembly plant in Seattle, one of 186 new manufacturing firms created in the state. Manufactured goods worth $200 million were produced by 1926. That year on the other, drier, side of the Cascade Mountains farmers harvested 7.4 million bushels of wheat.

An economic sea change in the Northwest was taking place, the shift from small manager-owned enterprises to large corporations, run by managers and owned, in the case of private utilities and Ford, "back East." Capitalism was changing. So was labor.[8] Dave Beck, a Seattle laundry truck driver and self-styled "labor capitalist" with no time for ideologies of the left, was organizing the teamsters. Warren Magnuson was an early member of Beck's union, which, with his help, would be a major force in state politics for another quarter century. Maggie would always be ready to help the powerful union boss.

Magnuson arrived just in time to leave his own mark on an even more turbulent and prosperous epoch in the state's history.

CHAPTER 4

Mr. Smooth

W arren Magnuson's buddies back in Fargo/Moorhead stayed in
touch with the pal they aptly called "Mr. Smooth," whose
reason for coming west, he said, was to attend the University
of Washington law school.[1] Whatever help he got from Bill Stern, it was
insufficient. Magnuson needed work. Coach Enoch Bagshaw arranged a
job for the football prospect, delivering ice, member of the Teamsters
Union. Frat house playboy, iceman, student, and pigskin hopeful, Magnuson was an extraordinarily active young man about Seattle.

His university grades showed it. Magnuson, who earned his keep with
off-campus jobs, paid enough attention to pass, but without academic
distinction. He was bad enough in philosophy to be humbled with a D
in the spring term of 1926. That fall, however, the scholar quickened
with As in math and economics, Bs in law and music. The balance of
his academic record from winter of 1927 until graduation from the law
school in the spring of 1929 was a yo-yo between A and D—mostly Cs.
The academic record slights the man's intelligence.[2]

Magnuson had no apologies for this lackluster performance when, a
few years later, he said he studied law rather than medicine, religion, or
engineering because he didn't feel "technically inclined, nor scientifically
inclined, sufficiently to enter those kinds of professions." Neither was
he so spiritually inclined: "A lawyer can be his own boss. The work is
interesting and not prosaic."[3]

But the law student certainly had other matters on his mind. Football for one. For the sheer physical joy of rough sport, Magnuson gave
himself after classes to the university's varsity squad as football's equivalent of cannon fodder, the "scout" team scrimmaging against the first
team in the role of the Huskies' next opponent. For all his athletic
ability, he was undersized for play in the powerful Pacific Coast Conference. Nevertheless, he had an obvious taste for the controlled brutality
of this sport. If he missed the glory of Saturday's cheers, he relished
the sport's essence, rough physical contact. The coaches liked it. Bart
Spellman, an assistant coach and father of a future Washington governor, John Spellman, became Magnuson's college helper and lifelong
friend.

"I turned out for football when I was a struggling law student," Magnuson told an early interviewer. "I was on the scrub team and we used to go to the stadium every night and let the varsity and the stars run all over us in order that they might get in shape for the enemy [Saturday's coming opponent]. The going was tough. Bagshaw gave us the devil. But I liked it and liked him and we came out of it better men."[4]

Girls were another academic distraction. "I think the only reason he married me is that I wouldn't go to bed with him," says Eleanor Peggy (Peggins) Maddieux, "Miss Seattle of 1927," graduate of Broadway High School that same year. They met at the Shoreham Hotel in Washington, D.C., where "Miss Seattle" had gone for a beauty contest and Magnuson was attending a fraternity convention. The hotel manager told Peggins of Magnuson's presence. They married in June 1928, honeymooned in the Canadian Rockies, then visited his friends and family in Moorhead.[5]

The *Seattle Post-Intelligencer* rhapsodized over their wedding under the headline "Absent Queen as Commoner Weds Lawyer," a catchy way of saying Peggins blew a gig as a model at the North End Industrial Exposition to make her match at the First Methodist Church. Peggins was described as a beauty with charm and a sparkling personality. Earlier the newspaper ran a full-figured photo of "Miss Seattle" accompanied by what newspapers of that obliviously sexist era called her "numbers" (measurements in inches of breast, waist, hips, thighs).

Back home in Seattle, where, despite the headline, Magnuson had yet to finish law school, they had an apartment in the Olive Tower. Peggins went to work in the office of the stately Sorrento Hotel on First Hill, earning wherewithal for their rent and food. She became friends with his college buddies, Mort Frayn, a Seattle book-publisher-to-be, and Joe Hughes of Wenatchee, who would return there to practice law. Both, incidentally, were lifelong and prominent Republicans. Magnuson never visited Wenatchee without a visit and a drink with "old broken ass," as Maggie called his pal Hughes, who injured his tailbone in a fall while they attended the university.[6]

The marriage would formally last six years. Peggins, who later became Mrs. Vance Sutter, reflects with fondness and no regrets: "He started running around on me as soon as we were married. He was really two people, a real rascal but also very sentimental and sensitive; very sophisticated in some ways, childlike in others. Physically, he was beautiful, a young god."

In fact if not in legal terms, their marriage ended a few years after it began, when Peggins returned to the Olive Tower after an absence of three days to find her husband in the embrace of her best friend. She removed her wedding ring, threw it at Magnuson, and moved out. At his request, the divorce was not final until after the 1934 election, when Magnuson was elected King County (Seattle) prosecutor. "I always teased him about saving his political career," says Peggins, noting the negative impact of divorce on a politician at that time. They remained friends for life.

Peggins says she took no contraceptive precautions during their marriage, yet did not become pregnant. Other women in Magnuson's life have said the same. He apparently was incapable of siring offspring.

Handsome, likable, and studious enough to master law school, Magnuson was probably destined for politics, as his early classmates forecast. But his first practical taste was drudgery, stuffing envelopes for the League of Women Voters. Al Schweppe, the University of Washington's law school dean, spotted the student as a comer. Even more fatefully, Magnuson sought advice about a political career from Scott Bullitt, the leading state Democrat, a partisan in the "wet"-"dry" polarities of Washington politics in the 1920s.[7]

Bullitt sized up the young law student as an astute politician in the making, recalled Dorothy Bullitt, Scott's widow and a lifelong friend of Maggie's. Warren Magnuson, she said, was an orphan who didn't know where he came from. "When he was graduated, the first thing he did was to go to Scott and tell him that he wanted to put his life into politics, asked him how to do it. Scott became his mentor, and Magnuson always gave him credit for being the ideal politician."[8] Scott Bullitt proceeded to recruit young Magnuson as a delegate to the 1928 state Democratic convention in Spokane. Magnuson may not yet have had a clear idea about party affiliation, but from practice and conviction he was truly a "wet."

At the time, Prohibition packed an emotional intensity akin to latter-day arguments over abortion. From the late 1920s until its repeal in 1933, the prohibition issue overshadowed the long wars at the ballot box and in the legislature between public and private power interests.

Bullitt, descended from Kentucky pioneers, was a "wet." His Democratic Party was a wreck, torn apart by "jealousies, factionalism and general incompetence," virtually displaced in the legislature by Republicans and a farmer-labor minority backed by the state's socialists. Between 1914 and 1930 only 72 of 873 House members were Democrats. The party had one Senate member in the legislative sessions of 1921, 1923, 1929, and 1931. Bullitt aimed to put the party back together and into political power. An extraordinary man, gifted with intelligence and courage, this was not a goal beyond his reach. He urged voters to join the Democratic Party, which emphasized "the man, rather than the dollar, human rights before property rights, equal opportunity for all."

The former prosecuting attorney in Jefferson County, Kentucky, Bullitt came from Louisville to marry Dorothy Stimson, daughter of an established Seattle timber family. Handsome, enormously charming, Bullitt quickly gained notice as a "rising star." An exceptional, if not unique, Democrat, given his wealth and social status, he lost his race for the U.S. Senate in 1926 against Republican Wesley Jones, the victim of "booze" (his pro-wet position) and reactionaries; he had called for the states to settle the prohibition question and had opposed the Ku Klux Klan. The Women's Christian Temperance Union, a mighty force for politics as well as sobriety, became his most formidable opposition.

The anti-booze forces circulated 21,000 pamphlets claiming Bullitt had a "bourbon cash barrel" in his Senate campaign against Wesley Jones, one filled by the "brewery, distillery and saloon interests"—forces of evil intent on destroying Prohibition.[9]

Magnuson recalled, years later, that delegates to the 1928 state Democratic convention argued back and forth for hours during the April heat and evening cool of Spokane trying to settle the party's position on Prohibition and the "Bone bill"—Homer Bone's proposal to allow public utilities to expand beyond their municipal boundaries.

"Amid the wildest confusion, political gunpowder exploded—the convention ran wild," reported the *Seattle Times*. "Militant delegates predominated and were in control." Not a picture of harmony. The delegates endorsed Al Smith for president, the Bone bill, and the repeal of Prohibition.

Scott Bullitt, gearing for a race for governor against the reactionary Everett industrialist Roland Hartley, gave the keynote address. The *Seattle Times*, not a paper overly comfortable with the "Bourbon" Bullitt, despite his social status, reported that his speech received "thunderous applause" from delegates, presumably both wet and dry. Bullitt could bridge his party's ideological gap, if not make peace with the WCTU.

"What I like about the spirit of the Northwest is that the people want to know what a man stands for—not what his ancestors stood for in years gone by," the *Times* quoted Bullitt as saying. The newspaper characterized Bullitt as "pro common schools and egalitarianism" and noted that "the anti-saloon league will fight him."

They did, of course, just as they fought against the 1928 Democratic presidential nominee, New York Governor Al Smith. Both Smith and Bullitt lost their elections. Bullitt, however, emerged as his party's national committeeman with entree to the rising eastern stars of the national Democratic Party, James Farley and Franklin Roosevelt.

It's not clear when Magnuson decided on a party affiliation. There is witness, however, to the notion that the decision was based on expediency as well as ideology. He consulted his friend and benefactor Bill Stern in Fargo. He noted the rising strength of labor unions and their Democratic Party allies. Stern, North Dakota's "Mr. Republican," advised him to go with labor and the Democrats. This he did.[10]

Magnuson stumped the state in 1928 for Bullitt, and worked the University of Washington campus for Al Smith, alongside his fellow student, the idealistic Marion Zioncheck. There's no indication the Bullitt-Smith losses gave him second thoughts about betting on the wrong horse. For a short time after his graduation in 1929, Magnuson worked in the law office of Judge Samuel Stern—no kin to the Sterns of Fargo. With strong recommendations from Schweppe and Bullitt, he was offered the job as secretary of the Seattle Municipal League, steady work. He might have sensed a gathering storm.

Wall Street was still roaring that year, stock prices rising until October. But in the state of Washington, by graduation time business indices were falling, unemployment rising, and six banks had closed their doors, prelude to an economic catastrophe.

"It was politics or starve," said Magnuson. It was politics. He took the job as Municipal League secretary.

CHAPTER 5

Depression

The economic depression of the 1930s crashed over the Pacific Northwest with the effect of a tidal wave on a bamboo village. With it came Franklin Roosevelt, the New Deal, Warren Magnuson, and the federalization of the Northwest economy. The Yakima Chamber of Commerce in conservative central Washington would appeal to Washington, D.C., for shipbuilding contracts at the Bremerton Naval Shipyard on Puget Sound. Such was the economic desperation. Other bastions of unfettered free enterprise tumbled under the crush of business catastrophe. They dropped ideology to shout for help from the federal and state governments.

When depression receded too many years later, the region had a new political and social landscape. Labor unions controlled a piece of the economy. The Democratic Party, with its radical left allies, became the overwhelming party of choice. Warren Magnuson, the most influential conduit between Washington, D.C., and Washington State, was in the midst of a fifty-year political career that would not end until the coming of Ronald Reagan in 1980.

Legislator, prosecutor, lover, and congressman, Magnuson would be as important to the development of the Longacres racetrack and Northwest Airlines—private enterprises—as he was to the Naval Shipyard, the Boeing Company, the viaduct between Seattle and West Seattle, Columbia River dams, and small-town post offices.

In 1933, at age twenty-eight, a freshman at the dawn of his political career, he was a leader in the most turbulent legislative session in the history of the state. Handsome as a Hollywood movie idol, gregarious as a department store greeter, Magnuson was a natural. He fit Stimson Bullitt's primary requisite for the ideal politician: he enjoyed people and they enjoyed him. He was flexible, close in feeling to the facts of human needs. With his uncertain background and determination to make good, he was a fit for a time when the facts of American human needs had never been so grim.

Maggie had acquired a taste for fast horses, strong whiskey, and beautiful women, vices in the judgment of some, but indulgences that never overrode his business as a politician. The women he loved, even those he left, adored the man. Nothing else in his personal life is quite so remarkable. Forty years after their affair, Magnuson would greet the grandson of Ms. Germaine Barry, telling the young man, "I'll always be fond of her."

With banks failing, and factories closing their doors, Magnuson took his first steady job as secretary of the Municipal League in Seattle.[1] He quickly established enduring contact with the city's movers and shakers, most of them, like real estate tycoon Henry Broderick, and banker Lawrence Arnold, Republicans. The job, he said, aimed to "spread the spirit of better citizenship." The organization favored a city planning commission, development of the Seattle port, and dams on the Skagit River to power Seattle City Light. He staged weekly luncheons with guest speakers such as Scott Bullitt and James Doyle, publisher of the *Seattle Post-Intelligencer*. Magnuson wrote and edited the *Municipal League News*, which, for reasons never explained, had its largest foreign circulation in the Soviet Union. He had an abiding problem: money.

So did virtually everyone else in Seattle. By 1932, unemployment in the state was estimated, unofficially, at between 25 and 30 percent. As Terry Pettus, a newsman-survivor, has noted, it was especially tough on the middle class. Working stiffs were accustomed to losing their jobs. Not so white collar workers and professionals who attached status as well as wherewithal to their employment. While Dave Beck's Teamsters, Harry Lundeberg's West Coast Sailors, and Harry Bridges's Longshoremen gathered their muscle, a mini-city of unemployed and shacks grew near Seattle's central waterfront. Residents called it Hooverville in dubious homage to the president, governed themselves in a civil manner, and managed enough food to survive. It was tough. "Four years in a depression is almost a life," said Pettus.[2] In fact, it was almost a revolution, with the West Coast waterfront seamen and longshoremen in the vanguard.

There was no safety net to catch those pink-slipped factory workers, laid-off accountants, and unpaid lawyers who were in social free-fall. The response of the Hoover administration was breadlines and soup kitchens, much of this administered by the Red Cross. Hoover abhorred the idea of a "handout." Unemployment insurance and social security, sixty-year-old social mainstays of industrialized Europe, had yet to become American law. For a large minority of Americans the early 1930s were years of bitter helplessness. Their money vanished in failed banks, farms were lost to unpaid mortgages, and many faced outright hunger. Yet there would be no violent revolution. There are still graying radicals around Seattle who will not forgive Magnuson for his role in preventing that ultimate social calamity, such as had taken place in Russia thirteen years earlier in 1917.

Magnuson's correspondence to and from homefolks doesn't give any hint of the desperation which he was avoiding and, in a sense, preparing to exploit as a candidate for the state House of Representatives from Seattle's Thirty-seventh Legislative District come election year, 1932.

His Fargo buddy Amos Tweeden writes "Mr. Smooth" of a summertime of sunshine, fun, games, and girls: "It grieves the men deeply that you and Jim [?] did not return [from the west] but then we had a better chance with the honeys."

"Sis," his adopted sister Clara Junkin, expressed pride in Warren's achievements and her dismay at the fall-off in trade at the Junkin speakeasy. Prohibition's repeal had yet to come.

"We're real proud to think how fast you are coming up out there," wrote Sis. "Junk [her husband] is busy. He plans on opening the place now . . . but business is bad. And the price of alcohol is so cheap one can't make anything. Business comes by streaks. And there's always someone who wants a nice place to sit down and drink."[3]

Magnuson left the Muny League in 1932 to become a special prosecutor probing "official misconduct" on a contract between King County and the Van Doren Iron Works and to pursue allegations of overpayments on X-ray machines for Harborview Hospital.[4] The heightened public exposure enhanced his prospects in a race for the state legislature. He already had a robust base of support in downtown Seattle from law school cronies and Muny League connections. It took little of his uncanny vision to foresee the shift away from the Republican Party to the left, in some cases to the extremes of the socialist and communist parties. He had no question about the political tide, and so advised Joe Hughes, his law school pal, a Republican candidate for the legislature from Wenatchee: "There is no doubt in my mind that the state is going Democratic by over a one hundred thousand vote majority. And you'll be left sitting on a rock in the middle of the Columbia River." He also chided Hughes for taking lightly the political aspirations of another college friend, Marion Zioncheck.[5]

Magnuson attended the 1932 Democratic convention, another brawl between "wets" and "drys," this time without Scott Bullitt. At the peak of his influence in the national Democratic Party, Bullitt died at his home in Seattle. This was April 1932, the depth of the Great Depression. "It was a staggering blow to his party," wrote political historian Fayette Krause, "a death that shattered any hope for cohesion and stability in the Democratic organization; there was no other figure of comparable stature."[6]

A new star was rising, however. Like Adolf Hitler in Germany and Franklin Roosevelt in New York, Warren Magnuson had discovered radio. He was amplifying his voice. His message, delivered through well-crafted, typewritten speeches, was straight from the Populist—New Deal playbook: support for a civilian conservation corps and higher wages for workers. In a roundabout way, he was pushing for a revitalization of capitalism; this at a time when many of his peers had well-founded doubts about its value:

> Business prosperity depends on wages. . . . Unemployment means no business, economic destruction. There is high pressure propaganda circulated by so-called civic organizations who use their puppets in public office to knock down wages. Public, beware! We're in a new era in our history. By 1930 we were near the destruction of the American system. . . . Business failed to revive the system. . . . Democrats saved the time with Franklin Roosevelt and the New Deal. . . . Future historians will point to the New Deal as being responsible for the greatest single advance in economic progress—shorter work weeks, better working conditions, better hours and more leisure and happiness for our people.[7]

Such was Magnuson's prescient rhetoric. His actions in Olympia during the state's 1933 legislative session are more significant. He won his seat in the House of Representatives in a walk, portent of his success at the polls for the next thirty years. Roosevelt won the White House and Homer Bone won the U.S. Senate seat. It was a political watershed, galvanizing new politics, and new friendships.

Bone's campaign manager, Saul Haas, met Magnuson through Scott Bullitt. Haas had come west from New York to attend Northern Idaho College, and edited the *Portland News* and the *Port Angeles Herald* before returning to Manhattan as a copy editor for Hearst's International News Service. He came to Seattle in 1921 as editor of the *Union Record*, a booster of Bullitt's race for the Senate in 1926. Haas and Magnuson thus began a friendship, initially a political partnership, that became a business partnership in 1935 when Haas purchased the nearly defunct radio station KPCB, changed its call signal to KIRO, and welcomed Magnuson as an investor. It proved to be an investment of considerable value, although Magnuson probably took the initial plunge into radio more from friendship with Haas than hope for a lucrative return. Their friendship lasted until the newsman's death in 1972. Once when they were together in New York, Haas took Magnuson to the city's Lower East Side, and left him standing on the sidewalk while he entered a run-down tenement building. Haas returned after a brief interlude without offering an explanation for the unusual visit. Magnuson figured that his friend had gone back to visit the grim home of his youth.

"I see you're making good," wrote Bill Stern from Fargo. "I know you can go a long way and listen to the advice of older men, even though you may not always use it. . . . Remember what the railroad conductor always says and watch your step. Let me know how things are going." Stern would very soon have more in mind for Magnuson than happy greetings.

Things were going swell. Olympia loomed as Magnuson's next great adventure, one he wished to share in part with a woman friend, Ethel Anne Farley. He pitched her qualifications as a secretary to the legislative hiring committee and noted "her democracy [sic] is above reproach. She is the former private secretary to Sen. James Reed of Missouri."[8]

Washington's Twenty-third Legislature, a sneak preview of the New Deal to come in Washington, D.C., convened January 9, 1933. The House had seventy Democrats, twenty-seven Republicans. So abrupt was the change from Republican to Democratic dominance, only a handful of legislators had prior experience. One of these precious few, George Yantis, an Olympia lawyer, was elected House Speaker. At once he addressed members on the gravity of their situation:

> These are not ordinary times. We find ourselves and our nation in common with other nations of the world in a condition which we had hoped had passed forever from the affairs of civilized people. May I offer a word of suggestion: we must be loyal to our country, our state, our principles. We must also be loyal to each other. Legislatures are always a hard place with few to commend us, many to condemn. . . . We are now in the same boat working for a common cause. Let us be loyal to each other.[9]

"This was the year of the big upheaval," recalled Charles Hodde, himself a former Speaker of Washington's House of Representatives, a lobbyist for the Grange at the 1933 session. "This was different, the problems severe. There was Hooverville in Seattle—unemployment was 25 percent to 30 percent. People were looking for something different."[10]

Relief for unemployed was most pressing. If anyone overlooked that fact, there were two hunger marches on the capital, wake-up calls for action. The first, January 16, brought over a thousand men, women, and children, most of them from western Washington, many in tattered business suits. Historian Gordon Newell says the typical marcher was thirty-two years old, three years out of work, with a wife and two kids, and had lost savings in a bank failure. Several carried banners, one said "Communist Party Leaders in the Struggle for Workers." No doubt the Communist Party had helped organize the march.

"We can't sit back and starve," said one. Indeed, they looked undernourished. Olympia barricaded itself against what appeared to be revolution. The capitol locked its doors, fearing violence. Instead, the confrontation was orderly. A committee formed from marchers' ranks met with legislative leaders. They demanded unemployment insurance. A second march, of more thousands, got shunted off by law officers to a cold winter's night in the Priest Point Park on Budd Inlet north of the city.[11] But the message was delivered.

"Sure, unemployment relief was most pressing," said Hodde. "But given the brand new 40-mill limit on property taxes recently passed by an initiative to the people, the '33 session also had to scramble and find a new source of revenue. These problems placed a premium on legislative skills. There were some very able legislators, some very stupid ones. Magnuson stood out.

"He was recognized as being very noisy and young, but knowing what he was talking about. He sat on the aisle about three rows from the back of the House chamber. When he talked, he waved his arms, walking up and down the aisles. The members listened. They were looking for a leader. He was one—someone who could say this is where we're going."[12]

He was a reformer, not a radical. Members of the communist-socialist persuasion, firm in their convictions that capitalism was beyond salvation, formed a substantial subcaucus inside the seventy-member Democratic caucus. They were heated in their expressions, but not very effective. As it always does in legislative bodies, the power to produce legislation moved to the center. The difference in 1933 was a center far to the left of the Republican-dominated 1931 session.

Howard "Mac" MacGowan, a one-eyed, $2,600-a-year star reporter of the *Seattle Star,* discovered Magnuson and thirteen other freshmen legislators living communally in the old Sylvester mansion near the capitol. Magnuson, wrote MacGowan, was the leader. Their aim, shades of the nineteenth-century rural Populists, was legislation allowing the Utilities and Transportation Commission to set the rates consumers would pay for gas, electric power, and telephones. Magnuson brought the bills with him from Seattle. He also carried the "Bone bill" and a measure to allow pari-mutuel betting on horse races, this one on behalf of racetrack entrepreneurs Bill Edris and Joe Gottstein of Seattle.

It was the start of a lifelong friendship and political alliance between Magnuson and MacGowan, an Oregon native, sometime student at Reed College who shipped out of Portland to see the world and soon thereafter emerged as a newsman to work for the *Paris Herald,* the *New York Sun,* the *New York Herald,* and the *New York Journal.*[13] It was an era of newsprint journalism and itinerant journalists. The latter have given way to the more immediate and glamorous stars of television. Mac had an eye for talent as well as news. So did Yantis. He made Magnuson chairman of the unemployment relief committee, de facto floor leader of the session's most important legislation. For a maritime equivalent, imagine an ordinary seaman promoted to skipper of a blue-water voyage.

The bill, a precursor of unemployment compensation to come later from the New Deal, was described by Speaker Yantis as "an act to relieve the people of the state from hardship and suffering created by unemployment." Left unstated was the idea that capitalism had failed and that the state needed to ameliorate its failure—an approach the communist-socialist subcaucus had to swallow. Too many of their constituents were hungry. It called for a $10 million bond issue and a commission named by the governor to shell out funds for work projects. It passed the House ninety to one, some credit to Magnuson's oratory. It had little more difficulty passing the Senate.

But the snag was a provision in the state's constitution limiting bonded indebtedness unless the state faced the threat of insurrection. House Bill 263 shattered the limit. The state Supreme Court, in its wisdom, if not practical experience, took note of the massive hunger marches, their potential for insurrection, and decided HB 263 met the measure of the constitution.[14] Governor Clarence Martin made Charles Ernst director of the relief operation and Dorothy Bullitt, widow of Scott, a member of the supervising commission. Magnuson would shortly become its attorney.

Work on the Emergency Unemployment Relief Commission, said Mrs. Bullitt, was exhausting; the pressure from those seeking money for their projects was constant for two years. Meetings in the governor's office each Tuesday lasted all day:

> There we were, a committee of five, plus a young lawyer just out of school . . . Warren Magnuson. . . . Maggie and I drove [to Olympia] to those meetings together. . . . His first marriage was a college something—I don't think it lasted long—and I don't think they had the same ideals. He had a funny growl of a voice that sounded artificial until you got to know him and knew it was real. He liked to talk things over with me. He opened up and told about his vision of the law and what was wrong with things.[15]

The *Star* front-paged legislative action on the relief measure, along with photos of Hollywood movie stars Claudette Colbert and Myrna Loy, and news that Adolf Hitler demanded German rearmament to "protect its borders." It editorialized a warning about the squads of private power lobbyists "buzzing around Senators and representatives" to kill passage of the "Bone bill" and companion measures setting utility rates. They lost. The public power measure passed after two days of debate—there is no accounting of the amount of free liquor—with senator-elect Bone himself lobbying the capitol corridors. He gave thanks to the freshman Magnuson for its passage. Joe Gottstein and Bill Edris, privately, did the same for his work on the pari-mutuel measure, the foundation for a horse breeding and racing industry as well as their Longacres track in a Seattle suburb.

Despite the legend, embellished by President John Kennedy, Magnuson did not create the Grand Coulee Dam through his legislative charms. As a legislator, he did add to the cry for federal money to construct this massive monument to the federalization of Washington State, the first of the dams that would electrify the Northwest and turn its arid central basin into a cornucopia. Public power advocates had urged its construction in north-central Washington since the end of World War I. President Hoover approved the project in principle, but never pressed Congress for the money. Franklin Roosevelt provided inspiration and money, $63 million, and construction began in September 1933. Grand Coulee fit the New Deal's scheme for recovery, a labor intensive project to provide cheap hydroelectric power for heavy industry as well as consumers.[16] It remains, churning electricity, a physical monument rivaling a pyramid or the main temple at Angkor Wat. Private power interests tried to kill it. The *Washington Post* called its construction a misuse of federal power. Even the *Bellingham Herald* called it a "folly"—there was no industry to use its electricity. The *Herald* failed to anticipate the aluminum plants that were to come soon after its completion, in time to make the materials critical to American war machines. Grand Coulee and the dams to follow, thanks to federal finance, would remake the Northwest. Magnuson and a few other visionaries understood this even before the first bucket of Grand Coulee's 10 million cubic feet of concrete was poured. He introduced the bill to divert $200,000 from the state unemployment relief fund for Grand Coulee construction. Opposition quickened. Ralph Nichols, a Seattle City Council member, summed up the case against it in a letter to Magnuson: Northwest electric power was already surplus; the money could be better used for irrigation—a diversion pushed by Washington Water Power; a state subsidy would be needed to make Grand Coulee power cheap enough to sell.[17] Dorothy Bullitt later recalled that the dam was presented primarily as an irrigation project to enhance its public acceptance.[18] Fortunately for the future of the Northwest, wiser heads knew better and prevailed. The dam became a triumph of New Deal ideology, a public work that hired the unemployed, generated energy, and opened new farmlands. In sum, it created wealth.

Moreover, the unemployment relief act helped shape the modern state. In addition to boosting Grand Coulee, the seed money built the Roza irrigation project, turning the semiarid Yakima Valley into the world's most productive apple orchard; the Deception Pass Bridge in Northwest Washington, a structure of awesome beauty and a latter-day tourist attraction; and Seattle's Washington Park Arboretum. As Mrs. Bullitt later explained: "The bridge, the dam, and the irrigation [projects] were necessities. The arboretum wasn't, but we needed some project in the densest population area of the state. . . . We chose the arboretum not for growing plants and trees, but to employ untrained men who could live at home and work in the city."[19]

Reformers in Olympia did not stop with the unemployment relief act. With scant press attention, they enacted another precursor of New Deal legislation to come. House Bill 14, providing a pension of $30 a month for citizens over sixty, did not sail so easily through the tumult. It stalled on a motion by Representative E. F. Banker, an Okanogan County cattle rancher who wondered "what's the rush" on such drastic legislation and moved to send it back to committee. He lost 73 to 25. Thus, months in advance of the New Deal, the nation had its first de facto "Social Security" law. Alas, it was somewhat hollow. Strapped for cash, the state left it to the counties to fund these pensions. But it was a mighty turn toward what most Americans now regard as a sacred birthright.

Gently prodded by Homer Bone, who came in person to lobby, the legislature passed the bill bearing his name allowing public utilities to expand across the state, taking over customers held by the private power companies. It did not come easily. *Ryan's Weekly* reported its passage after "a three day scrap. Maggie showed plenty of stuff on the ball. It was his fine work that passed the Bone bill." Bone telegraphed his thanks to the young legislator.

"We're having a very difficult time on taxation," Magnuson wrote Frank Bell, secretary to Senator Clarence Dill. "Sometimes the problems appear to be beyond solution—but we'll work our way out." The way out was passage of a gross tax on business and occupations, the "B&O tax." Magnuson said it was to be strictly temporary. Quite the contrary, it remains a staple of the state's tax base to this day.[20]

Outside the capitol, Magnuson spent time with other freshmen in the Sylvester mansion, sleeping on cots, sharing meals. He had money enough to live elsewhere and did, but he said he spent time in the commune "to learn the needs of the jobless." Despite the terrible economic conditions and the stress of a critical legislative session, he was experimenting and having a hell of a good time.

"You Republicans sure die hard," he wrote in a letter twitting his old buddy Joe Hughes. "Don't you know that from now on there will be only two major parties in the country—Democrats and Socialists. The Republican Party is in permanent retirement. Seriously, I wish you were here. I sure am having a great time and with the two of us together we could run the entire House. I am having some success at it, but with you added it would be a cinch."

Hughes responded, "We have found it necessary to cancel our sub-scriptions to all Seattle newspapers in order to keep from looking at your homely physiognomy every morning."[21] A brilliant trial lawyer, a Republican of strong conservative bent, Hughes remained Magnuson's lifelong pal.

Magnuson's Methodist marriage vows were in abeyance in Olympia, a sexual free-fire zone for legislators before that time and ever since. Ethel Anne Farley sent him a note, written, she said, while listening on the radio to the "theme song of all married men who trifle on their wives: 'Don't tell a soul we love each other lest they discover.' Damn all married men!!!" Later, apparently after the end of their affair, Ethel Anne wrote Magnuson: "I'm sorry personalities have spoiled our friendship. This is one of the principal hells of being a woman . . . however, if at any time it sounds interesting to talk to a female who neither drinks or smokes or who won't try to drag you down, call me up."[22]

Peggins, however, had yet to throw in her wedding ring. From Seattle this vivacious woman wrote her legislative representative: "Hello Man in the Moon. I'd like nothing better than to run down one of the center aisles [in the House] and greet the gentleman from King County (the one fair to see) with less propriety than is generally the custom on the floor."

Absent much response from her husband, Peggins again writes:

Hello. Ya might just write me a postcard, seein as how I love you somewhat. Just between you and me I'd sorta like you to come up and see me this weekend. Think ya can make it up to the city?—Your same sweetheart you've had nigh unto six years and the one you'll have for 60 more says here's somp'n for ya, X.
       P. Magnuson.[23]

The state legislature still faced unfinished business, ratification of the repeal of national prohibition and the creation of a new system for controlling and selling booze. It returned in a special session December 4, 1933, quickly approving a state monopoly on liquor sales. The Steele Act, named for its Senate sponsor, was drafted at least in part by Al Schweppe and pushed through the House by Magnuson, his last major act as a state legislator. It remains law to this day.

At the end of this historic session, Speaker Yantis took note of his twenty-eight-year-old colleague, Magnuson: "You remember I told you I was going to have to count on you for a lot of work related to revenue and taxation and also on the unemployment problems. You were a very important factor in the session and delivered the goods every time. . . . I extend my personal appreciation [and] I wish you every success. . . . you have the ability and the character to deliver at all times."[24]

CHAPTER 6

Young Man in a Hurry

Young Magnuson had aims on the King County Courthouse and beyond—to a future in the skies above. The world of the Depression around him in Seattle, soup lines and Hooverville, loomed dreary. Not Magnuson. He was flush with success in the 1933 legislature, confident of his political ability, ambitious, and eager to please. "The liveliest young man I ever met in many a long day," observed R. L. Rutter, the conservative Spokane banker.[1]

Unlike about 25 percent of the men in Seattle, he also had a job, attorney for the state relief commission, which had $10 million to spend for the creation of jobs—the measure he pushed through committee and out of the House of Representatives in Olympia. From the scant evidence he left behind, the job wasn't enough to engage the man. His sometime allies, left-radical Democrats, were busy organizing what would become the Washington Commonwealth Federation. Magnuson busied himself with private goals.

Back in Fargo, his mentor Bill Stern and Croil Hunter were forming a new airline to link the Midwest with the Northwest. Hunter would shortly become the first general manager of Northwest Airlines, owned at that time by two St. Paul millionaires. Stern would again be Magnuson's link to opportunity.

Shortly after the end of the 1933 legislative session, Stern wrote Magnuson to meet with Hunter in Spokane, advising "there may be work for you." Magnuson apparently missed the meeting but he grasped at the chance to take flight with the nation's newest transportation industry. Nothing this side of Hollywood would seem so glamorous to Americans of the early 1930s as travel in a flying machine. Given his vision, the young legislator foresaw profits as well as glamour. His own preference for travel remained streamlined trains.

"Dear Bill," he replied a few weeks later to Stern. "I haven't heard from Hunter. . . . Gov. [Clarence] Martin has asked the Congressional delegation to urge an air mail contract between Minneapolis and Seattle. . . . I assume Hunter wants some help on this move. . . . If there's any thing further to do along these lines for yourself or Hunter I would be glad to cooperate. I know most of our Congressmen and the two senators, one of whom [Bone] I know exceptionally well."

Congress was the key to the awarding of an airmail contract, the de facto federal subsidy needed to get a new airline off the ground. Hunter already had a proposition in the mail. He wanted Magnuson's help in extending the airmail route from Billings, Montana, to Seattle. The first step: creation of a committee to arouse Seattle's interest in an air route to the Midwest. "You'll be in a position to be of very material assistance," Hunter noted.

"I would be glad to be of any service, legal or otherwise, to your company in helping arrangements at this end," Magnuson wired Hunter. He followed with a note to Stern requesting that he contact Hunter to close his employment deal. Stern said he would "make it my business to see that you get a job" if they need a lawyer in Seattle. What they would get, however, was a lawyer-legislator with established connections to the state's New Dealish delegation to Washington. By November 1933, Magnuson had established himself with the fledgling airline, arranging a meeting for Hunter with Governor Martin, and winning the "wholehearted support" of Saul Haas, "Senator Bone's right hand man." He was mister-in-between for Northwest Airlines and the federal government.[2]

They needed a lobbyist to carry their demands to Washington. These were critical: funds for construction of airports and beacons to guide aircraft onto the airfields. Radio was primitive, the global positioning navigation system farfetched even for Buck Rogers, the futuristic comic strip hero of that era. To bulk up their case in Washington, civic boosters along the northern route formed the Northern Transcontinental Airways Association. R. L. Rutter, chairman of the Spokane and Eastern bank, was its first president. One of his first acts was to hire Magnuson to lobby for the federal money, "regardless of which company is given the [airmail] contract." The lobbyist's salary was $500 plus expenses. Northwest, which already had passenger service from St. Paul to Seattle, had an obvious edge in being awarded the contract.[3]

It also had Magnuson, a Northwest Airlines fixture, who had entree to the postmaster general, James Farley, a prime mover in the airmail contract. Sam Stern, Bill's brother, had written his friend Farley to introduce Magnuson as "one of the leading young Democrats in Washington state and a member of the Legislature," and to say that he would come calling. It worked, a lobbyist's dream come true. In April 1934, Rutter wired the word to his lobbyist, now returned to Seattle: "Thanks for the good work in Spokane and Washington and more power to you. . . .

Farley has agreed to let a 90-day contract for the entire route, Chicago to Seattle. Isn't that great news?"

Northwest was off the ground, flying new 192-mph Lockheed Electras and developing into one of the nation's major airlines. It has survived into the late twentieth century while Pan American, Eastern, Braniff, and other pioneers have crashed in red ink and vanished.

"I've been so intimately connected with [Northwest] problems, it has almost become a matter of pride to suceed," Magnuson told Hunter. "Local natives point me out as part of the organization, I have been talking and selling the airline so vociferously."

Lawyer Magnuson was handling airport leases for the airline, and working the back rooms of Olympia to forestall a tax on aviation gasoline, one with a $300,000 impact on Northwest Airlines. At the same time he was shamelessly plugging Puget Sound to the Northwest management. A Chicago-Seattle connection would "bring in a tourist trade to Puget Sound." The region could be America's summer playground. "I was a member of the last Legislature that liberalized some of our rigid blue laws. We expect to be able to offer good clean championship boxing and horse racing." Indeed, Magnuson had passed the pari-mutuel law and found the land in suburban Seattle for the Longacres racetrack owned by his friends Joe Gottstein and Bill Edris.

"The only opposition [to Northwest] I can see would be from the Boeing interests, which are quite dominant in our territory," he told Hunter. Boeing at that time was a corporate brother to United Airlines.

If there was any challenge to Representative Magnuson over a conflict of interest between his public service and private work for Northwest, it stayed muted. It would come two decades later in political campaigns, whispers, then editorials suggesting Northwest had bought the Washington politician. The politician did purchase Northwest stock after a discreet inquiry to Hunter, "I am now in a position [to purchase] the stock if it is agreeable to Mr. Lilly. . . . find out if it is possible for me to make that purchase."

R. C. Lilly, president of the First National Bank of St. Paul, was one of three major owners of the airline, according to testimony given by Croil Hunter to a Senate hearing on airmail contracts. The others were Shreve Archer and H. H. Erwin. Shares of its stock were strictly limited. Asked if any of these shares were given to individuals for services, Hunter answered emphatically, "No sir."

It was agreeable to Lilly. Magnuson purchased Northwest stock through a New York broker on the New York stock exchange and held it until he became chairman of the U.S. Senate Commerce Committee, when the stock was liquidated. For the chairman of the committee with a handhold on aviation, the conflict of interest would have been egregious, viewed by today's standards. It was already bad enough in 1935. It was not, however, a violation of any law or rule of the legislature or Congress. The crackdown on political conflicts of interest did not come into force until the 1970s, by which time Magnuson had sold his Northwest Airlines stock and removed himself from its board of directors. He made money from his private ventures, sufficient to accommodate a high-flying lifestyle that included Hollywood, Santa Anita, Churchill Downs, and Belmont as well as Seattle and Washington, D.C. But they did not make the man wealthy. He had a hardy appetite for work, but a limited desire for wealth—in contrast to his great congressional pal Lyndon Johnson, who did get rich in public office.

Magnuson had other private business, including legal work for S. S. Hahn, general counsel for the Scripps League of Newspapers in Los Angeles. The Scripps chain included the *Seattle Star*. He performed initial work for Scripps without charging a fee, a smart means of attracting the newspaper's support, even if done without design. Early in 1934 he was getting set to move up the political ladder, with a run for King County prosecutor, one of the most powerful positions in the state. Newspaper notice was part of the campaign machinery.

Saul Haas and the *Star*'s own Howard MacGowan, Magnuson's boon companions, surely provided encouragement and know-how for the race. Haas had managed Homer Bone's Senate campaign, then shifted from newspapers to radio, purchasing a bankrupt station located in the basement of the Cobb Building in downtown Seattle. His friends helped with finances. They included Magnuson, who invested $2,000. Eventually he would wind up with a four percent interest in station KIRO along with a friendly outlet for his views. MacGowan, the news veteran, was an all-purpose writer and intelligence operative. More encouragment came from downtown contacts Maggie made as Municipal League secretary, chief of whom was Henry Broderick, the commercial real estate magnate and staunch Republican. Broderick would not let partisan politics interfere with his judgment of political flesh.[4] By July 1934, Magnuson had made the decision to run. Democrats began to rally for their first chance in decades to hold the prosecutor's office.

The enthusiastic *Star* described Maggie as the "White hope" of Democrats and progressives, "short, handsome . . . so easy going you wonder how he ever did so much in so little time. . . . He won labor by moving the anti-injunction bill [allowing strikes] from legislative committee to passage—a bill blocked [by business] for 20 years," and he got the Bone bill through "despite many a cigar and bottle of whiskey passed out by the [private] power boys."

"The race will be tough," advised Ed Henry, the secretary, as administrative assistants were then labeled, to U.S. Representative Marion Zioncheck and, much later, a King County Superior Court judge. "So it will take a damned vigorous campaign, but I think you can do it. . . . I know Marion is for you. He thinks a lot of you."[5]

It came easier than Ed Henry figured. Maggie had looks, personality, a record of performance in Olympia, and something no Republican could match, a common touch. The campaign went smoothly. In its midst Peggins, still enchanted with her husband, needled the candidate, whom she addressed as "Mr. Rickles": "You might tell MacGowan there are rumors afloat that Magnuson was seen at a tea recently and I fear for the reputation of his protege. Is the red blood of the Magnuson headquarters paling to pink? Tea parties smack of Republicanism to me. Make the next one a cocktail party and retain the esprit de corps!"

Aided by tea parties, esprit de corps, and a fast-running Democratic tide, Magnuson won in a walk. When he first met the beautiful Carol Parker, just returned to Seattle from a singing engagement in Shanghai, he called himself the "persecuting attorney." They would go on from that meeting in the nightclub owned by bandleader Vic Meyers, Club Vic, to a fifteen-year relationship, although this did not quell his quest for other amours.

Shortly after his election, the new prosecutor slipped away for ten days in San Francisco and Los Angeles for a high time of girls and drink. He did not invite Peggins. Instead, in Los Angeles there was Florence Durkin, who came down with a bad case of the blues when Magnuson went back to Seattle. She wrote, "Warren darling . . . I certainly agree with you when you say so very few things in life are perfect and when people find any certain perfection it should not be cast aside. I would like to believe you do care a little because I developed a fondness while you were here that has rapidly developed into something pretty close to misery since you left. . . . I'll try to get my mind off how much I am missing you. [I] trust it hasn't been anything wrong that hurried you away. I'm looking for a letter or a personal appearance. Love, Florence." There's no indication Magnuson ever saw the woman again.

He did see Germaine Barry, a secretary in Sheriff W. B. Severyns's office, and would that spring of 1935, as quietly as possible, get a final divorce from the vivacious Peggins. Newspapers found out about the divorce action across Puget Sound in the Kitsap County Courthouse. Maggie shrugged at the publicity and said, "I guess it couldn't be helped."

Barry, in a letter, chided the prosecutor for his absence from the office he had just joined:

Dear High Flier, Flying again? Was she blonde or brunette?
>Remember my little man
>That lambs they gambol too
>Where do they end up, my little man
>They end up in the stew
>You may end up in it too.
>Je t'aime et je t'adore.
>>Germaine[6]

Magnuson also had an eye for legal talent and showed it in 1935 when lining up his staff of deputies. Jobs were scarce, so the hiring was easy. Ed Henry came back from Washington. Paul Coughlin, a major player in the public power movement, signed on as chief deputy, and Albert Rosellini, a young University of Washington law school graduate, got his call from "a guy named Magnuson" two days after the Democratic primary election.

Rosellini, a future two-term governor of the state, had missed by eighty votes in his race for the state legislature against "Tiger Jim" Murphy, a local boss in Seattle's Rainier Valley district. Magnuson was, nevertheless, impressed. "He wanted my help in the election finals," said Rosellini, still a vigorous warhorse in the 1990s. "He said I could have a job as deputy prosecutor if he won the election. That sounded good. He was a gregarious guy, as a boss easygoing, very politically conscious, an adviser to all his deputies. He did not flaunt his power, never made a big deal out of his position. He had a lot of friends."[7]

The new prosecutor inherited problems, a seaport with tenderloin and a Chinatown operating under an unofficial policy of "tolerance," provided the police got their share of the wages of sin. Reports to his office listed bars dispensing moonshine whiskey at 15 to 35 cents a shot. "Little Harlem" had moonshine, dancing, and "anything you want," meaning prostitutes. The Alameda County, California, district attorney, and subsequently U.S. Supreme Court chief justice, Earl Warren, tipped the prosecutor that "Madame Jessie" was violating the laws of the state by running a house that was not a tea parlor.[8]

One inside breakdown reported 900 prostitutes at work in the city and 221 bootleg parlors. Whorehouses paid $5.00 per month per woman to police, who gathered $275,000 a year in graft, a sum distributed among themselves and other public officials. No wonder there was a reaction against such "tolerance" by the city's expanding middle class, its citizens of propriety.[9]

The Reverend Mark Matthews, Seattle's male version of Carrie Nation, demanded the new prosecutor shut down the city's wicked ways and enforce its blue laws. Magnuson did so for a few days until the public uproar over the Saturday night and Sunday restrictions convinced even the staunch Reverend Matthews that Seattle had to go back to its hypocritical ways. The prosecutor and the preacher subsequently became good friends. Maggie had an extraordinary gift for turning an adversary into a confidant. "Futile" said Magnuson about efforts to shut down good times in the seaport. Seattle's "tolerance" policy, with lines running directly from the courthouse and the cop shop to the bars and whorehouses, would endure—even flourish—until the late 1960s, whatever the character or disposition of subsequent prosecutors. It was Seattle's way of dealing with its split personality, part seaport and tenderloin, part bourgeois respectability. A tough crusade against the hypocritical policy by the *Seattle Post-Intelligencer* in 1968 resulted in indictments against the incumbent prosecutor, sheriff, police chief, and lesser officers of law enforcement, closing the "tolerance" chapter in the city's history.

Magnuson, like his sucessors in the office, at least acquiesced in "tolerance." When clean government forces demanded a grand jury at the end of his tenure, Superior Court Judge Clay Allen cited the need to probe payoffs, payroll padding, employee kickbacks, and gambling, then qualified his remarks: "I'm not pointing an accusing finger at Maggie, but he was prosecutor during the malfunctions [*sic*]."[10]

Otherwise, his first year record was impressive. He won 316 convictions, lost 27, sent 123 men to the state prison in Walla Walla, two of them for hanging, and won praise from the city's stiff-necked publication of propriety, the *Argus*. One of these prosecutions, for murder in the first degree, was against "Mary Kelly," whose real name, probably Russian, was a mystery like much of her life. Mary personified the polyglot side of Seattle, the tough part along the flats below Queen Anne, First, and Capitol Hills, where the respectable folk domiciled. A soldier in the "Imperial Russian Battalion of Death," she served on the German front in World War I, married an American soldier in Vladivostok, and migrated to the United States after the revolution. She worked as a fisherman until uncovered as a woman, then moved into a tideflat shack along Seattle's Elliott Bay with one Otto Johanson. She described him as a "piece of human tideflat driftwood." Tired of her shackmate, Mary Kelly bashed his head with a sledge one January night, then slit his throat. She got $100 from his pockets, went downtown, got drunk, and then got chauffeured home to her shack in a 16-cylinder limousine. Her defense attorney described Otto as a "quarelsome fellow." Magnuson refused to ask the death penalty.[11]

He prosecuted relief chiselers and collected kickbacks from salaries of his deputies, sums ranging from $73.50 to $139.50 each month.[12] It was, explains Rosellini, a common practice in public office at that time. To the victor went the spoils. There's no accounting of kickback disbursement. Rosellini speculates that it went into political campaigns, Magnuson's as well as those of other deputies. "He wanted all of us to participate in politics," said Rosellini. He and Ed Henry would go on to the state legislature.

It may seem appalling in the 1990s, but until 1969 there was no law against a public prosecutor and his deputies also conducting their private law business. Magnuson did not neglect his side work as a lawyer-lobbyist for Northwest Airlines. Letters to Washington Senators Bone and Lewis Schwellenbach lobbied on behalf of airmail legislation and introduced the men to Croil Hunter. He helped on petty matters for the airline in Seattle, and—most egregious, considering his public position—waged a legal action against the Washington Aircraft Transportation Company for damages it did in a collision with a Northwest Electra. Magnuson informed Hunter, "They are liable. We are trying to get everything we can out of them."

He spent time at Holman Field, Minneapolis–St. Paul, where Northwest Airlines headquartered, while Paul Coughlin kept the courthouse store, seizing illegal slot machines, conducting the regular weekly poker games. Coughlin kept Magnuson informed by telegraph or letter, once complaining of a sore arm from pitching cards at the poker game.

The King County prosecutor was at Holman Field in early January 1936, when a strike force of the Veterans of Foreign Wars (VFW) stormed an "educational" meeting in Seattle sponsored by Communists. They came in swinging, violating property and civil rights. Even several conservative lawyers said the raid was unwarranted. In the absence of Magnuson, Coughlin filed charges against two of the raiders, Rae Miller and John Garvin. It was a bold action and Coughlin was nervous.

"I realize there may be considerable question as to whether I did the right thing," he wired Magnuson. "But public reaction has been more favorable than I expected." He waited for Magnuson's return to prosecute Garvin and Miller. There was a political furor over the charges, and Magnuson was especially sensitive: he had tentative plans to run for a congressional seat in the November elections. But he had no question about Coughlin's action. He proceeded with the prosecution.[13]

The North Seattle Council of Clubs blasted the prosecutor for coddling communists. They had cheered the VFW raid. Magnuson expressed his feelings on civil rights in letters to the organization and to Frank

Bayley, a leading Seattle attorney: "I am not a communist and I believe in upholding the constitution just as strongly as any member of your organization. . . . the issue in this case is not communism but the right of free speech and free assembly."[14]

If he was lax—"tolerant" was the semiofficial word—about Chinatown fleshpots, the prosecutor was rigid in his enforcement of the Bill of Rights, a civil libertarian by instinct as much as training. His VFW prosecution came as a watershed. Those who viewed communism as a greater threat than even unemployment marked the man as an enemy. It would so remain for his political career. But the Democratic Party's radical left took quick note of the young man's blow for constitutional rights. Talk about his lifestyle came tempered with respect for his steadfast action in the VFW case.

Professor Garland Ethel of the University of Washington wrote the prosecutor: "in these days of growing contempt for constitutional liberties and for fearless and impartial enforcement of the law your action against the VFW . . . is to be commended."

Hugh DeLacy, a left radical, told Magnuson, "I don't agree with your political philosophy, but I admire your efforts to protect these men [victims of the raid] as citizens."[15] DeLacy would soon become a leader in the Washington Commonwealth Federation (WCF), and later a congressman. He regarded Magnuson as soft on capitalism.

New Deal, New World,
the "Soviet of Washington"

N ineteen thirty-six is the swing year in twentieth-century politics, the year that brought an end to the world as structured in the aftermath of World War I, and the effective beginning of World War II. Isolationist America, mired in Depression, was still trying to cope with the catastrophic failure of laissez-faire capitalism. Adolf Hitler, the elected German chancellor, had already discovered the trick by putting men at work building roads and arms, the latter in defiance of the Versailles Treaty. The treaty, a mistake, imposed reparations, arms restrictions, and territorial subtractions on the World War I loser, Germany. Hitler also reoccupied the Rhineland, defying his own generals along with Britain and France. The European powers watched and shrugged, paralyzed by the dictator's brass and to a degree sympathetic with his potential as a force against the Soviet Union.

The League of Nations was a handsome building with a fat bureaucracy in Geneva, bankrupt as even the semblance of a vehicle for maintaining international order. By contrast, the United Nations today is a stanchion of world stability. The League of Nations and the democracies watched as a fascist army warred against the democractic republic in Spain. Germany and Italy, fascist dictatorships, sent warplanes, equipment, and troops to the aid of General Francisco Franco, honcho of the right-wing rebellion. It was their testing ground for the big war to come. The Soviet Union sent aid and agents to seize control of the Republican forces, a betrayal documented in one of the most important books of the century, *Homage to Catalonia* by George Orwell, the pessimistic visionary who subsequently wrote *1984*.

An alarm sounded when Hitler and Benito Mussolini, Italy's numero uno, signed an "anti-Comintern pact" aimed at preventing the spread of communism from the USSR, and, incidentally, to bolster their standing among anticommunists in the West. Stalin, the USSR's dictator, responded by pushing, through his agents, the antifascist Popular Front movement.[1] His idea was to ally communists with liberals and socialists of the Western democracies and work from the bottom up through

established political institutions in the fight against fascism. It was announced at the Seventh Communist Party Congress in Moscow in August
1935. Earl Browder, the party's American boss, brought the word back
from Moscow to New York, and the word would spread from there to
Seattle. Alliance, not a proletarian revolution, was the order of the day.[2]
The chief diplomatic agent was Maksim Litvinov, Stalin's foreign minister, an affable character in fact as well as in several subsequent portrayals
out of Popular Front Hollywood.

The Popular Front was a worthy movement prompted by the selfish
concerns of Stalin who rivaled, if he did not outdo, Hitler in wickedness,
but understood the ways of the chancellor better than the pols in London
and Paris. It had an enormous impact in France, some in England, and
more among the intellectuals and their journals of America's East Coast.
Indeed, it played, without fanfare, a role in the 1936 politics of Warren
Magnuson and Washington State.

The Popular Front doctrine meant that the Washington Commonwealth Federation (WCF), the state's left-wing, liberal-to-communist
alliance, would work strictly within the established and thriving Democratic Party, not as a third-party alternative. The WCF would later be cited
by the House Un-American Activities Committee as "communist."[3] A less
biased judgment would conclude that while it had many true-believing
party members, the majority were liberal Democrats searching for a way
out of the Depression's morass. The record also shows the preeminent
role of Communists in WCF politics, directly or indirectly responding
to suggestions (commands?) from Moscow. American Communist Party
semisecret members were disciplined, if misguided, in their devotion to
twists in the Moscow line.

Whatever the Kremlin's wishes, the WCF's mainstream expressed the
will of the state's left-liberal Democratic constituency, a potent body
skeptical of capitalism and pushed to the limit for action against the
consequences of economic depression. The alliance worked so well that
for the rest of the decade the WCF was the hinge on which state politics
turned. It shaped the Democratic Party's turbulent 1936 state convention
and helped promote Warren Magnuson from local to national politics as
a member of the 1938 New Deal Congress. It did so over the corpse of its
idol and personification, Marion Zioncheck.[4]

Magnuson probably eyed a congressional seat before leaving the University of Washington when he and his friend Zioncheck worked on
the campaigns of Scott Bullitt and Al Smith, the Democratic presidential
nominee. If so, Zioncheck beat him to Washington, D.C., winning the
First District (Seattle) seat in the 1932 Democratic sweep.

By 1936, Zioncheck, Polish born, Seattle reared, was publicly showing signs of the mental trouble that would cause him to take his own life. Maggie was talking openly about congressional ambitions, consulting with Governor Clarence Martin and Senator Homer Bone and joining the Washington Commonwealth Federation. He was also expanding his weekly forums from radio talks on station KOL to speeches across Puget Sound in Kitsap County, home of the Bremerton Naval Shipyard, another part of Washington's First District.[5] The prosecutor was, as they say in news business, "getting his voice," and it was exceptionally good to judge from the response in letters from listeners.

The radio speeches, initially flaccid and rhetorical, were sharpened to pointed expressions of populist and New Deal social philosophy. Magnuson wrote them himself on a manual typewriter. They boosted Franklin Roosevelt as the savior of capitalism. Business could survive only if people had jobs that paid wages sufficient to purchase industry's production. Social Security, unemployment insurance, and Civilian Conservation Corps (CCC) were cushions against another freefall of the economy, à la 1929. Playing to First District voters, the plurality of which were first- or second-generation Scandinavian Americans, Magnuson emphasized the introduction of these social tools sixty years earlier by the governments of Norway, Sweden, and Denmark.

"A democracy survives only when it adjusts itself to economic change," he said in a 1936 radio talk. "The world faces a machine age, fast moving progress that necessitates alertness to its consequences. Some countries fail. . . . The result is dictatorships and monarchies. Scandinavians faced the same problems and adjusted with unemployment insurance, public utilities, cooperative enterprises—far sighted reforms while we slept."[6]

His pitch went straight to the mark: an appeal to the pride of Puget Sound's Scandinavians and the defense of New Deal and state legislative reforms against conservative charges of "socialism." Maggie, the "natural," was maturing, but not enough to convince his deputies in the prosecutor's office that he was ready to challenge Marion Zioncheck for the House seat.

"He was charismatic, certainly ambitious," said his deputy, Albert Rosellini. "But we tried to dissuade him from the run for Congress. Frankly, we didn't think he could beat Zioncheck." They couldn't know that Zioncheck would defeat himself.[7]

No figure in the state's political history has so confounded friends and enemies as Zioncheck, a left-wing Democrat with the aims of a saint and, eventually, the antics of a madman. He was loved and hated in equal measure, now remembered, if at all, as crazy. Ultimately, like Jay Gatsby, he is a tragic figure, a man possessed to strive for goals he could never attain. He wanted to make the world good, kind, and fair, in contrast with his friend Magnuson, who aimed at making things as good for as many people as practical, given his skills, while enjoying himself in the process. At the end Zioncheck was a newspaper laughingstock, tragedy with a bitter twist.

Lean, dark, intense, Zioncheck came with his parents from Kety, Poland (near Krakow), in 1905 when he was four years old. Like Magnuson, he worked his way through the University of Washington Law School, then rode the Democratic tidal wave to Congress while Magnuson went to the state legislature. He went to Washington carrying the burdens of Depression suffering on his shoulders, almost Christlike. He carried his work to an equal extreme: a congressman who read and deliberated on every line of proposed legislation. It was too much of a load.

Early in 1936, Zioncheck told Magnuson that he might not file for reelection. He married Rubye Louise Nix, no Daisy Buchanan, and began making the papers. Marion and Rubye were arrested by Washington police for cavorting toward dawn one morning in the Capitol fountain pool. He was charged with being drunk and disorderly and placed in a Baltimore mental hospital from which, shortly, he escaped. Vacationing in Puerto Rico and drunk again, Zioncheck wrecked a car and demanded U.S. Marine protection from the local police. Back in New York, he and Rubye got top play in Gotham's many multiedition newspapers after an all-night drunk in a midtown nightclub. The stories said Zioncheck swilled scotch and soda all evening while dancing with the "club's chorus girls." In July 1936, Zioncheck announced he might run for governor.

Back home, the *Argus* sniffed at "our clowning Congressman" and predicted his days as an elected politician were numbered; that his influence in Washington, D.C., was nil. "He'll assume the role of a martyr," said the voice of Seattle's middle-class establishment.[8] Zioncheck wavered on whether to seek reelection to congress, but he accepted the endorsement of the WCF, whose socialist domestic policy and Popular Front foreign policy he preached as gospel. He would go to his death with the federation's imprimatur.

If Zioncheck is remembered only as a clown, the Washington Commonwealth Federation has been buried—no love lost to the state's political establishment—as "communist." That legacy from the witch-hunting House Un-American Activities Committee was oversimplification, if not libel. The federation's muscle came from its liberal members, like Magnuson and several of his deputies, and brought the organization to the peak of radical power in the state. Its roots go back to the nineteenth-century Utopians and later anticapitalist labor radicals. It was the crystallization of an alliance between socialists, farmers, liberals, and labor under the strong influence of Popular Front communism. It was the state's answer to its desperate times.

The alliance began with the Reverend Fred Shorter, chubby, pink-faced pastor of the Pilgrim Congregational Church in Seattle. The charismatic Shorter had the manner of a TV evangelist, the religion of a "social Christian." He gathered like-minded Christians, socialists, and liberals, including Howard Costigan, a barber by trade, and Zioncheck, under his umbrella and lost his congregation on middle-class Capitol Hill. They formed the Commonwealth Builders, a group aimed at curing the ills of the Depression. They helped elect Zioncheck and Senator Bone in 1932 and attracted the attention of Morris Raport, the Communist Party's Northwest organizer. The Builders loomed before Raport and the CP as the ideal vehicle to implement Popular Front policy of working from the bottom up inside the state's Democratic Party.

With Raport and Costigan pushing, the Commonwealth Builders emerged from a meeting in the Jade Room of the New Washington Hotel, reborn as the Washington Commonwealth Federation, the formal alliance of farmers, labor, liberals, socialists, and communists. Communist leadership was critical to building the organization, but it was never a mere front for the Kremlin. It was antifascist and pro–New Deal, on both counts in close accord with regular Democrats. The U.S. Communist Party at that time had about 51,000 members, about the same as the Camp Fire Girls. Anticommunists inflated its threat, which, at that time, was not overt subversion of the U.S. government, but the Popular Front, a political response to the challenge of Hitler.

The WCF's rank and file found the organization's chief reason for being summed up in a single radical issue, an elaboration of the old Utopian idea that each worker should produce only the equivalent of what he consumes. The idea was expressed as "production for use" and formally politicized as Initiative 119, to be submitted to the voters of the state of Washington for approval or rejection on the November 1936 ballot.

Initiative 119, if approved, would have created state-owned factories, state-owned farms, state-owned banks, state-owned insurance companies, state-operated medicine, and state-owned electric power.[9] It was a euphemism for socialism, possibly the only such radical economic change to reach a vote of the people in the United States, the basis for Democratic Party leader Jim Farley's overly quoted description of the "47 states and the Soviet Republic of Washington." The initiative failed at the ballot by a three to one margin, but ignited the most radical and riotous Democratic Party convention in the state's history, King County Prosecutor Warren G. Magnuson presiding.

The task of holding the party's conservative and radical wings together had gone from the deceased patriarch Scott Bullitt to the young up-and-comer Magnuson. If senior Democrats shied from the job, obviating the wrath of one or both factions, Magnuson went for it. It was a measure of his self-confidence, gained as prosecutor and as de facto floor leader for economic reforms in the 1933 legislative session. He was thirty-one years old and would play the role at the 1936 convention that had been undertaken by Bullitt eight years earlier in Spokane. His aim was to avoid an election year walkout by one of the two factions. He sought advice from Senators Bone and Lewis Schwellenbach and the conservative leader, Governor Clarence Martin. In the end he had to face and control the political turmoil by himself.

"A bird needs two wings to fly," Maggie told the 3,000 delegates when the convention assembled at the Morck Hotel in Aberdeen, Washington, May 23. "So does a political party." Lieutenant Governor Victor A. Meyers, the ebullient bandleader, nightclub operator turned politician, boasted that he was the only elected state official brave enough to come to Aberdeen that weekend. Governor Martin stayed away. So, apparently, did Zioncheck. There was no prayer, no singing of the national anthem. Delegates wore yellow or orange armbands—yellow for conservatives, orange for the lefties. Magnuson gave the keynote speech before chairing the showdown. He plugged the New Deal and its leader, FDR, who was facing his first reelection.

"Roosevelt has brought order from chaos," he said. "The Democratic policy is water power without profit, schools for all children, programs to cure unemployment. We'll support anything the convention passes on production for use [I-119]. Don't be afraid to face the issue because someone calls it socialist. Why quibble over terms? We Democrats have been left-wingers for 134 years."[10] He also warned that the pending left-right battle had to be settled if the convention meant to finish its business and draft a platform.

By the end of his speech, Magnuson's voice had dropped to a hoarse whisper. The delegates were opening their arguments, first by conservatives—among them Magnuson's great friend Joe Drumheller of Spokane. They failed in an attempt to block the seating of several lefties. The brawl continued over "production for use"—Initiative 119. The WCF group resolved that the socialist program "is the only solution for the condition confronting us. . . . industry cannot absorb the machine-made idle. There's no demand for their work." The resolution failed, the convention deadlocked. At one o'clock Sunday morning Magnuson left the platform for a back-room meeting with leaders from both sides. They returned to resume the convention with a Magnuson trademark: a compromise.[11]

The 1936 Democratic Party platform called for a social security program, unemployment compensation, aid to dependent children, public health programs, collective bargaining and labor arbitration, and federal aid for dams and irrigation. No problem. It also endorsed "in principle" the state socialism of Initiative 119—the compromise. WFC radicals had won "in principle," and conservatives had saved face by avoiding endorsement of the specific points of a party demand for socialism. At 6 A.M. Sunday morning, the biggest, most ideologically fractured, party convention in state history adjourned, leaving conclusions to be reached by the newspapers.[12] The *Tacoma News Tribune* headlined: "Demos Back Left Wing Platform." The *Bremerton Journal* called it "a bitter defeat for the reactionary wing of the party" and hailed Magnuson for his "brilliant work as chairman in spite of a deliberate attempt by the right wing to steamroller the convention into a disorderly uproar."

Magnuson returned to Seattle concerned about the left-right party split and sent a letter to delegates appealing for unity in the face of November elections. His reasons were not entirely unselfish. He was running for Zioncheck's congressional seat.

On June 2, barely rested from the shootout in Aberdeen, Magnuson wrote Spokane County Prosecutor Ralph Foley, father of later Speaker of the U.S. House of Representatives Tom Foley, that he was "seriously thinking about the race."[13] He made no mention of the incumbent. Given Zioncheck's adverse publicity, there was no need to do so. Foley's response was surely encouraging. Saul Haas was enthusiastic. He was FDR's state campaign manager, and Maggie promised to make the congressional race as much a campaign for Roosevelt as for himself. A vote for Roosevelt, he reasoned, would be a vote for Magnuson. The WCF, however, remained steadfast: Zioncheck was still its candidate.

In mid-July, Zioncheck, back home and smarting from the barbs of the New York press, gave a speech entitled "Who's Crazy Now?" at the Reverend Fred Shorter's new church, the Church of the People, in Seattle's University District. He attacked the practice of pork-barrel politics and told a reporter that while he might not be seated if reelected, "I'll take my chances."[14] He said he would run on an "anti-psychotic platform." The man was falling apart.

On August 1, after informing Zioncheck, Magnuson filed for the office of First District congressman. His notice could not come as balm to the anguished incumbent. Newspapers that week headlined: organization of the state into Public Utility Districts, citizen owned and operated electric utilities; severe fighting between Republicans and Fascists in Spain; and the Olympic Games in Adolf Hitler's Berlin. Photos showed Hitler looking on as Jesse Owens, an African American, is for the third time bemedaled with gold. The dictator is not smiling. On August 3, Zioncheck made his final announcement on his political plans. He would not seek reelection. Citing his "mother's ill health," he said he wanted to be "America's forgotten man." The WCF professed to be "astounded."[15]

On August 8, Zioncheck wrote part of his last testament before leaping, headfirst, from his office on the fifth floor of Seattle's Arctic Building. Newspapers reported he landed on Third Avenue in front of a car bearing his wife, Rubye. Magnuson, a few blocks away, was prosecuting a capital murder case in the King County Courthouse. His memory of that deadly juxtaposition seemed to stay with the politician all his life. He would tell the story repeatedly, sometimes to strangers. The *Star* said Zioncheck had been under treatment for manic-depressive illness, that "the little brother to the poor" had gone from a sober and hard-working congressman "to a carousing madman." His last words, left behind in the testament on his office desk, said, "my only hope in life was to improve the conditions of an unfair economic system."

Whatever his mental problems, Zioncheck was a sensitive man in a brutal occupation, a "zero-sum game" in the anesthetized description of social scientists, a game of winners and losers. In the face of Zioncheck's ambivalence—"I will run, I won't run"—and his sensationalized antics (possibly exaggerated), the prosecutor was openly testing the mood of the First District, standard operating procedure in politics. The response was positive, and then some. The *Argus* would always vacillate in its judgments of Magnuson, although one would never know it from this description of the prosecutor in May 1936: "Young Warren Magnuson has given this city a mighty able administration and with far less grandstanding than we have been accustomed to in this office."[16]

There's more than a hint in papers left behind that Magnuson felt a measure of guilt in the suicide of his be-demoned friend. His speech "in memoriam to my dear friend Marion Zioncheck, representative to Congress, 1932–1936," was effusive, emotional, and out of character:

> My classmate took the only way to end the frightful suspense of a threatened and impending insanity with the prospect of spending his years in confinement. . . . He wanted to lift the load that brings workers to their knees. . . .

He had a sense of failure . . . [and] the press distorted his escapades. He told me "I hate this cheap ballyhoo, telling people a pack of lies about what we're going to do for them in Washington. . . . I can't stand this game of decoying the voters."

He was the most brilliant of our young Democrats, passionately devoted to the idea of leadership. He felt the corporate structure must be made amenable to community spirit. He was opposed to the application of force by an armed minority. He believed the days of Cain and the exploitation of neighbors must give way to the Golden Rule.

Marion felt too profoundly and too intensely, a heavy responsibility to his fellow man. These are my impressions and recollections of our dead comrade. I give them to you with only one hope—that we shall continue together where he left off.

There's a curious twist in this peroration, a turn away from homage to Zioncheck to Magnuson's description of the "average Congressman":

His mind is a squirrel cage in which the animal goes round and round just as long as the big bosses put in a few nuts. The squirrels that stay in the longest are those who never do anything else but whirl the cage. . . .

Many a politician has gone to Washington saying "everything I have shall be given in the name of the people!" In short time he says to himself, "I can't afford to be left out of this. Everything I can get away with is mine." He tells constituents, "I've got you all there is to be had from the pork barrel. What more can I do?" Voters send him back.[17]

Apart from relieving any sense of guilt he may have felt after the suicide, Magnuson was drawing a distinction between the 150-proof idealism of the vanquished Marion Zioncheck and the base political instincts of a congressional survivor-to-be, Warren Magnuson. It was the young prosecutor's last look back. He was pushing ahead to the vacant congressional office. But it is fair to judge from his subsequent forty-four-year congressional career that a good measure of Zioncheck's idealism tempered this survivor. He brought home his share of the pork and then some. But his idealism would make this nation better for its working stiffs, housewives, immigrants, blacks. If, as his critics on the left would charge, he went soft on capitalism, he got a good price that accrued to ordinary Americans.

CHAPTER 8

Mr. Magnuson Goes to Washington

The tidal wave of change that broke with the Great Depression still ran fast through the summer of 1936, when King County Prosecutor Warren Magnuson began a campaign for Congress, his first, the most critical of his career. But a conservative undertow was developing. Democrats, even Magnuson, the most popular of them, could not take the election for granted.

Franklin Roosevelt, the most loved and hated American president since Abraham Lincoln, was nervous about his reelection, despite the assassination of his most feared rival, Senator Huey P. Long, the Louisiana Kingfish, a brilliant "share the wealth" demagogue with White House ambitions. FDR had another election fear, the attempt by Republicans to hang a Red label on the New Deal. He tried to laugh it off, telling a New York audience that it reminded him of the rich man who fell into a river and nearly drowned. When a fellow dived into the water and snatched him to life, the rich man berated his savior for the loss of his top hat.[1]

Besides, the *New York Herald Tribune*, a great if Republican newspaper, predicted victory for Alf Landon, the Republican nominee, in thirty-three states. This was in October, one month before the election.

Washington State's economy had marginally improved—a result of New Deal irrigation and dam building. Unemployment had dropped to its lowest level of the decade. The chambers of commerce could look over the shacks of Hooverville and boast of "a sturdy, God-fearing, people who have created a great empire in the Pacific Northwest." Trade value through Puget Sound ports hit $369 million; the lumber industry had 60,000 employed; 2 million acres of land awaited irrigation waters that would flow from Grand Coulee and Bonneville Dams.[2] There's no mention of the federal administration's economic initiatives in *The State of Washington 1936*. Implicit in this book's cheery message: who needs the New Deal?

Magnuson did not overrate the conservative backlash. Instead, after Marion Zioncheck's suicide, he quickly sought the endorsement of the Washington Commonwealth Federation. He wanted the mantle of left-wing respectability as well as the congressional seat of his ill-starred college classmate. He made a good estimate of the political tide.

The federation's leaders were not eager to transfer their endorsement from Zioncheck's grave to the vital Magnuson. In the wake of their triumph at the Democratic state convention, Howard Costigan, the WCF president, could boast, "It's up to the Democrats to woo us, not for us to woo them." Magnuson went wooing.[3] He wanted it both ways: recognition and help from Seattle's conservative establishment, his chief private client, Northwest Airlines, and from the communist-influenced left-wing alliance.

He met with Costigan and Morris Raport, the Communist Party's Northwest organizer, in a private home in Seattle's middle-class Montlake District, a neighborhood of tree-shaded streets near the University of Washington. Magnuson requested the endorsement. They balked. He reminded them of his strong support from the city's muscular waterfront unions, the Sailor's Union of the Pacific (SUP) and the Marine Firemen, Oilers, Watertenders and Wipers Union (MFOW), both well salted at that time with left-wing seamen, some of them Communist Party members. They still balked. Then he told Costigan and Raport of his backing by the antagonist of these unions, the Teamsters, and their boss, Dave Beck.

Pudgy, pink-faced Beck, a onetime laundry truck driver, had no time for labor radicals. "You can't beat bosses by destroying them," he said. His genius in organizing workers from Seattle's First Avenue—but not the waterfront below it—to Los Angeles warehouses came from skillful negotiations with business bosses. Some called it "price fixing" and "collusion." Regardless, it meant good wages and working conditions for his members, who were sales clerks and warehouse workers as well as truck drivers. Beck borrowed the notion of one big union from the Wobblies, labor radicals he detested. His manner and philosophy made Beck a most attractive alternative to Harry Bridges, his only rival as the West Coast's most powerful union leader.[4] Magnuson carried a Teamsters card. He got it during his college days as an ice delivery man and he remained allied to the Teamsters boss.

The waterfront unions weren't enough, but with Beck and the Teamsters on Maggie's bandwagon, Costigan and Raport caved. On August 22, the WCF gave its endorsement for First District Congress to Magnuson.[5] There was baggage attached, an effective seal of approval of the candidate from the Communist Party, a fact that got lost or ignored when witch-hunters came after WCF members in the anti-Communist purges of the 1950s. It wasn't lost, however, on his political opponents in 1936. For that matter, the WCF endorsement didn't sit well with all of those on the left. J. F. Cronin wrote the WCF, "I don't see why the federation has endorsed the pussy-footer Warren Magnuson without the slightest consideration for one [Democratic candidate] who has come up through the struggle, Harry Ault."[6] Cronin didn't grasp the idea of the Popular Front. It called for mainstream winners, not socialist symbols. Maggie was not alone among mainstream politicians seeking the Communist Party endorsement. Across the nation scores of others did so, many no doubt living to regret the fact.

That summer remained tumultuous. On August 14, members of the American Newspaper Guild went on strike against William Randolph Hearst's *Seattle Post-Intelligencer*. It was coincidence that Hearst had become stridently anti-Roosevelt and anti-Communist. Prosecutor and congressional candidate Magnuson steered clear, saying "my sympathy is with the strikers, but I must represent all of the people." Aided by Beck's Teamsters and Bridges's Longshoremen, newsmen won their strike, a major advance in the Guild's effort to organize newsrooms around the nation.

Candidate Magnuson, as he promised his pal Saul Haas, ran a campaign based on FDR and the New Deal. What he said in that campaign was the rough and ready essence of the political philosophy he would hold for the balance of his career in Washington, D.C. He promised pork for sure. He also explained his social ideas. He owed them to John Rogers and the Washington State populists as well as to FDR's New Deal.

"Historians will record in the future the greatest paradox is the hostility of business and wealth against Franklin Roosevelt," he broadcast through the user-friendly airwaves of KIRO. He reminded constituents, many of them still speaking their old-country language, that Roosevelt's programs were really "no new deal," Norway and Sweden had established the same policies sixty years earlier. "The time has passed when an [unemployed] man standing in front of a factory can be called a bum. The factory owner can now be called a bum." These campaign speeches, with scant variation, promised "water power for the benefit of people—without profit" and federal money for further development of the Bremerton Naval Shipyard.[7] He would deliver on both counts.

His chief opponent in the primary election, one Chris Wilkins, tried to go with the undertow, denouncing Magnuson for taking the endorsement of the "radical WCF" and boasting that he, Wilkins, was the only Democratic contender opposed to Initiative 119. Magnuson swamped him in the primary and faced off in the general election against Fred Wettrick, the GOP nominee.[8] He did not alter his appeal for votes, nor did he speak for or against the proposal for a socialist state embodied in the initiatives.

The general Republican Party line in this election was the "defense of American institutions" endangered by the Roosevelt administration. "Inspired Republicans must check the nation in its drift to collectivism and dictatorship. . . . All must stand fearlessly face to face with American tradition."[9]

"As a lawyer," said Magnuson, "I admire tradition, but I don't believe tradition should blind us to actualities. We need American horsesense not to be led astray by Red Herrings." Magnuson descibed himself as "a liberal—perhaps too liberal for some" but not a radical.[10]

He noted the "Red Herring of fear" in the campaign, then ignored it in a campaign speech written on stationery from the Olympic Hotel, his elegant new domicile owned by his good friend Bill Edris. Magnuson had been the one who located the farmland south of Seattle where Edris and Joe Gottstein built their Longacres racetrack. The speech:

> Labor wants the right to earn a decent and honest living for their families at decent wages. In the past, business has had it better than labor, but most employers know that better wages means better markets. Shorter hours and a shorter work week are the solution to machines throwing men out of work. A short work day and a five day week ought to be mandatory at prevailing wage scales. There must be compulsory arbitration [between unions and business]. I'll propose such legislation. I believe these views to be American views. They mean a solution to our economic problems. Any other inference [by this he meant the Communist smear by conservatives] placed on them is merely a smokescreen to missguide you.
>
> As for national defense—the First District first. Too many have a desire to go to Congress to be a statesman. We leave that to the senators. I'm concerned with being a good sincere worker for the welfare of the people of this district. I helped pass the [Homer] Bone bill. If approved in the November referendum it will allow construction of state transmission lines leading to all parts of the state. That means cheap electric power.[11]

It didn't pass, being turned down by voters along with I-119. The bid to make Washington a socialist state failed 370,140 to 97,329. Eugene Dennett, a WCF board member, blamed Communists for the loss, intentionally or inadvertently. The federation's Communist Party members placed themselves out front in the campaign for I-119, thus ensuring a negative public response.

In this "Olympic" speech Magnuson made a rare, if not his one and only, public reference to his origins. Referring to street gossip that "I don't even know my own name," he said "it happens to be true. I'm an orphan." He went on to give thanks to his adoptive parents and probably won a measure of the sympathy vote. Indirectly, it marked the distance traveled by the thirty-one-year-old politician from Moorhead, Minnesota.

Magnuson had a determined, if lightly skilled, general election opponent in Wettrick, a lawyer, forty-eight, best known for his work in the American Legion. The *Municipal League News* described the University of Washington graduate as "a tireless worker for American principles versus Communism who favors the deportation of aliens engaged in Un-American activities—a splendid record." The WCF, said Wettrick, was "Un-American," and Initiative 119, a "plan for state socialism."[12]

"Republicans would have you believe all Democrats are Red and that the Washington Commonwealth Federation is determined to turn this state over to Moscow," said Magnuson. "Not true. Democratic candidates do not necessarily subscribe to the beliefs of all their endorsing organizations. I work with any conscientious group that is trying to better the condition of mankind. These groups have aligned with the Democratic Party. Rank and file Democrats are just as American in thought and principles as other citizens."[13]

Wettrick was naive. One month before the election he wrote Bill Stern, North Dakota's GOP national committeeman, passing on what he regarded as damaging information about Magnuson. Did Stern know of his protégé's alignment "with the extreme left wing sponsoring the socialistic doctrine of production for use and other near Communistic proposals?" Any more such dirt? asked Wettrick. He promised to keep any reply from Stern confidential. Apparently there was none. The implied libel wasn't news to the Fargo banker.[14]

Wettrick lacked the savvy to slow Magnuson's march to victory, even with high-powered ammunition from an unexpected source, the *Jeffersonian Democrat*, the newssheet of a group of conservative Democrats formed by a onetime aide to the socially prominent Seattle attorney, Steve Chadwick. They issued a campaign call for Democrats to reelect FDR, but to "REPUDIATE Warren Magnuson whose record is a discredit to the Democratic Party."

The campaign blast was slanted, quite possibly in hopes of derailing a potential political rival before he gained the full power of a congressional office. Nevertheless, it was not, from a critic's vantage, without insight. It was the most telling critique of the politician at any time during his career, a shaft from the hunter's code: if you shoot at a lion, shoot to kill.

"Dear Maggie," the shot began. "We strongly object to an opportunist" and think "you should stay put as prosecutor. . . . We are just about through with you for you trifle with the right and pledge yourself to the left" and "you behave in such a manner we are driven to suspect a man's honor, integrity and loyalty to any party."

It went on: "Three years ago your heels were down, trouser cuffs frayed, shabby as the dickens. Your car was repossessed for lack of payments. . . . You drew a $200 a month salary from the Relief Fund [his salary as attorney for the Unemployment Relief Commission]. You joined the Democratic Party in 1930 when you saw a potential job in the offing" and "some of us think that you are really pledged to the Communist Party and you ought to get out of the Democratic Party."

The article continued: "Do the unemployed know you reside in a luxury suite at the Olympic Hotel? That it's true you backed up [Howard] Costigan's fee for radio broadcasts [on KIRO] so he would deliver the WCF endorsement? There are those who think you are not fit to wipe Marion Zioncheck's shoes."

The *Jeffersonian Democrat* concluded "it is better to vote for an honest Republican than a disloyal Democrat." They endorsed Wettrick for Congress. The article was unsigned.[15]

True, Magnuson was a once struggling law student who had moved up from residence in the Benjamin Franklin Hotel to the swankier Olympic after his divorce from Peggins. He had also lost his car, and he was frequently to be nipped for debts. He had hesitated before becoming a Democrat and did so, he told Stern, because of the rising power of labor. True, he had more than trifled with the right, Seattle's downtown business establishment. He had co-opted the movers and shakers from less talented rivals. There were more compelling reasons for the WCF to grant him its endorsement at the Montlake meeting, but it is possible that part of the deal was help in maintaining Costigan's radio talks; possible but not proven. That he was "pledged to the Communist Party" is patently absurd, if not deliberate malice.

Magnuson was a politician, which is to say an opportunist, eager for support from all quarters. The difference was his skill in tying bonds—making deals, if you please—from Seattle's waterfront up First Hill to the cloistered University Club. They obviously liked what they got. Opportunism is a two-way street. Whatever his deals, private as well as public, Maggie would never stray from the core principles laid out in this campaign, support for ordinary citizens and the Bill of Rights. At times he may have looked flexible, perhaps faking it a bit. At root, he was steadfast.

He made no response to the *Jeffersonian Democrat*, a pattern he was to keep in the face of campaign charges for the rest of his career. At the end, as he had figured, the conservative backlash was overrated, almost certainly inflated by the predominance of Republican-controlled newspapers around the country. They had misled the *Herald Tribune*. Roosevelt defeated Landon in the biggest landslide to that point in U.S. history. Magnuson defeated Wettrick by a two to one margin.

His mother came from Moorhead to Magnuson's postelection celebration at, where else, the Olympic Hotel. She described herself as "elated." The congressman-elect said he was "numb." He recovered shortly, resigned as King County prosecutor, and went off to Fargo to visit family and friends. He was already angling for a committee assignment on Naval Affairs, the better to bring home appropriations to his district's largest single employer, the Bremerton Naval Shipyard.

On New Year's Eve, the dead end of this pivotal year, Sam Stern, Bill's brother, wrote his pal Jim Farley, Democratic chairman and postmaster general, about his current guest, "a former Fargo boy Warren G. Magnuson, Congressman-elect from Seattle. He is a fine young chap . . . has lots of ability. You met him with me in Seattle in 1931. I wish when he calls on you, you would give him a little fatherly advice on the good old Farley way."[16]

Stern asked for Farley's help in getting Magnuson on the House Naval Affairs Committee and for two tickets to Roosevelt's inaugural celebration in Washington, D.C. A week later Stern informed Magnuson that Farley replied he would do "all that he could to get you on the Naval Affairs Commitee."

The new congressman's course was set.

CHAPTER 9

"Ensign" Magnuson

Handsome, blond, blue-eyed, and born to politics, Warren Magnuson took to Washington, D.C., like the cherry trees. He blossomed. His timing and connections smoothed a transition from state to national political life. His energy in the national capital, in Seattle and Hollywood, in hindsight looks almost superhuman.

Jim Farley complied with Sam Stern's request. He used his formidable influence to secure Magnuson a seat on the Naval Affairs Committee, whose chairman was Carl Vinson, Democrat from Georgia. Maggie would sit alongside another freshman, Texan Lyndon B. Johnson. Johnson was twenty-eight; Magnuson, thirty-two. They were "ensigns" in "Admiral" Vinson's navy, friends for life.

This was Franklin Roosevelt's Washington, not Herbert Hoover's—a city in fundamental change from the center of a laissez-faire capitalist federation to a seat of government suddenly concerned about every aspect of American society from Wall Street to Main Street. It was more the Washington, D.C., we know today, a strong central government—too strong, too centralized for its critics then and now—with proliferating alphabet agencies, a powerful executive, an active Congress, surrounded by battalions of lobbyists and journalists seeking to influence their actions. This was the New Deal government, a consequence of its rescue of capitalism. Networks of airplanes, telephones, and radios had shrunk the nation, enhancing its central government. Roosevelt greatly magnified his bully pulpit with fireside chats heard as clearly on a Cascade Mountain "spark-box" as in the Capitol itself.

Years later, when asked to explain his and Johnson's devotion to the New Deal, Magnuson said, "All of us are creatures of our times. We needed to do something [in the 1930s] no matter what it was called. It was a modest approach."

The Depression lingered. Almost as ominous was the potential of war in Europe from Germany, a dictatorship seeking to reassert itself as a great power, and from Japan, a new empire emerging from an old exclusive culture. Japan had invaded China. Germany made known that its territorial aspirations went from the Rhine to the Vistula. This was before the German appetite grew from its conquest of Western Europe,

Central Europe, and much of the Soviet Union. The real war was only five years away, but Washington wished to ignore it. New Deal policy in 1937 was neutrality, and a pox on those far places across the Atlantic and Pacific. The new congressman shared that policy.

Magnuson was so absorbed with his new job, he appears for a short while to have dropped his customary distractions. "The stallion," as his friend Bill Stern sometimes called Maggie, answered a query from Joe Roberts, a buddy from the Washington state legislature, about the "beautiful women in Washington." This was in January. "There are none—at least I haven't had any time to make any research," Maggie replied. "Besides, Old Lady Congress is quite a mistress."[1]

A month later he wrote another Seattle buddy, Army Seijas, an attorney, "you're going to have to look a long time before you see my maiden speech. From what I see around this place, the best way to kill yourself off, with constituents and colleagues, is to talk too much. I'm keeping my eyes and ears open, my mouth shut." He told Roberts he planned legislation placing all naval ship construction in Navy shipyards and noted, "you can understand what this would mean for Bremerton and Seattle."

As personified by Carl Vinson, Majority Leader Sam Rayburn, and Vice President John Nance Garner, Congress was a demanding mistress. This was thirty-five years before congressional reform diluted the power of seniority and committee chairmen. Power accrued only through seniority. Intellect and energy, hallmarks of Magnuson and Johnson, were secondary, if not incidental, to the stretch for clout. Patience was paramount. About twenty members ran the House, chief among them Speaker John Bankhead, Democrat from Alabama (father of Broadway's great Tallulah), and Rayburn.

If Magnuson has a rival in this century as the greatest legislator west of the Mississippi, it is surely Rayburn, the Southwest populist, FDR's main man in the passage of New Deal legislation. After Scott Bullitt and Homer Bone, he was the next great teacher for Magnuson, the Northwest populist.

Sam was son of a Confederate soldier who rode with General N. B. Forrest, the semiliterate cavalry warrior whose tactics were to be carefully studied by German blitzkrieg generals Guderian and Rommel. He grew up in a hardscrabble, east Texas family of Primitive Baptists with a profound mistrust of Wall Street and eastern financial interests. In church services Primitive Baptists, to the disgust of Southern Presbyterians and Episcopalians, washed each other's feet. Rayburn was raised arguing the Bible and responding to his parents' primitive discipline—the willow switch.

He went to the state legislature and became its youngest Speaker. He came to Washington with a dim view of the city's vices and a keen ear for the tutelage of his fellow Texan, crusty John N. Garner. He brought strong opinions.

President Wilson, said Rayburn, "is a cold eyed Presbyterian," and Washington a "selfish, sour-bellied place with everyone trying for fame, ready at all times to use the other fellow as a prize pole [pry-pole, a lever] for it." He immediately joined Garner's "board of education," an afternoon gathering in the Speaker's office for poker, storytelling, shoptalk, and bourbon. Of Rayburn, Garner said, "he stays hitched" (keeps his word). Of the "board of education," Garner said: "You get a couple of drinks in a young congressman and then you know what he knows and what he can do. We pay the tuition by supplying the liquor."[2]

Magnuson and Johnson were quickly admitted, tested, and taught. Rayburn said forget the flattery, drop the flowery speech, and learn to become receptive to the mood of other members. "If a man can't see, hear and feel, he is lost here," Rayburn instructed. "Man has to be led by persuasion, kindness and reason. Handle yourself well in committee duties. If you fall down in committee work or become self important, that fact will be noted. Other members will avoid you."

That advice is absurdly dated in this age of television politics and ten-second sound bites—spurs to self-importance, showboating. But these were Magnuson's tenets, if not before he joined Rayburn's board of education, then certainly for the balance of his career. He was not made for television, despite his stunning good looks. He was too modest, too given to persuasion and to low-visibility committee work.

"Sam Rayburn sprinkled Holy Water on Magnuson," said W. Feather-stone Reid, a longtime aide to Senator Magnuson.[3] The majority leader and Speaker-to-be did the same for his fellow Texan, L. B. Johnson. He gave both freshmen fast entree to the White House and to their hero, FDR. "Roosevelt sorta took me and Johnson in as young Congressmen," Magnuson recalled several presidents later.

> He was very, very, good to me—and, unlike some more recent presidents, he always cleared his bills with everybody before he sent them to Congress.
>
> I played poker with Roosevelt in the White House. He always paid off in checks—knowing we'd be reluctant to cash them, given his signature. I still have a couple for $30 and $60. Mrs. Roosevelt didn't like our poker games. She paced outside the room to show displeasure.[4]

Poker, Roosevelt's favored means of relaxation, was played in the president's second-floor study, his favorite room, with its ship models, sailing pictures, books, papers, and leather sofas. "Once, in that first term, there was a call to my office. A voice told the secretary 'this is Roosevelt calling. I'd like to talk to the Congressman.' She answered, 'yes sir, Mr. Napoleon Bonaparte.' She could not believe it was the President."[5]

Magnuson's main work came on the Naval Affairs Committee. The "admiral" ran a tight ship—no showboating by any subordinate, much less a freshman. His manner, however, was more akin to a country lawyer than a military martinet. His speech drawled and he forever chewed the end of an unlit cigar—a habit Magnuson may have acquired from the chairman. He called it "my Navy" and bossed committee members about like cabin boys. Magnuson and Johnson sat side by side on the lower tier of a committee hearing room in the Cannon Office Building. Vinson pretended he didn't know their names. He did hand out favors, usually junkets to naval bases, several of these in California. Magnuson used these free trips to visit his splendid and fast developing relationships in Hollywood.

Early on, the two freshmen had the audacity to question a witness. Vinson recessed the hearing. "I want to see you two young boys in the back room," he commanded. According to Maggie, "he let us have it—new members were allowed only one question, then two questions their second year, and so on. He called his new members 'Ensign.' Older members told us 'when he calls you Captain you have arrived.' "[6]

None of this shook Magnuson's self-confidence. In January 1937, he wrote George Vanderveer, the Seattle labor lawyer, "I'm getting myself somewhat adjusted to the angles incident to being a Congressman. . . . I'm feeling pretty good and think I'm going to like the work."[7]

Magnuson worked in Congress as hard as he played in Seattle and Los Angeles. This was very hard indeed. He lived by Rayburn's code: work hard, talk little, watch intensely. Later he would preach the same to younger members. At the end of his first term, a letter from the "admiral" thanked Magnuson for his work "on behalf of the Navy establishment. We have our differences [the Georgian had no tolerance for racial minorities] but in the final analysis, we all have the same objective—maintaining the Navy in the highest state of efficiency."[8]

Magnuson's objectives were more specific. The Bremerton Naval Shipyard, by 1937 the state's largest single employer, with a monthly payroll of $450,000, "is constantly on my mind," he said. Small wonder. Newspapers across the state as well as Puget Sound noted the naval bases as a magnet for federal dollars. They all clamored for more. So did Magnuson.

Working with Senator Bone, Maggie got $4.5 million for a new dock at the base and for the modernization in Bremerton of the aircraft carriers

Saratoga and *Lexington*—early mainstays in the Pacific war to come. He also called for the purchase of naval stores in Puget Sound and for the upgrading of the Naval Air Station at Sand Point on Seattle's Lake Washington. He pressed, sans success, for all naval ship construction to be done in Navy shipyards. He was persistent, if not a pest.

William Leahy, the chief of naval operations and Roosevelt's close military adviser, reminded Magnuson that "Seattle is not ignored" when the Navy transships to Alaska or overseas to the Pacific.[9] This naval hustle was in addition to serving the meat and potatoes, albeit rather large ones, to his constituency: Kitsap County wanted federal money for a new airport and for construction of the Tacoma Narrows Bridge between mainland Tacoma and the Olympic Peninsula. Various chambers of commerce wanted the congressman's help in converting the Moran estate on San Juan Island into the summer White House (a marvelous idea), and Seattle wanted the Army's Fort Lawton on Magnolia Bluff as grounds for a world's fair (a hopeless notion, given pending military demands).

The freshman handled requests for compensation for a WPA construction worker who lost a leg on the job and from the International Association of Machinists, who wanted the Army to purchase Boeing's new YB-17, "the only union-built airplane in the U.S." Seattle's Chamber of Commerce pitched for an airmail route (a federal subsidy) between Seattle and Alaska. Magnuson, a Northwest Airlines stockholder-attorney replied: "I want to assure you it will be a pleasure to work to establish the air route." He also noted that the Washington State delegation in Congress "works more harmoniously than any other state delegation."[10] That pattern would last, thanks to Magnuson and Senator Henry Jackson, until the 1980s.

Magnuson was accelerating the federalization of his adopted state. No single member of Congress from the Northwest would ever do more. In one of his most important efforts, the freshman congressman fell a step short of direct aid to Seattle. In 1938 he sponsored a bill creating the Alaska International Highway Commission to study, with a Canadian counterpart, the route for a road linking the continental United States with Alaska via Canada. His aim was for such a route to commence in Vancouver, 180 miles north of Seattle, but the commission stalled on a decision. With the start of World War II, the U.S. Army Corps of Engineers took matters unto their own bulldozers and cut a route from Edmonton, Alberta, to Fairbanks. Seattle got bypassed as a terminus, but the 1,500 mile road was completed in 1942—as much credit to Maggie as to the Corps.

Despite disappointment over the Alaska highway, feedback from the First District that first session was approving. George Crandell, a lawyer for the Letter Carriers Union, wrote in April 1937: "The boys at the table often speak of you. It's refreshing to contrast your record with that of Zioncheck . . . and there's no harsh criticism from even the hard-shell Republicans."[11]

Despite his concentration on domestic concerns and his professed neutrality, turmoil in other parts of the world kept intruding. Howard Costigan of the WCF asked Magnuson to propose an embargo against Germany and Italy to balance the administration's policy of neutrality in Spain's civil war. It didn't happen. In the wake of Kristallnacht, the night in November 1938 when Nazis smashed the windows of Jewish-owned shops in Germany, there was a flurry of letters from Jews concerned about the growth of anti-Semitism and a counterpoint from the Arab National League concerned about the growth of Zionism and Jewish migration to Palestine.[12]

Rabbi Stephen Wise wrote Magnuson that Hitler's takeover of Austria was "deeply troubling, an indication of further suppression of Jews." Magnuson said he would do all in his power to spare European Jews from "this barbaric oppression."[13] Taking sides early on the Middle East's major conflict, he signed a resolution urging Britain to keep the doors of its Palestinian mandate open to Jewish refugees.

A less partisan observer, Harry Kinnear, a friend from Seattle, sent his prewar impressions to Magnuson in a long letter from Berlin near the end of his extended tour of the world that began in the Far East in 1938:

> The Japanese have bombed Canton creating five million refugees. . . . Shanghai is terrible. There is smallpox and typhoid. People think China will win this war. I can't agree. The Japs are just one big family. . . . they think they know what they want and intend to get it unless Russia or someone stops them. All China is their goal, a market for their products. . . . However, the USA has no business going to war for our interests in the East. We don't need to "save face". The cost of war would be too great.
>
> I was glad to reach Berlin after a month in the USSR (terrible). . . . I liked Germany very much. In three weeks I can prove nothing [about Germany] that I have read in the papers. However, another visit may sharpen my eyes.[14]

Kinnear may have sharpened Magnuson's antiwar attitude. He would, three months before the Japanese bombing of Pearl Harbor, vote against the extension of the draft—it passed by a lone vote—and had favored the Ludlow Amendment, "one of the most difficult votes I've cast."[15] Long forgotten in the recurring debates over the president's power to declare war, Representative L. L. Ludlow proposed a constitutional amendment in 1938 which would have mandated a national referendum before a declaration of war. Despite Magnuson's support, Ludlow's pivotal resolution failed in the House.

The congressman had a more immediate concern in 1938, reelection to Congress in another year marked by bitter dissension within the state Democratic Party. Being a favorite of Carl Vinson and Sam Rayburn carried little weight with the First District, where the left-right split inside his party got down, at times, to a matter of jobs. Lillian Cloudy, a Magnuson ally, told him that Morris Raport, the Communist Party organizer, was clearing all applications for WPA road construction jobs and had just hired "Communist party organizers" for two such jobs.[16]

Republicans were hopeful. The split gave them a "wedge" issue, a chance to attract enough conservative Democrats for a 1938 comeback. It would not work in the First District despite an excellent candidate, Matthew Hill, a lawyer and GOP progressive. Magnuson had his own political cadre, apart from the party apparatus, another career-long characteristic established in his first term. He stayed in close touch with Saul Haas, Dave Beck, Bill Edris, Paul Coughlin, Ed Henry, and Mac MacGowan, the ex-reporter, world traveler, and would-be mining entrepreneur. Mac worked for Magnuson as the I&R platoon works for an infantry regiment: he was political intelligence and reconnaissance, inventor of the word—but not necessarily the technique—of the "Mc-Goozle," a political deal that leaves both parties happy or at least one of them happy and the other not mad.[17]

Maggie spent Christmas 1937 at home in Moorhead with "Mom" before returning to Congress and preparations for the reelection campaign. Haas warned his pal he'd likely have a primary election opponent. His letter also lamented the loss by their mutual buddy, Freddie Steele, a Seattle middleweight, to San Francisco's Fred Apostoli, in a main event fight in New York's Madison Square Garden. Haas noted, sourly, "rumor is that Freddie was licked not only by the other guy but by a Broadway blonde."[18]

Another buddy, Frank Bell, chairman of the U.S. Fisheries Commission, wrote to L. G. Wingard of the U.S. Bureau of Fisheries in Seattle, a member of the state Democratic Party finance committee. "I am very much interested in the reelection of Rep. Magnuson and Sen. Bone," said Bell, applying a tactless political squeeze. "The majority of the money you raise should go into the Bone-Magnuson campaigns. I'm just writing this letter so you will understand how I feel on the matter and not with the intention of dictating to you. . . . I hope you will do everything possible to divert funds to Bone and Magnuson."[19]

Bell, who would boast that he sometimes used Magnuson's office for his business in Washington, D.C., was the effective boss of his underling in the Seattle bureau. His fame and disgrace would come in the late 1950s after conviction for perjuring himself before a Grant County grand jury probing payoffs in the construction of the Grant County Public Utility District's Priest Rapids Dam. It was, in the last analysis, a heavier fall for the image of public power, the creation of the Utopian and Populist idealists, than for Frank Bell. He showed only common greed. Public power had exposed itself to be as capable of kickbacks and corruption as the hated eastern-controlled private utilities.

Secretary to Senator C. C. Dill at the creation of Grand Coulee, Bell, seventy-five, would be given a fifteen-year sentence, then paroled by Governor Albert Rosellini in the early 1960s. Public power would go on to show even more greedy judgment in its alliance with private power companies in the 1970s to construct nuclear power plants—the WPPSS ("Whoops") scandals of wasted money and collapsing bonds. Grant County and Frank Bell were a prelude to the largest bond failure in the nation's history.

Democrats had a replay of their 1936 state convention, this one a knock-down, drag-out affair in Tacoma. The left maintained control even after two hundred conservatives stormed the platform. State Chairman Elwood Caples was tossed from his platform perch amid the fistfights, token of the "bitter hatred between factions." The platform called for the federalization of banks and finance houses, nationalization of monopolies, better pensions, and increased unemployment insurance payments. "The only people happy about it are Republicans," reported the *Star*, although "many left-wingers didn't think the platform went far enough."[20] Magnuson kept a low profile, addressing a sideshow to the main event, a gathering of Washington Young Democrats, the organization that he and Frank Bell's daughter, Mabel, helped form after their graduation from the University of Washington. Maggie skipped the fistfights.

His campaign speeches were also a reprise, praise for FDR and the New Deal for saving the capitalist system. He got a warning about this from Frank Dean of Seattle shortly before the primary: "When you say we are saving capitalism, many heads shake. . . . Capitalist has a bitter taste in many mouths."

For the *Post-Intelligencer*, Magnuson outlined his record in the Seventy-fifth Congress. He claimed responsibility for $27 million in appropriations for the Bremerton Naval Shipyard and funds for defense of Alaska

as well as the initial appropriation for research to eradicate cancer—the
first of his efforts to push medical research. He also could boast of the
Canadian–U.S. Commission to study a U.S.–Alaska highway.

The GOP wedge was a campaign urging Democrats to split their ticket
and "vote American." They played heavily on the Communist Party's
Popular Front alliance with Democrats. Red-baiting, FDR called it. Jim
Farley wrote Magnuson asking full details of the Washington State situation, apparently nervous. He told Magnuson the 1938 election "is as
important as any in U.S. History."[21] It was a tough year. The Depression
had gone from bad to worse. Bonneville Dam was generating electricity,
but some of the sheen came off the New Deal as unemployment rose,
and relief payments remained static.

Nevertheless, Magnuson walked through the Democratic primary
election and left his opponent, James Hodson, smiling—a near perfect
McGoozle. "I appreciate the way you ran your campaign," Hodson wrote
Maggie. "It was a pleasure to oppose such a worthy adversary."[22]

Republican Hill challenged Magnuson to a radio debate before the
general election. He said they agreed on the need for a highway to Alaska,
funds for the navy yard, and the WPA, "but you won't disavow the
Washington Commonwealth Federation which is not consistent with
American institutions and ideals." Magnuson would soon come to dis-
agreements with the WCF, but he would never disavow the support he
got from the Popular Front organization.[23]

Maggie boasted to Bill Stern that he would win reelection by a two to
one margin, and so he did. He had easily passed a congressman's biggest
campaign hurdle—election after the first term. His letters during the
Seventy-fifth Congress frequently complained that he had "never been
busier." The wonder of Magnuson's prewar years is not that he would
declare himself busy, but that he could maintain the pace of his activities,
personal, political, congressional, and romantic. They were awesome.

Adonis from Congress

Tucked away in the papers Warren Magnuson left behind is a semi-facetious description of the ideal congressman, author unknown save for a first name, "Jerry." It could have been a description of Congressman Magnuson in his first seven years in Washington, D.C., perhaps the only reason the paper survives.

"The ideal Congressman," wrote "Jerry," "is a man of vision and ambition. He works all day, plays all night, entertains men and their wives without creating rumors; [he is] a man's man, a lady's man, . . . politician, polygamist, model husband, and, after a decent speech, a guzzler."[1]

Magnuson was such and more. As sometime campaign aide Gerald Hoeck, and others, note, "There were several Magnusons." The most visible and accountable was the congressman, a man of vision intimately tied to the needs and politics of his state. Not so visible was the night man, a Hollywood playboy, Longacres racetrack player, and the dutiful son with acute family problems. Out of sight—although political enemies claimed to have had a glimpse—was his work inside Congress on behalf of Northwest Airlines, and for Archer Daniels Midland (ADM), the General Motors of the Midwest grain industry.[2] Magnuson and Seattle had a special interest in Northwest Airlines. ADM's connections with the Northwest were embarrassingly scant.

ADM had Magnuson on a $200 per month retainer as an attorney;[3] nothing illegal in such activities at that time. The House of Representatives had no rules or laws on conflicts of interest. He did not get rich from this congressional sideline, as did his pal L. B. Johnson from extra-congressional activity. It did give Magnuson the wherewithal to care for an ailing mother and panicky sister, while supporting his own expansive lifestyle.

He was chided at least once by a political friend for his "playboy" activity, and years later it would be the flimsy substance of a futile campaign against his reelection. Most significant, however, is that none of this private activity made the slightest dent in his growing popularity at home or in Congress. In Washington, D.C., the column writers were calling him the "Adonis from Congress." He was expressing the popular will of the people of his state, which was antiwar and hungry for federal gravy. He was bringing home the bacon with the gravy, and sometimes along with his glamorous beauties from Hollywood.

"Hollywood?" wrote F. Scott Fitzgerald, who once worked there. "It's alright. It's a mining town in Lotus Land."[4] Most Americans were not so blase. The place was irresistible as the manufacturer, wholesaler, and retailer of American dreams. Magnuson found it in its heyday, the early 1930s. The fantasies it created sold like beer on a troopship. Films were an antidote to the troubles of the Depression, a magnet especially to small-town and country youth like Magnuson. It was the New Jerusalem for many of his generation.

Whatever his dreams, Maggie became acquainted with Hollywood and Los Angeles through S. S. Hahn, the Scripps Newspapers general counsel, and Mac MacGowan, who left the *Seattle Star* for a one-year stint on the *Los Angeles Record*.[5] Newspaper reporters, in that era before union wages and conditions, were professional gypsies. The nominal attraction became specific with Carol Parker after her return via Seattle from a singing engagement in a Shanghai nightclub. Parker met Magnuson, a fellow North Dakota native, in Seattle. A year later, while he was King County prosecutor, Magnuson began visiting Los Angeles, where Parker had become a contract starlet-singer with Paramount Pictures. Their relationship lasted, on and off, for fifteen years, and perhaps as many locales.

Carol Parker (now Cahill), a lively, attractive woman who retired to Ajijic, Mexico, played small parts in B movies. With Magnuson her role was larger. Maurice Rosenblatt, a friend, likened her beauty to that of a more famous movie star, Rita Hayworth. Carol made the nightclub and racetrack scene in Los Angeles, elegant parties in Washington, D.C., and Palm Springs, vacationed on Virginia Beach—one marvels at where Magnuson found the time—and visited art museums in Paris. Once she went with Magnuson to the U.S. Naval Academy at Annapolis. "They whistled at me," she says, pleased at the memory of the midshipmen. She wound up a movie career playing in westerns with handsome Buster Crabbe, the erstwhile Flash Gordon in the Saturday serials.[6]

Through Carol, Magnuson met Joyce Matthews, another starlet, and Mary Healy, a budding star from New Orleans. These relationships were apparently more than casual. Carol describes Healy as "very attractive, talented and smart." And Magnuson: "He liked being around stars, and Hollywood needed a Washington contact. Warren was very happy with his life, already proud of what he had done." He rendezvoused with Matthews, later the wife of comedian Milton Berle, at the Sherry Netherland Hotel in New York. Gene Markey, the film writer, wed Hedy Lamarr, the Austrian beauty imported to work in the fantasy factories. They stayed in close touch with Maggie. His relationship with Mary Healy became more serious.[7] Carol laughs at the rumor that Magnuson had an affair with Gloria Swanson, the silent film megastar and mistress of Joseph Kennedy, father of Maggie's pal John Kennedy, the future president. "That's far fetched. That would be like going to bed with your mother. How do such stories start?" Swanson was five years senior to Magnuson.

Carol Parker perfomed as a thrush with the popular orchestras of Ted Weems, Shep Fields, and Ted Fiorito, no longer household names. She says, "Warren's favorite song was 'Time on My Hands.' He said that was our song—but he probably said that to all the girls."

Al Cohn, a writer at 20th Century-Fox, and, later, writing coach at Metro-Goldwyn-Mayer, became a fast friend—Carol says his best friend in Hollywood. So did Sybil and Harry Brand, a publicity writer for 20th Century-Fox, whose boss, Joseph Schenck, was one of a half-dozen Hollywood moguls who owned and operated the film industry.[8] The most noted of these, Louis B. Mayer, entertained Maggie and Carol, as did the Brands. "Mayer adored Warren," she recalls. So did Mrs. Brand, who also hosted parties attended by Mary Healy and Maggie. "He was a darling, darling man; very close to Harry," says Sybil Brand. "They talked on the telephone every day. We would meet in Palm Springs where we had a home or in Seattle. Mary was a very nice girl. We were quite close for a while."[9] Mary and Maggie began to make the gossip columns that proliferated with the growth of Hollywood's mystique. They were pictured together in the *Seattle Star*.

Healy had been a singer in New Orleans' Roosevelt Hotel,[10] unofficial Louisiana headquarters for Senator Huey P. Long, where he drank, caroused, and bossed the great state of Louisiana. She became 20th Century-Fox's "Discovery of the Year" in 1939, with an image inflated by Harry Brand's prose: "a dainty little Southern girl, pert and piquant. She could have eight dates a night, seven days a week."[11] For a time, however, she appears only to have had eyes for Magnuson. Brand reported to the congressman that he had sighted Mary with columnist Jimmy Fidler in Pittsburgh, amid rumors that Maggie and Mary were about to get married. Carol Parker told their mutual pal, Al Cohn, the rumors were true. "Not true," Magnuson replied, although he did send "Mom in Moorhead" a photo of himself and Mary.

Walter Winchell, the Sunday night network radio gossip, reported wedding bells for the congressional Adonis. Ed Stone, editor of the *Seattle Post-Intelligencer*, wired Magnuson for story and picture and, by all means, name of the bride.

"Honest, Ed, that's news to me," Magnuson replied. "If it happens, I'll let you know. You know what [columnist Westbrook] Pegler says about Winchell: '15 minutes of hysteria, innuendo and inference about private lives that are either too big or too contemptible to talk about.' I don't know what category I'm in."[12]

At the peak of the Maggie-Mary-wedding-bells gossip early in 1940, Magnuson had as his guest in Seattle, Ruth Overton, of Alexandria, Louisiana, daughter of Senator John Overton, Democrat from that state, an ally of Huey Long's. This must have been unknown to Fidler, Winchell, and Ed Stone. Carol Parker would come to doubt there was ever anything very serious between her friends Mary and Warren.

When Parker's career stalled as a B-flick cowgirl, Magnuson appealed to Joseph Schenck ("Mr. Schenck" in his communications) to find a role for the starlet in an Irving Cummings production.[13] The movie musical role never materialized. The request suggested a working relationship between the congressman and the movie mogul, the most underrated of the studio bosses according to Hollywood historian Scott Berg. His biographer, Hank Messick, paints a less flattering picture of the Russian-born Schenck, who began an American show business career with the Marcus Loew theater chain, married the silent star Norma Talmadge, and in 1936 merged two Hollywood studios into 20th Century-Fox. Messick described Schenck as a "heroic hedonist," compulsive gambler, and pal of gangsters. Berg says Schenck, who favored a string of Hollywood beauties, took the fall for the other bosses when the Justice Department found the studios making payoffs to keep a mob-controlled union, the International Alliance of Theatrical Stage Employes. The other studio chiefs were married with children. The payoffs, protection from strikes, were made through one Willie Bioff, Al Capone's man in Hollywood. Schenck was charged with income tax evasion and sentenced to four months in jail in April 1941.[14] Magnuson dispatched his deepest sympathy to "Mr. Schenck" and advised the movie maker to "go get it [jail] over with—don't postpone the eventual day."

The mob had, indeed, moved west from New York and Chicago to the greener pastures of Los Angeles, no gangster more murderous and handsome than Benjamin "Bugsy" Siegel, a sometime hit man who would begin the development of Las Vegas as the greenest pasture of them all. Rumors about "Maggie and gangsters" would surface in political campaigns to come—rumors that were unsubstantiated, malicious, and ineffective. However, Carol Parker recalls one evening at the Ambassador Hotel in Los Angeles which might have revealed there was a flicker of truth to the gossip.

"He always stayed at the Ambassador when visiting Los Angeles," she says. "We had met there in the dining room for dinner. Two men approached and wanted to talk with Warren. They were polite. He said 'let's go to the bathroom.' They talked for a few minutes and the two men left. Warren said they were Bugsy Siegel—he was very handsome—and a gambler called Nick the Greek. They wanted Warren's help for a man in prison in Washington state. He said he told them 'I'll see what I can do, but don't know that I can do anything.' It was his way of dismissing the request."[15]

Magnuson's attraction to Hollywood is abundantly evident from letters left behind. Not so apparent is Hollywood's attraction to the handsome congressman. There has always been a draw between Hollywood's sex and Washington's power, says Scott Berg, Sam Goldwyn's biographer, and, beneath this, "a psychiatrist might say that politicians and movie people have a mutual personality disorder—excessive narcissism."[16]

Hollywood, however, had more immediate concerns. The studio moguls, nearly all of them Jews, were alarmed at Adolf Hitler's treatment of their European landsmen. They also faced the threat of antitrust litigation or legislation from Washington to bust up their patent monopoly of the film industry. Harry and Jack Warner, Louis Mayer, Goldwyn, Schenck, and Harry Cohn were vulnerable. They knew it. They needed all the help they could muster in the Capitol. They found an ally in Magnuson.

Al Cohn passed the word to Magnuson early in 1939 that Senator Burton K. Wheeler, a Democrat from Montana, was the "sub rosa leader" of the fight to thwart legislation aimed at breaking the monopoly, or possibly placing Hollywood under a government regulatory agency. Radio was regulated. Why not film? "Wheeler is friendly with the magnates," Cohn wrote Magnuson. "The industry is trying to beat the gun by the self-enforced divorce of production and distribution." Cohn finished his intelligence report with a racetrack tip and local gossip: "I'm tired of picking knives out of my back—the worst offender is your old pal, [Harry] Brand." In response, Maggie promised to come to L.A. in June to square matters between his two buddies. He said nothing about Wheeler or antitrust litigation.[17] Most likely, however, with the sub rosa, backroom talents of the young congressman, the studios were able to evade an antitrust reckoning for another decade. If justice suffered, art did not. The moguls and their monopolies made our greatest films.

A few months later, after L. B. Mayer hired a lobbyist named "Rosner," Cohn noted the man had the mogul "hooked" and wondered if Magnuson knew anything about him "except that he is a phoney."[18]

"You are correct on R," Magnuson replied. "Too bad men like Mayer are so gullible. You Hollywood people 10 miles outside the Los Angeles city limits are like country boys off the farm . . . but even stupidity deserves protection."[19] The exchange suggests that Magnuson would look into problems created by the inept lobbyist.

By the end of the congressman's second term, Seattle street talk, reinforced by the gossip columns, began to take notice of the Hollywood Maggie. It probably aroused nothing stronger than envy among the working stiffs in this unionized city, his core constituency. But not all of them approved. M. A. Niedfelt, a left-wing supporter, wrote Maggie a warning: "You have been playing around too much, breaking people's confidence in you. Keep this up and you'll soon be classified with the Wall Street vipers in Washington, D.C."[20]

Whatever the effect of his lifestyle on his health, it bounced harmlessly off his surging career. Part of the reason was his own skill in handling the romantic rumors. Magnuson had a way of curling the corners of his lips when something funny came to mind, usually in prelude to a joke or humorous tale. It is easy to imagine his quasi-smile when a group of Wenatchee city fathers, Republicans mostly, braced him on reports that he had delayed by days a return to Congress while romancing a starlet, Toni Seven, in Hawaii.

"It's true, I failed to get back in time for the opening of Congress. I was in Hawaii with my girlfriend," he said. "Had a fine time; ran into one of my fellow senators, a Republican. He was with his boyfriend." The room went still.[21]

And somewhere in the full rush of Lotus Land romance, Magnuson hit an emotional rock. He fell hard for one of the movie beauties—possibly Mary Healy, who would go on to marry fellow actor Peter Lind Hayes. He was, as they say in the novels, all broken up over the abortive romance. Al Cohn wrote to soothe his wounded feelings, tenderly: "I'm convinced your little experience with the God of love was salutary for your immortal soul. . . . I don't think you are ready for the double harness. You've got too much on your hands with your career and your taste in women has not fully developed, although I approve your selection of playmates. Anyhow, don't let it get you down, kid. I saw that lovely Erickson yesterday. She told me to tell you to hurry on down." Harry Brand wrote in consolation, "I have some new talent interested in congressmen."[22]

Nor would he take the final step, marriage, with Carol Parker. They flirted with marriage, and came close to it a few times during their fifteen-year relationship. Each time, he stopped short. Carol, like all of the others, adored Warren, despite his string of affairs with other starlets and those of lesser fame—some of them her friends. The most serious of these affairs, if not the most enduring, was with Senator Overton's daughter

Ruth, a Louisiana-Washington belle, not a movie employee. The affair was mutually intense; at the end poignant.[23]

"She was smart, sophisticated, and lived much of the time in Washington where her father was in the Senate," said Mrs. Herbert Kraushaar, a lifelong friend in Alexandria. "She was very lovely and gracious, outgoing but not pushy—a lady, a Southern lady."[24] "She was crazy about Warren," says Irv Hoff, Magnuson's magnificent administrative aide.[25]

Southern, indeed, in social attitudes as well as manner, and a tease to boot. "My dear Congressman," she wrote the Northwest liberal Magnuson after he voted for a federal law to prohibit a state poll tax, the device for keeping southern blacks away from the ballot box. "You have become their [blacks] chosen leader. I'm told that on a clear day you can see them swarming along the highways of the country like Black ants heading towards their Mecca, Seattle, their Messiah, Marse Magnuson."

Her letter continues: "We in Louisiana are looking forward to discussing the Negro situation in the Northwest. Should a crisis arrive over the weekend, you may reach me at the Ambassador Hotel in New York." And she adds a PS: "There's something about the Ambassador that puts me in a pretty suggestive mood." The letter was written on stationery from Senator Overton's office.

The big puff story from the agitprop division of the film factories in 1938 was the search for an actress to play the role of Scarlett O'Hara in *Gone with the Wind*, a romantic myth of the South during the nation's Civil War. Al Cohn wrote Magnuson in January: "My first candidate for Scarlett is la Belle Overton, the swamp angel. Of course, she'll have to get rid of that Louisiana accent and talk real Southern like 'you-all.' Otherwise we Northerners won't know what she is talking about." Overton was not an actress, but Cohn wasn't entirely kidding.

The affair went on and off, in the Magnuson pattern, from his homes at the Shoreham Hotel in Washington and the Olympic in Seattle, to New York and Los Angeles. Ruth appears less tolerant of Warren's other women than Carol Parker. In a dark mood near the end of the affair she wrote: "Maggie Dear, Things are pretty damned crazy around here. . . . I'd have given ten years of my fast ebbing life to have been under that table. Love, Ruth." There was no reply to this cryptic note, which apparently alluded to a dinner to which she was not invited. Maggie had another woman. Ruth soon went home to Alexandria to stay.

At least once before leaving Washington, Ruth offered to help Magnuson move a piece of hometown legislation blocked by her father in the Senate. Magnuson's bill called for federal help in reclaiming a barge owned by Puget Sound Bridge and Dredge but stranded by the Navy in the Aleutian Islands. Senator Overton was one of those Southerners so conservative he filibustered against daylight-savings time; said it would wreck his cows.

"Dad is blocking Warren's bill. I know how to get it loose," Ruth told Irv Hoff. "Tell Warren to call me. I'll handle Dad." But, Irv says, "I told Maggie I had it settled—all he had to do was to call Ruth Overton. He blew up. He said, 'stay out of my personal life.' I was crestfallen. The bill passed anyway—with or without Ruth's help—when Overton withdrew his objections at the last minute."[26]

Maurice Rosenblatt, an ex-GI just home from the South Pacific and freshly recruited as a lobbyist for the non-Zionist American League for a Free Palestine, recalls his first meeting with Ruth Overton and Warren Magnuson: "Rose Keane, a mutual friend, took me to the Shoreham. Ruth and Maggie were playing circus in Magnuson's apartment, a hell of a party with a dozen or so others. When the door opened I looked straight at a pair of legs—Maggie's. He was standing on his head. I joined the party. I still had New Guinea mud on my boots. Ruth was lady-like, Maggie was vivacious. I stayed until 2 A.M."[27] Rosenblatt and Rose Keane, a Broadway actress, went on to work closely with Magnuson on the creation of the state of Israel, but nothing more came of the senator's romance with Senator Overton's daughter.

"She was not old-maidish, but I don't think she ever had another serious romance, after she came back to Alexandria, after the Congressman," said Mrs. Kraushaar. "It was very very serious with Magnuson. She lived in the old family home, never married, not to the Congressman or anyone else. Her father, Senator Overton, ended it. He told her he did not think Magnuson would ever amount to anything. She could not go against her father's wishes." Ruth Overton died in a fire at her home in Alexandria in the early 1980s.

Charles Hodde, an old friend from the 1933 Washington legislature—himself a former Speaker of Washington's House of Representatives—reflected in the early 1990s on Maggie's days of wine and roses, wondering aloud how he could play so hard, yet do so much, and continually get reelected.

"He was quite a playboy, but they couldn't turn him out even if they disapproved of his life-style. He was too good, and it never bothered his work," said Charlie, a lifelong teetotaler. "Besides, he always brought home the bacon."[28]

CHAPTER 11

Horses, Flaxseed, and Dutiful Son

I n the late 1930s, federal bucks—the "bacon" brought home to Puget
Sound by Representative Magnuson—were hauling the nation out of
its depression, equipping it for a war that an overwhelming majority
of Americans did not want. Seattle was booming. So was Magnuson, a
second-term congressman favored by Sam Rayburn and Franklin Roosevelt, a romantic adored by Hollywood starlets, an attorney with close
ties to Seattle's gambling demimonde, and an adopted son with a troubled family.

The federalization of the Northwest economy which began with the
New Deal and the Grand Coulee Dam was nearing its peak and there
were no complaints, even from the most conservative business quarters.
Magnuson was the personification of this new manna from the Potomac,
and, as such, it was convenient to overlook his excesses in Congress and
his unconventional lifestyle. It was also easy because most of his side
ventures and family troubles were unknown outside his loyal circle of
political pals.

The family troubles began during 1937, his first year in Congress.
Clara Junkin—"Sis"—divorced her bootlegger husband. Magnuson subsequently learned his mother had a serious illness. In January 1937, "Sis"
told him they were having a tough time meeting mortgage payments on
Mom's house in Moorhead and they were three years in arrears on their
property tax payments. Worse, wrote Sis, victim of an internal disease, "I
have had such peculiar dizzy spells for a couple of days [and] the words
just seem to dance on the paper."[1]

Magnuson promised to take care of matters. He would pay the back
taxes, and Bill Stern would take over mortgage payments. Apparently, he
didn't come through. In June, Sis wrote that Mom planned to sell her fur
coat for money to pay the taxes. "She tries not to worry, but I know how
she feels," said the daughter, who was out of a job at the time.[2] Magnuson
settled the matter by wrapping up the taxes in a new mortgage. He was
also thinking about moving Mom and Sis to Seattle, his political base,
the locale of his business sidelines—radio and horse racing.

His ties to Joe Gottstein, Bill Edris, and their Longacres racetrack went
back to its origins with the passage in the 1933 state legislature of a

measure allowing pari-mutuel betting on race horses. It was Magnuson who found land for the race course in the valley south of Seattle. He became an investor—"part owner" he would claim to some—of Longacres and a resident in Edris's Olympic Hotel, where he got user-friendly rates, as low as two dollars a night for a time.

Gottstein was a formidable character, an all-American football player at Brown University who became what one former employee called a "benevolent dictator" as boss of the racetrack, a man accustomed to having his way.[3] When Maggie came home from Washington he usually lunched at the Olympic with Gottstein, Edris, and their close pal and police department ally, Ernie Yoris.

Yoris was chief of detectives, a friend since Magnuson's days as prosecutor. He liked cockfights, despite their illegality, and a good story. Carol Parker described the detective as likable but rough: "If you were his prisoner you would shake in your boots. He was very, very close to Warren even after Warren went to Congress. This didn't puzzle me. After all, Warren had been prosecutor, Ernie was a detective. Besides, they were both Scandinavian."[4]

These friendships were good for business at Longacres. This was still the era of the "tolerance" policy, when law officers might be persuaded to look the other way at violations of local gambling ordinances. There were bookmaking places in Seattle and "race" wires to serve them names of starting horses and race results from tracks around the nation. Bookie parlors operated, discreetly, under a tolerant police force—at least until the racing season opened at Longacres. For those weeks the bookies closed their shops. Longacres thus averted competition for its gambling dollar. To remain open, the bookies risked a police raid, which was embarrassing for managers and their sometimes distinguished clientele. No such raids could be made without clearance from the chief of detectives.[5] For decades, this was Seattle's way of coping with a social contradiction: a high-minded view that gambling was evil versus a down-to-earth recognition that a lot of responsible people liked it and aimed to wager. Longacres closed in the early 1990s, partly a victim of the liberalization of state gambling laws and the introduction of a state lottery.

Magnuson showed unusual sensitivity about the professional fate of Ernie Yoris when a wave of civic reform threatened the tolerance policy and the incumbent law enforcement establishment. Yoris survived each threat, to Magnuson's relief. There are strong indications that Maggie had an interest in a race wire, the Northwest News Company, as well as the racetrack. Northwest's chief officer, one Jack Meehan, was a consummate and highly skilled horse player, and also a pal of Ernie

Yoris. At one point, in March 1941, Magnuson requested a favor from Meehan.

"I owe Joe [Gottstein], that is, the mutuel department of the Washington Jockey Club [Longacres] $175.50," the congressman wrote the horse player. "Transfer anything I may have due [from Northwest News] to Gottstein. I'm a little short. I bluffed a little too much in that last poker game."[6]

The Meehan-Magnuson relationship surfaced a few years later when a future political opponent, Governor Arthur Langlie, said he had checks written to Magnuson from the Northwest News Company. He accused the congressman of an "association with bookmaking." Magnuson said the relationship was "that of a lawyer and a client." In October 1942 he got $1,000 in legal fees from Northwest News, described as disseminating "horse race betting information." No more was heard of the matter.

At least one of his inner circle, Mac MacGowan, didn't like the looks of the congressman's racetrack crowd. In midsummer 1941, there was heat on Seattle police and B. Gray Warner, Magnuson's successor as King County prosecutor, from a probe by federal Treasury agents. MacGowan called it a "fishing expedition" by the T-men. Warner was quizzed about his campaign contributions. Mac informed Maggie that "Yoris is okay" (safe from the probe) but that Ross Cunningham, sometime aide to Governor Langlie and longtime *Seattle Times* political reporter and editorial-page editor, "thinks the worst people in the world include Joe Gottstein, Bill Edris, Dave Beck and Frank Brewster,"[7] the latter Dave Beck's chief Teamster lieutenant, another horse player. The heat passed with no arrests, no indictments. Tolerance prevailed.

Magnuson's money problems went beyond Longacres. While he was working out the purchase of property on Bainbridge Island's south shore, he got another notice of insufficient funds in his account at the Pacific National Bank. Fortunately the bank's executive vice president, Casper Clarke, treated the overdrafts with gentle reminders. Magnuson would, eventually, come up scrambling with sufficient money.

Mom and Sis, along with a lifestyle out of a Hollywood film script, kept Magnuson in worrisome money trouble. The situation in Moorhead was worsening, with Sis a constant nag to her brother. Mom, she complained to Magnuson, wouldn't allow her to learn typing. Instead, she told her daughter to marry the first man she met with a few dollars. Mom was deeply ailing, demanding round-the-clock care from Sis. She'd like to "go out to a show with a young man," Sis told Magnuson, "but Mom can't be left alone." Her daily routine revolved around Mom's care and feeding. "It's a hell of a job," she said, "and I'm about nuts. I have all of my life wanted to get away from this damned town, but I'll do whatever you want—leave and find a job or stay with Mom."[8]

Magnuson replied that if his mother failed to improve, Sis should place her in a hospital, "regardless of expense." He subsequently sent checks to Sis for mortgage payments and for nursing care. He also noted, "I'm financially pressed." Nevertheless, later that year, 1941, he moved Mom, Sis, and his sister's daughter, Loretta, into the small compound on Bainbridge Island (a house and a small cottage on five acres) that he had purchased through Henry Broderick. Wherewithal for this extra expense came in part from work in Washington on behalf of Archer Daniels Midland (ADM).

The Minneapolis grain company and vegetable oil processor, founded in 1840, already had a history as a major player in Midwest politics. More recently, it has helped bankroll the presidential campaigns of Richard Nixon and Robert Dole and, like the garbage octopus, Waste Management, Inc., occasionally sponsors enlightened programs on public television, labeling itself "Supermarket to the World." Washington, D.C., is a critical factor in the firm's profits and losses. ADM began talking with Magnuson in late 1940, at the peak of his family troubles in Moorhead.[9] It's a fair guess that Magnuson's friends in Fargo and the Northwest Airlines executives in Minneapolis provided introductions. Initially, Tom Daniels, the ADM vice president, played it rather coyly.

"Because of our growing interest in the Northwest, the company would like to hire Rep. Magnuson as an attorney to handle certain problems," said Daniels. "The fee would be a flat $200 per month." That was no small change in 1941 dollars, and Magnuson indicated an interest. The "certain problems," however, had almost nothing to do with the Northwest, but much to do with Argentina.

"Entirely satisfactory with me," said Magnuson of ADM's offer. For the next two years, even during his Navy service on an aircraft carrier in the Pacific, he was ADM's man inside Washington. They got their money's worth. Magnuson worked to secure rationed materials, and to thwart a tax on flaxseed, as well as a move to prevent trading in flaxseed. ADM was especially demanding that he beat a proposed reduction in the duty on Argentine flaxseed. The State Department was pushing the duty reduction as a means of arresting the Latin American nation's tilt toward Nazi Germany.

"Make a careful study and resist in every way possible such a reduction," Daniels instructed Magnuson. The congressman noted some of his colleagues "seemed to be sucked in by international diplomats instead of paying attention to our own country. The Argentine diplomats have done a lot of social work." Whatever the outcome concerning the flax duty, Argentina remained neutral in World War II.

One of Magnuson's Washington State colleagues, Representative Knute Hill, proposed a bill forbidding trade in flaxseed. "We are very much opposed," said Daniels. "I can take care of the bill very easily," replied Magnuson. As for the proposed tax on flaxseed, Magnuson informed Daniels, "a great deal has been done to forestall the tax. I am constantly pounding away on the theory that our domestic needs will be greater in the next four years."

By 1941 both ADM and Northwest Airlines were feeling the crunch of restrictions on tools and equipment as the federal government shifted material priorities to the preparations for war. They were constantly appealing to Maggie for help. Northwest needed authorization for purchase of new passenger planes and for a new route to New York City; ADM needed approval for equipment for plants in New York and New Jersey and the State Department's okay on a license to export soybeans to Cuba. "We're having a hell of a time with the Cuban soybean situation," Maggie informed Daniels. He took the matter directly to Cordell Hull, Roosevelt's courtly secretary of state. ADM appreciated his work.

"Those who had a long, tedious, difficult time getting priority ratings for equipment supplies didn't have a Mr. Magnuson to handle the matter for them in Washington," wrote Hunter Goodrich, ADM's general manager late in 1941. "I get along just fine with the boys on the [federal] priorities board," Magnuson informed ADM, also noting, "the war situation is black . . . those in the know are expressing grave concern."

"All I want for Northwest Airlines is a fair advantage," Maurice Rosenblatt quotes Maggie as telling a hearing on aviation priorities.[10] Maggie would go on to bigger and more laughable malapropisms.

The 1940 election for Magnuson's third term in Congress seems but a ho-hum episode, barely mentioned, in a hectic career. Behind the scenes it was another matter. What captured public attention was a battle in Congress over a bill tailored to deport the Australian-born Harry Bridges, boss of the powerful and left-wing International Longshoremen's and Warehousemen's Union (ILWU), scourge of the West Coast steamship companies, rival to Dave Beck's Teamsters. Maggie kept his solidarity with Seattle's working waterfront by voting against the measure on grounds it was unconstitutional, which it almost surely was. Nevertheless, he got a fire storm of protest. Apple growers in Wenatchee said longshore strikes crippled their overseas sales. C. Arthur Foss, the Foss Tugboat owner-skipper, said Bridges damaged West Coast shippers. Most of the protest echoed C. W. Stults of Seattle, who urged Magnuson to "deport aliens who do not support our form of government and are trouble-makers."[11]

Joe Gottstein brought the most critical word to Magnuson: "It was a terrible mistake to support Bridges. Don't mention it anymore as it has roiled up [Frank] Brewster and [Dave] Beck and many of your friends." Public sentiment had shifted, said the horse track impresario, to "Old Glory," away from Howard Costigan and the Commonwealth Federation. He cautioned, "be careful about tie-ups with the CIO or any other Wobbly organization."[12] The irony is that Bridges and the other Seattle waterfront unions—the sailors, cooks, and marine firemen, the militant left edge of the American labor movement—created a situation that allowed the more conservative, business-oriented Beck and his sidekick Brewster to position themselves for good contracts with business. Beck appeared much the lesser evil, when viewed from the Rainier Club down Columbia Street, than Bridges and his brothers on the waterfront.

Beck's power in Seattle paralleled Maggie's rise in Congress. The labor boss frequently requested favors of his congressman, once to intervene in the pending deportation of a Teamster official in Portland, another time to secure a place in Naval ROTC for his son. Before his fall from power, Beck became a regent of the University of Washington, a prime status symbol in Seattle's downtown establishment. Requesting Magnuson's help on a private real estate project at Snoqualmie Pass, Beck listed as character references university president Raymond Allen, Seattle-First National Bank president Tom Gleed, *Seattle Post-Intelligencer* publisher Charles Lindeman, and Spokane's Joe Drumheller. None had ever gone to work with a longshoreman's hook or without a coat and tie.

There is further irony in the aftermath of this emotional political issue. Bridges's longshoremen became exemplars of racial integration, earning prime wages and top working conditions. Their leader would become in the 1970s a West Coast labor "statesman" as tight with the steamship companies as Dave Beck had been with his dairy, beer, and laundry truck owners. Like Beck three decades earlier, Bridges eventually became a working buddy of men with soft hands, dressed in three-piece suits.

Oddly, like Fred Wettrick a few years earlier, Steve Chadwick, the properly mannered and formally attired attorney, asked Bill Stern, North Dakota's "Mr. Republican," to ask Magnuson to support his bid to re-place Lewis Schwellenbach in the U.S. Senate. Schwellenbach resigned to become a U.S. District Judge.[13] He was apparently uninformed about Magnuson, who was also considering a run for the Senate that summer of 1940. Mac MacGowan pushed for it, but Bill Edris and Joe Gottstein were opposed to Maggie's race for the Senate. They were exasperated by his vote against the deportation of Harry Bridges.

MacGowan the politician, however, had a better sense of the possibilities than Edris the clever entrepreneur. It appeared to be a grand opening. There might be opposition in the primary election from Frank Bell, the Grant County wheeler-dealer, but Mac MacGowan said Maggie would have the blessings of both Senator Bone and the outgoing Schewellenbach, who might agree on Magnuson but otherwise were in a backstage feud—a possible reason for Schwellenbach's decision to leave the Senate for the judiciary. By midsummer, Magnuson had left a firm impression that he would be a candidate for the Senate, not for reelection to the House. What most emphatically changed his mind was opposition from John Boettiger, erstwhile supporter who sought revenge for Magnuson's reappointment of George Starr as Seattle's postmaster. Postmasters were mighty pieces of political patronage in those days before corporate subsidies. Boettiger, no run-of-the-press newspaperman, was President Roosevelt's son-in-law and publisher of the *Seattle Post-Intelligencer*.

"I told you over the telephone about a month ago I have been seriously considering filing for the [Schwellenbach] vacancy," Magnuson wrote the president. "In view of the fact that the P.I. has made it more or less obvious whom they are supporting, it has been generally assumed that the candidate mentioned is the administration's choice for this vacancy." Magnuson then asked for Roosevelt's "help with my decision. Our loyalty to you and conflicting local interests make the situation somewhat difficult."[14]

No help from the White House was forthcoming. Maggie weighed a decision. Bill Edris advised him it would be a tough fight: "Maggie, you haven't worked on a campaign in a long time. This means doing everything and working from early to late—let's quit monkeying around and start doing something."[15] In midsummer, lacking a response from Roosevelt, Maggie made up his mind: it was not his time for a Senate race. Boettiger had his revenge.

Magnuson's race for reelection to Congress was a reprise of 1936, Fred Wettrick again the Republican nominee. Without bothering to campaign much, Magnuson won by a three to one margin. With liberals like Magnuson, Ed Henry, and Paul Coughlin bailing out of the Communist-tainted Washington Commonwealth Federation—but never repudiating their former alliance—Wettrick was shorn of the "anti-American" issue used against Maggie in the previous campaign. Besides, how could one label "un-American" the pal of Lawrence Arnold, the conservative head of the Northwest's largest bank, Seattle First-National, and Henry Broderick, the canny real estate mogul?

The Democratic Senate nomination went to Representative Mon Walgren, onetime Everett jewelry store owner, who, like Maggie, relished poker, whiskey, and high living. Walgren defeated Steve Chadwick, the self-proclaimed Jeffersonian Democrat turned Republican, in the November election to hold the seat.

Roosevelt's quest for a third term dominated political news. Polls up to election eve showed he had a tough race against Wendell Willkie, the Wall Street lawyer from Indiana whose major clients were the private-power holding companies, scourge of Homer Bone, Sam Rayburn, and Warren Magnuson. When Willkie, perhaps carried away by his campaign, reversed course and indicated sympathy for public power, Ed Flynn, the Democratic national chairman, described him as a "self-made proletarian."

That fall, the Cincinnati Reds, behind Bucky Walters and Paul Derringer, won the World Series, sharing headlines with Roosevelt, Willkie, Hitler, and Mussolini. In Washington State, that autumn was more significant for the emergence of two new political personalities. Henry "Scoop" Jackson would share with Magnuson preeminence in Northwest politics for the next four decades, yet rarely drink anything stronger than Coca-Cola. Republican Arthur B. Langlie, like Jackson a northwesterner of Scandinavian heritage, would challenge Magnuson for preeminence.

The election was nearly a Democratic rout. Scoop Jackson, the shy-looking Snohomish county prosecutor and onetime Everett newsboy, easily defeated Payson Peterson. Peterson would become a perennial candidate for Congress, the state's version of Minnesota's Harold Stassen. "Scoop and Maggie" were to become the most powerful Senate combination in the history of the West, rivals to the congressional clout accrued by seniority to their southern colleagues. Langlie prevented the rout by narrowly defeating Clarence Dill, the favored Democrat, for governor. The difference was a few hundred votes, and Democrats would contest the election.

Langlie, the Seattle mayor, was up from the ranks of the city's reformist Cincinnatus Society, a group Charles Hodde called "so ethical they think they could re-write the Bible to make it better." A stern Presbyterian despite his Norse ancestry, Langlie had no tolerance at all for Seattle's "tolerance policy." He was a confirmed teetotaler, particularly disdainful of hard-drinking Magnuson and his racetrack cronies. Eventually he would put their conflicting lifestyles to an election test. First he had to get seated as governor.

Although there's no evidence Magnuson played a part in the plot, Mac MacGowan kept him apprised of the Democratic scheme to prevent Governor-elect Langlie from taking office in Olympia until the resolution of an alleged vote fraud. The legislature would refuse the office to Langlie, pending a recount of the vote. In the meantime, Lieutenant Governor Vic Meyers would take the governor's chair, "Smith Troy [the attorney general] gets the Highway Patrol and the Highway Commission, the Auditor [Cliff Yelle] gets purchasing. It will probably work because all members of the Legislature will get some loot. The problem is press support for Langlie."

It didn't work. Dan Markel, a *Post-Intelligencer* reporter, informed Magnuson that the Democratic leadership "bungled the job" and got outmaneuvered by Langlie. Instead of leaking "dabs" of a report on election irregularities, the leadership made the whole report public. Some Democrats were "hypnotized by the Republican call for bi-partisanship." Some were double-dealing: Vic Meyers got cold feet because of a potential threat to a bill which would give him a job in the interim between legislative sessions; Joe Drumheller, the Senate leader and Maggie's main man in eastern Washington, "played tight with Langlie while pretending hostility"—or so Markel saw the debacle.[16]

Magnuson's only comment on the abortive plot was "too bad the legislature is mismanaged." He added that "you can't be fish and fowl—you will lose Democratic friends and the respect of Republicans."

And he mentioned again how busy he was in Washington, D.C.

CHAPTER 12

Commander Magnuson

The beginning of Magnuson's third term in Congress, the twilight of America's professed neutrality in a bellicose world, was a contradiction. The congressman from Washington State's First District was a dove in hawk feathers, a peacenik doing everything possible for defense of the nation's Pacific flank while casting critical antiwar votes. Maggie was having it both ways by appeasing those opposed to U.S. involvement in war—perhaps assuaging his conscience—and by boosting Puget Sound's economy with increasing federal appropriations for its shipyards, naval stations, and the Army's Forts Lewis and Lawton.

In 1940, while Hitler's Luftwaffe was trying to bomb Great Britain into surrender, the Boeing Airplane Company had to double its plant capacity to build B-17s ordered by Maggie's pal, General H. H. "Hap" Arnold, chief of the Army Air Corps. Knowing where Boeing's bread would be buttered, the congressman made a point of friendship with General Arnold. The Navy ordered $10 million in new ships from the Bremerton Naval Shipyard, and by 1938 electricity generated by federal dams on the Columbia River was serving a new Northwest industry, the manufacture of aluminum, a light metal essential in the construction of military aircraft. The dream of Homer Bone and Warren Magnuson for cheap, nonprofit power was enriching the region in a manner they never anticipated. "Help wanted" ads, rare as flamingos on Puget Sound five years earlier, filled the back pages of Seattle's newspapers. By 1940, Seattle's business index had boomed to 117.9, the level of 1929, the last year before the big crash.[1]

President Roosevelt had "McGoozled"—the perfect Magnuson word for it—a decidedly unenthusiastic nation into providing military aid to Britain through what he called "lend-lease." In exchange for the use of their military bases in the Caribbean, he loaned U.S. ships and money to the British. Magnuson likened the lend-lease to loaning a garden hose to a neighbor whose house is on fire. The United States would become the "arsenal of democracy." The "garden hose" began to pour in 1941, a de facto, if not de jure, violation of U.S. neutrality in the European war. By that time Roosevelt would be reelected to an unprecedented third term.

Puget Sound was getting its share of the war business with Maggie as middleman. The Boeing Airplane Company got a $60 million contract for 300 B-17 bombers early in 1941, a major breakthrough for the aircraft manufacturer, the foundation of America's effort to defeat Germany through strategic bombing. A note from Lawrence Arnold, a hunting pal, a conservative, and head of the region's largest bank, Seattle-First National, said "everyone at home thinks you are doing a splendid job."[2]

"I've been busier the past four months than ever before," Magnuson wrote Joe Gottstein. "Mail has tripled, there are constant committee meetings, everyday someone in Seattle comes with problems. . . . The old hometown should be booming. If not, it's not my fault." But he was not too busy for friendships and local politics. He advised Gottstein to proceed with a libel suit against the *Spokane Spokesman-Review*, the anti-public power voice of conservatism in eastern Washington: "letting these things go gives the newspaper psychology the license to continue vicious presentations."[3] Gottstein later settled for a letter of apology.

At the request of Boeing's conservative management, Magnuson had lobbied his buddy General Arnold for purchase of the four-engine B-17. Boeing feared competition from California's nonunion Douglas Aircraft, which paid lower wages and sold a cheaper bomber. After a day spent with Arnold, Maggie assured Boeing that the general was convinced that the "superiority of Boeing's work" would offset California's lower wages.[4] The B-17s would carry the brunt of America's air war against Germany.

Threat of war changed the region's politics as well as its economy. But the congressman faced a two-edged sword with the issue. Despite the dependence of "3,000 to 4,000 Seattle families" on the B-17 contract, polls showed an overwhelming margin of opinion against war. "Keep us out of war!" was the one-line postcard Mabel Green sent her congressman in 1940. A year later the mood shifted somewhat. Arthur Brine, a Maggie stalwart in Port Orchard, wrote "although we want to stay out of war, a great majority want to see Hitler stopped. . . . the local Silver Shirts cannot be found anymore."[5] Silver Shirts were native fascists, boosters of Adolf Hitler.

None of this shook Washington politics so much as Hitler's crucial pact with Joseph Stalin in 1939. Agreement between these two abnormal personalities but absolute dictators was the marauding tiger lying down with the hungry bear. In the geometry of politics, it was the equivalent of a squared circle. It took the U.S. Communist Party two months to get the signal straight: U.S. foreign policy under FDR was no longer "antifascist." Suddenly it had become "pro-imperialist." That was the new party line from Moscow, and American Communists had to obey or quit. The pact caused an immediate loss of membership in the American Communist Party.[6] It rattled the Popular Front to its foundations in Washington State. Abandoned by liberals, the Washington Commonwealth Federation (WCF), the Communist-influenced critical mass of the state's Democratic Party, began its meltdown into the party's pariah, eventually hounded almost from memory by headline-hunting professional anti-Communists. The WCF's liberal members began to take a second look at their strange alliance and leave the organization. Among them were Ed Henry, Paul Coughlin, and Warren Magnuson. The crusty Arthur Brine summed it up in a letter to Maggie: "That political acrobatic feat by Russia has blown the pants off all sorts of political groups. I'd hate to be in your shoes and have to find an answer [to its meaning]."[7] What it meant was that Germany and the USSR were temporarily dividing Eastern Europe between themselves. That is, until June 1941, when the Nazi tiger would turn with fury on the Russian bear.

Early in 1941, Magnuson summed up results of his work on behalf of the Northwest from his seat on the Naval Affairs Committee, all of it war related whether he wanted the conflict or not: employment at the Bremerton shipyard up from 2,500 in 1937 to 12,000; Puget Sound shipbuilding contracts worth $400 million; appropriations for Navy bases at Sitka, Kodiak, and Unalaska in Alaska (but not Willapa Bay), and for housing projects in Seattle at Yesler Terrace and Sand Point and in Bremerton; monies allocated to enlarge the naval torpedo station at Keyport, and to build the highway to Alaska. Maggie was a prime mover of the latter. Missing from his list of federal funds for the Northwest is his sponsorship and passage of appropriations for cancer research, the first of his landmark bills for medical research.[8]

"Washington has the most liberal Congressional delegation. Seattle, the greatest city in the Northwest, is represented by the youthful, good-looking, Warren G. Magnuson, a champion of labor, a brilliant orator," reported Richard Neuberger, a Portland journalist and Oregon senator-to-be, for the *Progressive* magazine. Banker Joshua Green, no friend of labor, but warm with Maggie, said, "you're doing a fine job in Washington." No doubt he had noted the bump in Seattle's business index.

"Congress is working," Magnuson wrote a friend in Los Angeles. "It takes a long time for the boys to get moving but once we think someone is encroaching, things begin to happen."

At the behest of Los Angeles pals, he also sponsored a bill to create a Naval Academy on the West Coast—an Annapolis of the West, with California the preferred locale. The Navy wasn't interested. Nor did allegiance to Puget Sound divert his attention from California projects, especially if his Hollywood pal, Al Cohn, turned on the charm. Maggie had suggested that the 20th Century-Fox film writer might be wise to slip the attention of the Dies Committee by changing jobs. Representative Martin Dies, a right-winger from Texas, was on the hunt for lefty pinkoes and had big eyes for Hollywood. Cohn became a Los Angeles police commissioner, and, thanks to Maggie, the city's unofficial ambassador to Washington, D.C., where he pushed the wares of Douglas and Lockheed aircraft companies seven months before Pearl Harbor. Maggie wrote Al that Douglas was due to get orders for sixty DC-4s, and Lockheed would get orders for eighty Constellations—both four-engine transports of advanced design, some of them still flying at the close of the century.

Al Cohn, like at least three of Maggie's buddies in Seattle, Saul Haas, Mac MacGowan, and Roy Peterson, eventually became a Collector of Customs; Cohn in Los Angeles, most likely with further push from the powerful young congressman.

Magnuson informed Cohn that officials were privately giving a "black picture of the war situation." The English were under German air bombardment and nearly isolated by a Nazi submarine blockade. Only American intervention, already partly initiated through Roosevelt's lend-lease, could save the Mother Country. The English, said Maggie, needed a four-engine bomber, and the office of priorities management, "a mess, everyone running around like mice," needed better organization. Finally, on second thought, "there's strong opinion England can't be saved even if we do help. . . . tell Carol to drop me a note."

He still firmly opposed U.S. participation in the war, even announcing in early August to Burt and Mary Farquharson, WCF pioneers, "you can count on me to vote against the extension of the draft." When Julius Madison, a Maggie loyalist in Carnation, wrote "its no business of ours to mess in the circus of insanity in Europe," Magnuson replied, "I wholly agree. I wish a majority of Congress felt the same. There's hysteria in Washington. It's a good thing Congressmen have to go home and face the people."[9]

None of this feverish 1941 activity distracted him from personal affairs and constituent business. He took time to purchase through Henry Broderick the Bainbridge Island home for Mom and Sis, to congratulate Saul Haas for jacking up station KIRO to 50,000 watts, and to acknowledge his dividend of $6.89 as a stockholder.[10] He intervened in Seattle on behalf of Charlie Kamm, his former congressional secretary, fallen on hard times and too much strong drink. Carol Parker and Ruth Overton seemed to be his most important, although not necessarily exclusive, romantic interests that last year before war.

Hitler, the spellbinding orator and creepy personality bent on accumulating more living room for his German subjects—and death to those people he regarded as inferior—gave the world another acrobatic shock. Dismissing his pact with the paranoid Stalin, he invaded Russia in June 1941. Magnuson said, "Everyone hopes Russia and Germany will knock each other out. But military experts feel the German machine can overrun Russia at will. . . . If Germany and Japan conquer Russia we are in a worse position in the Pacific than in the Atlantic."[11] The stunning invasion prompted another amazing ideological U-turn by Moscow, naturally, by the American Communist Party, and by the WCF, perhaps the most solid evidence of its knee-jerk connection to the Kremlin's international party line. The "pro-imperialist" foreign policy of Roosevelt would again become labeled "antifascist." Saving the Soviet Union from the German invasion became paramount.

On February 27, shortly after the WCF's annual convention, the federation's new president, Hugh DeLacy, wrote a stinging admonishment to Magnuson for his vote in favor of granting additional war powers to President Roosevelt: "It's not pleasant to tell you of our acute disappointment at your 'aye' vote to give the power to wage undeclared war, the power of dictatorship over the resources and people of America, into the hands of a single man whose mind is no longer on his people or peace."[12]

Magnuson's vote was to ease restrictions in the neutrality act that allowed Roosevelt to provide U.S. Navy escorts for vessels bucking Hitler's undersea blockade. It was a major, if sneaky, step toward U.S. participation in the war. Senator Burton Wheeler denounced the change and the Navy for acting "aggressively" in the Atlantic war. The WCF's Moscow-influenced party line on war stated that imperialist, fascist, or fascist-leaning nations were having at each other and that this was no business of America's. Moreover, DeLacy wrote, "under the pretense of fighting Hitlerism 6,000 miles away, [the bill] HR 1776 gives us Hitlerism at home" (FDR).

Magnuson gave DeLacy a calm, civil reply, indeed his stock response when questioned, or in this case attacked, about a controversial vote. He had given the vote a great deal of thought: "I believe we are all trying to reach the same objective, but I disagree with your conclusions. If you feel this is a deviation from my long consistent liberal record, I'll have to accept that as your honest opinion. I will also vote for the Ludlow Amendment. I'm sorry we disagree."

DeLacy, a Phi Beta Kappa and subsequent lecturer in literature at the University of Washington, followed the Communist Party line. An honorable idealist, he eventually explained, "I guess I might be said to be a communist. I became convinced in the Depression that the proper solution for problems facing the U.S. people was a socialist reorganization of our society."[13] He would go on to be a one-term member of Congress from Seattle, then fade into obscurity in southern California with the anticommunist purges of the 1950s. One wonders how his loyalty to a party line could survive yet another twist from its creator-enforcers in Moscow.

DeLacy wrote Magnuson again in July 1941, one month after the German invasion of the Communist motherland, headquarters for the Communist International whose Popular Front had played a role in Washington State politics. The party line had switched and so had the WCF. It now favored the war: "With U.S. aid, the Chinese, British, and Russian people will smash Hitler. . . . Roosevelt's pledge for aid to China, USSR and Britain must be carried out without delay."

DeLacy added, without any hint of apology, "We [the WCF] now accept the necessity of Roosevelt's foreign policy."[14] The Brits and Kuomintang Chinese, overnight, were no longer imperialist fascists.

Magnuson's response to this breathtaking ideological flip-flop was gracious. He did not gloat: "I appreciate your communication on the international situation. . . . I entirely agree with your conclusions." Those conclusions, of course, were the same as held by Magnuson in February, when he caught the WCF wrath. His reply was also characteristic: forget the grudge. Forgive. His vote may be needed on another day. It was a quality that came from a gentle nature and a shrewd understanding of practical politics, a main key to his success as a legislator.

Even before the German invasion of Russia, Magnuson was privately talking war but voting peace, if the latter can be considered the goal of his continued promotion of U.S. neutrality. Like his committee seatmate, Lyndon Johnson, Magnuson had the rank of lieutenant commander in the naval reserve. In April when he got a $6.89 dividend from his stock in station KIRO, he also sent a personal, confidential letter to Governor Langlie, also a reserve naval officer: "I've talked with Adm. [Chester] Nimitz about this and he said that we should take active duty in the Navy together in the Northwest. It would set a good example. Mull it over."[15]

Langlie sent a terse reply one week later: "thanks for the invitation, but I can't leave office." Magnuson, however, appeared to have his mind set about active duty. There was already street talk about the possibility of his resigning Congress to join the Navy. In late July he advised Mac MacGowan, "spike those reports of a [congressional] vacancy if I go into the Navy." He did not intend to resign from Congress, but there was ample evidence across the Atlantic and Pacific that he might be needed elsewhere.

Japan, controlled by an aggressive military clique, loomed as much a threat in the Pacific as did Germany in Europe. Nazis mastered Austria, France, the Netherlands, Belgium, Denmark, Norway, Poland, Czechoslovakia, and most of the Soviet Ukraine. Less visible than these bloody conquests was the human nightmare unfolding in Europe's Jewish ghettos and Heinrich Himmler's concentration camps. The secret of Hitler's murder of Jews and other European *untermenschen*—secret because the dictator did not aim to arouse international opinion—was leaking from escapees and reliable observers. By 1941 the horror began to touch members of Congress and the administration. There came a rush of Jews seeking refuge in the United States, many of them to become inadvertent victims of the Great Depression.[16]

Citing the nation's soaring unemployment, President Herbert Hoover placed a sharp curb on immigration in 1930. Roosevelt, pressured by Congress, eased the restrictions in 1935, when Hitler's murderous intent was not yet clear; matters did not seem so grim. When the economy nosedived again in 1938, Roosevelt renewed the restrictions. By that time, Hitler had unleashed his Nazi thugs on Jewish businesses. He had shown his hand.

Abetting these barriers to Jewish refugees was a potent streak of anti-Semitism in the United States. Race-hate preachers such as Father Charles Coughlin and W. D. Pelly, founder of the Silver Shirts, shared the airwaves with *Amos 'n' Andy*, and were precursors of tamer radio demagogues of the 1990s. Coughlin and Pelly said straight out what the latter-day ideologues say with innuendo, yet even a respectable conservative like Seattle's Steve Chadwick, national commander of the American Legion, argued that "with 13 million unemployed, immigration must be restricted." For too many in Europe, the consequences were fatal.

In 1938, Rabbi Stephen Wise wrote Magnuson that Hitler's takeover of Austria was "deeply troubling, an indication of further suppression of Jews." Magnuson replied that he was willing to do all that he could to spare European Jews from "barbaric oppression." His initial act was to sign a statement urging Britain to keep Palestine open to Jewish refugees.

The dreadful situation came closer to the congressman when a constituent, Dr. H. Schoffman, requested Magnuson's help in gaining an exit from Vienna for his wife's parents, Leopold and Laura Lederer. They were supposed to sail from Lisbon, Portugal, to America on the SS *Exeter*, passage paid in advance by the Schoffmans. The problem was a U.S. visa. "I'm doing everything possible," Magnuson replied to one of many communications from Schoffman. He appealed to the State Department's visa section, which in turn noted that all U.S. consular offices in Austria and Germany were closed. The Lederers needed to reach the U.S. consul in Lisbon. But first they needed a U.S. visa to gain an exit permit from Vienna.[17] It was life or death, and Catch-22.

The flurry of communications between Magnuson and the exasperated State Department reached a climax in August 1941, when A. M. Warren of the visa section wired, in essence, forget it: "I regret there is nothing more I can do." As an anticlimax, the State Department billed Magnuson $8.31 "to cover cable charges from the Lederer traffic." Maggie mailed a check in that amount to Cordell Hull, the stately secretary of state. He could only guess, and hope, at the fate of the German couple.

Half a century later, another daughter of the Lederers, Anna Joachim, an old woman living in Seattle, told of their fate. She had difficulty recalling Magnuson's role on behalf of her parents and would only say her father and mother were murdered in Vienna by Germans, "but that was fifty years ago."[18]

For all of his sense of the inevitability of war, Magnuson made one critical vote he may have come to regret. As promised to the Farquharsons, he voted against Roosevelt's request for a thirteen-month extension of the draft, the most critical defense issue facing the nation in that critical year. Without the extension, most of the early draftees would be leaving active duty in October. Graffiti—"OHIO"—punctuated the tents of Army camps. This was short for "Over the Hill in October." FDR wanted an indefinite extension. Speaker Sam Rayburn said no, but that he might push a thirteen-month extension through the House. He knew the vote would be close. When, on August 12, at the end of the roll call, draft extension prevailed by a lone vote, 203 to 202, Rayburn slammed down the gavel and announced "the bill is passed." Opponents raged about his fast gavel and his subsequent refusal to hear a motion to reconsider the bill. Mothers in the House gallery moaned and wept, but its passage gave the nation a three-month lead to prepare for the inevitable.[19] Japanese war hawks gave the vote a different meaning, a sign of the deep division in U.S. society over war. It may have encouraged Pacific aggression.

Back home after the congressional recess, Magnuson explained his "no" vote, saying General George Marshall, the army chief of staff, had doubts about the wisdom of a draft. "It's the wrong approach," Maggie told home folks. "We need to build a professional Army." There were other pressing constituent matters in those final months before World War II. Ken Schoenfeld, a furniture manufacturer, complained to Maggie that "labor has taken over my place and must be controlled." John

Schermer, a deputy prosecutor, wanted his help securing a state Liquor Control Board listing for the T. W. Samuels Distillery. Sheriff Bill Severyns wanted his friend to get the army off his back. Colonel Ralph Glass, commander of Fort Lewis near Tacoma, had begun the first in a series of military requests for a shutdown of Seattle's whorehouses, all of them citing one poetically named the Dainty Rooms. Whatever their boon to a soldier's morale, the women were infecting troops with VD. The sheriff, somewhat defensively, said, "I've got a 100 bed clinic for whores in the city jail." He added, somewhat wistfully, "You know, Maggie, this is your town as well as mine. Please help."[20]

It all changed on December 7, 1941. The Japanese attack on Pearl Harbor, America's chief Pacific military base, shook the nation like nothing since the Confederate shelling of Fort Sumter, the first gunsmoke of the Civil War. December 7 was "a day that will live in infamy," said Roosevelt in his address to Congress, December 8. It happened to the apparent surprise of the Army, Navy, Marines, and the Roosevelt administration. One year earlier Admiral Yates Sterling, a Pacific fleet commander, told the *Seattle Star*, "the Japanese are not likely to send a fleet to attack Pearl Harbor. It's too far away."

There was fear of a Japanese invasion of the Northwest. Magnuson shared it. Before flying back to Washington for the declaration of war, he told a state legislator in Raymond, Washington, that the Navy was considering a base at Willapa Bay on the state's southwestern coast, part of his all-out effort to gain protection for the nation's Pacific flank. Under military orders, Seattle went to blackouts at sundown. Newspapers dropped advice to the lovelorn columns for "What To Do If Bombs Fall Here" (i.e., take cover).[21]

Farewell to American neutrality; no further contradictory votes from Magnuson. The congressman, as he would put it, "crystallized." He wired the Seattle newspapers that he was flying back to Washington with ten other western congressmen and that he would vote "aye" on Roosevelt's pending resolution for a declaration of war. He did and three days later, along with Lyndon Johnson, went to the office of Admiral Nimitz and requested assignment to active naval duty. Both congressmen had their papers in order. "We want to go to war," said Magnuson. "Nimitz initially balked—you two guys here again? But he signed the papers. We didn't resign from Congress—we just went." In fact, they were granted leaves of absence. Their salaries dropped from $10,000 a year to $3,000.[22]

Nothing better illustrates the difference between these two masters of Congress than their political use of subsequent wartime experiences. For the immodest Johnson, it was rank exploitation. On the basis of one harrowing bomber run in the South Pacific, he puffed himself into a flesh and blood John Wayne and so ran for the U.S. Senate. Magnuson apparently saw weeks of heavy combat with Admiral William "Bull" Halsey on the aircraft carrier *Enterprise*, yet rarely spoke of it, although he did make limited use of his experiences in one election campaign.

His service record says he was dispatched on March 19 to the *Enterprise* as an observer and subsequently, April 30, ordered to duty on the West Coast with the Bureau of Navigation. The carrier and its crew won a Presidential Unit Citation for action "in nearly every major carrier engagement" from December 7, 1941, to November 15, 1942. Maggie missed the pivotal battle of Midway by one month. It's apparent that the Navy considered Magnuson and Johnson of greater value on the Naval Affairs Committee than as observers of warfare. But as Committee Chairman Carl Vinson noted in a letter to Magnuson, the combat experience added greatly to his value as a committee member.[23]

He had a close brush with fame or worse when "like a dummy" he volunteered to take part in a surprise raid on Japan led by air ace Jimmy Doolittle from the aircraft carrier *Hornet* on April 18. Flying twin-engined B-25 bombers, the raid did little damage to Japanese home islands, but hit the bull's-eye with American morale. Like nothing else, it showed the range of U.S. power even in the war's initial stage. Landing in Chinese airfields, fifty-five of the eighty airmen survived the raid and returned to combat duty. Magnuson told his wife Jermaine years later that he had been accepted as a participant in the raid, but the stormy seas prevented his transfer from the *Enterprise* to the *Hornet*, and lost him a place in history as a participant in the raid subsequently described in the book *Thirty Seconds Over Tokyo*.[24] As an honorary member, he would join survivors of the mission in their annual reunions. He never mentioned this, however, except to his closest associates.

He had a mighty fling in San Francisco before departure for the South Pacific, a high time that left appreciative, but forlorn, love letters from several admirers in his wake.[25] His papers give only indirect reference to time under fire. Instead, they reflect a keen interest in the business affairs of the congressional office he left behind in the care of two exceptional secretaries, Claire Atwood and Mary Turnbull Ferrandini. They loved Magnuson, as would two generations of staffers to come.

Newsweek magazine, in February 1942, pictured Claire and Mary and explained how the office operated in Magnuson's absence: "The girls sit in on meetings of the Naval Affairs Committee and through mail keep Magnuson informed on all legislation. . . . Before leaving he had paired his votes on important pending legislation. . . . The girls handle requests for materials with the War Production Board [WPB] and will go to Seattle if the 1942 campaign is tough." Maggie didn't intend to give up his seat come war or elections.

He still had a $200 per month salary from Archer Daniels Midland (ADM), the grain company now more concerned with war-scarce materials for their processing plants than with Argentine flaxseed. Claire and Mary carried on the ADM business, working their charm on the WPB. "I got a good priority [for materials] for ADM on steel," Mary informed Maggie. "Knock off a few Japs for me." Magnuson had his Seattle law partner, Bruce Bartley, and Bartley's bright new counsel, Max Nicolai, transfer his ADM money to the Pacific National Bank.

Mary told Julius Madison that Magnuson was "in the thick of things," and that on one day his carrier had endured two attacks. Bill Edris relayed a letter from her boss, telling of "pretty tough action, but I'm okay." Mary summed it up in another letter to a supporter, "Really, isn't he a great fellow? He could have claimed deferment as a member of Congress. Instead, he is doing two jobs for his country at the same time."

Early in 1942, Mary wrote a long, chatty letter to her boss expressing her concern about his safety in combat: "but you always come out on top and enjoy a real fight better than anyone we know. . . . I've forwarded the ADM money. . . . Carol [Parker] is lonesome and invites me to come stay with her in New York. . . . Lou Small [a Hollywood publicist] is hanging around the office. He's the biggest blowhard of all the pests to date. . . . you got another 'prize' from White—you held out on what happened that night!"

Ida White, a young Seattleite, had a raging crush on her congressman, fervently expressed in a small volume of passionate letters. Mary twitted her boss about "that night," which might have been a figment of Ida's active imagination. Ida wanted Magnuson's photograph, the picture of a dashing Naval officer, strikingly handsome in uniform, wearing a David Niven streak of mustache. Mary said no. It did not slow the determined Ida White. Inspired by the dashing Maggie, she informed him of her venture into song writing. Their titles suggest their content: "Beautiful Miami and You," "My My Miami," and "Sweet Dream Boy."[26]

Answering Mary's epistle on Ida White, Magnuson sent an undated letter, written on lined paper, to Claire and Mary, addressed to routine business and instructing them to "give all the help you can to Scoop [freshman Representative Henry Jackson]. He's alright. I've had several letters from Carol. She's a good trouper and not afraid of work. I was worried about her but I know you kids will keep in touch. . . . There are lots of nice islands out here. Maybe I could be the Swedish king of Pogo

Pogo and go into the coconut business. . . ." He also told them: "The censorship is very strict . . . I feel fine. I've lost ten pounds. . . . I hope you girls practice running. If this keeps up for long I might be chasing you all over the office when I get back—I might be able to catch one of you. Be sure I'm paired on all important votes. [Washington state congressmen] Coffee and Jackson can do that."

Harry Brand wrote from Hollywood that Carole Landis, a studio love goddess, was knitting socks for Commander Magnuson. Mary reported to Brand that her boss was in the midst of South Pacific shooting. In a reminder of the mood of those times, there is a letter from Watson Barr, a Seattle attorney and college classmate: "You probably recall Takahashi from the university. He was picked up for aiding Japanese in securing supplies. It was a surprise. I've known him for years and thought surely he was an American at heart. It shows you never can trust these slant eyed rats."[27] Barr also told of going to the cockfights with Ernie Yoris.

Sentiments such as Barr's, a mix of racism and fear, were the norm in 1942, shared by Magnuson and an overwhelming majority of West Coast citizens. They underlay the massive removal of Japanese Americans from the West Coast to relocation camps—some would say "concentration" camps—on the other side of the Cascades, a shameful, patently unconstitutional episode in Northwest history conducted with the approval of its elected officials, with a single exception—Tacoma Mayor Harry P. Cain, a Republican conservative.

Magnuson had been on sea duty less than three months when the *Seattle Post-Intelligencer*, whose publisher, John Boettiger, was the president's son-in-law, editorialized: "Rep. Magnuson has proven one of the best go getters Washington ever sent to the capitol. But the Navy should bring him home to the First District. The Navy now should be able to spare him."

On July 1, Roosevelt ordered all congressmen in service to return to their congressional seats. Magnuson had, as he told his office, "been in the thick of it," fighting in the South Pacific. Now House Speaker Sam Rayburn was demanding the return of his House members. Roosevelt complied. Magnuson and Johnson got back in July, to the relief of Mary, Claire, and Maggie's First District constituency, but too late to file for reelection with the secretary of state in Olympia. No need to bother. Henry Broderick, the Republican real estate tycoon, made the trip and paid the $100 filing fee, a sum Magnuson later repaid. Maggie's popularity was greater than ever.[28]

CHAPTER 13

War, Politics, and McGoozle

P olitical ambition usually doesn't make any sense," Representative
Magnuson mused to his chief political operative in Seattle, Mac
MacGowan.[1] Approaching the flood tide of his career, Magnuson
was back in the Capitol from sea duty, quite proud of what he had done,
yet reluctant to talk much about it and determined not to use it for
political campaign fodder. Campaigns were coming, but for what?

In those years, 1942–44, the war seemed to grind on forever. In retrospect, its end was fixed in 1942, a year after the United States entered with
a total commitment to win. Even before the factories and shipyards began
their deluge of war machinery, long before the power of the Columbia
River was used to produce material for nuclear bombs at the secret arsenal
at Hanford, Washington, the Axis fate was sealed. A marginal U.S. force
of aging aircraft carriers and nearly obsolete aircraft stopped a Japanese
invasion of Midway Island in June 1942, destroyed the heart of its carrier
fleet, and sent the empire into decline.[2] Hitler's blitz through the Soviet
Union stalled in the streets and factories of Stalingrad on the Volga,
prelude to a three-year retreat to his bunker and suicide in Berlin. A
British attack at El Alamein about 60 miles east of Cairo sent General
Erwin Rommel's strike for the Mideast oil fields into reverse and defeat.
If we did not recognize the terminal significance of these Allied victories,
perhaps there were too many notices of death and "missing in action"
from the War Department to next of kin.

The mortal consequences of war reached Magnuson even after he
returned to the Naval Affairs Committee from the *Enterprise*. A folksy
letter dispatched to his dear friend "Jug"—Captain George R. Newgard
of Chehalis, Washington—came back unopened, its envelope stamped
"Killed in action, Guadalcanal."[3] Newgard's body lies alongside other
American infantrymen in graves on the South Pacific island, harvest of
the other critical American victory in 1942.

With a war record to punch up his proven skills and connections
in Washington, Magnuson attracted pressure and speculation about his
political future. Ed Stone, editor of the *Post-Intelligencer*, wrote that his
position in Seattle's First District was "impregnable." No doubt of it. The
larger question was whether to seek the governor's office in Olympia or a

Senate seat in Washington. These races were far down the road in 1944, but not far enough to obviate the pressure.

No sooner was he back from war when George Allen, an official of Sick's Brewery, owned by Emil Sick, wrote: "Emil and I consider you the only citizen of the state who can head the ticket and wrest the governor's office from the Republicans. . . . the state must be saved first [and] a routine candidate will lose to Langlie."[4]

"I'll think it over," replied Magnuson, who had other matters in mind, favors for Bart Spellman, his former coach, and Dave Beck, and a poignant request from Germaine Barry, a sometime flame. She wanted help in getting her brother Rod into officer candidate school. Barry told of visiting Mom on Bainbridge Island and noted, "She misses you." So, too, did Germaine.

"I'm sorry our meeting in San Francisco wasn't more pleasant, but I chose to remember only the pleasant memories of our association which are many," she wrote. "I've enjoyed the few hours we've spent together. Everything looms pleasant through the softening of time."[5] They apparently had met before Maggie shipped out to the South Pacific.

Magnuson replied that Barry's letter "made me feel better to know how you feel." All was forgiven for a weekend gone wrong. Rod Barry won admittance to officer candidate school.

Late that summer Magnuson and Lyndon Johnson made an inspection of bases in Alaska, returning with a report that charged a lack of cooperation between the Army and Navy allowed a Japanese aircraft carrier and its escorts to slip away, unharmed, from Dutch Harbor.[6] The Army, said these two members of the Naval Affairs Committee, failed to inform the Navy of its contact with the enemy vessels. The Army commander was subsequently relieved of duty.

Much of the congressman's time in 1942 was spent in work on the highway to Alaska and setting the stage for successful passage of repeal of the Chinese exclusion clause from immigration laws. For this he won warm praise from John McCormack, the House majority leader and a Thursday night poker table companion, and lifelong gratitude from Chinese Communist rulers-to-come, Mao Tse-tung and Chou En-lai. He spent vacation time at Virginia Beach with Carol Parker, who had come to Washington to fill a temporary staff vacancy.

Mary Ferrandini, on leave from the Washington office, had charge of the reelection campaign in Seattle, such as it was. Magnuson seemed almost unconcerned. Mary saw it as a de facto contest between Magnuson and Langlie, a test of strength between two possible opponents in 1944. Mary also had personal problems. By October her marriage to Ralph

Ferrandini was at an end, because, she told the Boss, he couldn't adjust to her more powerful position and felt insecure.[7]

If Magnuson was cool about reelection, Hugh DeLacy was nervous. Magnuson's opponent, Harold Stewart, was a Bainbridge Island businessman opposed to wartime strikes and the forty-hour workweek. Apart from Stewart, DeLacy needed Magnuson's help in other congressional campaigns. Three weeks before the election he wired: "The campaign is at a critical point. Imperative you come home."

"I'm busy repealing the vicious poll tax," Magnuson replied. "I'm coming home ten days before the election. So is Mon [Senator Walgren]."

Magnuson defeated Stewart by a two to one margin. Otherwise, DeLacy's premonition of trouble for Democrats panned out as feared. Two of these congressional incumbents lost to Republicans—Knute Hill and Martin Smith. So did the former senator and champion of public power, C. C. Dill. Dill blamed it all on Washington Water Power Company, and its virtual house organ, Spokane's *Spokesman-Review*. He told Maggie, "they spread the craziest rumors about me. Water Power put up all the money—they will never forgive me for the Grand Coulee Dam. It compelled them to lower their [power] rates."[8]

The election kicked off a renewed stream of career advice to Magnuson. Lois Ogilvie, state director of federal housing, told Maggie, "I hear nothing but good things about you—your future is in national politics."[9] She advised against a race for governor, "even though you could beat Langlie." Perhaps tilting his hand, Magnuson told Ogilvie, "I'm inclined to agree with you on the governor's race, but no decision has been made."

His mother died early in the spring of 1943, despite his effort to improve her health by moving the family to Bainbridge Island. Magnuson suffered the loss of his adoptive parent, a woman Carol Parker described as hard and tough. He told friends, "She got along splendidly for a couple of years. She enjoyed herself. She was 78 or 79 years old, but you know she lied about her age. She said she was 73 or 74. But she was the same old girl right up to the end. She was feeling well until the day she died. Thank God she didn't suffer. It was over in ten minutes."

He found comfort in Ruth Overton, Carol Parker, and a new romance, Elvira Wildman, who soon left New York to run a model agency in Chile. From the Crillon Hotel in Santiago she wrote Warren: "come to see me. Are you married or in love? Take my advice. Fall in love but don't marry. In Chile or New York I'm looking forward to seeing you real soon. Maybe we can get drunk together for old times sake."[10]

Magnuson never hid his love of women or strong drink. Neither was it much publicized until Arthur Langlie, a teetotaler who banned whiskey from the governor's mansion, and a praying Presbyterian, made it a campaign issue in 1956. Nevertheless, his after-hours pursuit of happiness was not a secret. Knowledge of it invited this note of advice from one M. N. Ryder of Raymond, Washington: "You are doing a great job down there [*sic*]. I am going to give you a tip as I have been marred [*sic*] 4 times . . . : just let them alone. You cannot find one like your good old mother. . they are all out to catch you. Just be a friend and No More and you will not have headaches. . . . they cannot be honest. They will try to borrow money off you and never pay it back."[11]

A less charitable view came from August J. Martin of Seattle, who told Magnuson that his spreading reputation caused people "to sour on democracy. Say goodbye to you political career. . . . you are not a states-man but a mere utensil of the blocks [*sic*] that decide public policy."[12]

"Warren enjoyed drinking," said Carol Parker. "He just enjoyed it. He wasn't trying to suppress anything. He liked bars, the atmosphere. He was very happy with his life, very proud of what he had done."

Apart from the pursuit of happiness, Magnuson appeared uncertain about what he would do with himself under the pressure to run for governor or senator. "Political ambition usually doesn't make any sense," he told MacGowan during a period of stress. He aimed to hold decisions in abeyance and stick to his job as a congressman.

As such, he had to handle the backlash of a Federal Security Agency report on Seattle's war-stimulated tenderloin which landed on local offi-cials with the impact of a Japanese firebomb. The report alleged: "gam-bling, prostitution and vice are running rampant in Seattle. Police are doing little about it. Certain groups are taking graft, several policemen are part owners of gambling or whore houses." It claimed that "the madam of the Dainty Rooms, 606 7th Ave. South, discussed freely with [undercover feds] the hour at which officers from the morals squad would be visiting their house," and went on to say, "It's apparent that the police, although aware of the damage to the war effort, are not willing to take any action towards removing this menace."[13]

Magnuson expressed his concern to the agency's Charles Taft "about federal officials taking sides in local issues." Taft said there were seventy brothels in Seattle, including the Lux Rooms, New Weller Hotel, and Dainty Rooms, dispensing a high rate of venereal disease to servicemen. He suggested "rest camps" for employees of these establishments, hook-ers servicing the servicemen, and noted, "Mayor Devin may be a grand chap, but the City Council may be paid off." Magnuson grumbled but the federals prevailed. Seattle's red-light district became a casualty of war, off-limits to soldiers and sailors, shut out of business.

The war effort raged beyond Seattle's tenderloin. Maggie got a progress report from one of his former shipmates on the *Enterprise*, Commander R. W. Ruble, promoted to executive officer on the *Hornet*. "We can be proud of our service on the 'Enterprise,'" wrote Ruble. "But the days of a shoestring operation are over—we've got more men and weapons. The real purpose of this letter, however, is that I want you to get Jane Russell into the WAVES. Send her and 1990 others down here. Do that and I'll manage your next campaign."[14] (Jane Russell was a leading sex goddess in 1943 Hollywood. WAVES was the Navy's female auxiliary.)

"Good to know you're getting a good deal of men and equipment," answered Magnuson. "As I look back we didn't have a hell of a lot, did we?" He duly noted that the House "turned down a bill the other day allowing WAVES to go overseas. Sorry."

Major Joe Roberts wrote his buddy Maggie on Christmas Day 1943, from the Italian front, accompanied as he wrote by background music from 105 howitzers: "War is hell, cold and wet. I think of that delightful day when you and I can laugh together across a table at Maison Blanc [a Seattle restaurant of that period]. . . . the Luftwaffe is coming, so back to that muddy, smelly, hell-hole of a slit trench."[15] Magnuson was well into the New Year when the letter arrived, another pivotal election year. Time for a decision.

Earlier, Tom Smith, the King County Democratic chairman, had implored him to run for governor and not merely lead a Democratic ticket. Smith wanted to run for Maggie's vacant congressional seat. He thought he deserved it: "I've worked too hard, given up too much and have too much at stake to be dealt out."[16] Magnuson said it would be hard to give up his seniority on Naval Affairs; much depended on the outlook of the war. Matters had not "crystallized."

More serious urgings came from Smith "Smitty" Troy, the state attorney general and a Maggie ally. Democrats needed Magnuson, the most popular one of them all, to lead the ticket as a candidate for governor and the party to 1944 election glory. "Someone simply has to do it and you're the guy," wrote Smitty from a Tennessee army camp. "If not we're all out on our ears."[17]

"I've tried to stay aloof from discussions, concentrating on my work," Maggie answered Smitty in midsummer. "I can assure you there's plenty of work. Republicans have offered little in the way of a constructive program. The best they can do is criticize President Roosevelt and he is still the strongest presidential candidate."

Roosevelt had a critical decision of his own: whether to seek a fourth term in the White House and to do so while in drastic physical decline, a fact observed by the political operators around the presidential court, including Democratic National Chairman Frank Walker and Ed Flynn. They were already plotting the replacement of Henry Wallace as Roosevelt's potential running mate. These urban pols regarded Vice President Wallace as a flake, unstable. They rightly feared Roosevelt would not survive a full term and did not want the erratic Wallace in the White House. They would, of course, succeed.

Magnuson, by contrast, was a practical visionary, a politician attuned to the possible, not the wish. A cynic might call it scheming when he touted to Smith Troy the possibility that Senator Walgren would make the race for governor against Langlie: "Rumbles indicate Walgren might be the one to do battle with Langlie. Mon might not be such a bad selection. He could run without resigning from his senate seat until sworn in as governor. If Mon is able to appoint his successor it would really be an ideal picture." In MacGowan's parlance, it would be a perfect McGoozle.

Smitty balked: "You have a far better chance of knocking off Langlie than Mon. . . . Langlie has to be liquidated above all things. Mon hasn't the poise and ability you possess. . . . you must be our next governor. You are our White Hope!"

Polls reported by Al Rosellini showed Magnuson far ahead in any contest for the Democratic nomination for governor. Despite the numbers, Magnuson replied to Smith Troy in late fall, "master minds of our party conclude we should let the matter rest in the status quo and discuss several candidates for governor." He surely had Walgren in mind as one of those other possibilities, perhaps the only other possible candidate. He noted that his speech to the Spokane Chamber of Commerce was panned by Ashley Holden, as having left a "poor impression."

Magnuson never named the "masterminds" who were diverting the heat laid on him to run for governor. Holden was political editor for the anti–public power *Spokesman-Review* and, much later, publisher of a smalltown newspaper found guilty of libeling state Representative John Goldmark, the pro–public power chairman of the House Ways and Means Committee.

The backroom speculation among these serious politicians figured Eric Johnson would be the Republican candidate for the Senate seat held by Homer Bone. A native of Washington, Johnson was the highly popular president of the U.S. Chamber of Commerce. Amid the talk, war still raged. Germany and Japan were on the defensive, but fighting with such determination that Magnuson would tell the *Post-Intelligencer* in the spring of 1943: "An invasion of the West Coast is, of course, likely. It would be fool-hardy, but face saving. The Japanese are desperate.

An air strike against Puget Sound is more likely, but we are adequately prepared."[18]

Magnuson got an odd request from Hugh DeLacy at the peak of this warfare. He wanted the congressman's help in getting veterans of the Abraham Lincoln brigade out of Army cook-tents and into combat.[19] It was a most peculiar discrimination, charged DeLacy. At the time of Pearl Harbor these veterans of the Spanish Civil War were the nation's only combat-seasoned line troops. Mainly from idealism and left ideology, they had fought with Republicans against a Fascist rebellion supplied by Adolf Hitler, the latter for reasons of his own. He wanted to prolong Spain's civil troubles for as long as possible to distract attention from his aggressive military buildup.[20] There were 500 brigade veterans in the U.S. military, another 300 in the merchant marine. Despite their experience, they were shunted out of combat units into service units; in effect, peeling potatoes instead of killing enemy troops.

Failure to make better use of these seasoned soldiers was a sign of the distrust with which military commanders held left-wing ideology. One stunning exception was Marine Colonel Evans Carlson, a field observer in the 1930s of Mao Tse-tung and his Eighth Route Army, Chinese Communists. Carlson instilled in his Marine commando battalion Maoist military tactics and the U.S. Constitution. Eventually, however, he became suspect for his sympathies with the "Red Chinese" military tactics—anti-Communists of the 1950s allowed no deviation. He is remembered today by survivors of "Carlson's raiders" with something close to adoration. His basic military concepts are part of the Marine Corps manual.[21]

Magnuson, sympathetic and occasionally outspoken about the need to normalize relations with "Red China," stayed "busy as a bird dog" between committee work in Washington and requests from buddies back home. Bruce Bartley, his Seattle law partner, wanted help getting material priority from the War Production Board to expand Seattle's Model Laundry, a business backed by Maggie's landlord, Bill Edris, and Teamster boss Dave Beck. "I know, Maggie, you won't be doing anything wrong to give it a hell of a boost," said Bartley. He also requested a "word to the Federal Communications Commission" on his efforts to purchase a 250-watt radio station in Bremerton. Political advice? Certainly: "if you want a Senate seat, it's a matter of now or never."[22]

It came to this—"crystallized" in Magnuson's vernacular—in the spring of 1944, when Senator Homer Bone confided that he would be named by Roosevelt to the U.S. Court of Appeals in San Francisco. Magnuson acted as if his ambition had already been determined. He would seek Bone's seat. On April 15, days before a public announcement of Magnuson's candidacy, Bone gave his blessings: "I am mighty glad you're going to run for the Senate." The pressure of a race for governor shifted to Walgren. It looked like the start of a beautiful McGoozle.[23]

At the end of May, Magnuson wrote Anna Roosevelt Boettiger at the White House that he had filed for the Senate. Senator Walgren had filed for governor. Maggie had a primary opponent, ex-Representative Martin Smith of Grays Harbor, and told Mrs. Boettiger: "Smith has been nasty, but I'm used to that in campaigns. He's giving Republicans ammunition to use against me in November." Anna, presumably with the knowledge of her father, the president, replied with warm approval of the news.[24] But that was a switch.

In the wartime absence of her husband, John Boettiger, Anna had taken over as de facto publisher of the *Post-Intelligencer*, and she was having terminal trouble with the boss of bosses, William Randolph Hearst. The "chief" had turned against President Roosevelt's New Deal and the *P.I.*'s liberal tone. Anna complained in a letter to her mother that Hearst, from his office near Columbus Circle in Manhattan, was dictating stories to be played in the newspaper. Some of these she questioned. Was the Office of Price Administration infected with Communists? she asked Mrs. Roosevelt. In January 1944, Anna looked with disfavor on Magnuson as a Senate candidate because he was too close to Hearst, who had just dispatched Charles Lindeman to Seattle, as "acting publisher." Anna described Lindeman as a man with a "terrific hatred of the New Deal," a personal enemy doing everything in his power to undermine her work. In fact he came to usurp Anna's job—which he did. Anna went back to Washington to serve her adoring father as the White House hostess, and by May had reversed her position on Magnuson. All was well with his Senate candidacy. It did not go well with John Boettiger, who lost his *Post-Intelligencer* job to Lindeman, took a $40,000 severance payment from Hearst, and, in October 1950, jumped to his death from the seventh floor of the Weylin Hotel in Manhattan. The note he left behind said, "I have reached the end of the road."[25]

Allied troops were approaching the Rhine, and Boeing was at work on its new Superfortress, the B-29, when Lieutenant Colonel Harry P. Cain, the former mayor of Tacoma, on military duty in Europe, took the Republican nomination for the Senate. Republican surrogates, including Maggie's close friend Mort Frayn, would carry the campaign for the absent candidate. Eric Johnson never showed up for the race. Fulton Lewis, Jr., the news commentator, called Cain, the lone politician opposed to internment camps for Japanese Americans, courageous and extraordinarily able. Oddly, he had also called Magnuson "one of the ablest men in

Congress." Bone told Maggie, "Cain knows as much about the problems in Washington as my poodle dog knows about differential calculus."

Magnuson easily defeated Smith in the primary. Cain loomed as more formidable. Indeed, Maggie's bosom pal Frayn, president of the University of Washington Alumni Association, declared shortly before the election that polls showed Cain a cinch winner.

Once again, it wasn't close. But it was not without edgy moments. The ever hostile *Spokesman-Review* attacked Magnuson as a "New Deal rubber stamp" and a "shirker" for coming home to Congress instead of staying in warfare with the *Enterprise*. Cecil Copeland, Seattle commander of the Veterans of Foreign Wars, responded with a statement saying Magnuson had been ordered back to the Congress by the secretary of the Navy after seeing action in raids on Wake, Gilbert, and Marshall Islands. Ohio Governor John Bricker, the GOP vice presidential nominee, campaigning in Seattle, called Maggie "unpatriotic" because he had said the Nazis were holding off on a peace deal in hopes of getting a better one from Republicans in the new administration. Magnuson personally screwed up by writing a letter of condolence to Guy Scoles, a constituent, on the death of his son in combat. He erred. The son was wounded, but alive, and Guy slashed Magnuson for causing him "unwarranted grief."[26] Nevertheless, Maggie won the race by over 50,000 votes. Hugh DeLacy, not Tom Smith, won Maggie's First District congressional seat, despite a "Communist" label laid on him by the *Argus*. Henry Jackson had a closer call against the once and future perennial, Payson Peterson. The big upset was Mon Walgren over Arthur Langlie for governor, a win that unleashed a new round of musical chairs speculation: who would Walgren name to his Senate seat, and would Langlie give Magnuson extra seniority by naming him as Bone's replacement before the end of 1944? His successor, Magnuson, assured, Bone resigned his seat shortly after the election.

For a while at the end of 1944 there were two Senate vacancies from Washington State. The *Seattle Star* reported a deal already cut that would have Walgren name former governor Clarence Martin as his senate replacement. "Not true," said Walgren. "There's no deal. I've been too busy running." A frightfully ailing Franklin Roosevelt defeated Tom Dewey for a fourth term with Senator Harry Truman as his running mate. Frank Walker, the new Democratic Party chairman, and Flynn had succeeded in their internal skirmish to remove Vice President Wallace from the ticket.

Magnuson reshuffled his local patronage, replacing one buddy, Saul Haas, as Collector of Customs, with another, Mac MacGowan. The bigger news, however, was a $1 billion order for Boeing B-29s; and the "faster than sound" German V-2 rockets assailing London. Langlie came under a newspaper barrage calling for the appointment of Magnuson to Bone's unfinished term.

"Name Magnuson Now," screamed a page-one *Star* headline November 16. "It would be the proper, economical and sporting thing to do before Jan. 1." Another newspaper editorial huffed that it would "be a blotch on an otherwise good job as governor" if Langlie did not give Magnuson the jump ahead in seniority.

Langlie obliged on December 13, naming Magnuson to Bone's unfinished term, moving him ahead of fifteen other senators elected in November. As the governor explained: "the decision was based entirely on the possibility that the people of the state might benefit from seniority privileges." Besides, he said, with no major legislative business pending, it would be an empty honor for any Republican replacement. The Langlie-Magnuson political rivalry, momentarily put aside, would not climax for another decade.

There's an odd footnote to the 1944 election and the subsequent scuffle over vacancies in the state's congressional delegation. Shortly after the election, Magnuson received a "private and highly confidential" letter from Representative John Coffee, a left Democrat from Tacoma, a graduate of the University of Washington and Yale, and a onetime secretary to Senator C. C. Dill. It was also poignant, revealing rival ambitions over the Senate that escaped publicity during the campaign—and thereafter.

Coffee reminded Magnuson that it had been his lifelong ambition to be a U.S. senator, specifically one replacing Homer T. Bone, his brother-in-law. "It has meant everything to me and I do believe I am ideally equipped for that post," he said. But he wanted to avoid a primary election showdown with Magnuson, "one that would have damaged all Democratic candidates." Thus, he skipped the primary. Then he went to the crux of his message: "I decided against the primary race with great reluctance when you assured me you'd try to persuade Walgren to appoint me to [his vacant] Senate seat. You assured me categorically you'd front for me on this point. I am counting on you Maggie. I am counting on you to keep your promise."[27]

Coffee's letter is painfully sincere, but too much time and politics has passed to know how much—if any—pressure Magnuson laid on Walgren to name the congressman to the Senate. Whatever the commitment, the call was Walgren's, and instead of Coffee he named his secretary, Hugh B. Mitchell, a Montanan educated at Dartmouth College and a former Everett newspaperman. Apart from his personal trust in Mitchell, Walgren was put off by the hint of a scandal in Coffee's office regarding army contracts at Fort Lewis.

John Coffee won reelection to his House seat and returned denouncing our "wretched appeasement of General Franco," an unregenerate left-liberal possibly frozen in the Popular Front.

Magnuson took his oath of office just before the Christmas holiday. He described the ceremony in a letter to his friend, Judge Homer Bone:

> My poker playing friend Scott Lucas [an Illinois Democrat, member of the Senate Naval Affairs Committee] took me down the aisle. The Vice President [Henry Wallace] gave me the oath of office. After it was over Wallace said he didn't know whether we were moving on to a poker game or merely trying to get into your late celestial body. It isn't much different except the seats are harder and the employees bow about four inches lower than in the House. Everybody talks at once. The roll call asked for "Mag-NEW-son" and he explained that he wanted to keep the Swedish influence in the body as long as Walgren had gone on. I was assigned your old office. . . . If you have any problems or cases of scotch, please write your senator.[28]

Bone replied to his "charming and able friend" that he had twisted a few arms in the state over Magnuson's early appointment. "I wanted you shoved up as many grades as possible and it would have been a stupid thing for the governor not to appoint you and aid the state."

A few days later Judge Bone sent another note to his successor: "Cain would have been a misfit in that position."[29] Perhaps he was thinking of the contrast with Senator Magnuson, for those times—if not now—a nearly perfect fit.

CHAPTER 14

Senator Magnuson

"Civics books tell you about the machinery [of government] but they never let you know that human beings were what made it run; they talk grandly of a government of laws, not of man, concealing from the idealistic and the young the too harsh fact it is men who make and administer the law and so, in the last analysis, it is the men who will determine whether laws will function. They made it all so unreal, somehow and it wasn't unreal at all."—Senator Lafe Smith of Iowa, sounding like Warren Magnuson, in Allen Drury's best-selling novel about Congress, *Advise and Consent*

Vice President Harry S. Truman had lunch with his friend Warren Magnuson, the freshman senator from Washington State, on April 12, 1945. It was the senator's fortieth birthday, his fifth month as a member of the upper chamber of Congress. Truman, the choice of Democratic bosses to replace Vice President Henry Wallace on the 1944 presidential ticket, was just as green in his new job. For both, as well as the rest of the world, it became a pivotal day in another watershed year.

After lunch they returned to the Senate chamber, Truman to preside and complain in a letter to his mother about a "windy" speech from a midwestern senator, Alexander Wiley of Wisconsin. At session's end, he repaired, probably with Magnuson, downstairs to Sam Rayburn's "board of education." The Speaker had bourbon on his table. Before he got to partake, Truman was called to come at once to the White House. There, about 5:30 P.M., he was informed of the death in Warm Springs, Georgia, of President Franklin Roosevelt.[1]

A few weeks earlier, the war still raging in Europe and plans for an invasion of Japan abuilding, Roosevelt had called Magnuson to the White House for a highball and a talk. The president, sick unto death, lay flat on his back on a sofa, asking Maggie for items of gossip off the Washington merry-go-round. Then he got to the business: "What is going on with Columbia River power development? What can we do from the White House?" Magnuson departed in amazement at Roosevelt's concern about Northwest power projects, shaken by the grim pallor of the most important individual in the world.[2] Then the president died.

Harry Truman, an unsuccessful farmer, failed haberdasher turned professional politician in Kansas City, was the president of the United States. The news sent Nazi propaganda minister Joseph Goebbels into a fit of exultation. Inaccurate as usual, he told Hitler this was a turning point in the war. Magnuson, who would never know his real father and scorned the man who gave him a name, took Roosevelt's death as a son feels the loss of a father. He was disconsolate, telling Sis a few days later, "I had a very sad birthday. It seems like misfortune dogs all of my birthdays—I'm almost afraid to have one."

Current historians are far kinder to Truman than his contemporary critics. He is now generally acknowledged to have been one of our best presidents. In April 1945, he was regarded lightly, if at all, by most observers—a tool of the corrupt Pendergast machine in Kansas City, a pipsqueak, utterly unprepared for leadership of the nation, much less the nontotalitarian world. Some of his supporters considered the new president a temporary White House aberration, pending election in 1948 of a substantial Republican, Governor Tom Dewey of New York or Senator Robert Taft of Ohio. It was a gross underestimation.

Magnuson wasn't fooled. Stunned by the death of his political idol and teacher, he waited two weeks before passing his judgment of Truman on to Harry Brand in Los Angeles:

> The trouble is that too many people compare Truman to Roosevelt. Fellows like that [FDR] come only once in a couple of centuries. Roosevelt was our greatest president. Any comparison of Truman with the average run of Presidents will find him more than holding his own. . . . I had lunch with him the next day [April 13] with a small group of senators. He was sure a scared guy with the terrific responsibilities he knew he had. That, confidentially, is the best indication I know that he will be a good president. He knows what a job he has to do and knowing it he will delegate authority and accept good advice. . . . I'm certain the Senate will have a lot more lead parts in the new show. His [Truman's] only contacts and immediate friends exist in that body.[3]

Smart, earthy, decisive, Truman liked the taste of bourbon and the reading of American history. He had virtually no indoctrination for his new job. The Axis powers, Germany and Japan, were yet to be vanquished. There was the Potsdam Conference with Churchill and Stalin to maintain the anti-Axis alliance—especially to secure Soviet support for the all-out assault on Japan—and the attempt to arrange peace for Europe while converting to a peacetime economy at home. In sum, he was to lead the nation into a new world order.

Adolf Hitler shot himself to death April 29 and the German army surrendered a few days later—one down, one enemy to go. On July 16, the day after his arrival in the Berlin suburb of Potsdam, Truman was told that American scientists had successfully exploded an atomic bomb in the desert near Los Alamos, New Mexico. It was, and remains, the ultimate weapon in the human arsenal. Nothing, after the defeat of the Axis which it hastened, has done so much to change world politics. In the few weeks after Roosevelt's death, Truman must have been briefed on the "Manhattan project" to build the bomb, a secret guarded tighter than Fort Knox. Asked by a Los Angeles pal early in the year about reports of a strange supersecret factory near Oak Ridge, Tennessee, Magnuson said he would look into it, but he figured that it was akin to the secret munitions plant built by the federal government on the semiarid desert near Hanford, Washington, and powered by electricity from Grand Coulee Dam.[4] Both plants were, of course, manufacturing atomic bombs.

Truman's decision to use the bomb came with characteristic dispatch and no second thoughts. A Boeing B-29 dropped an atomic bomb on Hiroshima, Japan, August 6, 1945, laying waste to a city of 550,000 and ending one era while ushering the world onto a new stage—this one marked initially by high hopes and nerve-racking uncertainty. Heirs of the atomic age have disparaged Truman for use of the bomb on Japanese civilians. The president's view: the bomb spared an invasion of Japan at an estimated price of 500,000 to one million U.S. casualties, while sparing Japanese citizens caught between warring armies. Although control of the bomb would be a dominant concern of Magnuson's for decades to come, he shared Truman's view of its use. And, lest it be forgotten, so did an overwhelming majority of Americans in that summer of 1945. With the bomb, the war was over. The long nightmare of material shortages, the War Department telegrams regretting the deaths of husbands, sons, and brothers, ended with the mushroom cloud over Hiroshima. The United States was at a new beginning, a superpower virtually unrivaled. Most Americans knew this. Doubts about the bombing of Hiroshima would have to wait for years to come.

The immediate question was how to control this new instrument of almost unbelievable destructive power. It was most clearly perceived by those who made the bomb, one of whom, the physicist Frederick Reines, wrote Magnuson three weeks after Hiroshima, "I'm compelled to tell you that this must be recognized as not just another weapon."[5] Reines also raised the question haunting control of the bomb: how to cooperate with the Soviet Union, now masters of the Eurasian continent from Central Europe to the Pacific.

"I don't propose that we did a bad thing in using it against Japan," Reines wrote the new member of the Senate Naval Affairs Committee.

"It saved allied lives and, yes, even Japanese lives. It was a blessing for humanity. Now we are in a grotesque situation. If we must fight the Soviets, now is the time to do it. In four years, they will have the bomb. But no reasonable man can subscribe to any form of this bloodletting. The only alternative is a heroic effort to get together [with the Soviets], remove distrust."

This was advice that Magnuson would live by for at least the next two years. Reines was dead accurate in his forecast of Soviet production of the bomb. His hope for allaying suspicion of the Soviets and international control of the bomb was not yet forlorn. U.S.–Soviet relations had yet to freeze into superpowers divided by what Winston Churchill would soon call the "iron curtain." Euphoria over winning the war carried optimism about the future, the promise of a better world and more material goods. Most Americans rallied behind the idea of a United Nations to bind the new world order.

Magnuson reflected this view in a letter written shortly before the nation's first peacetime Christmas in five years: "As an alternative to force, conscription and war, we should try harder to settle disputes in a peaceful fashion, make every effort for success of the UN. We must not fail the UN as we did with the League of Nations." However, he wasn't tossing caution to the wind. Replying to a constituent who demanded that we keep the bomb an American secret, Magnuson replied that since we would not for long hold a monopoly, "we should seriously consider making atomic knowledge available to the United Nations at the proper time and under proper conditions."[6]

At the end of this year, a watershed both for himself and the nation, Maggie summed up in a letter home: "[We have reached] a new stage of political and international affairs. Politically we are still in the horse and buggy days compared with developments in science and machines. With high speed airplanes and the atomic bomb the theory of national barricades no longer exists. We must evolve."

He also noted the disintegration of our other wartime ally, China under the Kuomintang regime of Chiang Kai-shek. It has left us, he said, with a Hobson's choice: "The U.S. wants to see a great Chinese democracy, but it cannot possibly be a democracy in terms of the American conception. If the Communists win in North China it will be a Communist country. If the Kuomintang wins [its civil war against the Reds] a semblance of a dictatorship will be set up."[7]

Never, however, did he subscribe to the myth that the Chinese Communists were pawns of the Kremlin, part of its insatiable urge for world

Emma Magnuson and the child she adopted in infancy and named Warren Grant Magnuson. Moorehead, Minnesota, 1907. WGM Papers, UW Libraries

Magnuson, the Western Union delivery boy. On his rounds he met the Stern family in Fargo, North Dakota. WGM Papers, UW Libraries

MAYOR DORE

VIC

SENATOR DILL

WARREN MAGNUSON

F.D.R.

En route to a landslide election, Franklin Roosevelt motors through downtown Seattle with Mayor John Dore and Sen. Clarence Dill on his left. Behind Dore is bandleader Vic Meyers. To Dill's left, in a polka-dot tie, is Warren Magnuson, up and coming. WGM Papers, UW Libraries

Carol Parker, Paramount Pictures starlet, warms up to Buster Crabbe, cowboy, erstwhile "Flash Gordon" of the Saturday serials. Paramount photo via Carol Parker Cahill

Croil Hunter and Magnuson, years after Hunter, with Maggie's critical help, got Northwest Airlines airborne. WGM Papers, UW Libraries

Portrait of young Warren Magnuson.
WGM Papers, UW Libraries

Hugh DeLacy, leader of the left faction of the Washington Commonwealth Federation, member of Congress—a good man, say those who knew him, despite his adherence to Moscow's party line. WGM Papers, UW Libraries

Rep. Marion Zioncheck, Sen. Lewis Schwellenbach, Prosecutor Magnuson, 1934.
WGM Papers, UW Libraries

Maggie and Mon Wallgren, pool-playing, fun-loving
pal of Harry Truman, a former senator and governor,
1949. WGM Papers, UW Libraries

Lt. Commander Magnuson, at ease during the "thick of action" in the South Pacific aboard the carrier *Enterprise*, March 1942. WGM Papers, UW Libraries

Home from the war by order of President Roosevelt, Maggie, the naval person, looks as fit for Hollywood as for Congress. WGM Papers, UW Libraries

Peter Bergson, key lobbyist for the creation of a "Free Palestine," and his two best advocates in the Senate, Magnuson and Guy Gillette of Iowa. WGM Papers, UW Libraries

Smiling senators Hugh B. Mitchell and Magnuson flank a somber Rep. Henry Jackson and Gen. Mark Clark, 1946. WGM Papers, UW Libraries

The Senate buddies, before they split: Magnuson and Sen. Joe McCarthy on his right. Others (left to right): Harry Cain, Washington; Irving Ives, New York; Henry Cabot Lodge, Massachusetts; William Jenner, Indiana. WGM Papers, UW Libraries

Ida White, songwriter and superfan of an uninterested Magnuson. WGM Papers, UW Libraries

Irv Hoff, cowboy turned college registrar, first in a succession of invaluable administrative aides to Senator Magnuson. WGM Papers, UW Libraries

Walter Winchell, inventor of the modern "three-dot" newspaper column and its make-or-break practitioner, and his friend of convenience, 1950. WGM Papers, UW Libraries

President Truman signs a much-desired Alaska railroad bill while Magnuson and Representative Jackson grin approval. WGM Papers, UW Libraries

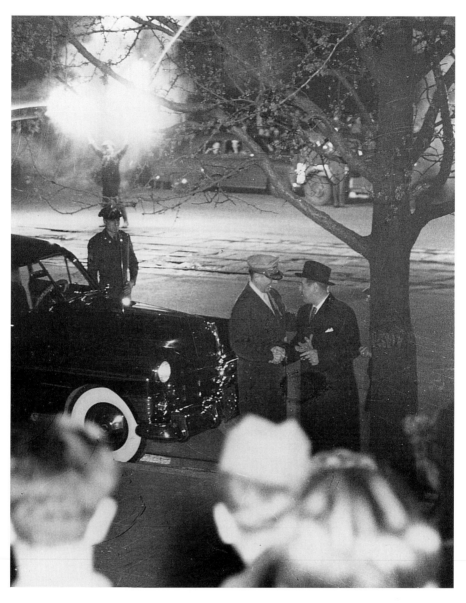

Gen. Douglas MacArthur just before he says so-long to Senator Magnuson
and to his U.S. Far East Command, 1951. President Truman's notice of dismissal
came during MacArthur's talk with Maggie. WGM Papers, UW Libraries

June Millarde (Toni Seven) and Bill Stern, two of Magnuson's
boon companions, together sometime in the 1950s. WGM
Papers, UW Libraries

Morrie Forgash and Jessie Robertson, Maggie's indispensable assistant.
Forgash grabbed the check for Magnuson's mammoth party at the
Harry Matthews–Rocky Marciano championship fight in New York.
WGM Papers, UW Libraries

Magnuson and Adm. Lewis Strauss eye a model of Maggie's maritime wish, a new nuclear-powered U.S. freighter. Maggie would later say of the haughty Strauss: "Only man I ever saw who could strut sitting in a chair." WGM Papers, UW Libraries

Democrat Magnuson and pal Bill Stern, "Mr. Republican," back home in Fargo. WGM Papers, UW Libraries

Two presidents and a prime mover: (left to right) John Kennedy, Magnuson, and University of Washington President Charles Odegaard, Seattle, 1962. WGM Papers, UW Libraries

Viewing an early model of Seattle's Space Needle: (left to right) Eldon Opheim, port director; Roy Peterson, collector of customs; Al Rochester, city councilman; unidentified; Magnuson; John M. Haydon, port commissioner. Courtesy William Peterson

Magnuson and his one-man "I&R" platoon, Howard MacGowan, 1959. WGM Papers, UW Libraries

Commerce Committee conference, 1961: (left to right) Edwin Johnson, Thurston Morton, Magnuson, and George Smathers. WGM Papers, UW Libraries

Gerald Grinstein, successor to Irv Hoff and architect of Magnuson's revival after the near loss in 1962. WGM Papers, UW Libraries

conquest. That myth would prevail among some sober U.S. policy makers, as well as professional anti-Communists, up to the end of the war
in Vietnam in the mid-1970s. It would provide emotional fuel for the
anti-Communist hysteria of the 1950s after the Kuomintang, corrupt
and ineffective, left the Chinese mainland to Mao Tse-tung and the
Communists. Senators Cain, Jenner, Knowland, and McCarthy would
accuse Truman's administration of having "lost China" as a result of
treason in its ranks. The resulting abuse of civil rights dwarfs the loss
of historical reality.

Magnuson kept his emphasis on U.S.–Soviet cooperation given the
new reality: the United States, had to share superpower status with the
Soviets. "There are great differences," he said, "between our two governments, but each of us loves our land, [and] none want to see it
destroyed in atomic warfare." He would even entertain the idea of a
mixed national defense force—Americans and Soviets soldiering side by
side—as "logical but probably politically unacceptable."[8] He was at this
time a proto-peacenik, perhaps a shade closer to the discarded Henry
Wallace in his international outlook than to his pal Harry Truman in the
White House.

Magnuson's optimism was not shared by all of his constituents. There
were acute postwar anxieties as war materials production slacked and
civilian production lagged; there were nagging racial fears, like those seen
lately in California's 1994 initiative against illegal immigrants. Several
constituents urged the senator to see that Japanese Americans shipped
out of the state to "relocation" camps in Utah and Idaho be forbidden to
return to their homes, and instead sent to Japan. Magnuson finessed
these racist entreaties by saying they should be allowed to return to
their homes only if they swore loyalty to the United States, a nearly
meaningless condition since only a handful had ever foresworn such
loyalty. They were Americans, many had served with valor in the U.S.
military.

E. J. Hansen of Tacoma urged Magnuson to ship American blacks to
Liberia "while we have the money and ships." Magnuson replied gently
to this old racist idea: "As citizens we have inalienable rights—protection
of life, liberty and property." The idea is totally unacceptable, said Magnuson, unless black Americans wish to go to Africa "as some European
Jews wish to go to Palestine."[9]

The Zionist dream of a Jewish homeland in Palestine, a British mandate, was already a half-century old. It became compelling to Americans
when newsreels and photographs complemented eyewitness accounts

of Hitler's systematic murder of millions of European Jews. Magnuson's Jewish friends and acquaintances lobbied steadily for his support for a homeland among the predominantly Moslem Arabs of Palestine. To void friction with the Arab population, the British aimed to stop Jewish immigration or hold it to a minimum. They had critical Mideast oil to protect. Almost as cool to the idea was Truman's State Department, soon to include Secretary George Marshall, and elements of the defense establishment, most notably James Forrestal. Anti-Semitism may have tainted the dispute. Nevertheless, there was genuine argument over the nation's strategic interests, a fear of the long-term consequences of an Arab-Jewish conflict. Undersecretary of State Loy Henderson warned that a partition of Palestine into Jewish and Arab parts would never be workable. Evidence remains that he was not entirely wrong.

But public pressure, spearheaded by Jewish backing of the Democratic Party, made support of a Jewish state irresistible. It brought its focus to Washington, D.C. Max Silver, a Seattle furrier close to Magnuson, queried the senator shortly after Roosevelt's death: "anxious to know if you had an appointment to speak with the President with regard to our problem in Palestine. . . . hundreds of thousands of Jews in Europe are desperate to go to Palestine and start life anew."[10]

"I did speak to the President with regard to Palestine," Magnuson answered Silver, a campaign supporter, on July 21, 1945. "We are certainly working like hell on it in the Senate," he reported, with "nothing less than four conferences in the last two weeks—a most interesting evening with David Ben Gurion. Palestine will be discussed at Potsdam." Magnuson left no record of this meeting, or for that matter any other White House meetings, apart from what he put in private letters. However Eben Ayers, an assistant press secretary to Truman, noted in his diary that Senators Magnuson, Guy Gillette, and Owen Brewster met with Truman again on the Israeli issue the week of September 14, 1945. Subsequently, a news outlet close to Gillette reported Truman had urged British Prime Minister Clement Attlee to allow the migration of 100,000 Jewish refugees to Palestine. It was a leak, and Truman was angry. Ayers quotes the president as saying "the whole meeting was confidential and nothing was to have been said publicly about it." When Gillette denied the leak, Truman said, "Who else could it have been?" Ayers wrote, "He indicated Gillette would never get to see him again."[11]

Maurice Rosenblatt and Rose Keane, guests at Magnuson's "circus party" with Ruth Overton, had come calling that night in 1945 to lobby the senator on behalf of the American League for a Free Palestine. The league favored an Israeli state, but one distinctly different from the kind proposed by Silver and the Zionists. The league wanted a secular democratic state as opposed to a Jewish democratic state. At that time the distinction was obscured by the overriding need to find refuge for Holocaust survivors. It's unlikely Magnuson would have regarded the difference as significant, improbable that he made such a distinction.

Rose Keane was the most important connection between the league and Magnuson. A Missouri-born Broadway actress married to Herman Shumlin, a leading theatrical producer, Keane is described by Rosenblatt as "red-haired, vivacious and shapely; a do-gooder, rather than a confirmed political lefty like the rest of her Broadway crowd." The crowd included Lillian Hellman, whose plays were produced by Shumlin; Hellman's lover, Dashiell Hammett, the hard as a rock mystery writer; and humorist Dorothy Parker. Rose most likely met Magnuson through the senator's off-Broadway connections in Manhattan after she began discreet, voluntary lobbying on behalf of the American League for a Free Palestine. It was Rose who recruited her friend Rosenblatt, the ex-GI and aspiring journalist, as a lobbyist in Washington for the league.

Ben Hecht, the journalist-playwright (*The Front Page*), screenwriter, and mainspring fund-raiser for the league, described its aim in a letter to Magnuson: "to rebuild Palestine within its historic [mandate] borders with the Arab population as equal partners in a Democratic state based on the four freedoms."[12] What Hecht did not say is that the league was also funding the Irgun, a semi-outlaw Jewish army which seemed intent on driving Palestinians from the mandated territories. But first things first, and as Rosenblatt observed, on behalf of Jewish Holocaust survivors Magnuson was urging Truman to recognize a state of Israel, never mind its ideology. It is impossible to measure from the record Magnuson's influence on Truman's historic decision. Judging from relations between the two men, one can speculate that it may have been critical.

Silver, prominent in the state as a businessman and as a Democrat, was disconsolate when he wrote to Magnuson in October: "I'm at a low ebb. The British don't seem to give a damn about the fate of distressed Jews in Europe. . . . [Drew] Pearson says Truman is against a Jewish homeland." More significant than Silver's despondency, however, was the absence of any correspondence to Magnuson from citizens of Arab heritage.

"The Arabs were not a factor in the debate over recognition of the state of Israel," says Rosenblatt, a key participant. "Our fight was with the State Department and the British." When it was done—when Truman decided to grant U.S. recognition to the new state in May 1948—the American League for a Free Palestine closed its Washington office, a five-story mansion at 2315 Massachusetts Avenue, making way for the Israeli embassy. To honor the occasion, there was a farewell party at the Waldorf Astoria in New York with Maggie as the featured speaker. The senator teased Rosenblatt for ordering a salami sandwich in the swank hotel dining room. His speech, said Rosenblatt, was brief and pointed: this was a beginning, not an ending. The drama of Israel had just begun.

"Maggie was not what you'd call a great orator, but he had a gift of saying the appropriate thing at the right time," said Rosenblatt. "He was, of course, correct." Subsequently, there was a warm exchange of letters between Rose Keane and Magnuson. "How nice to see you—you were so good!" wrote Rose. However, Rosenblatt says their relationship was strictly political. As such, it was quite important. Rabbi Franklin Cohn of San Francisco proposed that Magnuson become the first U.S. ambassador to Israel, a flattering suggestion that Maggie probably did not take seriously.

The bomb, the United Nations, and the Jewish state were certainly matters of concern to Magnuson, if one is to judge from his letters and speeches. Of more immediate urgency to the senator and his constituents was the reconversion of the state's economy. The Columbia River dams at Bonneville and Grand Coulee gave it the prime stuff of economic success: cheap power. The Seattle Chamber of Commerce provided an insightful transition plan. Outlined to Magnuson, it called for retaining as much as possible of the existing war industries, chief of which were Hanford and Boeing's military contracts. The chamber saw a better future in more highways and more irrigation of the dry but fertile Columbia River Basin. That meant more dams. Another part of the plan called for increased transpacific trade through the Seattle gateway.

No single person in the state's history would have as much to do with implementing this general economic strategy in the heavily federalized Pacific Northwest as Magnuson. The senator already had set Northwest Airlines' sights on a route to the Far East by way of Seattle. He was becoming as critical to the development of the Columbia dams and Columbia Basin irrigation as Henry Ford had been to the production of automobiles.

"The dams," said Irv Hoff, when asked what he considered Magnuson's greatest achievement as a legislator.[13] By 1954 there were eight federally subsidized dams on the Columbia River whose prime mover at the source of funds in Washington, D.C., had been Warren Magnuson. None of them, incidentally, bear his name. One would be named for Senator Charles McNary of Oregon, Magnuson's Republican counterpart in dam-boosting on behalf of public power and a skilled legislator (Senator Alben Barkley, Democrat from Kentucky, called him a legislative genius) who had a way with President Roosevelt. "Kilowatts means jobs—it's as simple as that," said Magnuson campaign materials of the early 1950s. Not so simple is the way dams transformed the Northwest economy, enriching it with the production of aluminum, microchips, wheat, apples, and potatoes; results beyond the wildest dreams of C. C. Dill, Homer Bone, or Rufus Woods, the early Columbia River visionaries.

Along with this zeal for dams and economic development, there was an orphan's insecurity. Maggie was doing well financially. He wanted to do better. Late in the winter of 1945 he borrowed $20,700 at four percent interest from Bill Stern's Dakota National Bank and used it to buy 900 shares of Northwest Airlines, which he had represented as an attorney. Years earlier he had told Stern, "You are quite right that the boys will be surprised to know that I am one of the heavy stockholders of NWA, so I won't be peddling apples like many other broken down politicians when I get thrown out of office."[14] Collateral for the loan was shares of Northwest that he already owned.

The stock purchase might be described as a gamble for Magnuson, the horse player and poker master. It led him to his first public criticism over a conflict between his public office and his private business. Having pushed the airline toward the Orient, he now pushed Washington for federal approval of its proposed route from Seattle to Japan. To this end he worked closely with Lawrence Arnold, chairman of the powerful Seattle-First National Bank, as well as Northwest's Croil Hunter. In October, Arnold wrote his duck-hunting companion Maggie, "I agree with you. The business interests of Seattle should pull together on this one [the NWA route via Seattle to Japan]." Arnold said that he had instructed all bank officers to "do everything to help Northwest Airlines without making it too obvious—Seattle-First has no other airlines business except NWA." This meant quietly applying pressure through their extracurricular activities in clubs, churches, and civic organizations. He added, perhaps nervously, "I haven't heard any criticism regarding your attitude on this situation."[15]

The *Post-Intelligencer*, however, had referred to Magnuson's unusual "personal position" in the Northwest Airlines affair. Drew Pearson would finger Maggie for having secured the Seattle-Tokyo air route for Northwest through his influence with President Truman. Magnuson was sensitive about this publicity despite the absence of Senate rules on conflict of interest, allowing as much to Lawrence Arnold. Whatever it meant for Magnuson's private gain, however, the route was critical to the development of Seattle as a Far Eastern gateway, a major step for the remote, rain-stricken Northwest corner toward becoming an economic rival to

San Francisco. It was a major strand in the developing trade bond between Japan and Washington State.

When the flurry of nonlethal criticism about his conflict faded, Maggie wrote banker Arnold, "regardless of what attitudes others take, no-one has been stronger for an Oriental route than I. I'd been doing a lot of quiet work on this even before the criticism started. As a matter of fact, I'm probably the only one who could get this done."

That last sentence was an uncharacteristic boast. A great part of his enormous skill in what sociologists call "human relations" was a native modesty. His working legislative maxim could have been "give credit, don't take it." Maggie knew how to give praise in order to get things done. Thus there is no legacy of a "Magnuson" dam on the Columbia. What counted was accomplishment. Never mind glory. Yet his stealth in working Washington—no footprints, no speeches—surely helped to cover his Northwest Airlines bet. There is irony in the naming of a dam for McNary, the Republican minority leader and Wendell Willkie's vice presidential running mate in 1940. No less than Maggie, he was a modest man, loved by his colleagues, who rarely heard him speak from the Senate floor.

Lawrence Arnold, architect and builder of the Northwest's largest bank, had boosted his business, as well as the Seattle economy—the two, more often than not, were in concert—by working with Magnuson. The air route affair done, he could laughingly complain to Croil Hunter that he was "peeved you didn't make me purchase several thousand shares of Northwest Airlines stock several years ago."

But the first transition priority was Boeing. Army orders for B-29s dropped from 122 per month in August 1945 to 22 per month. Lines formed at state unemployment offices. Boeing laid off 20,000 workers, half its labor force. Primed by defense jobs, Boeing being the most significant employer, the state's population had jumped from 1.7 million in 1940 to 2.2 million in 1945. Initially, there was skepticism about whether the economy could afford work for all the newcomers. "I tell you folks, the best thing you can do is to go back to Iowa," a speaker told a mass meeting of unemployed in Seattle.[16]

Even before this Boeing bust, Senator Hugh Mitchell had held hearings in San Francisco and Seattle on the problem of reconverting the aircraft industry. Now Magnuson went to work, as usual behind the scenes in Washington, seeking at least a partial restoration of the B-29 orders. He failed the immediate objective, but he would succeed in positioning Seattle and Boeing for increased military purchases from the newly created U.S. Air Force—a separate branch with its own power to draw on federal appropriations. Boeing's engineers soon had a vastly improved bomber, the jet-powered B-47, off the drawing boards and ready for production. Ironically, the B-47 created an even graver crisis for Boeing/Seattle, inadvertently congealing the company, the city, and the generals into what Richard Kirkendall, professor of history at the University of Washington, characterizes as the "metropolitan-military industrial complex."[17]

The Air Force, citing concern for the vulnerability of Seattle to long-range bombers, wanted the B-47. But they wanted it built in Wichita, Kansas. At the time, 1949, Boeing/Seattle was still too shaky to lose 15,000 jobs. Its new civilian craft, the Stratocruiser, wasn't making money. The B-47's successor, the eight-engine B-52, was not yet ready to fly. Further, Boeing/Seattle reasoned, if the Air Force aims to have the B-47 produced in Wichita, why won't they demand the same of the B-52? The Seattle Chamber of Commerce, joined by those in Tacoma and Spokane (military contracts were a state issue, not merely local), mobilized behind Boeing. Magnuson was point man. The city and the state might suffer the loss of B-47 production, but not the greater loss of the B-52.[18]

Magnuson's files are several inches thick with communications from civic leaders urging action for Boeing/Seattle, strange as this may seem to a later generation given to scorn federal largesse. Out front, Maggie persuaded Air Force Secretary Stuart Symington to meet with leaders in Seattle to discuss the economic impact of his decision to move production to Kansas.[19] But according to Hugh Mitchell, the critical move was made behind the scenes without fanfare or press releases.

Mitchell, a warm, thoughtful progressive with a gentle manner and an easy sense of humor, had returned to Congress in 1948 after losing his Senate seat to Harry P. Cain in 1946. Senator Cain, incidentally, had no part in the Washington push to save Boeing.

"We got called down there to the Pentagon, Scoop [Representative Henry Jackson], Maggie and myself to discuss the situation," Mitchell recalled. "Boeing was vital to all of us. They told us the bad news. Scoop and I did what we could which wasn't enough. What saved the situation was Maggie's influence with Harry Truman. He went to the White House and saved the B-52 contract for Seattle. Otherwise it was lost."

Mitchell says that years later he asked Boeing officials if they had knowledge of Magnuson's intervention with Truman on the B-52 contract. "They had no knowledge of it," said Mitchell. "Maggie never blew his horn. What he did probably saved the company in Seattle."[20]

Irv Hoff, Magnuson's administrative aide, can't remember what Magnuson said to the president regarding the B-52. "He had a way of doing things on his own," Hoff recalled. "He'd say, 'Well, let's think about that.' A week later he'd say, 'I ran into Truman. The problem is all solved.' He had his way of addressing people at the right time, in the right way. I'd always push. He'd say don't do things so fast. I'd get peeved. A week later he'd do it—problem solved."

"The senator from Boeing" came to be the derisive label applied to Henry Jackson, but it more aptly fits Magnuson, who pressed General Hap Arnold to purchase B-17s, fought against B-29 cuts, and finally, through Truman, got Boeing to keep B-52 production in Seattle while it developed the line of commercial jetliners that would dominate the world market for nearly half of the twentieth century.

Nevertheless, as far as Magnuson was concerned, Boeing/Seattle's needs in those early postwar years were not consonant with the growing clamor over a potential military threat from the Soviet Union. He deplored the war talk and defended U.S. aid to Britain and France, the two allies exhausted by war. Andrew Babcock of Carnation, Washington, sent a letter to Maggie typical of this prelude to the cold war: "The U.S. and Britain are giving in to the Soviets. If we tell Russia where to get off, she'll get off her high horse. If not, we've got to fight. Let's do it while we can beat them."[21] Magnuson's response to such correspondence was also typical: "I'm concerned about war talk. It must stop or eventually such rumors will begin to represent public opinion and war would be inevitable. . . . we've got to deal with the Russians."

From this point, early in 1946, Magnuson privately divided his colleagues, and probably others, between those he judged to feel that a war with the Soviets was inevitable and those, like himself, who felt it could and must be avoided.

Even after Winston Churchill's cold war curtain-raiser in Fulton, Missouri, March 5, 1946, Magnuson held to the idea of cooperation rather than confrontation with the Soviets. In his address at Westminster College, Churchill, the once and future British prime minister (he had been dumped by the Labour Party in 1945), called for a British-American alliance to hold the West against an "indefinite expansion of [Soviet] power and doctrine." Europe was now divided from the Baltic to the Adriatic Sea by an "iron curtain," said Churchill. President Truman, at his side on the platform, apparently agreed. Magnuson did not.

"I'm a great personal admirer of Churchill, but I can't agree with his proposal for an Anglo-American military alliance," he wrote three months later. "International disputes should be ironed out through the United Nations. . . . I'm against appeasement, but we've got to understand the vast differences between our governments." Again, he hammered against war talk: "Talk that we may be on our way to World War III must stop. Governments reflect the people and if they [people] want war, they'll find it. We must talk peace and work for it—this can't be accomplished through fear, suspicion and war talk."[22]

Maggie had met "Winnie" Churchill at the White House, where they joshed about their respective feminine nicknames. Churchill advised the senator that "Maggie," like "Winnie," was a campaign asset. Privately, Magnuson wasn't enthusiastic about "Maggie." Friends and lovers always addressed him as Warren.

For reasons that will likely be forever debated, the national mood was drifting away from Magnuson's international sentiments. Confrontation with the Soviets was overtaking the idea of cooperation. History was changing course, a fact most vividly reflected in the election of 1946. Detractors, such as J. C. Anderson of Seattle—"a former supporter [who now regarded Magnuson as] a cheap politician and grafter at a time when we need statesmen"—told the senator that he was lucky not to have had to stand for reelection in 1946.[23]

In fact, relief at not having to run for reelection every two years, Maggie told his old pal Evert Arnold, was about the only difference he felt in being a senator. "Otherwise, it's about the same old story. I'm busier than the devil. I still have my hair, but I'm getting a senatorial stomach [pot belly]." He didn't have to tell Arnold that it wasn't all work.

His standard route had expanded from Seattle, Los Angeles, and Washington to Manhattan, where he would lunch with a new pal, Walter Winchell, and meet with Madame Chiang Kai-shek, Mr. and Mrs. Norman Winston, and at least once with Gloria Swanson, the fabled film star and friend of Joseph P. Kennedy. The orphaned boy from the Red River Valley had developed a taste for conspicuous consumption—custommade shirts from Budd, 590 Fifth Avenue, at $10.50 each. Winchell, chairman of the Damon Runyon cancer fund, and Mrs. Frank "Chris" Delany pressed the senator for federal research money, while hosting luncheons at "21" and the Stork Club.[24]

Early that summer, Magnuson, President Truman, and his host, Governor Mon Walgren, forever to be called Truman's "crony," broke from state affairs to go fishing on Puget Sound somewhere between Olympia and Point No Point on the official state boat. Magnuson later confided that he feared adverse publicity if they returned without a catch, "so we did procure two or three good salmon—like women on their ages, I'll never admit whether I caught them myself, or whether I helped someone else pull them in."[25] On their return to Olympia, Truman was photographed, grinning ear to ear, displaying a fish as though it was his own catch. It wasn't. Skunked after several hours on the Sound, Truman decided to take a nap. While the president slept, Magnuson spotted a nearby boat, manned by sons of Scandinavia fishing out of their Seattle enclave, Ballard. They had just hauled in a large salmon. Maggie moved the state boat alongside, and asked to buy the catch for the benefit of Governor Walgren and President Harry Truman, his boatmates. The fisherman complied and Truman got his picture in the papers with a twenty-pound salmon.

A few years later at a political rally in Ballard, Magnuson was accosted by the same son of Norway, who alleged that the senator almost busted up his marriage. How on earth could he have done such? "Vell, I toll yew," replied the fisherman, who explained that he had been sharply rebuked by his wife when he came home, sans fish, but with a whopper of a tale: He had sold his catch to the governor of Washington, the president of the United States, and Senator Magnuson. Hearing such a tale, she accused him of spending an afternoon at a Leary Street tavern, and, worse, lying.[26]

Carol Parker remained Magnuson's closest female companion. But there were other friends. Chris Delany invited Magnuson and Ruth Overton to New York for fall parties. A month later she wrote Maggie, "I'm terribly worried about our darling Ruth. She has been through a bad time." The trouble could have been love. Mrs. Eve Brooks of Vancouver, arranging a meeting with Maggie, wondered, "Are you married? Rumor has it that you are." Magnuson wired back, "Rumors entirely erroneous. Love."[27]

Betty Hutton, Hollywood's "blonde bombshell," wrote Maggie in the spring of 1945—the peak of her reign as queen of Paramount musicals—for advice on how to secure federal funds to provide a suit of clothes for each man leaving military service. She noted this was customary for convicts leaving prison. Accordingly, servicemen should get equal treatment. Could she discuss this issue with the senator personally in Manhattan June 15? Magnuson promptly said "yes" to such a discussion, although he forewarned that he wasn't exactly certain he could help promote the suit of clothes project.

They did meet at the Waldorf Astoria the weekend of June 15 and perhaps again on the weekend of July 21. He had spent an earlier evening on the latter weekend dining with Madame Chiang Kai-shek.

"I was pleasantly surprised at the Hutton gal," Maggie wrote Al Cohn in Hollywood. "You know how you hear things. From what I'd heard my impression was that she was a jumping jack. On the contrary, very pleasant, intelligent and damned attractive."

Cohn, who probably engineered the liaison, noted that like Carol Parker, La Hutton was on her way to Europe to entertain troops. "Maybe she'll meet Carol and they can trade notes."[28]

Nothing came of Hutton's proposal of civilian suits for ex-soldiers.

CHAPTER 15

The "Pol's Pol," the Playboy's Playboy

The 1946 "off-year" elections shook the nation's Congress and statehouses like nothing since 1932. With memories of capitalism's collapse fading, it was Republicans in, Democrats out, an abrupt rebuke to fourteen years of New Deal–Fair Deal recovery. Senator Magnuson and President Truman survived, but they weren't on the ballot. Representative Henry "Scoop" Jackson barely withstood the challenge of Payson Peterson, a perennial candidate. Senator Hugh B. Mitchell did not, losing to the erratic Republican Harry P. Cain.

Scoop and Maggie were the only Democrats remaining in Washington's congressional delegation. Suddenly the 1950 election looked dangerous, if not to Magnuson, then to his Seattle braintrust, Bill Edris, Mac MacGowan, and Bill Lindberg. The result was an upgrading of Maggie's staff. Henry Owen, the chief business officer of KING radio and TV, recruited Irv Hoff, the University of Washington registrar of students, to become Magnuson's chief aide. Magnuson hired Jessie Robertson, a clerk on the staff of the state legislature in Olympia, as his secretary. They were the "second generation" of a succession of superb staff assistants working for Magnuson and the committees that he chaired—staffers generally rated by their peers as the best on Capitol Hill. Jessie and Irv were smart, savvy, and loyal, in the last analysis probably indispensable to Magnuson's political career, given his high-flying lifestyle off the Capitol campus. Hoff remained as Magnuson's "deputy senator" for fifteen years, never returning to the university. It was a remarkable career change for the astute Hoff, who grew up in McCall, Idaho, and worked as a cowboy and cattle rancher in Oregon and Idaho until 1934, when he sold his stock and went to college. As a graduate student and assistant registrar at the University of Washington, he reorganized the school's enrollment system, then served as registrar for five years until hired by Magnuson.

"Hoff was intelligent, competent and his word was good," said Norm Schut, the labor leader in Washington state and onetime aide to Congressman Thor Tollefson. Jessie answered the letters, Irv handled the facts, and Maggie worked the politics—a superb legislative combination.[1]

Blame for the political upheaval of November 1946 ranged from the unpopularity of Harry Truman to the scarcity of meat in grocery stores.

In fact, the country was making the adjustment from war to peace, from primitive capitalism to two-fisted labor agitation. Strikes were frequent as workers tried to make up for wages sacrificed during the war. And they were frequently violent. There was conflict within the labor movement between the conservative American Federation of Labor (AFL) and the militant, Communist-tainted Congress of Industrial Organizations (CIO). Overriding was a general feeling that labor had grown too big for its Levis and that labor was to Democrats what Wall Street was to Republicans. Redress was needed.

"It's a good thing you weren't running," Charles Clise, a Seattle real estate magnate wrote Magnuson after the election. "There's too much government control. We've drifted into a government by fiat—an example is the Columbia River Valley Authority [CVA]."[2]

"No question," Magnuson answered. "The election reflected the reaction of voters to bureaucratic administration and the economic upheaval after five years of total war." As a footnote, he added, "CVA won't pass."

Even as a footnote to the development of the Northwest, the CVA is significant as an expression of the region's populist philosophy. The central authority would have controlled irrigation, land-clearing, flood control, reforestation, and electric energy production. Banks, private power companies, and newspapers saw the CVA as a threat to private interests. C. J. Zintheo, an engineer with the Natural Resources Development Agency in Seattle, saw it as a way to equalize the bounty of the great Columbia. He noted the opposition in a letter to Magnuson, then added, "It is much more important to have a great many of our people in moderate circumstances with regular incomes. . . . than for a large number of people working for a mere existence for large corporations to accumulate large fortunes for a few, who do not put money in general circulation in the community where it is made but support another class of people in idleness."

For most Democrats, the election of 1946 looked like Thermidor, the radical reaction to the French Revolution. But not to Magnuson. Having boosted his staff with Jessie and Irv, he left his bright-lights, Budd shirts lifestyle unchanged. Nor did the GOP election sweep affect the clarity of his vision. He predicted the Eightieth Congress would "do nothing," much as Harry Truman's winning 1948 campaign rhetoric would charge. In fact, "do nothing" is not quite fair as a pejorative for the Republican Eightieth Congress, given its approval of the landmark Taft-Hartley labor act and the Marshall Plan for aid to war-ravaged Western Europe.

Magnuson adjusted easily to the new Washington representatives, one of these being Thor Tollefson, who defeated John Coffee, a left Democrat tied to the CIO, for a seat from Tacoma. Coffee suffered from exposure of a contract for Fort Lewis awarded to one of his prime campaign contributors. He would also be fingered by Magnuson's friends in Los Angeles as having whispered rumors about the senator's "crooked" side dealings with Joe Gottstein, Dave Beck, and Bill Edris. Magnuson apparently made no response to the rumors, but he did extend his help to Tollefson, who had backing from the state AFL and had hired as his legislative aide Norm Schut, a young AFL union leader. Decades later Schut recalled Magnuson's welcome to the new congressman.

"Maggie called first, wanting to know if he could do anything for Thor," said Schut, later prominent as the leader of the state employees' union in Olympia. "He was most helpful getting Thor a seat on Merchant Marine and Fisheries Committee, which handled vital interests of Puget Sound. That was for the good of the state. Republicans controlled the House, but, what impressed me, Magnuson had pull all over the place—on both sides of the aisle. He was very quiet, nonpartisan, doing everything behind the scenes. He had great influence with President Truman, but he had influence everywhere. He was a long-term player, a team player. He handled himself in order to be able to work with everyone—a pol's pol."

Apparently Maggie was just as cooperative with the other freshmen Republicans, although a bit different with Harry Cain. Magnuson seemed puzzled about the man he had defeated in 1944, who would become one of Joe McCarthy's second-string Red-baiters, then wind up in the 1970s as a civil libertarian supporting Senator Henry Jackson for president.

"Confidentially," Magnuson wrote Henry Broderick shortly after Congress began its eightieth session, "I don't know how it is going to work out with our friend from Tacoma [Cain]. I have been deliberately more than cordial. Of course, it takes a little time to get adjusted here to the fact that Democrats and Republicans don't hob-nob together on a friendly basis. But the best interests of the state require a great deal of cooperation of all representatives, regardless of party. You may be sure that I'm going out of my way toward that end."

He stuck to his word on this collegial approach even as he gave special attention to the other delegation Democrat, Henry Jackson. At the end of the Eightieth Congress he wrote to each of the Republican members (Homer Jones, Russell Mack, Walt Horan, Tollefson, and Cain), commending them for rising above party obligations in order to "discharge our common obligation to the people." He noted that "the interests of our state and region were placed above partisan politics in many instances."[3]

There was no reply from Harry Cain. Others responded cordially. Thor Tollefson and Homer Jones expressed gratitude to the delegation's senior member for his "personal kindness" and the cooperation of his office—much credit due to Irv Hoff, the new administrative assistant.

As Hoff described his working relationship inside the Senate office, his job was to supply the facts, then "when the timing was right" Magnuson moved to push the legislation. How did he know the proper timing? "The Boss would say to me, 'Don't get nervous. I can just feel it when the time is right,'" said Hoff. "I've never seen anyone else with such instincts, so good at making deals. And those instincts were on the side of the underdog. He was always on the side of the underdog."[4]

The weekly White House poker game continued to flourish under Truman as it had under Roosevelt, although the venue was revised. "Truman is fixing up a place in the [White House] basement so we can go down there since he can't go out without a lot of secret servicemen," Magnuson wrote another Truman poker pal, Governor Mon Walgren. "[Senator Scott] Lucas and I told Harry as long as he is getting $75,000 a year [the presidential salary] he shouldn't play so tight. . . . I haven't been doing so well." Later he wrote Walgren: "Lucas and I spent a very pleasant weekend with Truman on the [Presidential] Yacht. I need not tell you what we did for 48 hours other than eat. Lucas and I didn't do so well."[5] Despite the luck of the cards that weekend, many years later Magnuson would characterize Truman as "a great president but a lousy poker player—he didn't know when to quit."

Privy to the president's poker table, magnanimous to Republicans, seemingly irreplaceable to the state's economic powers, Magnuson would appear to have peaked as a legislative artist. This may explain the measure of the man taken by the *Yakima Republic*. The newspaper, a major voice of central Washington conservatism, was also a major beneficiary of Columbia River Basin irrigation projects watering the apple and cherry orchards, greening the desert with wheat and potatoes.

"Even Republicans," the paper editorialized, "return from Washington saying the man has influence." He is "everybody's friend" and "he looks like Van Johnson [a movie idol] about to kiss Jennifer Jones [a movie goddess]. . . . Oh, he can pretend he's just a young fellow groping through the wilderness of the Atomic Age . . . but Magnuson is a sharp and calculating politician [who has] been at this game for many more years than his appearance would suggest, a very smooth character to be sure, a trader, a dealer who has missed few bets. He's not a bad senator, except that he adds a vote and a voice to a party that holds some of the prize crackpots of all time."[6]

Not all of the crackpots in this Eightieth Congress were Democrats, as that otherwise excellent description of Magnuson implied. Republicans had a fair share, all of them determined to curb labor through the measure proposed by Senator Robert Taft of Ohio and Representative Fred Hartley of New Jersey, and to thwart the real or perceived threat of communism, whether from the Soviet Union or the Columbia Valley Authority. Magnuson, the legislative ally to President Truman, needed all of his highly touted skills in these legislative fights.

The Taft-Hartley labor law and the Marshall Plan are enduring monuments to the Eightieth Congress, the former our basic labor-management law for nearly half a century, the latter possibly saving Western Europe from Communist control.[7] By contrast, the bitterly debated CVA proposal is hardly remembered, despite its enormous impact on the politics of the Northwest, particularly Washington State.

The United States had already spent $3 billion for foreign war relief by the spring of 1947, an expense duly noted by Magnuson's constituents and fiercely defended by the senator. Now Truman wanted $17 billion for the European Recovery Program, and he wanted it named for Secretary of State George C. Marshall, an advocate, not its prime mover.[8] Thus the Marshall Plan. Magnuson never seems to have questioned its need, and it is safe to assume that he helped sway Republican as well as Democratic votes toward its adoption. Senator Arthur Vandenberg, the critical Republican vote, initially balked, saying it would bankrupt the nation.

"It's an odd thing that Congress can take out of the pockets of my wife and myself $400 to give to those people against our wishes and with no opportunity to vote," G. P. Fishburne, a constituent, complained to Maggie. Magnuson reaffirmed his support: "The Marshall plan will stabilize a very shaky international situation. It is much cheaper than the collapse of the countries of Western Europe." That notion prevailed. Eventually Senator Vandenberg became persuaded to Truman's view that if Europe "went down the drain" so would the U.S. economy. The Marshall Plan won congressional approval.

Taft-Hartley was bitter and more divisive, but Republicans had the votes to "curb the power of big labor." The emotional furor over this measure obscured its legal complexity. Oversimplified (only a labor lawyer would do justice to a full description), the act outlawed closed (union only) shops, held unions liable for breach of contract, required them to make financial reports, and held their leadership to an oath that they were not Communist Party members. Joe Drumheller, Maggie's chief political agent in eastern Washington, warned the senator he should "keep away from Taft-Hartley." Instead, in early summer 1947, Magnuson addressed a prolabor crowd of 35,000 in New York's Madison Square Garden. "The crowd," Maggie wrote Al Cohn, "was so large it overflowed into the street. . . . people are really up in arms about this! Taft-Hartley swings the pendulum too far the other way. It's not workable and can never be enforced."[9]

Truman wavered over a veto. His labor secretary, Lewis Schwellenbach, the former senator from Washington State, opposed the veto. Clark Clifford, Truman's adviser from St. Louis, insisted that a veto would reunite labor and bring it back into the Democratic fold after the 1946 defections. Politics aside, the president, like Magnuson, regarded it as a bad bill. He issued a veto message, an act of conscience that would indeed provide a political reward in the 1948 election. Thor Tollefson, mindful of his AFL support, voted on the losing side to sustain the veto. So, of course, did Magnuson.

"I voted against the bill because I feared it would cause more strife than it would cure," Magnuson told J. W. Clise, a conservative critic who told him the nation needed more than Taft-Hartley: abolition of the forty-hour workweek and an end to featherbedding, "which can only weaken us in the international struggle we are now engaged in."[10]

These critical issues of peace and labor did not distract Magnuson from his own enduring legislative concern, federal funding for health research and hospitals. "He was a nut about it," recalls Hoff. Defending health appropriations, Magnuson said "a nation is no stronger, no more progressive than its people. I support health legislation with enthusiasm. It helps bring the well-being of the nation to a higher standard." A cynic would suggest that it also brought him closer to the lords and ladies of Broadway, Walter Winchell, chairman of the Damon Runyon cancer fund, and Mrs. Mary Lasker and Mrs. Chris Delany, the socialite-philanthropic boosters of cancer research. In fact, his legislative attachment to health issues began in 1937 when he was discovering Hollywood, not New York, and continued until 1980, the end of his time in the Senate. By the mid-1970s Maggie had been prime mover of legislation creating the National Institutes of Health, largest medical research enterprise in the world. He had fed millions of dollars into Veterans Administration health services, community health centers (Odessa Brown in Seattle's Central Area, an example), hospital construction, and medical education. A major beneficiary of the latter, the University of Washington Medical School, could have been called "the college that Maggie built." Instead, they merely named it for the senator. Maggie said he was honored.[11]

That public recognition was unusual. Apart from his modesty, Magnuson's way of doing legislative business made such recognition difficult. Until the voting climax, he operated off the Senate floor, out of sight in the corridors and workrooms of the Congress—"kitchenwork" is what Magnuson called it. Joe Miller, a sometime Magnuson campaign aide, and a veteran Washington lobbyist on behalf of labor and small timber mills, recalls a request from Mary Lasker for Veterans Administration research funds. Miller took the request to Magnuson, who said "fine." He would amend the Veteran's appropriation, adding research monies, but only with agreement from his Republican counterpart, Senator Everett Dirksen. Miller, only mildly daunted by the overwhelming personality of the basso-profundo orator from Illinois, went down the corridor of the Senate Office Building to Dirksen's quarters.

Agreement was quick and easy. "Dirksen said simply, 'If it's good with Maggie, it's okay with me,'" Miller recalled. "And we got it. Mary was very happy, I was proud of my role. Maggie had . . . Maggie had gravitas."[12] Under Magnuson's aegis as chairman of the Appropriations Subcommittee on Labor, Health, Education and Welfare, the Veterans Administration medical research budget rose from zero to $50 million between 1956 and 1966.

The health "nut" was never so enthusiastic about Hugh Mitchell's—and public power's—dream of a Columbia Valley Authority, modeled after the enormously successful Tennessee Valley Authority which had replaced the coal-oil lamps of southeastern American farmhouses with electric lights. The CVA would have consolidated twenty separate federal agencies, including the Corps of Engineers, Bureau of Reclamation, and Interior Department, under one administrative authority, a federally appointed commission.

CVA died with Thermidor and the defeat of Mitchell in 1946. But to the abject astonishment of pollsters, political columnists, editorial writers, and Republicans, Thermidor was short-lived. It lasted only two years. The conventional wisdom prior to the 1948 presidential election was overwhelming: Tom Dewey would be the next president, Republicans would continue to have majorities in both houses of Congress. The day before the election a page-one *Post-Intelligencer* news story reported "a Dewey victory for the nation's highest office is generally conceded everywhere." Inside, a smaller item reported, "Dewey will retain James Forrestal as Secretary of Defense." The newspaper's lead editorial that Monday told voters the election was the "last chance to evict the curious and corroding coalition of Marxists, labor bosses and professional politicians

[of] the Truman administration which has failed abysmally in foreign affairs."[13]

Preelection prognostications flopped like beer at a temperance picnic. *Newsweek* polled fifty national political writers shortly before the election. All fifty predicted Dewey would win the White House. However, they did not comport with political intelligence coming back to Magnuson, nor did they influence Harry Truman, who whistle-stopped across the country attacking the "do nothing Eightieth Congress" and drawing big, enthusiastic crowds to the back of his railroad club car, the "Magellan." Magnuson traveled to Spokane with Carol Parker to join Truman on the train for the trip across the state to Seattle. Later he described the president as "in one of his [emotional] upswings—looking fine and in good spirits." Carol drove back across the state with Mac MacGowan, who suffered from poor depth perception. He was blind in one eye, the result of an industrial accident in his youth. "I was a little scared," remembered Parker.

But not Truman. Even then, midsummer, Truman was pretty sure that he would win reelection. Nor was he daunted when Clark Clifford showed him the *Newsweek* poll of writers. "I know every one of these 50 fellows," said Truman. "There isn't one of them has sense enough to pound sand in a rat hole."[14]

"A political miracle," declared the *Post-Intelligencer* two days after the election when figures showed Truman elected president and Democratic majorities in the House and Senate. Actually, the election results had more to do with administration price controls, and the reunification of labor behind the Democrats, than with the supernatural. Magnuson seemed no more surprised than Truman with the election. He wired his buddy Lyndon Johnson, winner in the Texas Senate race by mere double digits, congratulating him on the "landslide." Johnson showed it to the press. Skeptical observers, noting a considerable graveyard vote in south Texas, turned Maggie's telegram into a derisive sobriquet—"Landslide Lyndon." Hugh Mitchell returned to the House of Representatives, and the CVA came back from the dead.

This time the CVA fight was rejoined with increased ideological kick. Truman made its adoption part of his reelection platform, a campaign promise. Phil Weyerhaeuser, heir to and boss of the industrial timber giant, decried it as "Communism on the Columbia." "Socialism" and "totalitarianism" shrieked the *Spokane Spokesman-Review* and the *Seattle Times*.[15] Ideology aside, CVA loomed as a financial threat to the investor-owned utilities, Washington Water Power and Puget Sound Power and

Light being most dominant. What Water Power wanted—or didn't want—the *Spokesman-Review* would make known. Puget Power had good friends at the *Times*.

This issue should have been a natural for Magnuson, the public power apostle of Homer Bone. It was not. There were complications, not the least of which was his seat and power on the Appropriations Committee chaired by Senator K. D. McKellar of Tennessee, a covert enemy of TVA, which he regarded as a federal intrusion on states' rights. Maggie would have been loath to stir the wrath of this vindictive relic of Reconstruction politics. Nor, as Joe Miller speculates, would he have gained satisfaction in the potential loss of political influence to a centralized commission commanding bureaucrats scattered through the federal agencies along the Columbia. For ideological as well as business reasons, such as investments in Puget Power, Magnuson's Republican friends in downtown Seattle were opposed to the CVA and so informed the senator. In response, Maggie gave little more than lip service to the CVA bill. It never would emerge from a House committee. It's a pity, given the later plight of the mighty Columbia, a river suffering from conflicting political and economic interests of the expanding population it must serve.[16]

On the face of it, Maggie had enough business in Washington, D.C., defending a beleaguered president, defending himself against increasingly hawkish constituents, and working for health care and constituent demands. His pace, however, seemed to accelerate after his fortieth birthday. His physician warned he might be risking heart failure at the rate he was running. The senator couldn't be slowed, joining H. J. "Tubby" Quilliam and Bruce Bartley in a new enterprise,[17] Music, Inc., and playing the gaming tables at Bugsy Siegel's Flamingo Casino in Las Vegas (a $1,500 plunge on one weekend) as well as the horses at Bowie, Laurel, Belmont, and Del Mar. Apart from Carol Parker, there was time for a pair of new flames, June Millarde and Austine McDonald. Carol, frustrated for want of a marriage proposal from the senator, wed a Northwest Airlines pilot, a match that lasted only nine months. Maggie hired a lawyer to handle her divorce, but they were never to wed. As she explained, "It seemed like something always came up."[18] The bachelor senator remained in a swing between Washington, Seattle, Los Angeles, and Manhattan. The senator was part playboy, and growing vulnerable to the application of that pejorative.

Music, Inc., the Muzak ("elevator music") franchise for the Northwest, struck a sour fiscal note. It did provide employment for Sis, who remarried and began a recovery from alcoholism. Bruce Bartley was going in the other direction. By mid-1947 his accountant informed Magnuson the firm wasn't making money. Tub Quilliam was at the end of his rope with Bartley, who "got stiffer than a goat and made all sorts of assertions to Scoop Jackson." Bartley, Tub told Maggie, "is not loyal to you and cannot be trusted when he is drunk." Magnuson seems to have tossed up his hands at the music enterprise, suggesting that it be sold at cost to Harry Brand in Hollywood.

"Are you and Austine marrying as all suspect?" Winchell inquired in October 1947. Walter, an ex-vaudeville stage entertainer, invented the gossip column, perfected it in William Randolph Hearst's *New York Mirror*, and then expanded it in the 1940s to include national politics. Broadway press agents were his prime sources of information, until his contacts broadened to include Washington political operatives in Congress, the bureaucracy, and the White House. Not the least of these tipsters was J. Edgar Hoover, boss of the overglamorized G-men. They gave Winchell the inside dope; he provided them with oceans of swell publicity. Maggie was part of the Winchell-Washington symbiosis.

Austine McDonald of Warrenton, Virginia, had been wed to Oleg Cassini, another Hearst columnist. Described as elegant, stylish, even haughty, Austine had her own column of Capitol gossip in the *Washington Times-Herald*. She did not marry Magnuson but would later wed W. R. Hearst, Jr., his father's successor as head of the Hearst Corporation.

"She was really stuck on Magnuson," said Irv Hoff. "He made little effort to reciprocate. When he began dating June, Austine turned vindictive."[19] June Millarde, better known by her starlet moniker, Toni Seven, made a bigger hit in Hollywood as a 1940s pinup girl than as an actress. She topped Lana Turner, Betty Grable, and Carole Landis—Hollywood's leading love goddesses of the 1940s—as the GI's favorite pinup girl in a poll conducted by army newspapers. She entered Magnuson's life as Carol Parker and Austine McDonald were fading out, eventually moving to a home in the Washington area, and accompanying the bachelor senator to social functions in Seattle as well as the nation's capital.

By the time June settled into the Washington scene, items popped up in the *Times-Herald* about the senator's absence from the convening of the Eighty-first Congress. He missed President Truman's speech to Congress and, these items indicated, was nowhere to be found. The *Post-Intelligencer* followed the *Times-Herald*'s lead with a page-one, above-the-fold pinup picture of the sparsely clad Toni Seven, "a golden-haired, heiress-actress." And it claimed that rumors were flying that "she is romantically linked to the 43-year-old senator." The newspaper quoted Magnuson as saying his one-week delay in getting back to Congress was the result of "snowstorms" in the western mountain passes. June said, "Why all the fuss?"

A fuss it was. Toni Seven was not even close to having been the first or the only romance in the bachelor senator's life, but she was the first to come under the glare of newspaper publicity, stories all the more heated with photos of the starlet as a pinup. It was Magnuson's first bitter taste of a press more concerned with his private life than his work as a legislator. He didn't like it, and noted in a letter to his sympathetic buddy, Joe Hughes, "It started with the *Times-Herald* which employs one of my late friends. It was very embarrassing to June. She feels terrible."

The Toni-Maggie items gathered momentum with *Confidential* magazine, the flagship scandal sheet of the 1950s, selling a menu of sex and anti-Communist jingoism. *Confidential* hit the stands in May 1955 with a four-page splash on "the senator and the starlet," claiming "the cross-country romance between Senator Magnuson and starlet Toni Seven has had Washington buzzing for years." "The buzz," said *Confidential*, came from those "wondering if the senator will ever make an honest woman of Toni, the gal who tossed a budding film career into the trash can to spend her time soothing Magnuson's brow and performing other comforting services for so many years." The rest, accompanied by photos of Toni suitable for the bulkhead of a ship's forecastle, was innuendo, smut, and "snowbound," the tale of Magnuson's absence from duty at the start of the 1949 session.

Carol Parker, whose books and phonograph records had been shipped from Suite 823 in the Olympic Hotel to an apartment in New York, wrote Magnuson to express sympathy over the nasty rash of publicity. "Newshounds are on your neck again," she wrote. "I'm just writing to say I hope you can and will find happiness you richly deserve." And "your kindness to me will always be remembered," she promised; "recall me as one of your dearest well-wishers and admirers. Please be happy."[20] Seattle newspapers were reporting "wedding bells" for Maggie and June, who had an inheritance from her show business parents, June Caprice and Harry Millarde.

"Not true," said Magnuson of the marriage reports. "We are very close friends." They lived separately in Washington, but did entertain together, both there and in Seattle, where she duly impressed Magnuson's buddies and their wives. "June was a good lady," said Irv Hoff. "She drank too much, but she was always loyal to Maggie."

"What has Toni Seven got that I can't fix," huffed Miss Bobby Roberts, Apt. 3033, St. Moritz Hotel, in a note to Magnuson. "Join me for a cocktail when you visit New York."

Magnuson visited New York frequently, staying at the St. Moritz on Central Park South or a few blocks away at the Sherry Netherland Hotel on Fifth Avenue. It is doubtful he and Bobby ever had the cocktail, but the story of Magnuson, Toni Seven, and "snowbound" had a life of its own. For example, on December 23, 1963, a month after he succeeded the assassinated John Kennedy as president of the United States, Lyndon Johnson called a grieving Larry O'Brien to chastise the congressional liaison for the absence of fifty-six Democrats at roll call. O'Brien, Jack Kennedy's last campaign manager, said they had been "snowbound." A tape recording of the Oval Office telephone conversation can be heard in the LBJ Library at the University of Texas.

The president said it reminded him of a time when Sam Rayburn asked that he recommend a congressman to chair a committee investigating the FCC. "I told him Magnuson was a young, liberal Congressman, the man to chair the committee. I called Magnuson. He said he was snowbound and couldn't get back. But he was whored up out there in Palm Springs with a movie star," Johnson told O'Brien in this distorted and exaggerated version of the old tale. "When I told Sam Rayburn, he said I'll never put a snowbound member on a committee twice. Now you go meet with those Democrats who were absent. You smile, act polite, shake their hands, then cut off their peters and put them in your pocket."

"Yes, Mr. President," answered O'Brien. He sounded drained.[21]

CHAPTER 16

Cold War, Monkey Business

The cold war arrived with a whimper, not a bomb, early in 1947 when America's British allies, the dominant world power for almost two centuries, informed Washington they could no longer play that role for want of men and money. They publicly announced a withdrawal of troops from India, Ceylon, and Burma, and privately informed President Truman's State Department of withdrawal from Greece and Turkey. They would turn over Palestine, where Jewish settlers were in rebellion, to the United Nations.

Harry Truman and his wise men, George Marshall, Dean Acheson, and the Soviet expert George Kennan, reckoned the United States had no choice but to fill the power vacuum, or face a world tilting toward the increasingly aggressive Soviet Union. Truman addressed Congress somewhat obliquely, saying the United States should help "free people to maintain their free institutions and national integrity against movements that seek to impose upon them totalitarian regimes." There was no mention of the Soviet Union. There was a specific request in this historic speech for men and money to "assist Greece and Turkey." Greece would soon be engaged in a civil war, Whites against Reds, the latter apparently getting little aid from Big Brother in Moscow.[1] Turkey appeared menaced directly by the Soviets. If this does not mark the unofficial start of the cold war, it surely brought an end to America's brief postwar flirt with isolationism.

Apart from ideology, fear of communism grew from our new place in the world and from the power, overt and covert, of our hard-to-get-along-with intractable rival, the Soviet Union. This fear would soon increase to a panic, producing one of the darkest chapters in American history since the witch trials in Massachusetts, coloring—or discoloring—American domestic politics for ten years and foreign policy for the next forty years, until the collapse of the Soviet system. It was an ironic episode in our history, given the panic's timing at the peak of American economic and military power. Domestic communism, diminished to near political impotence since the signing of the Hitler-Stalin pact in 1939, loomed to many as a greater threat than the Red Army. The panic crystallized in a hunt for Communists and Communist sympathizers, real or imagined, for exposure if not prosecution. It was a high time for scoundrels bearing false witness, a terrible time for the accused and for those torn between loyalty toward democratic institutions and old friends. It became the stuff of hot Republican politics, climaxed by the McCarthy era, so named for its prime advocate, Senator Joseph McCarthy, a Republican from Wisconsin.

The high tide of McCarthyism was preceded in Washington State by a legislative committee, chaired by state Representative Albert Canwell, a Spokane Republican, investigating communism at the University of Washington.[2] Results were mixed. Three teachers, professed Marxists, lost their jobs. One of them was Joseph Butterworth, a withdrawn, self-effacing expert on the poetry of Chaucer, a lesser threat to the American way of life than the legislature in Olympia. Three other teachers were suspended. Another of the accused, Melvin Rader, a brilliant, much-beloved professor of philosophy, came back to haunt the Canwell Committee. Rader proved that he had been falsely charged with participating in a Communist meeting by a professional anti-Communist witness. For writing an exposé of this false witness, *Seattle Times* reporter Ed Guthman, later an aide to Attorney General Robert Kennedy, won a Pulitzer Prize. Canwell failed to win reelection to the legislature, but his committee, despite the egregious blemish of the Rader accusation, had magnified the stigma of even the most remote Communist connection, not to mention party membership. The stigma was politically incorrect to the point of criminality. It was a fearful time for those with such connections, accentuated by the heavyweight anti-Communist guns of Hearst's *Seattle Post-Intelligencer*.

Having promoted the legislative hearings, behind the scenes in Olympia and on its news pages, the newspaper then editorially judged them a great success, since they had exposed the few potential threats to the American way of life without jeopardizing anyone's civil rights. Naive, said the editorial, "to believe any person subscribing to the violent doctrine of Communism would shed his opinions like an overcoat once in the classroom." Even more naive, however, to think that freedom of expression and association, as guaranteed by state and federal constitutions, had not been chilled by Canwell's scattershot Commie hunt.

One so endangered, Senator Warren Magnuson, the Communist Party's de facto candidate for Congress in the absence of Marion Zioncheck in 1936, faced an election in 1950. Mac MacGowan warned the senator in April 1950 that Canwell aimed to run for the Senate, using the Red scare, and that Republicans might claim Magnuson had attended Communist meetings. It was even possible, said MacGowan, they unknowingly had attended such meetings. Vulnerable to the charge of flirting with heresy, Magnuson bent with the panic, appeasing the *Post-Intelligencer* by having its editorial on Canwell's probe of the university reprinted in the Congressional Record, then writing the editor, Ed Stone, in praise of its good work.[3] The senator faced trouble enough from his left-wing associations. But more trouble, in the judgment of Irv Hoff and Bill Edris, was fallout from his extravagant extracurricular lifestyle. In Magnuson's reelection case, Republicans had more than McCarthy going for them. There was publicity about Toni Seven and rumors of Magnuson's undue influence for and private gain from Northwest Airlines and KIRO radio.

"Bill was very disapproving of Warren's lifestyle by this time [1950]," said Marge Edris, the businessman's widow. "He was too important to lose in an election, but there were too many girls, too much Hollywood—too much monkeying around. Girls loved him to death, but he never bought them gifts. He had the most beautiful disposition of any human I ever knew. He drank a lot, but he handled booze as well as anyone I ever knew. Still, there was too much Hollywood, too much monkeying around."[4]

Early in 1949, Edris warned Maggie that his love life was "making the Seattle papers every day. . . . June [Toni Seven] should talk no more." Hearst's Sunday newspaper supplement, the *American Weekly*, is "out to do a Toni-Maggie story and if they do, it will add to an already bad situation."

"Don't be a stallion all of your life," came the warning from his Fargo friend, banker, and adviser, Bill Stern. A Seattle constituent, John F. McKay, claiming he was "snubbed" by the senator, wrote a blistering critique of his personal conduct in May 1949: "You are drunk with power, egoism and self-esteem—utterly devoid of statesmanship. Your discourtesy shocks even habitues of Skid Road. Some men go to Washington, D.C. to grow up, some to swell up. You have swollen to the point of bursting." It must have stung, but Maggie only noted that "McKay seems a little touchy."

The bad situation was made worse by the folding of the *Seattle Star* while the *Post-Intelligencer* made its turn to the crusade against communism. Citing irreconcilable differences with W. R. Hearst, John Boettiger, FDR's son-in-law and Anna Roosevelt's husband, had quit as the newspaper's publisher after discharge from the army. In his wake came *Post-Intelligencer* editorials telling northwesterners that the newspaper's "only concern was Americanism," shorthand for anticommunism. Magnuson could no longer count on its support. The *Seattle Times* was staunchly Republican, the *Spokane Spokesman-Review* a mouthpiece for privately owned power companies. Given these journalistic circumstances, Hugh Mitchell urged Magnuson to join him in an effort to purchase and revive the *Star*, a newspaper that leaned, if it leaned at all, in favor of liberal Democrats such as Magnuson, Jackson, and himself. It came to naught; as Mitchell explained, "we could not raise the money."[5]

Walter Winchell, with a radio-newspaper audience of millions, swam on the tide against communism, taking tips from J. Edgar Hoover, and warning, in his creative slanguage, against "comrats" or "comsymps" in your church or under your bed and against appeasement overseas.[6] In the minds of these crusaders there was a vast conspiracy in the land, leaving liberty and property, if not life, at risk. In fact, there were very few Communist Party members, all of them shadowed by J. Edgar Hoover's diligent G-men. In Washington State the critical influence that Communists had exerted on the Democratic Party of the 1930s Popular Front amounted to little more than a faded or blocked memory. Perhaps the very lack of evidence inflamed the idea of an internal Communist threat.

"The FBI says that one-tenth of one per cent of the U.S. population is Communist," said Maggie in an American Broadcasting Company radio debate with Senator Karl Mundt, a South Dakota Republican. "To combat this small group many in Congress would jeopardize the freedom of 99 per cent of the U.S. people." Maggie was the clear winner on this radio broadcast, January 31, 1946.

But Magnuson, the postwar peacenik favoring international control of the atom bomb, cooperation with the Soviet Union, and all-out support for the United Nations, also felt the heat. In September 1950, he joined a Senate majority to approve the McCarran Act "for control of subversive activities," the legislative equivalent of using a pile driver to crack walnuts.[7] The measure was premised on a Communist conspiracy to establish a Communist dictatorship working through "Communist fronts." Any "contribution to the overthrow of the government for a totalitarian dictatorship" became unlawful, punishable by ten years in prison and a $10,000 fine. To implement this broad, inexact mandate, the bill created a Subversive Activities Control Board, later chaired by Harry P. Cain. The board was supposed to decide whether an organization should be designated "subversive." It was more enduring as a monument to panic until its death for lack of funds and interest in 1973. One liberal admirer wrote Magnuson that he should be ashamed of his vote for passage of the McCarran Act, and this he may have been. Perhaps to atone, he was quietly active in saving the professional careers of persons falsely, or laughingly in several cases, accused of being Communists or Communist sympathizers, several later to become prominent in Northwest law and education. He worked especially hard for adoption of Truman's Fair Employment Practices Act, a proposal for minority employment rights, a prelude to the civil rights acts of the 1960s.

If Magnuson was nervous about reelection, so too were several of his friends prominent in Seattle's downtown business establishment. As a practical matter, they needed his services in Washington, D.C., more than they needed to serve their more conservative ideology. John L. Scott, a leading establishment light, wrote to refute certain rumors and to pledge his political loyalty to Maggie. D. K. MacDonald, the insurance broker, vowed his loyalty in a letter to Senator Harry Cain's secretary, with a copy, naturally, to Magnuson.

Odd as it seems, there was talk that Cain, with two years left in his term, might up and challenge Magnuson in 1950. This was "as punk an idea as could be dreamed up," MacDonald wrote. "If this is the best Republicans can dream then they'd better stop dreaming . . . [and] if Harry Cain goes against Magnuson, Harry would lose," he predicted. "Maggie gets a lot of Leftist votes, but there are also a lot of Republicans who are Magnuson advocates. Cain against Magnuson is a screwball idea. Magnuson is an excellent senator who gets results for a lot of people."[8] He might have added: didn't Maggie save Boeing for Seattle—for its insurance salesmen, real estate developers, car dealers, and bankers as well as for its working stiffs?

The senator's labor support was solid, especially along the waterfront. In October 1949, five hundred delegates to the National Maritime Union (NMU) national convention gave Magnuson an honorary membership. He leads, said the NMU, "the fight to keep U.S. vessels" manned by American crews, "a fighting champion of liberal legislation for higher wages, more Social Security, better housing, greater civil liberties and economic security."[9] His membership book number: 40290.

Yet for Maggie, the nation, civil rights, and a measure of public sanity, the worst was to come. Chiang Kai-shek's Kuomintang Nationalist regime in China, America's nominal World War II ally, was finished. Having lost the "will of the people," as Confucius would have noted, it folded under its own corruption and the stronger, more dedicated force of Mao Tse-tung's Red Army. Nationalist remnants took the government treasury, much of it supplied by the United States, and fled to Taiwan. With Chiang's collapse, the most vociferous critics of the Truman administration could, with a twist of geopolitical logic, charge "we lost China," and lost it because of Communists in the State Department and other branches of the administration. How China became ours to be "lost" never came to be questioned in the heat of this advanced projection of an internal conspiracy—a trifle risky to ask such questions in those days.

On June 24, 1950, the day after the University of California fired 157 employees for refusing to take an anti-Communist oath, and three Hollywood writers—not including Al Cohn—were consigned to federal prison for refusing to tell the House Un-American Activities Committee whether they had been members of the Communist Party, President Truman was informed that Communist North Korea had invaded South Korea. Maggie began to despair.

Truman had tried to beat the congressional Commie hunters to the punch by issuing a "loyalty program" for federal employees. Under this executive order, anyone could be fired if there were reasonable grounds to question his loyalty. The order, said Clark Clifford, was "a response to the temper of the times . . . a political problem." He added: "My own feeling was there was not a serious [conspiracy] problem. I felt the whole thing was being manufactured." The president "thought it was a lot of baloney. But political pressures were such that he had to recognize it."[10] So, of course, did Magnuson.

Truman, as usual, reacted without hesitation to the Korean invasion, moving our military into the war under the flag, and nominal support, of the United Nations. Magnuson was among a small group of senators called into the Oval Office to discuss the invasion at its outset. Several argued against U.S. intervention. Truman stopped them short: "I've already decided whether we'll participate. You have to decide how we're to do it." The *Post-Intelligencer*, in its new editorial page policy, reacted with sour disdain to the war, the administration, and the United Nations: "We should let Red China in—and leave the U.S. out." Stone sent Maggie another editorial, punctuated with boldface type, blasting "the blundering and disloyal foreign policy leading us to a complete disaster." America was "a vassal of the U.N. and its mongrel flag" and it was "imperative that we extricate ourselves from this situation at once." Stone added there had been an "80 percent favorable reaction to the editorial." In the same spirit, Stuart Thompson of Seattle wrote Magnuson: "the U.S. is being made a sucker. The U.N. is a dead duck . . . we are feeding and defending people who won't defend themselves."

Magnuson apparently made no reply to Ed Stone, but he did answer Thompson, defending the United Nations and denouncing the drift to isolationism: "It's unworkable. Scientific change makes isolationism a thing of the past. We're confronted with the fact of the necessity of living, the best we can, with other peoples of the world." But he did note, "I'm aware of the sentiments you mention."[11] This was an understatement.

On the face of it, Maggie, an inside wheeler-dealer, playboy pal of a semidiscredited president, and sometime leftist, looked ripe for plucking by any Republican this side of Harry Cain in the 1950 election. What wasn't apparent is that the senator had more going in his favor than had yet met the public eye: businessmen indebted to him for unpublicized Washington influence, militant labor backers, and a critically important buddy with a seat in the U.S. Senate. Maggie was a drinking and poker pal of Senator Joe McCarthy, whose name, alas, will outlive Magnuson's in American history.

On February 2, 1950, McCarthy, a nondescript senator from Wisconsin, addressed the Women's Republican Club of Wheeling, West Virginia, denouncing officials of the Roosevelt-Truman administrations as traitors and then crying havoc, raising in his hand a paper he claimed to be a list of 205 Communists in the State Department. With that gesture the McCarthy era began. The anti-Communist religion had found its Saint Paul. The facts—there was never substantiation to any but a few of McCarthy's charges—were of less importance than the message of unseen subversion at the heart of America's democracy. McCarthy was a liar, a political con man, whose time had come. Facts be damned.

"Everybody in the Senate felt a little heat in those days," Magnuson remembered:

> I knew McCarthy real well when he came to the Senate [1946]. He was an Irishman with a sense of humor. A grand guy. In fact we had a summer place that we rented together in Virginia Beach, both of us bachelors. We'd go down there together. We were great pals. Then, all of a sudden, he got involved in this communist thing and he completely ignored me. He never threatened me and I suppose it was because of our prior relationship. He didn't turn on his pal. He ignored me. Something possessed him.[12]

Characteristic of Maggie, a politician loath to speak ill of his fellow men, especially fellow senators, that description of McCarthy is charitable. A different view, however, comes from Magnuson's staff and other friends.

"A skunky guy, a bad guy," said Irv Hoff. "He was a pretty good pal of Maggie's, then he got off on the Communist hunt. It was the first time anybody read about him—what he said had little authority in fact. That list of Communists he flashed in West Virginia was completely spurious. A lot of people took a drink with him, went to the races with him. He started destroying himself at the Monocle [a watering hole near the Capitol favored by lobbyists, newsmen, and politicians]. He'd drink from noon until late afternoon." Hoff describes McCarthy's personal habits and private conduct as despicable, saying the senator once had sexual intercourse with a woman in a room in a house amidst a private party. McCarthy liked to show his manhood.

Carol Parker, accompanying Magnuson, met McCarthy at a Florida racetrack. "I hated him for what he was doing to all those people [accused of Communist sympathies]. Yet Warren and McCarthy were friends. They were so friendly, I thought . . . Hmmm. I guess that's the way things work in Washington—but how could Warren be friends with such a person? McCarthy was like a car out of control going downhill."[13]

Under Magnuson's patronage, Featherstone Reid went to work on the Capitol police force, assigned to the midnight to 8 A.M. shift in the Senate Office Building. "McCarthy would come in sometime between two A.M. and three A.M., drunk. I couldn't stand the man. He was jovial but, I thought, off his rocker. He would say nice things about Maggie. One morning I said, 'I hope you don't say any bad things about Magnuson.' He replied, 'Well, why should I ever do that?' Some mornings he'd come back to the office building with Roy [Cohn] and [David] Schine."[14]

Cohn and Schine were the senator's accomplices in civil rights mayhem, "cleansing" official American libraries in Europe of "subversive" literature, bringing charges against government officials suspected of leftist deviation. Schine became McCarthy's undoing when the senator turned on the U.S. Army for denying special privileges to his newly drafted aide. The Army-McCarthy hearings were televised, witnessed by millions who began to see the nation's most feared politician in much the same light as had Irv Hoff and Carol Parker.

Before his fall, however, McCarthy took a toll. Defeat of eight Democratic senators is credited to his crusade. The collateral damage on personal lives is not so readily quantified. By any measure, it was considerable. Walter Lippmann, the columnist antithesis of Walter Winchell, said the senator set back civil rights in this nation by a decade—such was the price for the assault on a near phantom, domestic communism. In the last analysis, says his biographer Richard Rovere, McCarthy was a champion liar who could say things without fear and with utter abandon, packaged as a hail-fellow-well-met. Like more notable villains of this century, he came with an abnormal absence of sensitivity. He did not seem to understand how much pain he caused his victims.[15]

By design, McCarthy would be the top Republican hit man in the 1950 elections. Irv Hoff and Magnuson's Seattle pals figured Maggie had more to fear from his publicized action as a politician-playboy bouncing between Hollywood movie stars and Manhattan socialites, drinking a lot, sleeping a little. "Maggie was going to hell," said Hoff. "He wasn't attending to business. It was hard to keep him on business. There was too much Hollywood." Hoff put out an urgent call for Gerald Hoeck to help in the campaign. Hoeck, the best and most creative ad man of his generation in the Northwest, went to Washington to meet a reluctant Magnuson and gather campaign material. Maggie had to be pushed.

"Finally he agreed to meet at 10 A.M. on a Sunday morning in May," said Hoeck. "When I knocked, a big guy in a cowboy hat came to the door, ushered me in, offered a drink. It was Bill Douglas, the Supreme Court Justice from Yakima. Maggie wasn't there. He finally showed up, looking worse for the wear of the previous evening, needing a drink. He had been out all night." The campaign slogan that came out of their talks was honest and to the point: "He gets things done."[16]

Mac MacGowan thought Maggie faced a greater threat from the Red scare than his lifestyle. In a letter to Magnuson, April 26, 1950, he predicted state Representative Al Canwell, the anti-Commie crusader, a precursor to Joe McCarthy, would run and throw the Red book at the incumbent Democrat. "Communist [informers] will probably place you in a couple of Communist meetings," said MacGowan. "This of course is nuts. But it's entirely possible you and I have been in Communist meetings—in fact, I remember one." No such specific charge was ever made. But there were hints and campaign innuendo.

Al Canwell—"Let's get the Reds out of government and the government out of the red!"—lost the Republican Senate nomination to W. Walter Williams, a prominent Seattle businessman, leader in the Chamber of Commerce, an associate in clubs and civic uplift with John L. Scott, Henry Broderick, Lawrence Arnold, and Boeing's Bill Allen. Williams had been urged to make the race by Governor Arthur Langlie in order to restore "morality in government." Urbane, well financed, honorable, but not much known outside Seattle, Williams made little of Magnuson's private business dealings and public flings with starlets. He did acquire a letter lost from Magnuson's office in which the senator appeared to have signed on the advisory committee of an alleged Communist front organization. Hoff got the FBI to declare the apparent endorsement invalid, scant comfort for a nervous incumbent. Magnuson still faced a strong tide of anticommunism, grief over the Korean War, and disenchantment with the United Nations. He was an internationalist. The tide was isolationist.

The attempted assassination of President Truman by Puerto Rican nationalists one week before the election increased the tension for Democrats, who loomed in the conventional wisdom as big losers from Maine to the state of Washington. While reminding voters "he gets things done," Magnuson warned that reelection of a Republican Senate under the influence of Senator Robert Taft would mean a return to isolationism.

Governor Langlie, surely looking ahead to 1956, joined Williams in the campaign. Throwing a shot at bachelors Jackson and Magnuson, Langlie declared, "They can't understand the concern expressed by parents. How can they? They have never experienced the joy and responsibility of parenthood." Williams blasted Truman's plans for "socialized medicine," warning that the Democratic tendency toward "socialism destroys opportunity for youth." Williams did a bit of Red-baiting on his own, addressing an audience in Yakima: "Not that I accuse Magnuson of Communism; personally I doubt that he is. Of course, I don't know that he isn't. . . . he has placed national security in danger by allowing and encouraging Communist infiltration into government."

Magnuson noted in his campaign that Williams was so busy talking about communism he hadn't told voters much about himself. Despite the campaign's nasty tone, Maggie wouldn't back down on his defense of civil rights: "Our problem is to keep America strong without ourselves becoming a police state. . . . a lock-up of all the Reds would damage us and help the Russians. We must proceed by the constitutional processes."

The toughest shots came from the editorial pages. While acknowledging that Hugh Mitchell and Warren Magnuson were not guilty of outright subversion, the *Seattle Times* said they were "guilty of giving protection to leaders of the Communist line of thought in this state over the years." Thus they were guilty by association since they had knowingly worked with Communists and other leftists in the Democratic Party of the 1930s. The *Post-Intelligencer* noted Magnuson's vote for the McCarran Act, before dismissing it as "too little, too late. He has followed Truman down the path that leads to socialism. . . . Magnuson is on the wrong team. He's pro-Truman. Williams will check the travel to socialism [for] he knows the value of a dollar."

Magnuson's campaign brain trust, Irv Hoff, Gerry Hoeck, Mac Mac-Gowan, Scoop Jackson, and Jackson's aide John Salter—a "pixy Machiavellian" in Hoff's apt description—met with the senator in his Olympic Hotel suite. All agreed that it was time for a counterattack. Jackson, Hoff recalls, was adamant: "Williams is trying to paint you Red." Maggie kept silent while they talked. Finally, said Hoff, he got up, walked to an open window and started saying, "the sonsofbitches, the sonofbitches." "Scoop and Salter began to beam—they had got their point across, or so they thought for a few seconds," said Hoff. "Their beams faded when they saw the Boss shoo away a couple of pigeons eating apples he had left on the window sill. The sonsofbitches were pigeons, not Williams."

Hoff recalls the campaign as poorly planned and disorganized. Mac MacGowan remained optimistic. "We'll win, unless there is an unexpected disaster," Mac told Hoff. And what would such a disaster be? "An endorsement by the *Post-Intelligencer*," cracked MacGowan, tribute to the newspaper's swing to the right in the wake of Anna and John Boettiger. Yet at the campaign's end, the *Times* noted Magnuson "has the jitters." For the first time in eighteen years, the politician feared an election loss.

It came down to low comedy on election night in Suite 823 of the Olympic Hotel, where Magnuson awaited an election result he feared. He got drunk. While Walter Williams served coffee and cookies at his campaign headquarters, Magnuson, according to Joe Miller and Gerry Hoeck, consumed stronger stuff. He was "totally blasted by 5 P.M.," despairing at news that three of his Senate pals, Francis Myers of Pennsylvania, Millard Tydings of Maryland, and Scott Lucas of Illinois, had been defeated. All were Democrats.

"I'm next," Magnuson repeated into the evening. Apart from the impending hangover, his problem was the commitment to a West Coast radio interview with newscaster Chet Huntley, a University of Washington graduate and an early Seattle radio newsman who had moved to a bigger market in Los Angeles and would eventually anchor the NBC nightly news from New York. The interview was scheduled for 8:20 P.M. Miller and Hoeck forced Magnuson into a cold shower. Hoff ordered hot coffee and instructed Magnuson to tell Huntley, "It's only 8:25. Polls have just closed. It's too early to tell." Huntley called at the scheduled minute and Magnuson, under Hoff's coaching, repeated his election night mantra three times: " . . . too early to tell."[17] Apparently, it was sufficient to dissuade Huntley from further pursuit of political analysis from Suite 823.

Alas, a Republican tide was running. Taft beat labor to win reelection in Ohio. McCarthy had done his GOP job. Democrats were tainted with treason, none more than Tydings and Helen Douglas in California, who lost the Senate seat to Richard Nixon. Fortunately, the tide stopped at the Washington state line and Democrats gathered at Magnuson headquarters on the second floor of the old *Seattle Star* building to make what the *Times* called "merry." One of them got so merry he tumbled down a flight of stairs. Otherwise, there were no significant casualties. Jackson and Mitchell won reelection and so, by 60,000 votes, did Magnuson. As one Republican supporter noted, Maggie didn't win because he was a Democrat. Labor and hard-core Democrats formed the base of his support, but farmers and Seattle's business leaders realized they needed him in Washington. They conveniently overlooked his excesses of flesh and ideology to make certain he would return. Invisible in this campaign was the extraordinary organizational effort planned and pushed by Irv Hoff. Maggie had a silent army of support from the courthouses around the state to its capitol. Without it, his fears might have materialized. Wisely, Magnuson had ignored the charges about his Popular Front past.

Sobered by early morning, Maggie pitched for a bipartisan foreign policy and said he would return at once to Washington, D.C., to make sure Alaska would become the forty-ninth state. By narrow margins, Democrats had control of the House and Senate. Three years later Magnuson would speak of Walter Williams as "my friend" and warmly endorse his nomination as undersecretary of commerce in the Eisenhower administration. Williams wrote Langlie thanking him for campaign help "openly and under cover."[18]

Oddly, there was scant mention of McCarthy's role in the Republican victories and then only in wary editorial columns. But his impact wasn't lost on Senator Owen Brewster, the Maine Republican, who was chairman of the GOP Senate Campaign Committee. Brewster declared Joe McCarthy "decisive" in their Senate election victories and lamented the fact that the Red-baiter hadn't been deployed in other states. Better campaign use of Joe McCarthy, said Brewster, would have won Republicans control of the Senate.

McCarthy could have altered the vote in the Washington State campaign, from which he was conspicuously absent. Magnuson, as the *Seattle Times* suggested, was vulnerable to charges from his left-leaning past. Instead, said Maggie, "McCarthy ignored me. . . . One thing led to another and he went crazy. He started to drink a great deal. He didn't do this hard drinking before. . . . He didn't have any friends in the senate. He died of liquor."[19]

Magnuson returned to Washington, D.C., fears abated, and stronger than ever. "Government morality" unchanged, Governor Langlie sent Magnuson a cold note giving formal certification of his reelection. The governor did not offer congratulations.

CHAPTER 17

Maggie, Scoop, and Overdrafts

Throughout the 1940s and early 1950s, Warren Magnuson had the political and social life of a dream come true. He was a man with friends, lovers, and an extraordinary power to do, as he saw it, good. If not a household name across the country, he had emerged from the power lanes of Congress to became a national political figure in the Democratic Party. But the dream, like legislation before an appropriations committee, came with a fiscal note and seemed to be chasing him with a due bill. Jay Gatsby, the bootlegger with a touch of class, would forever stretch for the unattainable. Maggie was meeting his goals. His trouble was paying the bills. In those years he got into the habit of floating loans at banks in Seattle, Fargo, and Washington, D.C., and then neglecting to pay them off at their designated time. He routinely bounced checks, and his banker friends just as routinely covered the overdrafts.

Consistently overdrawn at Seattle's Pacific National Bank, Magnuson got a friendly, ever-so-diplomatic notice from its president, Charles Frankland: "You will recall this note was taken out nearly two years ago and our records show that we do not have your financial statement on file or collateral to secure the note. It has come up for possible criticism from time to time, but I have dissuaded the examining committee from listing it on the basis that I know you had substantial means and could liquidate the obligation." There's a handwritten postscript: "Warren, I know you will understand such bank procedures and payment are necessary."[1]

To this notice and others like it, Magnuson replied with the same excuse: "too busy." This was not an overstatement. Apart from Senate duties, he was a member of the 1952 Democratic Party platform committee, a main speaker at the Chicago convention, the western states campaign manager for Adlai Stevenson, his party's presidential nominee, and the wheel around which Washington State party politics now turned.

"Dear Chuck," he wrote Frankland. "I have been extremely busy all during the past several weeks. I have therefore paid little attention to my bank statements." The senator then goes on to request another loan from Pacific National, of $3,500, which he promises to cover in "two or three weeks."

The Stork Club, "21," Sherry Netherland, and St. Moritz in Manhattan, the Ambassador in Los Angeles, and the Flamingo in Las Vegas, with its gaming tables and his companions, came at a price he would have to scramble to meet.

But Frankland's assessment of Magnuson was correct. The senator had means. At the start of 1949 he listed assets as $2,000 in cash, $66,000 in stocks and bonds, a $3,000 car, and property worth $5,000. His income included $5,000 in legal fees, these apparently from the partnership with Seattle businessman Bill Edris, and salary and dividends totaling $23,200. The dividends came from 3,500 shares of Northwest Airlines, 63 shares of the Washington Jockey Club (Longacres racetrack), and 400 shares of KIRO radio.

The senator submitted this financial report to the Seattle-First National Bank in order to open an account for the Melody Company (also called the Music Company) in which he was a partner with H. J. Quilliam and Joe Gibson. Bruce Bartley, his former law partner and a partner in the Music Company, was no longer a part of this Muzak enterprise. Magnuson frequently requested Quilliam to pay his bills at the St. Moritz and Sherry Netherland, hotels anchoring Manhattan's Central Park, with money from the Melody/Music Company.[2]

At the outset of his career, eyes on the future of the skies, Magnuson invested his legal fees from Northwest Airlines into the airline's stock. He would hold this stock until 1955, when he became chairman of the Senate Commerce Committee. To avoid a possible conflict of interest, he then sold the stock, which traded on the New York Stock Exchange. He had a similar vision of the potential of radio. Along with Hugh Mitchell, he made a modest investment in Saul Haas's low wattage station, KIRO, in the early 1930s. Initially, it may have been as much a favor to his friend Haas as it was a prudent investment. Subsequently, however, he aimed to increase his KIRO shares, driven—if driven at all—by the need to fund his expansive lifestyle. He was obviously a favored investor.

In May 1945, the senator informed R. H. Butterwick, vice president of Bill Stern's Dakota National Bank, that 200 shares of Queen City (KIRO) stock would be sent to the bank in care of Magnuson. Butterwick was instructed to pay "the individual" delivering the stock "an agreed price of $20 per share." Magnuson noted that "$20 a share doesn't represent its true value, but some of the owners wish me to have more stock in the station." Collateral for the $4,000 loan to purchase the KIRO stock was 2,700 shares of Magnuson's Northwest Airlines stock. Further, he instructed Butterwick, "after the stock is purchased in my name, it should be sent to Louis Lear, Green Lake State Bank, Seattle, in order that he might affect direct transfer to my name, so I can take advantage of a dividend to be declared shortly."[3]

Maggie got a double dip from the purchase: a cut-rate price on KIRO stock plus a quick dividend from a split in the radio station's shares of capital stock. As a result of the split, Maggie's 200 shares, purchased in January 1946, multiplied to 500 in May. The transaction might be considered a gift from Saul Haas to his pal Maggie, but it did not violate any law on security sales. A few years later in 1953, KIRO swapped some of its stock for prime property at the top of Seattle's Queen Anne Hill. Haas wanted the land for a television studio and transmitter, should the station be granted its request to the Federal Communications Commission (FCC) for a television broadcasting license.

By that time, 1956, Commerce Committee Chairman Magnuson had a hand on the funding of the independent agency, the FCC. This gave him second thoughts about his KIRO stock ownership, and a possible conflict of interest. He expressed this concern in a letter to George Hardgrove, the KIRO board chairman, asking whether he should sell the stock.

"Don't sell," answered Hardgrove, "unless you really need the money. We have never sought for the company any advantages from either political party. Certainly, we have never asked you to use any influence on behalf of the company and furthermore, don't intend to. . . . [F]urthermore, we all know you would not think of doing so."

Magnuson kept the stock. KIRO got the television broadcasting franchise. In partnership with Bruce Bartley and Ted Pruitt, he got a $15,000 bank loan and purchased station KBRO in Bremerton. Yet, betraying his sensitivity to charges of a conflict, he made a rare breach of candor, telling an inquiring constituent a little white lie: "I have no interest in a radio station." They later sold KBRO to Jack Rogers, a Kitsap County weekly newspaper owner, and Bartley told Maggie that, given his meager law practice, "I would be very interested in [being] U.S. District Attorney. . . . Am permanently on the wagon and have been for four months."[4]

In August 1961, *Broadcast* magazine reported Magnuson owned four percent of KIRO's stock and described the senator as "a reasonable guy, easy to get along with—but no lobbyist for industry." It noted that he backed the nomination of Newton Minow, critic of television's "vast wasteland," as chairman of the FCC; that he "pushed legislation for educational TV and always has the votes."

Magnuson's KIRO holdings did not diminish his affection for the Bullitt family, owners of KING Broadcasting. Mrs. Scott Bullitt's chief business officer, Henry Owen, was one of Maggie's main fund-raisers. The relationship was strictly proper, and once, when Magnuson hinted his displeasure with newsman Chuck Herring, Owen ignored the implications. Herring had aroused Maggie's anger, but he remained a mainstay with the station.[5]

Whatever his failings of the flesh, the senator was not for sale, as *Broadcast* clearly implied. Ross Cunningham, editorial-page editor of the never friendly, frequently hostile *Seattle Times*, and a critical acquaintance of Magnuson's from the days of the radical 1933 state legislature, addressed the character question in blunt terms: "He is not venal."[6]

Nor did the senator have time, much less energy or inclination, for greed. Facing him in 1952 were internal Senate politics (the choosing of a Senate Democratic leader); a presidential election; home state politics (strategy over finding a challenger to the increasingly strident Senator Harry P. Cain); and the routine flood of requests from constituents and others.

Maggie's image as a political figure of national stature lagged behind the portrait of the state pol who brought home the bacon and had a ball in the process. But some of that gap narrowed when Senator Leverett Saltonstall, a Massachusetts Republican, went off the record to tell a Harvard Club gathering in Seattle "a word about Warren Magnuson." Reported Saltonstall: "He is one of the ablest senators in Washington and is hard-working, well-informed and aggressive—this is strictly off the record."[7]

Tapped for the Democratic Party's 1952 platform committee, Magnuson plugged for public power for the West, "equal pay for equal work regardless of sex," and a repeal of the Taft-Hartley labor law. His speech to the Chicago convention aroused the partisan audience. It was aimed at holding unity between the party's southern and western wings: "The Republican platform is the most reactionary in the party's ruthless history. . . . they plan to rob the South and the West of public power built by the people for the people. . . . they want to divide the West and the South and send them back 50 years." One critic called the televised speech "socialistic." Most critics cheered. There was a lot of talk about Maggie for vice president. His name was entered and withdrawn, probably at his request. The ticket needed and got a southerner, Senator John Sparkman of Alabama.

Shortly before the party's July convention, Magnuson told the *Spokesman-Review* Adlai Stevenson was "a slight favorite to win the Democratic Presidential nomination from Estes Kefauver," the Tennessee senator at least initially favored by Maggie. They were kindred spirits in the Senate club. Meanwhile, back in Washington State, Irv Hoff and John Salter were organizing in meticulous detail a Democratic campaign. Hoff's dispatches to the Democratic National Committee on candidate prospects are crisp with insight. Maggie's assistant was determined in 1952 to avoid the disarray of the 1950 campaign. The key, he said later, was to organize in advance; they needed to draft a "blueprint" for the campaign before otherwise cool heads got tired and confused. After much discussion, he would sell the idea to Henry Jackson. In front of this back-room planning and discussion, and ultimately the man calling the shots, was the well-seasoned Senator Magnuson.

As he would tell the bankers, he was a very busy man. But Magnuson was never so busy as to neglect constituent requests, especially if they called for medical research. Capitol Hill's major health facilitator, he was continuously routing money into hospitals either from federal funds or from the Damon Runyon memorial cancer fund, chaired by Walter Winchell and directed from the Astor Hotel in New York by John Teeter. Typical is a request from Maggie to Teeter for $25,000 for Swedish Hospital in Seattle, "a fine institution with an excellent staff." Swedish got the money.[8] Answering appeals from Mary Lasker, Teeter, and other health advocates, Magnuson pushed into the 1950 federal budget $37 million for cancer research, $29 million for heart research. If for no other reason, Mrs. Lasker, widow of an enormously successful Manhattan advertising master, adored Magnuson.

The free-trade visionary, Magnuson, stepped up to help Seattle's pioneering effort to open the door to commerce with Japan, the recently defeated World War II enemy. Seattle's Japan Trade Fair, held for two weeks in June 1951, was that nation's first opportunity to exhibit its goods in the United States since the 1930s. The fair had blanket support from the city as a "goodwill gesture on the part of the people of Seattle to the people of Japan." John Haydon, a Port of Seattle employee, late of the air war over Germany, and later a port commissioner, was its ramrod. Magnuson coordinated with the State Department and got the Senate Finance Committee to get a duty exemption for Japanese goods shipped to Seattle for the fair. The fair, said Maggie, was good for the nation, "great for Seattle." A magnanimous gesture, it placed the Northwest seaport in the forefront as the port of entry for Japanese products, a mainstay of the city's economy for the balance of the century. At Haydon's request, Magnuson then went to Japan as the city's goodwill ambassador.[9]

By coincidence, and not the design of President Truman, Magnuson was in Japan in April 1951, meeting with General Douglas MacArthur at the American Far Eastern commander's headquarters in Tokyo. Their private talk was interrupted by an aide with an urgent telegram. As Magnuson recalled the incident, MacArthur read the message in a few seconds and the two men continued their talk. Hours later, outside the military headquarters, the senator learned that the message said, in effect, "General, you're fired." The president had dismissed the American potentate for insubordination, an act that set off a fire storm of protest, launched a MacArthur for President campaign, and set a mean tone for the 1952 elections.[10] But there were more mundane matters pertaining to the Far East, along with Alaska, demanding Magnuson's attention.

A year after MacArthur's dismissal and the first Japanese trade exhibit, Seattle's seafaring unions (the Sailors' Union of the Pacific; Marine Firemen, Oilers, Watertenders and Wipers; and the Marine Cooks and Stewards) shut down the city's waterfront in an internal fight over "jurisdiction," the legal way of saying control of jobs. Marine Firemen feared the sailors were after their engine room jobs; cooks feared both unions. Firemen, armed with tire irons and baseball bats, patroled the waterfront around the clock, lest the topside sailors try to seize their places below deck. It never came to violence, but it brought a deluge of requests to Magnuson for a settlement. Letters came from every maritime city from Longview to Seward, Alaska, all saying the Alaska/Northwest economy was at risk. Vessels with cargo from the Far East were being diverted to California. Alaska chambers of commerce demanded a congressional investigation. Instead, Magnuson dispatched Max Kampelman, a sometime aide to Hubert Humphrey and future head of the Arms Control and Disarmament Agency, to find out what the strike was all about. He was to contact only John Salter in Seattle and work strictly without publicity. Maggie had to move carefully; he was a hero to all three unions, each of them a mighty source of political support. Eventually, with his quiet help, their disputes were resolved, no jobs were snatched, and waterborne trade resumed—the chambers of commerce's requests fulfilled.[11]

No request was stranger than Vaughn Evans's inquiry about the senator's relations, if any, with Kathleen Blethen, estranged wife of Frank Blethen, publisher of the *Seattle Times*, a newspaper generally hostile to Magnuson. Evans, Kathleen's attorney in divorce proceedings, said Blethen's lawyer claimed Mrs. Blethen had spent the night with Magnuson at the Shoreham Hotel. True, asked Evans? "Untrue and preposterous," replied Magnuson. Mrs. Blethen, he said, came to Washington with her widowed sister-in-law to get information on her brother, victim of a Japanese kamikaze attack in the South Pacific in World War II. Maggie's office booked them a hotel room—not at the Shoreham—and secured train reservations for their return trip to Seattle. Frank Blethen had dispatched a note thanking Magnuson for helping his wife. Evans replied a few weeks later that the divorce had been settled out of court and that he figured Blethen's accusation was phoney, "probably meant only to embarrass you and give you some adverse publicity."

"Dear Vaughn," answered Magnuson, "in a way I'm sorry it [the divorce] is settled because I could have retained you as an attorney, filed suit [against Blethen] and collected enough to make a good down payment on the paper itself."[12]

Despite all of their disdain for his politics and lifestyle, the *Times* was not reluctant to call on Magnuson for help of a most delicate nature. Elmer Todd, the newspaper's attorney and a minor stockholder, wanted Maggie's help to "locate someone off on a spree . . . in a bad crowd." Todd's letter was carefully worded, but the someone was, apparently, one of Blethen's sons, a prodigal. Magnuson once mentioned the request, and said that he had done his best on behalf of the Blethen offspring. He did not disclose the result of his efforts.[13]

Joe Drumheller, the wealthy scion of a pioneer Northwest family and Maggie's de facto agent in eastern Washington, appealed to Magnuson to intervene with Clark Squire, the regional federal tax collector, on behalf of "a couple of our pals, George Manos and Sam Salinas." Manos ran the Spokane racetrack, Salinas played the horses and made other bets. They owed the IRS $26,000, which Squire wanted to collect all at once rather than in installments as the two gamblers requested. Drumheller explained the facts of Spokane life:

> You haven't had a chance to spend much time in Spokane and you naturally would not know some of our inside set-up. I'm speaking particularly about Skid Row. For many years gambling, etc., has been headed by Manos and Salinas. There are others, of course, but the solid citizens of the community have looked for these two to keep the rackets clean and to give folks a break. They have done a dam good job of it. Their word is their bond and while their activities may be frowned on by the blue-noses, you and I both know that such people are essential in a city of this size. . . . we are just lucky to have a couple who are on the square. Both these men are good friends of mine and have always come to me for advice and will back anything I advise. If you could convey to Clark that you know Sam [which you do] it would help a great deal.[14]

Magnuson did so and the Internal Revenue collector complied with his request. There was no further explanation of the "etc." part of the gamblers' operation.[15]

Magnuson, of course, was familiar with such "tolerance" policies. He had been the prosecuting attorney in a seaport city with a transient population of seamen, loggers, and mill workers along with an upper crust occasionally hankering for the illicit pleasures of Chinatown. Word of Maggie's connection with the demimonde got around. Early in 1952, Crown Publishers issued *USA Confidential*, by Jack Lait and Lee Mortimer, Hearst newsies who boasted in the book's foreword, "we got our training on fast dailies." Their style was *New York Mirror* Winchellesque, "hot journalism" that doesn't let facts bar a salacious story, or a cynical observation. "Should we sue for libel?" Bill Stern asked Magnuson in April, shortly after the book's publication. They would have needed to get in line.

Lait and Mortimer were out to take the sheets off Reds, traitors, mobsters, "dope pushers and their sucker allies," plus "unbridled, hopped-up, sex crazy and perverted youth." Small matter if there really wasn't much beneath the sheets in pit stops made on their unusual exploration of the nation. They provided sleazy entertainment. Reaching the Pacific Northwest they found "rampant radicalism and wild jackassism in both parties." Its politics were "as cheap as Chicago." Seattle "smells of fish," a surprisingly accurate observation for this book. "Orientals slink" through the city's foggy alleys, just as they did in the Charlie Chan movies of that era. There are bookies at Green's Cigar Store, hookers at $20 an hour or $100 for the night, as any hustling cabdriver could have told. Local youth held "sex orgies in Golden Gardens," a fantasy, as was their notice that Dave Beck ran the town with Hugh Mitchell as his representative in Washington while Henry Jackson served as fish-magnate Nick Bez's "legman." A legman in the journalism of that time gathered facts and coffee for stars like Lait and Mortimer to process.

"Bill Stern, the Republican boss of North Dakota," said *USA Confidential*, "is Warren Magnuson's foster father. . . . [T]he enormously wealthy Stern supports his socialist adopted son in lavish luxury. They split power, patronage and perks of the Pacific Northwest. Magnuson is the gay blade of the Senate." By "gay" they did not mean homosexual, the word's meaning having shifted radically since 1952. "Magnuson votes pro New Deal, leftist and pro-crackpot." They hinted, broadly, at a sinister connection between the senator and the underworld, reporting that Bugsy Siegel's girlfriend, Virginia Hill, had moved to Spokane after the gangster's murder. Spokane, they said, is a "rube burg, a mobster concentration point," apparently oblivious of the role assigned Manos and Salinas. Magnuson, they said, had introduced legislation to "allow Virgina Hill's Nazi boyfriend to remain in the U.S."[16]

Siegel, who broke into the mob as an assassin, was himself victim of a Mafia gunman. Stories conflict on whether he had any Spokane connections. Veteran police reporters say that he did not, and newspaper morgues are absent any local notice of the gangster's presence around

Spokane. However, Mary Lou Bekkala, in a Seattle newspaper interview, says her father, a bootlegger, worked with Siegel in Spokane in 1935. Other natives swear they saw the flamboyant Siegel drive about town in his roadster, Virginia Hill at his side.

Regardless, after Siegel's demise, Virginia Hill bought a $31,000 house in Spokane and wed Hans Hauser, a German alien, and a Sun Valley and Mount Spokane ski instructor. Either through intervention with the Immigration and Naturalization Service or a special bill—Irv Hoff has no recollection of the latter—Magnuson did get Hauser a stay of deportation in 1946. Four years later, Hauser's stay was rejected. He left the country, soon followed to Salzburg, Austria, by Hill, the glamorous native of Bessemer, Alabama, an ex-mob moll now targeted by the IRS for payment of back taxes. She died there, "bored with life," an apparent suicide. Spokane's manufactured notoriety as a "mobster concentration point" was more writer's fantasy than fact, according to the city's veteran crime reporters. Such as it was, the Spokane "mob" was local and tolerated.[17]

Magnuson never filed suit for libel against Crown Publishers. He had more pressing matters in the Senate, supporting Lyndon Johnson, his congressional "classmate" over the Alabama Democrat Lister Hill for Senate Democratic leader; and boosting Mon Walgren, the defeated Washington governor and Harry Truman's nominee for the National Security Resources Board.[18] It was a losing fight on behalf of Truman's "beloved crony" (in the Republican press, Truman never had friends, he had "cronies") that brought Magnuson and Jackson to a breaking point with Washington's junior senator, Harry P. Cain.

Cain opposed the Walgren appointment with a vengeance. The gravel-voiced former Tacoma mayor linked Walgren, an amiable ex-Everett jeweler, to the state's leftist past and charged that he was "soft on communism," a code phrase suggesting treason. Beyond Walgren, Cain charged the ex-governor's buddy Nick Bez as being the "financial angel of Yugoslav communists." Bez, a primitive capitalist with the physique of an Alaskan brown bear, told Magnuson, "Cain had better prove those statements in my presence . . . otherwise there is going to be a bloody nose the next time we meet. I'm willing to meet anytime, anyplace." Drew Pearson wrote that Walgren "won" $50,000 in a dice game with Johnny Meyers, a publicist hired by Howard Hughes, the aircraft and machine tool entrepreneur. Pearson later learned, and so reported, that the source of the $50,000 dice game item was Cain himself. The columnist apologized, but the damage was done. Magnuson said Cain's charges were absurd, but it left the question of "Mon's competence and experience." He doubted he could move the appointment out of Judiciary Committee.

In fact, he couldn't, despite the president's full support—a rare instance of Maggie's failure to turn the Senate to his will.

The easy-going, pool-playing Walgren was captured in a column by Joseph and Stewart Alsop after the committee's judgment. They saw him in a Washington hotel sitting room "with a crimson enamel cigarette case boldly inscribed 'I swiped this from Harry Truman' displayed on a table." The Alsops continued: "In any county building, or state capitol or congressional haunt, you could duplicate this plump, neatly tailored, nearly gray-haired politician with the round, smooth, eupeptic face, unravaged and unilluminated. . . . All about him is commonplace. . . . One begins to see Walgren as he is—good friend, good fishing and poker companion, amiable without being uncomfortably witty, kindly without being alarmingly large-spirited, easy going, easily pleased, fitted for politics by the habit of joining. If his character seems a little blurred, why, so are his convictions."[19]

Nevertheless, in helping deny the federal appointment of Walgren, the good old boy from Everett, Cain inflicted a mortal wound on his own Senate career. Letters likened his committee antics and charges to those of the late Marion Zioncheck. "Has he gone crazy or just plain nuts?" asked Frank Miller of Port Orchard. *Time* magazine, the tacitly Republican organ, declared Cain one of its prime "Senate expendables." John Coffee, the former congressman, asked Magnuson, "How long are we going to have to endure Cain's rantings?"[20]

It would not be for long. The larger question: who would be the 1952 Democratic Senate candidate against Republican Cain? The obvious possibilities were Representatives Mitchell and Jackson, both Northwest progressives with solid reputations for integrity and competence. Jackson told Maggie at the start of the election year that he had "pretty definitely decided" to make the race against Cain, although he was not yet ready to make the decision public. Magnuson made it known that he didn't want a primary race between Scoop and Hugh, the senior senator's authority coming from the strength of his own political organization in the state. The informal "Maggie party" was based on a coterie of friends who extended first loyalty to the senator, and was financed by trade unions and nominally Republican businessmen indebted to Magnuson for their Capitol connection. This was political fallout from the federal impact on the state economy under the Roosevelt and Truman administrations. It was a pattern to be followed by Scoop Jackson, says Ancil Payne, aide to Mitchell at that time. The fallout from these personal Jackson-Magnuson organizations, Payne concludes, was a "state Democratic Party that was never again worth a damn."

Payne said Jackson appeared to have the better state campaign organization in 1952 and had no interest in being governor. Mitchell said there was no pressure from Magnuson: "The truth is that I wanted to run for governor. I thought I could accomplish more in Olympia than in the Senate."[21] So it was settled: Jackson to run against Cain, Mitchell to seek the governor's office. If he did not push these decisions, Magnuson might have nudged them in his gentle manner. He clearly looked kindly on Jackson, his Scandinavian landsman who went from Everett to Congress overly endowed with the Protestant work ethic. Maggie probably heeded an alarm from Seattle attorney Ken MacDonald, who wrote: "Don't let Mon run for governor. Mon will injure the Democratic ticket. He will give Cain an issue with which to batter Jackson."

Mitchell, who would become a successful Seattle businessman but never a spellbinding campaigner, fared ill, running against the McCarthyite tide of 1952. His opponent in the primary election, Albert Rosellini, the state Senate majority leader, made the most of Seattle-Spokane newspaper editorials savaging Mitchell for his "socialist" CVA legislation and his "softness" on Communism. A week before the election, a page-one *Post-Intelligencer* editorial slammed the Americans for Democratic Action (ADA) as "the Socialist outcropping of the Democratic Party. Hugh Mitchell wears its label. He is for the CVA which is about transferring the state's bountiful resources to a bureaucracy 3,000 miles away that cares less about the state." The ADA, in fact, was the rigorously anti-Communist, progressive wing of the party. The cry for "states rights" was a convenient cover for private power interests who feared and fought the CVA as a massive encroachment of publicly owned electric power.

Senator Joe McCarthy came to Seattle shortly before the election to debate the state's leading stand-up comic, Lieutenant Governor Victor A. Meyers, in a show rigged for laughs by the Seattle Press Club. A typical Meyers one-liner: Q: "Vic how do you stand on the CVA?" *A:* "I'm alright on that one." McCarthy did not appreciate the laughs. He was described as looking weak and subdued. Later he got fighting mad when KING-TV refused to allow him airtime for a televised address after he refused to allow their attorney to censor parts of his speech they considered libelous. The *Post-Intelligencer*, however, carried a reprint of the text, which described two members of Drew Pearson's staff as "ex-Communists," and allowed that a vote for Mitchell or Jackson "will give assistance to the Communists." Plugging Harry Cain, McCarthy labeled Jackson "soft on Communists."[22]

Mitchell won the primary election, but the Rosellini campaign effectively cost him the governor's race to Arthur Langlie, the GOP incumbent.

In the words of Langlie's biographer, George Scott, Mitchell was "tarred a pink."[23] Rosellini initiated the unusual paint job. Langlie completed the smear. Mitchell never recovered in the general election. The "soft on communism" charges flared again two years later when Mitchell ran unsuccessfully for Congress. This time Magnuson and Jackson issued a joint statement saying the charges were "crude distortions and falsifications of the facts . . . made for his opponent by local and imported henchmen."

With expert campaign help from John Salter, his longtime aide, Gerry Hoeck, Irv Hoff, and Joe Miller, Jackson demolished Cain, who could have been a model for the *USA Confidential* portrait of Northwest politics as "wild jackassism." Jackson had slipped past the left-deviationist charges. He stuck with Hoff's campaign blueprint by refraining from striking back at Cain for the "soft on Communist" charges until the end of the campaign. Nevertheless, as Mitchell and others have noted, the "Commie" innuendoes—hadn't Jackson sponsored the "Communistic-Socialistic" CVA legislation?—scared Jackson, perhaps coloring the balance of his career. Once perceived as a "liberal" on the race issue, Alabama's George Wallace lost a primary race for governor to a determined segregationist. He vowed never to be "out-niggered again" and went on to become governor and a leading opponent of integration. In that same spirit, Jackson may have felt no one was ever going to out "anti-Communist" him again. He went on to be a leading advocate for Pentagon appropriations and anti-Soviet sentiment.

No one was ever going to outdo Jackson in his zeal to defend the nation from the Kremlin's ideology and military power. Jackson, aided by a new generation of voters, defeated Harry Cain. But he apparently learned a political lesson from the campaign. A progressive liberal on domestic issues, he became a dedicated cold warrior with a Manichaean view of the postwar world. The subsequent Jackson-Magnuson partnership was an unparalleled Senate powerhouse, an odd combination of disparate personalities who worked together, with rare exceptions, as smoothly in the U.S. Senate as quarterback Jim Zorn and receiver Steve Largent did in Seattle's Kingdome. The exceptions were connected with differences on the cold war and were never much publicized. Scoop and Maggie harmonized despite contrasting Senate manners.[24]

Early in the presidential campaign, Magnuson worked with Adlai Stevenson, the Illinois governor and Democratic nominee, and Stevenson's campaign chairman, Wilson Wyatt, to develop a western states campaign strategy.[25] Stevenson attracted a new following of Democrats with his wit and eloquence. They would later form a cadre behind Jack Kennedy. Failing to carry his home state, the governor lost badly to a

Republican tide and Dwight Eisenhower, the general who had led the nation to victory in Europe in World War II. Eisenhower had promised to extricate the country from its war in Korea, and he looked like a man for the times. The nation settled down to relatively tranquil years, comforted by a massive outburst of consumer goods, simple fads like the hula hoop, even more simplistic television programs, and the grandfatherly Eisenhower. A majority of the '50s generation were said to be silent. In such times, lulled by affluence and this new miracle of entertainment from television, why get stirred up?

Republicans won the House and Senate. The *Post-Intelligencer* said voters had "registered disapproval of a federal super government." Barry Goldwater defeated the Senate Democratic leader, Ernest McFarland. The new Senate Democratic leader, Lyndon Johnson, realized he had a dangerously loose cannon in the Senate ranks. Joe McCarthy was anything but silent, accusing General George Marshall, and lesser figures, of the treason of "coddling Communists," and threatening critics with a Communist accusation. Marshall's military protégé, the new president, loomed as the only political figure with sufficient authority to challenge McCarthy. But Eisenhower kept his silence. Johnson had a major problem.

"Lyndon came to me and said 'don't you think we should do something about that fellow?' " said Magnuson. "I said, 'sooner or later we've got to.' I had a little hope that he'd get better and sort of repent. He didn't. He got worse. Johnson decided to go ahead. We had a [Democratic] Policy Committee meeting and decided to turn it [McCarthy's conduct] over to Senator John McClellan's investigations sub-committee."[26]

The upshot was the Army-McCarthy hearings in the spring of 1954, the televised exposure of the Wisconsin senator's antics and his aides, and the beginning of the end of the nation's McCarthyite nightmare. McCarthy subsequently suffered censure by his Senate peers, a humiliation from which he would not recover. He died three years later.

Those devastating hearings, watched by millions of Americans, overshadowed House Un-American Activities Committee hearings in Seattle in which a former Northwest Communist, Barbara Hartle, cited scores of persons for having been Communists or having Communist affiliations. Some took the Fifth Amendment, refusing to say whether they were now or ever had been party members; some repented of their past as Communists; and some never were—except in Hartle's imagination. The hearings were an anticlimax, an extra curtain falling on a political drama long past prime time.

CHAPTER 18

The Sinner and the Saint

I n 1956 the irresistible force collided with the immovable conscience. Senator Warren Magnuson, escalating in power as the new chairman of the Senate Commerce Committee, got an election challenge from Washington Governor Arthur B. Langlie, second to none in moral outrage and Presbyterian conviction. Against all the advice from his political allies, Langlie decided he had a responsibility to rid the Senate of the "morally bankrupt" Magnuson. He made the decision, said his administrative aide Norm Schut, after "consulting with President Dwight Eisenhower and God."[1]

The two leaders were stark contrasts with nothing in common, save their profession, their Scandinavian ancestry, and their political roots in Seattle. This was insufficient to make them like each other. Politics, to Magnuson, was the doctrine of the possible, the attainable. To Langlie, politics as practiced by Magnuson fit Ambrose Bierce's cynical definition as "the conduct of public affairs for private advantage."

Their seaport city, an emerging rival to San Francisco in the mid-1950s, was itself divided into contrasting personalities, symbolized by First Avenue just above the waterfront, and Fifth Avenue up toward First Hill. From the city's enduring Pike Place Market downhill to the heart of Skid Road (the "original" Skid Road, citizens boasted), First Avenue was lined on either side by taverns, 24-hour movie theaters, hotels (survivors of the gold rush with weekly rates), and pawnshops stocked with an exotic array of goods exchanged by seafarers for the pleasures of the street. The hard-knuckled maritime union halls were on First Avenue or just below it on Western Avenue. A blown-up photo portrait of Magnuson hung on the wall of the Sailors' Hall next to a crude painting of a seaman martyred in the 1934 waterfront strike. The air smelled of creosote pilings and salt breezes. First Avenue was Maggie's side of town, no place for ladies and perhaps not gentlemen. Yet the senator, bestriding two worlds, lived uptown at the elegant Olympic Hotel, which bordered on Fifth Avenue. This is where society matrons shopped at I. Magnin and Frederick & Nelson and went for entertainment to the Fifth Avenue Theater, a first-run movie house with an interior design taken from Hollywood's image of the Chinese imperial palace of the Ming dynasty. The lawyers, insurance brokers, and shipping agents, dressed in conservative suits, had offices in buildings along the street. Protestant churches, not union halls, were the institutional bulwarks of Fifth Avenue. This was the heart of Seattle's bourgeois propriety. It reflected Arthur B. Langlie, the politician of propriety who reviled the life and works of Magnuson and who could not have looked with delight on the gin mills, hockshops, hookers, and cheap hotels of First Avenue. Langlie believed in clean living as well as clean politics. The Magnuson-Langlie election enlarged these social differences.

Langlie is still remembered in Olympia as the governor who refused to allow whiskey, the fuel of legislation, in the governor's mansion. Maggie never had far to reach for a strong drink. Republican Langlie, by all accounts, was an excellent chief executive, despite his rigid personality. Nevertheless, he fought further federal intrusion into the Northwest, especially as conceived in the Columbia Valley Authority. He subscribed fully to the Republican Party line of 1956 that the election poised "liberty against socialism" with no more vivid personification than Langlie versus Magnuson. In the words of the *Post-Intelligencer*, it would also be a "clash of political giants."

Magnuson posed more than a threat to liberty in Langlie's view; he was a threat to clean government, and clean living. There were unverified rumors about Magnuson's outside financial interests, his Hollywood connections, and his starlets, particularly Toni Seven. This was not the right stuff of a clean politician, and Langlie set out to demolish the senator in a well-written campaign pamphlet titled "The Myth That Is Magnuson."

"Once upon a time," said the pamphlet, "there was a senator who loved the purr of a Cadillac, the genial clink of ice cubes late at night, the beguiling flutter of a petticoat. Sometimes, however, these 'hobbies' were so pressing that it was hard to attend to the affairs of state in Washington, D.C." The pamphlet described Magnuson's career as "absolutely Hollywoodian, with guys, dolls and gangsters and an unsuccessful marriage and all the other elements of a cheap film production." It quoted from a magazine article by Richard Neuberger, the Portland journalist who would become an Oregon senator, saying Magnuson's "fondness for models, starlets and svelt society editors" had more than once distracted him from his $15,000 a year job on the federal payroll. The campaign shot concluded, "Magnuson seems to have a very social life and he certainly appears to be busy for us . . . but what has he really done for us?"[2]

The answer was plenty, and it came catalogued in a brochure prepared for Magnuson's campaign. It is a summation of his two decades in Congress, a remarkable, if not unique, record; not the mark of a man all-consumed with guys and dolls, or supported, like the Wizard of Oz, by a propaganda machine. Approaching the 1956 election Magnuson had cosponsored and pushed bills to give statehood to Alaska and Hawaii (he would no longer be subtitled "the senator from Alaska"); a constitutional amendment to give equal rights to women; bills to create a Civil Rights Commission, to outlaw lynching, and to build more dams for the Columbia River Basin. Earlier Magnuson pushed through bills to give federal aid to education, improve Social Security, and establish the National Institutes of Health to research the causes of cancer, heart disease, and communicable diseases. He had cosponsored the landmark Fisheries Act that created the U.S. Fisheries Commission and had led the fights for McNary, Hungry Horse, Chief Joseph, The Dalles, Ice Harbor, and Detroit Dams. Those dams irrigated a semiarid desert in central Washington and provided energy for Northwest factories and homes. They created an economy which otherwise would not exist. No wonder Irv Hoff would call them Magnuson's greatest achievement. As the brochure put it, Maggie was proud of his fights against the Taft-Hartley labor act and for the Federal Employment Fair Practices Act. He could have boasted of his influence in saving Boeing for Seattle and his role in the pivotal Japan Trade Fair. He might have wooed the state's sportsmen, a powerful lobby group, by boasting of his passage of a bill to retain the Fish and Wildlife Service as a single agency within the Department of Interior. The Wildlife Management Institute called this a "complete victory for conservationists and sportsmen."[3]

This numbing recital of legislative achievement was dismissed by Langlie as the creation of press agents. By no means did it include mention of his outside interests or his friends in Hollywood; apparently at that time there was no talk of his Manhattan connections. Indeed for most citizens it was a time when a politician's private life was more a matter of his own business than the business of the public.

Dick Neuberger had also noted that the "dashing bachelor" Magnuson might be helped at the polls by rumors of his Hollywood playmates.[4] In retrospect, the journalist might have observed that Democrats uneasy with their vote for Magnuson could offset any embarrassment by supporting Scoop Jackson, whose personal habits reflected a Langlie lifestyle. Obviously, Langlie thought otherwise about the consequences of Maggie's playboy image. But he had no sense of the political reality of Magnuson.

"At times people like myself must be an awful bother," the real estate dealer John L. Scott, a ranking member of the state's business elite, a Republican, wrote Magnuson. "We're always asking for things. You never once sidestepped a request. Come hell or high water, I'll always vote for you."

Langlie didn't get it—the fact that many of his social peers were indifferent to the senator's lifestyle as long as he provided them with a Capitol influence. He didn't understand how Maggie had bridged the gap between First and Fifth Avenues. His aides, however, understood. "We all urged Langlie not to make the race," said Norm Schut. "But he abhorred Magnuson. When the stories broke about Maggie and Toni Seven, he had decided to run. I told him it was a mistake; that he was going to get beat. He said if he didn't run he'd be unhappy. He was bound and determined to expose Maggie, believing that he was a total crook, morally reprehensible. He didn't understand how Maggie had co-opted even his [Langlie's] own supporters."

Schut provides a vivid illustration of the Magnuson co-opting technique. Once, when Seattle advertising man Fred Baker flew to Washington, D.C., on business, the senator met him at National Airport, drove him to his hotel, and later in the evening took him to a reception at the White House hosted by President Truman. Recounting the flattering treatment, Schut quotes Baker as noting, "How can you beat a man like that?" Baker was one of Governor Langlie's most influential advisers.

The governor, who prayed frequently but abstained from alcohol, may have been deafened by the clinking of Maggie's ice cubes. It was a time when the senator was drinking heavily, as observed by Schut as well as Bill Edris. Apart from partisan charges, there is scant evidence to indicate that whiskey interfered with his legislative duties. Magnuson, like Winston Churchill, had an extraordinary capacity for liquor. "As best I could see," said Schut, "it might have been a problem. But while he had lapses, he did so much good while he was on the ball, he made up for them. Besides, he had a superb staff, the best I've ever seen."

But Maggie's lapses into strong drink might have looked to Langlie like a political death wish. Homer Bone warned the senator not to take a challenge from Langlie lightly. "He is formidable," wrote Bone. "Start planning now."[5]

If the governor found advice from his friends in Olympia and Seattle discouraging, there was President Eisenhower and his top aide, Sherman Adams, urging Langlie to make the race. Through White House push, Langlie became the keynote speaker at the 1956 Republican National Convention. *Time* had him on a preconvention cover, noting that he was favored by the president and a good governor for the state of Washington. His speech, calling for the need for "spiritual inspiration," was a bomb. Adlai Stevenson, again the Democratic presidential nominee, called it "an example of administration smug, self-righteous complacency." *Time's* claim that Langlie was "presidential timber" carried little weight with the state's farmers and union workers. The *New York Times* came closer to the mark, describing Langlie as an "earnest, hard-working, humorless [person] . . . who makes a great point of publicly consulting his conscience."

There was preconvention talk early that summer of Magnuson as a "favorite son" nominee for president at the Democratic gathering. Maggie didn't seem to make much of it, but a home-state supporter, Arthur Garrett, wanted none of it. In a letter to Senator Jackson, Garrett's message was: Maggie "No," Scoop "Yes." For president, he wrote, "you are our best candidate," perhaps planting a seed. Garrett went on to say that Magnuson needed to play ball with the state Democratic organization if he wanted to defeat Langlie.[6]

The *Washington Star*, noting the critical importance of the Magnuson-Langlie race to GOP hopes of controlling the Senate, said those who had heard Langlie's "sermonizing" convention speech would be "astonished at the governor's mud-slinging campaign, roughest in the nation." The governor had expert campaign advice from Murray Chotiner, architect of Richard Nixon's below-the-belt campaign against Helen Douglas in 1950. Chotiner subsequently advised GOP campaigners on the prime "need to deflate the incumbent opposition." Tear down his character.[7] The governor's men took him very seriously in Seattle.

Propelled more by conscience than Murray Chotiner, Langlie's campaign strategy, as one surprising critic noted, was to go after Maggie "with a Bible in one hand, slinging mud with the other." It was as if a Fifth Avenue minister had gone for a brawl with a First Avenue longshoreman. That critic was Harry P. Cain, the former senator, who advised Sherman Adams to supply Langlie with issues to replace the smut and sanctimony.[8] Stranger than Cain's apparent disaffection from the GOP candidate was Langlie's failure to play the "Commie card" against Magnuson as it had been played with success four years earlier against Hugh Mitchell. In the wake of Joe McCarthy's censure, charges of left-wingism may have lost their primal appeal.

If McCarthyism was finished as a political issue, the charges of booze, girls, and shady business never had any life at all, at least when thrown at Magnuson. They probably backfired. Early in the campaign, the senator's office was warned that he would be smeared on "morals" grounds; that Langlie intended to make heavy use of *Confidential* magazine's story on "The Senator and the Starlet." Maggie's secretary, Jessie Robertson, told an Olympia friend that June Millarde (Toni Seven) was "a very nice girl just trying to get along. She spends three days a week working for the

Red Cross. . . . Senator Magnuson is a single man and it would be rather strange if he did not like women and enjoy their company."

"Do you want your senator to go out with boys instead of girls?" Magnuson answered Langlie's campaign charges to the delight of his audiences. "My mother always said boys should go out with girls, not other boys." The line, delivered with an understanding nod, always got a laugh. Maggie was a man's man and a ladies' man. Most of his constituents knew it and approved. Addressing Langlie's frequent identification with the Almighty, Maggie got his biggest campaign laugh by warning a downtown audience that if they wanted a senator to last beyond the coming spring, they'd better vote for him, because "Langlie won't be down here after Easter."[9]

When he crossed the Cascades to campaign in Chelan County, his central Washington campaign chairman, Charles Cone, would introduce the senator with the story about an easterner who asked a rancher how to treat a rattlesnake bite. "Well," said Cone, a future superior court judge, "the rancher told him that you cut the flesh and suck out the poison. If it's in a place hard to reach you get a friend to suck out the poison. But the easterner asked, 'What if the snake bites you on the ass?' Well, the rancher answered, that's when you know you've got a real friend." Then: "Ladies and gentlemen, here's a real friend, Warren Magnuson."[10]

Harder to laugh away were Langlie's innuendoes of back-room business deals that conflicted with Magnuson's public office. Rumors about Magnuson's Northwest Airlines connection were rampant, but unconfirmed despite the efforts of Langlie's campaign sleuths. They were apparently not aware that Magnuson sold his airline stock after becoming chairman of the Senate Commerce Committee in October 1955. He did not want the appearance of a conflict of interest, despite the absence of any congressional rules limiting a member's private business.

In place of evidence, Langlie demanded Magnuson turn over his income tax returns. Initially, Maggie refused. Instead he said, "I've made a few investments in my life. Not too many, but they've turned out well. All of them had been made long before I went to Congress."

That was not quite true. And Langlie said so, again demanding his income tax returns. Indeed, the senator had made subsequent investments in station KBRO and the Melody Company. He may also have been a partner/attorney in other ventures with Bill Edris, his great friend and astute Seattle businessman.

A flock of newspaper editorials followed Langlie's call for Magnuson's tax records like seagulls trailing a garbage scow. The challenger assembled them into a half-page newspaper advertisement. The *Aberdeen World* said,

"Senator Magnuson has not been frank with the people of the state." The *Anacortes American* wondered, "What has Senator Magnuson attempted to conceal?" The *Yakima Republic* declared that, given Maggie's silence, "voters must accept the senator for what Langlie makes him out to be."

The *Ellensburg Record* came close to journalistic truth, writing that there had been "a lot of talk about Magnuson having a salary from a race track information sheet [and] about his owning $40,000 in stock of Queen City Broadcasting Co. when that station is seeking a new TV channel," and that he had been reported to have held "a lot of Northwest Airlines stock [*sic*] which has extensive dealings with the government."[11] Once questioned about the *Northwest News*, the racing sheet, Magnuson said that he had been paid legal fees.

The senator fretted over the income tax issue, discussing it late in the campaign in the Olympic's Suite 823 with Gerry Hoeck, Joe Miller, Irv Hoff, and John Salter. Hoff and Miller remember their surprise when Magnuson said he had decided to release the tax records. They disliked the idea, fearing it might provide Langlie with knockout campaign material. "Remember Billy Conn," said Miller, referring to Conn's loss to Joe Louis in June 1941 by a KO after leading the heavyweight championship fight into the late rounds on points. Magnuson handed the returns to Salter for inspection.

As Miller and Hoff recalled, Salter, the Scoop Jackson aide helping the Maggie campaign, perused the tax returns, then looked up, astonished, and said, "Maggie, you're a [*expletive*] piker!" He had expected the senator to be a man of greater means, unaware that he had sold the Northwest Airlines stock. Magnuson stated publicly that he would release the tax returns "to persons with a legitimate and sincere interest" for their inspection if so requested. The income tax issue died alongside the playboy issue.

President Eisenhower campaigned in Seattle two weeks before the election, pulling an overflow crowd into the Civic Auditorium. Langlie gave the introduction, an attack on Magnuson as a senator who was "not a real success at anything." Ike called Langlie a "man of honesty and integrity." Yet despite his enormous popularity and his easy election victory, Eisenhower lacked coattails. Neither he nor God, as perceived by Langlie, could offset Hoff's astute campaign organization that added extra labor muscle when Washington State Republicans tried to pass a "right to work" initiative outlawing closed union shops and emasculating the union movement. Ike couldn't help Langlie any more than Langlie could help himself. Besides, Eisenhower had more serious matters with which to contend. A week before the election, Soviet troops marched into

Hungary to restore a puppet regime, and Britain, France, and Israel went to war with Egypt to seize the Sinai Desert and secure the Suez Canal. Adlai Stevenson said, "The world is on the brink of war again." But it had no impact on the Senate race in Washington State.

In frustration, Langlie told a friend Magnuson was "morally bankrupt —a divorced man whose personal life is one of debauchery. Yet, these things I cannot get to the people." He said he was fighting a "righteous cause," but that he was "prepared to accept God's will."[12]

God's will on behalf of Langlie, if such it was, amounted to a majority vote in only one county, tiny San Juan. The governor was politically crushed. Maggie never before or since had such a lopsided election victory. Nor had his personal life ever been so treated to public exposure. No matter. Symbolically it was a clear triumph of First Avenue over Fifth Avenue; the sinner over the saint by a margin of nearly a quarter of a million votes. Langlie took the loss with grace, joking with the Olympia press corps and displaying a telegram from June Millarde which said, "Governor Langlie, I'm glad you lost." The subsequent news stories identified June Millarde as "Toni Seven, who was romantically linked to Magnuson." It was one last hit by Langlie. Maggie had no further comment.

Harsh as it had been, Langlie's campaign against the less publicized aspects of Magnuson's life never got much beyond innuendo. In fact, this multifaceted senator delighted in pleasures of sport and flesh, appetites undiminished since his youth at the University of Washington. Maggie got one hundred choice tickets from Jack Hurley for the heavyweight title fight between Seattle's Harry "Kid" Matthews and champion Rocky Marciano in New York. Hurley, an acerbic denizen of the Olympic Hotel, and a pal of Maggie's, managed and trained Matthews. Morris Forgash, a Manhattan businessman, paid for the tickets and threw a prefight party at the Waldorf Astoria for the hundred guests, who included Stub Nelson, political editor of the *Post-Intelligencer* and a favorite of Magnuson's. Matthews lost by a KO in the second round after leading on points. Years later, the pain gone but the memory fresh, a clear-eyed Harry Matthews, fighter turned locksmith, could laugh about the bout: "We fought to a draw. I won the first round [on points], Marciano won the second [by KO]."[13]

At the end of 1954, George Killion, president of the American President Lines, invited Magnuson aboard one of his ships for a Pacific cruise. The senator accepted. Killion also wanted legislation allowing the sale of the vessels *President Wilson* and *President Cleveland* from the Maritime Administration to his line.

Forgash, Norman Winston, Mary Lasker, wealthy Manhattanites, and Killion were genuinely fond of Magnuson. A major contractor, Winston also wanted to construct housing at Kelly, Brooks, and Lackland Air Force bases in Texas." They took him under their wings," said Irv Hoff. Winston was an extraordinarily rich internationalist who "knew everybody," and frequently entertained on his yacht on Long Island Sound, Maggie among the guests. Forgash had a New York business which had been boosted by the Commerce Committee's legal designation of freight forwarders as common carriers. It made a favorable difference in his business rates. Forgash was also a yachtsman, owner-skipper of the *Natamor* docked in Miami. In March 1954, Magnuson hooked up on the *Natamor* with an old friend, Elvira Wildman, then a businesswoman in Havana. Mrs. Lasker pressed Magnuson for cancer research funds.[14] All were helpful with campaign contributions, but their main interest, said Hoff, was "the enjoyment of being at least at the periphery of a king-maker, Magnuson. If they, or anyone else, had requests, the Boss would listen. He'd help if the request was reasonable and in the public interest."[15]

Looking at Magnuson was like inspecting a diamond. If Langlie could perceive only the First Avenue reflection, others saw a radically different person. There is an amazing analysis of Magnuson made in 1955 by Mrs. V. C. Evans, an admirer and a chance acquaintance who had once served as personnel director at the Naval Air Station in Oak Harbor, Washington. She based the eight-page character profile on his photograph and handwriting. Marked "personal and confidential" and sent to Magnuson, it said, in sum:

> You have a forceful, clear-cut personality. You can put things together with a sense of rhythm and smoothness. . . . Ideas come faster to you than subordinates can carry out. Your analytical ability is strong. You always need to know "why." You have a true love of beauty and harmony. You are tactful, warm-hearted, far above average in intelligence and have a desire to share everything, time energy and ideas. You can say a great deal in a few words . . . a born leader, an optimist. You have yearned for success . . . there's a need to reach the top. You are light on your feet, graceful, but sometimes sell yourself short. . . . [O]thers realize your power more than you.[16]

There are few who knew Magnuson, even his ideological opposites, who could disagree with this uncanny portrait of the politician. Oddly, it doesn't conflict with Langlie's hard-shell Presbyterian view of Magnuson. The trouble with Langlie's perception is that it was too narrow. It was also politically unproductive, if not politically motivated.

Not even the effusive analysis by Mrs. Evans pictures Magnuson as a scholar. However, he read books, probably more than the average politician. His library was large, filled mainly with works of history and biography. He had a great interest in books on Abraham Lincoln and on his hero, Franklin Roosevelt. There are several Bibles in the collection, and, slipped in among these serious volumes, a copy of *USA Confidential*. It is not the collection of an uneducated man. In his later years Maggie seemed to intentionally play down his erudition.

Early in 1954, replying to a query from Northland College of Ashland, Wisconsin, Magnuson listed the books that had "influenced his thinking": the Bible, *The Decline of the West* by the German philosopher Oswald Spengler, *The Education of Henry Adams*, and books by Elbert Hubbard, an eclectic, if not unique, influence. Unlike Adams and Spengler, Elbert Hubbard will never be mistaken as a major factor in twentieth-century thought. His turn-of-the-century books dealt mainly with the lives of great philosophers, writers, and musicians. They were books aimed at individual uplift, a trait they share with the writings of Horatio Alger. Hubbard's comments about Ludwig van Beethoven must have hit home for the orphan boy from Moorhead, who did not know his parents and did not like his adoptive father.

"Have you ever shared the mocking shame and biting pain of a drunkard's household?" wrote Hubbard on Beethoven. "Relationship is a matter of kinship, not blood. . . . do we wonder at the question who is my mother and [who are] my brethren? Beethoven was one of the plain people of the earth. . . . the only aristocracy he acknowledged was the aristocracy of the intellect."

American Prime Time

S enator Magnuson could have felt invincible, returning to Congress in 1957, carried by the overwhelming approval of his constituents; a ring-wise legislator, well schooled in addition to his natural talents. He was chairman of the Commerce Committee, the clearinghouse for legislation affecting the nation's commercial businesses and its economic arteries—airlines, railroads, highways, and shipping.

His private life was beginning to crystallize around a single mate, a beautiful Seattle widow named Jermaine Peralta, and a crisply defined code of conduct. Magnuson's personal letters reflect a shift to monogamy with the woman he would eventually wed, a Seattle native, graduate of Garfield High School, and a model at Adrians of Beverly Hills, a fashion salon. They met at the Olympic Hotel, where Jermaine worked in a jewelry shop after her return to Seattle.

"My philosophy of life," Magnuson explained in a letter to Clara Walker of Riverton, Wyoming, "is not complicated. Be steadfast to friends, tolerant of those who oppose you, respect the aspirations of all Americans. Be helpful to fellow citizens."[1] He was living those words. It was a good time for Senator Magnuson.

It was a good time for the nation. Dwight Eisenhower, elected to a second term, presided over a country at peace with the world and at the peak of its domestic affluence. A generation of Americans said to be "silent" was changing the national landscape by moving to the green suburbs surrounding our urban areas, a passage speeded by construction of four-lane interstate highways. Ford and General Motors ruled the international auto market. Nissan and Honda were strange, foreign words, rarely uttered.

The internal Communist witch-hunts had subsided as the nation's attention shifted to the potential threat from the other superpower, the Soviet Union, and its mighty ally, "Red" China. This happened quickly when economists discovered an arms buildup against Moscow and Beijing was far better for business than the pursuit of left-wing college professors and Hollywood screenwriters. Politicians were shifting with the new focus. Boeing and Bremerton were beneficiaries of the change.

If President Truman checked the spread of communism in postwar Western Europe, Turkey, and Greece with the Marshall Plan, President Eisenhower prevented a possible Soviet military invasion of Europe through a massive buildup of American forces in NATO, the reinstallation of a West German army, and an armistice in Korea. For the first five years of the 1950s the Soviet threat in Europe was taken most seriously by his top military commanders—his comrades in arms in World War II—if not by Eisenhower himself.[2] By 1957, they could relax somewhat. Some, including Vice President Richard Nixon, pressed for U.S. intervention in Vietnam, where a nationalist movement led by a charismatic Communist, Ho Chi Minh, was driving a spike in European colonialism, forcing a French retreat back to Europe. President Eisenhower did not want American troops in a jungle war on the opposite side of the planet. It was not in the national interest, which, in fact, did lie across the Atlantic. Would that his successors had seen it so clearly.

This landscape of American serenity wasn't without its seismic rumbles. The Supreme Court's 1954 decision in *Brown v. Board of Education* ended nearly a century of "separate but equal" common schooling, a decision culminating three years later in the racial integration of Central High School in Little Rock, Arkansas. Eisenhower dispatched the 101st Airborne Division to keep peace in the city against a defiant governor, Orval Faubus, and his white segregationist constituency. It was the gravest clash between federal authority and states' rights since the surrender of the Confederacy at Appomattox Court House. Less conspicuous were the "sit-ins" of blacks in segregated public facilities, dime-store lunch counters and city parks; blips on the society's Richter scale, but certain stimulants to the conscience of a Northwest populist such as Warren Magnuson. American apartheid was beginning to crumble.

In the midst of the Little Rock school crisis, the Soviet Union launched a soccer-ball-sized satellite that orbited earth, emitting a high-pitched "beep-beep" that shook the nation like nothing since the Japanese bombs at Pearl Harbor. If the Soviets could place a satellite into earth orbit, they could fire a nuclear weapon into New York or Washington. A comparable reaction today would be the arrest and debriefing of a space alien. The country went into panic over science. Concern with space rocketed to the top of the national agenda, a change bearing extensive repercussions. Eisenhower engaged a science adviser, James Killian of the Massachusetts Institute of Technology, and soon thereafter, so did Congress. Dr. Edward Wenk, chief engineer in the design and testing of the *Nautilus*, the first U.S. nuclear-powered submarine, became adviser to Congress on science and technology, an office created with the blessing of Magnuson and the Commerce Committee. Senator Lyndon Johnson, the majority leader, became first chairman of the Committee on Aeronautics and Space, matters at the top of the scientific pecking order.

Near the bottom was the science of the oceans—oceanography. Senator Hubert Humphrey, Democrat from Minnesota, moved to change this, introducing a measure calling for an integrated study of the oceans. As head of the Commerce Committee, where it was referred, Magnuson pushed the bill that within a few years would lead to the establishment of the National Oceanographic and Atmospheric Administration (NOAA).[3] An aide, Featherstone Reid, describes Magnuson, the extraordinary legislator, as a "romantic" about water. The senator could also be described as the father of NOAA. Integrating the ocean research and pursuing the money to fund it, Magnuson brashly played the Soviet card: "We're competing with the Soviets in the oceans as well as in space." It was a new fact of American life, a core part of the cold war: by raising the Soviet threat you could move mountains or budgets. By June 1959, in articles written for the Hearst newspapers, Maggie called it "The Wet War—a Struggle for the Oceans," and contrasted the $8 billion space budget with the $8 million allocated for ocean research. He even sounded biblical: "What will it profit if we win the skies and lose the oceans; if the oceans are infested with Soviet submarines?"[4] In addition to funds for more subs and research, Maggie pitched for an expanded fleet of new vessels for an American merchant marine still sailing the Liberty, Victory, and C-3 veterans of World War II.[5] This would be good business for the underemployed shipyards of the South and West Coast. Not so apparent, but equally significant to the nation's higher education, Maggie ensured that federal funds from the National Science Foundation would be parceled in grants to colleges and universities rather than in fellowships. Fellowships, he reasoned, would tilt the federal largesse overwhelmingly to the eastern Ivy League colleges. Grants would spread the money to public schools around the nation, not the least of these being his University of Washington.

Although his impact on national policy had greatly increased, Magnuson insisted on seeing himself as a "local" politician, representative of the people of one state. The *Seattle Times*, not the *New York Times*, was "his" newspaper, Magnuson lectured an aide as he dismissed a profile request from the most influential organ of American journalism. He eschewed a high profile for the "kitchenwork" of the committee and the cloakroom, where he attended to the needs of friends and constituents. He remained acutely sensitive to home folks. In a staff memo "re expenses" written soon after his reelection in 1956, Magnuson said, "Don't send unnecessary telegrams. Write them in ten words or less. Eliminate words not essential to a clear meaning of the message. The people of the state notice these things." Those, incidentally, are words for other writers to live by.

Seafirst Bank's (Seattle-First National) Lawrence Arnold appealed for help early in 1958 on the sale of Boeing 707 jet passenger craft to Northwest Airlines. "Bill Allen and Wellwood Beale [Boeing's top brass] would be most grateful for any assistance in the sale, a very substantial piece of business." Maggie replied, noting, "I'm glad the president [Eisenhower] bought those 707s today—I worked on this one."[6] One of these craft would become Air Force One, the presidential jet, which was eventually replaced by a bigger Boeing plane, the 747.

The senator stayed close to his friends in Manhattan. Norman Winston, the megamillionaire builder turned salesman of U.S. goods in Western and Eastern Europe, kept the senator informed on progress at trade fairs in Moscow and Brussels. Early in 1957, with Jermaine as hostess, Magnuson entertained Ruth and Frank Stanton at the Palm Springs, California, retreat he eventually would purchase from Bill Edris. Stanton, chairman of CBS, had business with the Federal Communications Commission. Winston had a vital interest in building contracts on U.S. military bases.[7] Magnuson's columnist friend Drew Pearson chided Maggie, "a fine senator 99 percent of the time," for having a "weak spot re TV." Pearson wrote that Stanton's CBS had been quick to affiliate with KIRO when the Seattle station got its television license in the late 1950s; a natural partnership since KIRO had long been a CBS radio affiliate. Despite Pearson's innuendo, it's doubtful Haas needed help from Magnuson or anyone else in his connection with Stanton. The politically astute newsman had charms of his own. The columnist also noted the failure of a 1956 Commerce Committee investigation to uncover "glaring scandals" in the FCC. In one of these alleged scandals G. T. Baker, president of National Airlines, claimed seven senators, including Magnuson, approached FCC members "in behalf" of a losing applicant for a Miami television license. A National Airlines subsidiary got the license, despite what Baker said was "wire pulling" by the other side. The White House denied such outside pressure. In behalf of his committee and the seven senators named by Baker, Magnuson categorically denied any interference at any time.[8] Nevertheless, his financial interest in KIRO, the CBS affliate, and friendship with Stanton, the CBS chairman, left the senator open to such attacks. He had a weak spot. In fact, his relations with Winston and Stanton went beyond professional concerns. They had mutual interests and personal attraction. It was the same with George Killion, head of American President Lines (APL).

Later in 1957, with Jermaine, Magnuson would cruise around the world on an APL passenger liner, courtesy of the astute Killion, who began to press the case for a renewed China trade on his Senate buddy. It was akin to preaching Catholicism to the pope. Magnuson had a lifelong interest in China. His feeling that Chinese made especially good American citizens led to his successful fight early in his congressional career to repeal their exclusion from U.S. immigration. Killion noted the senator's urging of air routes to Red China and reminded him that it was also time to start steamship connections to the forbidden [by the State Department] Communist empire.[9] Both air and sea connections would come in time, but not without a frenzied emotional controversy. There were still many Americans, possibly a majority, who felt that a perfidious Truman administration, not a Communist revolution against a corrupt regime, caused the United States to "lose China." Magnuson never fell for that historic absurdity—had China been ours to lose?—and, probably because of his friendship with Joe McCarthy, never suffered from it. But for two decades his was a lonely voice that the powerful lobby of the Kuomintang—the Chinese nationalists ousted from the mainland to Taiwan—and their many political friends would attempt to throttle. Throughout the China controversy, Magnuson maintained a warm friendship with Madame Chiang Kai-shek, tribute to his personal charm and understanding.

Brock Adams, then a rising Democratic star in Seattle, later a congressman and secretary of transportation, remembers the bitter response attending a debate before the Women's University Club in Seattle in 1956. Alongside Magnuson, he faced off against University of Washington professors George Taylor and Donald Treadgold, respected scholars hostile to relations with Red China. Adams and Magnuson pressed the case for a China trade—good national policy and good for business in Seattle to boot. The audience, like most other Americans, sided with Taylor and Treadgold, leaving the politically ambitious Adams with the uncomfortable feeling of hanging out on a limb.[10]

But it wasn't a unanimous judgment. Fred Haley, a Tacoma candy manufacturer with an eye on Far Eastern sales, a liberal Democrat unaffected by the China lobby, wrote in the *Argus*: "Magnuson has done the nation a service by bringing to its attention the ridiculous position of the administration on trade with China. Everybody else is getting a share of the China market. So should we."[11]

China, like health research, dams, commerce, and communications, remained a highlight of Magnuson's political vision. Of all the major players in twentieth-century American politics, none had a clearer understanding of the Chinese dilemma, and—just as important—held on to public office. In November 1945, Magnuson could see that "China is unable to maintain a stable government. The U.S. wants to see a great Chinese democracy, but it can't possibly be democratic in terms of the American conception. If Communists win North China, it will be a Communist country. If the Kuomintang [Nationalists] win, a semblance of a dictatorship will be set up."[12] Communists, of course, won in 1949, providing Republicans with a potent campaign issue for the next two decades. Magnuson's seatmate, Henry Jackson, fast becoming a leading Senate voice on national security, steered clear of the China controversy.

The 1958 election was a breeze for Jackson, an established figure of probity and common sense. Aided by a political tail wind, union workers aroused against a business-backed initiative to eliminate closed union shops in the workplace, Jackson won a lopsided victory over Republican William "Big Bill" Bantz. Newspapers began to talk of Scoop as a potential Democratic vice presidential nominee. It was a big year for Democrats across the nation. In Massachusetts, John Kennedy won election to a second term in the Senate.

It was not that good for Brock Adams, a stalwart in Magnuson's 1956 campaign against Arthur Langlie as the organizer of Young Democrats across the state. Adams, the President's Medal winner for scholarship and student activities at the University of Washington, returned to Seattle from Harvard Law School as a prime contact with the ambitious Senator Kennedy. Adams was the only student in the University of Washington's history to be both student body president and the top scholastic graduate in his class (1950). He was equally ambitious, requesting Magnuson's support in a race for King County prosecutor against the Republican incumbent, Charles O. Carroll. It placed Magnuson in a tricky position. Carroll, Maggie's college acquaintance, had carried on Seattle's tradition of "tolerance" toward the city's tenderloin activity. And Carroll was close to Magnuson's Teamsters Union pals, the boss, Dave Beck, and his assistant Frank Brewster, as well as to the city's downtown business establishment. Maggie tried to discourage Adams as "too young." Adams persisted until he got a major favor—the campaign help of Magnuson's excellent assistant, Irv Hoff, and Hoff's wife, Florence. Maggie laid low, but the campaign brilliance of the Hoffs nearly pulled it off for the youthful Adams. Mindful of Magnuson and the power of the city's business establishment, and the Teamster muscle, Adams downplayed the

President Lyndon Johnson signs the Civil Rights Act, July 2, 1964. To his rear: Dr. Martin Luther King, Jr. To the right: House Speaker John McCormack and Magnuson, "capstone" of the legislation. WGM Papers, UW Libraries

Warren and Jermaine cut their wedding cake for best man President Johnson and Lady Bird Johnson, 1964. WGM Papers, UW Libraries

Stan Barer, first of Magnuson's "Bumblebees" and clerk assigned to prepare Title II of the Civil Rights Act. WGM Papers, UW Libraries

Senators Jackson and Magnuson flank Sam Volpentest, some-time tavern-keeper and all-time savior (with Maggie's help) of Washington State's Tri-Cities. WGM Papers, UW Libraries

Herb Legg, political agitator, philosopher, innovator, and Democratic State Chairman, circa 1961, with Magnuson and the peerless Edward R. Murrow of CBS and Bellingham, Washington. WGM Papers, UW Libraries

Mrs. Albert Lasker, the whip behind Magnuson's appropriations for medical research, presents her friend with the Lasker Award, medicine's answer to the Nobel Prize. WGM Papers, UW Libraries

Senators Magnuson and Jackson, Gov. Dan Evans, and entrepreneur Zollie Volchok honor Seattle patriarch Joshua Green (seated). WGM Papers, UW Libraries

Magnuson squeezed extra unemployment benefits from House Ways and Means Chairman Wilbur Mills (center), whom, to the distress of aides, he addressed as "Orville." HEW Secretary Ribicoff smiles. WGM Papers, UW Libraries

Boeing officials, including designer Maynard Pennell (second from right), show Magnuson their proposed Supersonic Transport in a pitch for federal funds— prelude to one of Magnuson's rare Senate defeats. WGM Papers, UW Libraries

Reps. Mike McCormack and Lloyd Meeds huddle with Maggie
at the 1972 Democratic National Convention. McCormack was
one of several promised Magnuson's seat, should he leave it
prematurely, by Gov. Dixy Lee Ray. WGM Papers, UW Libraries

Magnuson and Republican Congressman Joel Pritchard, a key
player in Magnuson's bill to save marine mammals in Puget
Sound. WGM Papers, UW Libraries

Magnuson in Beijing, July 1973, with Vice Premier Chou En-lai. The joke? Only Maggie or Chou could tell, and they never talked. WGM Papers, UW Libraries

Magnuson, the longest active yet still politically viable advocate of normal relations with China, gives a plaque to Deng Xiaoping during the Chinese leader's visit to Seattle in 1979. WGM Papers, UW Libraries

Banquet buddies: Magnuson, President-elect Jimmy Carter, and Ralph Nader, the dynamo forcing corporate responsibility, November 1976. WGM Papers, UW Libraries

Warren and Lyndon—Magnuson never addressed him as "Mr. President"—
confer in the Oval Office aboard Air Force One. WGM Papers, UW Libraries

Vice President Walter Mondale swears in Magnuson as Senate President Pro Tempore—the peak of the senator's ambition—January 1979. Mrs. Magnuson is approving. WGM Papers, UW Libraries

Warren and Jermaine with Virginia and Jim McDermott when it appeared both politicians would triumph in the 1980 election. They didn't. WGM Papers, UW Libraries

Seattle Post-Intelligencer editor Lou Guzzo with Magnuson, Jermaine, and Harley Dirks, the "booze and shoes" merchant from Othello, Washington, turned invisible Senate power as clerk of an Appropriations subcommittee. Mrs. Dirks is at Harley's side. WGM Papers, UW Libraries

In happier times, Gov. Dixy Lee Ray poses between Senator and Mrs. Magnuson during a Democratic dinner. Ray would later call Magnuson a "dictator." The senator privately referred to Ray as "Madame Zonga."

Magnuson's vision of Christmas Eve in a small village. Like another master of politics, Winston Churchill, Magnuson painted for relaxation and did so from his own visions.

Twilight of a forty-eight-year political career: Magnuson in his office in the Old Senate Office Building at the close of a ten-hour work day. WGM Papers, UW Libraries

tolerance policy as an issue. It screamed for attention, but he lacked evidence tying Carroll directly to any legal indiscretion. He lost to the powerful Carroll by only 12,000 votes, a showing sufficient to make him the Democratic Party's crown prince and a sure contender for U.S. district attorney after the 1960 election.[13]

In the aftermath of the 1958 election, Magnuson's up-and-down relationship with Hearst's *Seattle Post-Intelligencer* took another swing. Ed Stone, the editor, said he was exasperated at the senator for "dealing exclusively with the *Seattle Times*. . . . If you think we are amenable to being kicked around, you are mistaken." Royal Brougham, the newspaper's venerable sports editor, followed a few days later with a note saying Stone killed an item in his column telling of Magnuson's help in getting a Russian baseball team to play in Seattle. "He [Stone] has a gripe about something," said Brougham.

Magnuson did not reply to Brougham's tip that Stone was angry, but later he gave the *Post-Intelligencer* an interview sure to raise hackles, if not newspaper circulation, in Seattle. He proposed trade with China, an end to "the most stupid policy we could follow [which] is to pretend 700 million people in the world don't exist."[14] Despite the city's proximity to China and its history of a lucrative China trade (Pier 91 was the West Coast depot for silk traffic), the idea of normal relations with China in late 1959 remained repugnant to the vast majority, including a lot of Seattleites who would later profit from such commerce.

Harry Bridges's longshoremen's union, however, began a China-trade clamor. Louis Goldblatt, the leftist, and therefore suspect, secretary-treasurer of the longshoremen, proposed to Vice President Nixon that representatives of the shipping industry go to China to explore the potential of trade. "There's no question that the overwhelming interest of the shipping industry is for an end to the China trade barrier and a revival of normal trade with China," wrote Goldblatt, copies to Magnuson and George Killion.

"An appeal to Nixon is futile," Killion wrote Magnuson. "Senate hearings on the West Coast are a much better alternative."[15] As a footnote he said he was interested in the secretary to Maggie's good friend, former Assistant Defense Secretary Anna Rosenberg, and earlier, as an adviser to the Pentagon on manpower, a prime mover behind the racial integration of the U.S. military.[16] Killion said the San Francisco Chamber of Commerce looked favorably on China hearings.

"The [China trade] movement is gaining momentum," Maggie wrote Killion. "I see the signs in the State Department and when you get them to move—that's something. We might hold hearings if I can come up with enough [Commerce] committee members to make it official. Otherwise, it might look self-serving in view of my prolonged activity in this field." He also reported the name of Anna Rosenberg's secretary, Mariam [Chickie] Chaikan, the attractive former lobbyist for the American Committee for a Free Palestine.

If the China story did not assuage the feelings of the *Post-Intelligencer* editor, Maggie had other means. He extended to Richard Berlin, chief executive of Hearst Newspapers, entree to friends among the state's leading political and business circles. Berlin thanked him, saying, "I didn't realize you had so many warm friends in high places." And late in the summer of 1959, prelude to the coming election year, Bill Edris allowed that he had a good talk with Charles Lindeman. "I think you'll get a better go in the P-I in the next election," Edris wrote Magnuson, a politician with other nagging problems that year.

Maggie's leg was in a cast and his ego somewhat bruised by wags who didn't want to accept the fact that he had dropped a case of salmon on his foot, breaking bones. There was the matter of rent for Mrs. Helene Cordery at 415 East 52nd Street, Manhattan—$270 for the month of February. Helene, a vestige of his life before Jermaine, was in Mexico and hadn't met the bill. She was also nagging for an introduction to Frank Stanton at CBS.[17] Years later he would advise a young aide, "Never have a girlfriend in Manhattan—too expensive. Find somebody down at the Agriculture Department." Presumably, Agriculture employees were not long off the farm and not likely to have cultivated expensive tastes.[18]

Throughout the 1950s, Magnuson kept a good measure of the Commerce Committee action focused on East-West trade, stimulated by reports from Norman Winston and his own travels to the Far East. All the while he worked for the creation of NOAA and ocean research. Otherwise, the committee had yet to distinguish itself in that pleasant decade of U.S. world supremacy as a protector of American consumers and as a vessel for uniting American society. Instead, the Commerce Committee was known for its staff freebies and its use as a magnet for members' campaign contributions. Vested interests were most influential, their lobbyists comfortable with committee staff, which consisted of six clerks. The revolution had yet to come. When it did, the staff increased to 120.

Nevertheless, Magnuson's influence inside the Capitol flourished, a function of his easy style in concert with extraordinary legislative skills. Irv Hoff, nearing the end of his tenure as Magnuson's chief aide, says Lyndon Johnson told him, "Maggie can smile though more legislation than any other senator can get through by wheeling and dealing. Most legislators are burdened by 100 pounds of hate on their backs. Maggie doesn't hate anybody."[19]

"He had a casual way of doing business," says Featherstone Reid, an aide for nearly thirty years. "He gleaned intelligence from casual contact on the Senate floor and in the cloakroom or over poker at the Burning Tree Country Club [where he did not play golf]. He was trained in the old school. You served an apprenticeship and waited your turn. He would tell each new senator, 'If I can be of help to you, let me know.' He meant it—and nobody, absolutely nobody, was ever better at counting Senate votes."[20]

Magnuson, the "local politician," kept his state at the forefront of his interests. Nothing served the state so much as hydroelectric dams, the source of cheap electric power and good jobs: Northwest prosperity. Chief Joseph, McNary, and Ice Harbor Dams are direct products of federal funds provided by Maggie's clout. He helped mightily with other dams built by Public Utility Districts on the Snake and Columbia Rivers. How did one senator manage such monumental public works? There was, of course, his institutional power as chairman of Commerce Committee and the Appropriations subcommittee on Health and Education. More important was his well-honed legislative manner.

"His colleagues would say, 'We know Maggie has problems with his constituents. We've got problems he'll help with.' And they would help," said Hoff. "He got those dams started in the Rivers and Harbors subcommittee of Appropriations. Chairman Carl Hayden [Democrat, Arizona] would open requests for pet projects. The key, Magnuson understood, was to get planning money, initially a modest sum, then to get a little more money each session, allowing the project to balloon. Eventually so much had been invested, the project had to be completed."[21]

The *Reader's Digest*, in an article hostile to public power, noted the process: "The Northwest cries 'power shortage—build more dams!' And Congress, bit by bit, seems to oblige."[22]

There was give and take inside the Appropriations subcommittee. Once Senator Richard Russell, Democrat from Georgia, wanted a $250,000 addition to the budget for a dredging project in Georgia. Magnuson approved. Maggie wanted $1 million for planning the Ice Harbor Dam. As Irv Hoff tells it, "Russell objected: 'You're setting a precedent.' Magnuson said, 'No. You just set a precedent by getting additional money for your dredging project.' Maggie got the money."

Lyndon Johnson subsequently mentioned a newspaper headline— "Maggie Unfreezes Ice Harbor"—in a birthday greeting to his old pal. "I heard in Texas you campaign for reelection on the slogan 'My daddy told me never to trust a man who wouldn't take a drink," Johnson wrote, adding, "whether you are unfreezing Ice Harbor or explaining the facts of life to the people, you'll always find me a Maggie man. . . . I don't know of any better man to be by my side in a tough spot than you. The state can be proud of the Magnuson contribution to the party and the country."[23]

Johnson's chief counsel, Harry McPherson, a Texan educated at the University of the South, says his immutable image of Magnuson came from the Senate floor fights over Hells Canyon, the giant chasm forming the border between Oregon and Idaho; debates on best use of its Snake River water carried the regional battle between public and private power to national headlines. "Hells Canyon" is a metaphor for this classic division: Republicans pro–private power; Democrats, populists and conservationists—the proto "environmentalists"—favoring, in this instance, a publicly owned high dam in the canyon.

The clash between these conflicting philosophies went back and forth in the 1950s, to the advantage of Idaho Power Company, the private utility, with Eisenhower's election. Idaho Power wanted three smaller dams, privately financed, in Hells Canyon instead of the one high dam, à la Grand Coulee, that would also serve navigation, recreation, irrigation, and flood control. The debate, now drawing national interest, came to a focus on the Senate floor in exchanges between Idaho Power's Senate champion, Herman Welker, Republican from Idaho, and Magnuson.

"I've always advocated [sic] the government not getting into the power business, the law business or any other business," said Welker, smarting from an earlier exchange with Maggie.

"My policy is for government to go where private enterprise won't," replied Magnuson. "I still stick to it. Without the federal government going into the Columbia River we would not have our dams—the basis of our economic foundation, the basis of thousands of jobs, hundreds of corporate enterprises. It has given us the cheapest hydro power in the world."

"Will the senator yield to a question that these dams were paid for by the American taxpayers?" said Welker.

"I will not yield to that," replied Magnuson. "It was not paid for by American taxpayers. The federal government loaned us money to build those dams. We're paying it back with interest."

"Since you believe in federal control through the Columbia Valley Authority," Welker answered, "would you not agree to have timber, minerals, all the natural resources given by God, controlled by the government of the U.S.?"

"There is no comparison," answered Maggie. "Private firms have developed timber and mines and have done a good job. But 20 years ago private power did not do a good job developing dams—it couldn't have built Grand Coulee."

And later Magnuson, eloquent and detailed in his knowledge of the Hells Canyon proposals, said despite Idaho Power's charge of "creeping socialism," their proposed three dams would cost more to build, and would cost those consumers "forced by Idaho Power to buy their electricity or use coal-oil lamps" 6.69 mills per kilowatt hour—about double the cost of power coming from the established Columbia River dams. Backed by the administration, Idaho Power prevailed.[24]

But Magnuson wasn't finished with Herman Welker, who carried President Eisenhower's fight to "privatize" (sell to private interests) publicly owned facilities, most conspicuous being the hugely successful Tennessee Valley Authority. Maggie listened to Welker's privatization rhetoric with growing irritation. Finally he got to his feet on the floor and roared at Welker: "Are you going to add Fort Knox to the privatization list?" Stunned by the tone, if not the content, of Magnuson's attack, the Idaho senator left the Senate floor in tears. Irv Hoff asked for an explanation. Welker said, "Maggie just kicked me one right in the crotch."

"My image of Maggie is this magnificent populist arguing with passion for the public interest over corporate profits," recalled McPherson, who likened him to Hollywood's version of the idealistic senator played by James Stewart in *Mr. Smith Goes to Washington*.[25] Maggie's skills in debate and oratory on the Senate floor were overshadowed by his "kitchenwork" in the back rooms and committees on behalf of Northwest dams, although not lost on the perceptive and admiring McPherson.

As essential as these dams were to the Northwest economy, it became equally important to arrange with Canada an equitable sharing of Columbia River water. The river comes out of the Rocky Mountains in eastern British Columbia and into Washington State at Kettle Falls. Joined by the Snake River, it curves west toward the Pacific, forming the natural border between Oregon and Washington in an immense and beautiful gorge. Under Magnuson's aegis, Howard MacGowan and his young attorney, Gordon Culp, a former member of Senator Jackson's staff, began work in 1959 on the U.S.–Canada treaty to coordinate water storage in Canada and power generation downstream in Washington. Five dams on the Middle Columbia in Washington State—Rocky Reach, Rock Island, Wanapum, Wells, and the notorious Priest Rapids—agreed to compensate British Columbia for construction of three new storage dams in that province. Negotiations between the provincial and federal governments of Canada and the half-dozen private and public utilities in Washington State were complex, but once done Maggie carried the treaty through the White House and Senate. The agreement, lasting for the balance of the century, was a model of international cooperation; for that matter, the model of a proper "McGoozle," a win-win situation for both sides, the U.S. and Canada.[26]

The Central Intelligence Agency tipped Maggie on another power scheme during the U.S.–Canadian negotiations, this one the far-out brainchild of one Arkady Markin, who identified himself as a "Soviet power engineer." He was apparently attracted to Magnuson's international reputation for dam building. The Soviet scheme: dam the Bering Strait between Alaska and Siberia and then pump warmer Pacific water into the Arctic Ocean in order to soften the Arctic climate. In a footnote to this message, the CIA correspondent, one Paul Borel, said Markin, the alleged "power engineer," was really a reporter with knowledge of Siberia. There's no record of a reply from Magnuson, a man with his hands full of problems arranging a Columbia River treaty; no indication of the CIA's interest in the mad Russian scheme.[27]

Seattle, Maggie's adopted hometown, was the city with most to gain from cheap power from the dams and the Canadian treaty. Barely one hundred years old, the seaport was about to attempt to shake its provincial image with a world's fair, an effort founded on Senator Magnuson's mighty ways with the appropriation of federal funds. In Seattle the senator raised eyebrows when his name appeared along with the "Edris Corp." on an office door in a building at 1012 Fourth Avenue. Asked to explain, Magnuson said Edris and he had the office "in a legal capacity," even though he had long ago ceased to practice law. "I still hang my hat in the place occasionally when I'm home." Whatever other functions the small office may have served, it gave Magnuson a place to get away from his official office—and its telephones—in the federal courthouse on Fifth Avenue, a few blocks south.

There was no total escape from his past lifestyle, however. June Millarde (Toni Seven), whose pinup pictures had graced the front pages of Seattle's newspapers and fueled its political gossip, was passé in Magnuson's love life but still in need of his help. Broke, thirty-six years old, and ineligible for an inheritance for another four years, she asked Warren for a loan and a private talk. The upshot was a $550 loan. As a friend, Warren was forever faithful. The tone of this exchange between tongue-in-cheek Bill Edris and Jessie Robertson regarding the Palm Springs away-from-it-all retreat of choice for Hollywood elite suggests Maggie was also forever preoccupied with Senate work.

"You're working for a no-good so and so—you fill in the blanks," Edris wrote Jessie. "His pool breaks down [at the home in Palm Springs] and he leaves me to fix it. Who in the hell does he think he is? Come time for campaign funds and I won't know who in the hell he is. He can go to hell. . . . I see by the papers he is busy pressuring the FCC in behalf of his friend [Saul] Haas—you sleep with dogs, you get fleas. . . . Tell him [Bill] Perlberg got $150 from [Charles] Lindeman, part of a football bet."

Perlberg, a Hollywood producer, took Lindeman, the *Post-Intelligencer* publisher and a new member of Maggie's Seattle crowd, on a football bet while at the Palm Springs home. Maggie, no doubt, did nothing to impede KIRO from acquiring its television broadcast license, despite Edris's feelings about Haas, the KIRO chairman.

Jessie Robertson replied to Edris that "the boss" had seen his letter, and knew his judgment was sound and that he would do a good job fixing the swimming pool. She then said, "The boss is working like a horse on committee agenda work, 9:30 am to midnight. Sometimes I wonder why anybody wants these jobs—how lucky you are to loaf and play in the sunshine in Palm Springs."

"Just kidding!" replied Edris to Jessie. "You're losing your sense of humor." The loyal Jessie closed with another note: "I enjoyed your letter—but there was just a grain of truth in it. Still, we love you and send love and kisses." There was nothing said about help for Saul Haas on the TV license, or the fact that behind the scenes Magnuson successfully pushed for a ban on liquor advertisements on television. He did it with friendly persuasion, rather than a federal law or a ruling by the FCC. "Maggie called down all the television-radio network executives and told them they ought to voluntarily agree not to advertise liquor and to tone down their beer ads," recalled KING Broadcasting's Ancil Payne. "They concurred."[28]

Magnuson subsequently rushed to the side of newspapers, at the urging of Lindeman, opposing a measure to ban liquor ads in newsprint publications. He doubted the measure's constitutionality. In a letter to the Seattle publisher, Maggie noted his "responsibility" for a voluntary agreement to ban liquor ads on television and to keep beer ads "in good taste," a small matter of national interest, perhaps, but moves worth major fortunes in advertising revenues to newspapers. In a backroom conversation with TV executives, he had shifted millions of dollars in ad revenue from television to newspapers. Such was the man's Capitol influence, a source of some wonder.

"Maggie didn't get his way by making speeches," said Irv Hoff, musing on that influence. "Once at the University of Washington in the '50s

Magnuson and Jackson were giving back-to-back speeches to students, Jackson first, a good speech, full of facts and logic. The students gave him a mild, polite response. Maggie got up, talked without any specifics, and held the students in the palm of his hand. He got a standing ovation. Amazing. Later I asked him about speeches. He said, 'the purpose of a speech is not to give information but to make people like you. If I can go out with people feeling I'm a good fellow, that's my objective.' "[29]

Maggie got his way, in some critical part, because he made people—fellow senators—think him a good fellow. Without that good fellowship, he could not have wielded the power of the Commerce Committee—the stick that brought sweet reason to the network executives on the liquor issue.

The decade of the 1950s closed with Magnuson more influential than ever, a "local" politician inevitably drawn to issues shaping American society. The temper of American blacks seeking civil rights rose dramatically with their sit-ins and marches. Their mood carried the sentiments of white liberals like Harold Bailey, who expressed outrage over white southerners' treatment of blacks. Magnuson replied that the 1957 civil rights bill was "the strongest bill that could be pushed through Congress against Southern opposition." And he added in a prescient footnote, "I have either been the original sponsor or co-sponsor of all the civil rights bills which have been before Congress since I first came here. You may be assured that my concern for individual liberties shall continue and that my efforts to guarantee them shall not abate. The limitations of my office allow no more."[30]

In 1959, Magnuson helped block a bill pushed by Senator William Jenner, Republican from Indiana, that would have placed limits on Supreme Court powers regarding civil rights. He joined Senator Hubert Humphrey in sponsoring a series of measures "to guarantee liberty, equal opportunity and equal protection under the law to all American citizens." These were mild precursors to the monumental legislation he and Humphrey would push into law five years, and an epic tragedy, later.

CHAPTER 20

Camelot and Comeback

E arly in the New Year, 1960, Senator Magnuson got a note and a clipping of his column from Joseph Alsop, the well-connected, well-informed Washington newsman. The note offered "apologies for my presumption." The column screamed alarm at a widening gap between U.S. and Soviet intercontinental ballistic missiles. Magnuson replied that the "missile gap" was indeed alarming, but equally alarming is "our lag in submarines and deep sea research."[1]

It was a preview of the stuff to come in the 1960 presidential campaign. Democrats had a national security issue with which to challenge the Republican administration of President Eisenhower and Vice President Nixon, an issue just as potent and just as phony as the GOP charge that Democrats "lost China."

After a decade of abuse for being "soft on communism" if not the "party of treason," it was comeback time for Democrats, the upshot of an informal alliance of Pentagon sources eager to boost defense appropriations, defense hawks inside the Senate caucus, and journalistic hawks like Alsop, outside.

Chief among the Senate hawks were Stuart Symington, Democrat from Missouri, the former Air Force secretary, and Washington's Henry Jackson, now established in his second term. Symington was a presidential hopeful that year. Jackson already had eyes on the Democratic vice presidential nomination. They lagged behind the frontrunners, John F. Kennedy and Lyndon Johnson.

Whatever the U.S.-Soviet gap in subs and ocean research, the ICBM "missile gap" was nonexistent, an illusion so far as the most sophisticated instrument in our intelligence arsenal could divine. Eisenhower, Nixon, the GOP presidential nominee-to-come, and Allen Dulles, the CIA boss, knew this but couldn't say how they knew. To do so would have disclosed the existence of the U-2, America's high-altitude photo reconnaissance aircraft, then flying over the Soviet Union in search of ICBM launch sites and finding none. While the administration remained silent about intelligence gathered from these illegal overflights, Democratic hawks were free to fire at will at Eisenhower and Nixon for their tolerance of such dangerous vulnerability. The president placed what he considered best for national security ahead of election-year politics. Nixon would pay the price.[2]

Although it would prove less potent than the missile gap, Republicans still had the China card to play against Democrats. A nasty argument broke out inside Congress when Senator Hugh Scott, the Republican minority leader from Pennsylvania, is alleged to have called Senators Claire Engle, Gale McGee, William Fulbright, Mike Mansfield, and Magnuson, and Representative Charles Porter (Democrat from Oregon) "jackasses" for their tolerant attitudes toward Red China. Porter, even more outspoken than Magnuson on the need to establish relations with China, seemed to exult in the clamor raised by Scott. It elevated the issue. Scott denied he had called the men jackasses, but certainly questioned their liberal views about China. Porter called for a national debate with Scott—NBC promised free airtime—claiming "our China policy is obsolete and dangerous. It leads to World War III and away from effective disarmament." Oddly—for public sentiment was still overwhelmingly on his side—Scott dropped the subject, refusing to debate Porter, a volatile liberal.[3] This came as a relief to Magnuson, if not the other Democrats. The less said the better. China was still too hot an issue to handle by Democrats trying to hold majorities in the Congress and to win the White House in 1960.

With Magnuson and Jackson, Washington State had the major bases covered in the presidential election to come. Magnuson was ambivalent at the 1960 Democratic National Convention, officially neutral but privately leaning toward his old friend Johnson for the Democratic nomination; Jackson was outspoken for his 1952 Senate classmate, Jack Kennedy.[4] Accordingly, John Salter worked for Kennedy while Maggie's aide Irv Hoff worked the western states for Johnson, advising Johnson's aide Bobby Baker where to find delegates in Idaho and Montana.

What Hoff could not do, and what Johnson wanted more than anything else, was to deliver Magnuson's open endorsement. "The Boss said the best he could do was to walk down the middle," explained Hoff. "The Johnson people were plenty sore at me for failing to deliver. But Magnuson had other considerations: Scoop wanted to be Kennedy's vice presidential running mate, and Maggie really liked Jack Kennedy—even if he regarded him as a Senate 'show horse.' They had a lot of things in common—they liked girls and a drink and a joke. Despite their differences in work habits, they were compatible. Both were blithe spirits. They really liked each other."[5]

Salter, Jackson's longtime administrative aide, was one of a handful of political operatives at Kennedy's first presidential planning session at the Kennedy estate in Hyannis Port, Massachusetts. In addition to Salter, Kennedy had young Brock Adams, a connection to young Democrats in the West and older delegates who would attend the party's convention in Los Angeles in July 1960. Hoff, Salter, and Adams were the best and brightest Democratic campaigners of their generation. Whatever happened in Los Angeles, the state was well covered.

What happened, however, was a split in the Washington delegation. A liberal hard core stayed with Adlai Stevenson, a presidential loser in 1952 and 1956, despite Adams's insistence that Kennedy would win the nomination and had the best chance to become president. A conservative group supported Johnson, Magnuson's choice until the the roll call showed the inevitable: a Kennedy nomination. But Maggie steered clear of a nasty squabble between Zelma Morrison, the Democratic national committeewoman, and Luke Graham, the state party chairman. With Jackson's vice presidential hopes at stake, it was no time for internal political warfare.

Outside the convention hall, Los Angeles society, mostly movie professionals, opened its doors to the convention stars. After one party, Hearst columnist Louella Parsons, dispenser of gossip and overseer of Hollywood mores, wrote of "the magnetic man from the Apple State, Warren Magnuson." George Smathers, the Florida senator with playboy tastes and a close friendship with Jack Kennedy, asked Magnuson to second his nomination as a favorite son candidate, even enclosing a suggested speech, citing Smathers's "effectiveness, integrity and devotion to duty."[6] Magnuson would not take his attention from the advancement of Johnson and Jackson.

Ironic as it may appear to later generations, Johnson was the "southern candidate" for the presidential nomination. The time has passed since southern states were part of Franklin Roosevelt's grand coalition of northern liberals, western farmers, and southern segregationists. Kennedy, a big hit on television in contrast with Magnuson and Johnson, had soundly defeated Hubert Humphrey in the winter-spring presidential primary races. He came to the convention with greater delegate strength, despite the enormous power Johnson exercised as Senate majority leader. One of Johnson's preconvention moves was to divide the power of Senate baronies, the committees, into subcommittees, each with a chairman. Thus Wyoming's McGee and Indiana's Vance Hartke became chairmen of Commerce subcommittees, nominally beholden to Johnson for their new status. It would not affect either the outcome in Los Angeles or the authority of committee chairman Magnuson.

"You know why we're getting licked?" the Senate majority leader remarked to an aide before the first and final roll call July 13. "The 'boy' [Kennedy] is out getting laid all over town while his people are working their asses off. I'm working my ass off while my people are all off getting laid all over town."[7]

Kennedy was so confident he remained calm through the convention roll call, which commenced at 10:07 P.M. Jittery nerves, not calm, is the usual state of candidates whether the stakes are for the courthouse or the White House. Brock Adams was equally confident and working furiously to shake Washington State delegates away from Governor Stevenson. Mississippi, New Jersey, and Florida gave their votes to favorite sons. Adams was frantic when the roll call reached Washington. Here was the opportunity to give Kennedy the nomination and enhance Jackson's chances for the vice presidential nomination. Seattle attorney Dan Brink and his Stevenson delegates were not to be budged. There was one surprise shift, however.

"All right, I voted for your man—now let's see what he's going to do for Scoop," a Kennedy stalwart, Joe Miller, quotes Magnuson as shouting into his ear on the convention floor. Maggie voted for Kennedy over Johnson, and the delegation knew it. They also knew he would never have gone against Johnson, save for the sake of Jackson's vice presidential bid and his intelligence that the convention fight was virtually finished. Washington left the balloting climax to Wyoming. The delegation leader, Mike Manatos, a Johnson backer, seized the time.

"I recall that my contribution to the hasty conference on the floor was that we would be absolutely foolish to pass up this opportunity to nominate the next president," said Manatos, later a key aide to President Johnson. "It was obvious it was going to be John F. Kennedy. Right behind us was the District of Columbia delegation, and if we didn't nominate Kennedy, they sure were going to."[8] Wyoming gave fifteen votes to Kennedy and, as the press said, bedlam ensued on the convention floor. So did the question of a vice presidential nominee.

Several years later John Salter would tell the *Argus* that Robert Kennedy offered the vice presidential nomination to Senator Jackson.[9] But at the time others were also under consideration, a spur used to stimulate delegate interest in the nomination of John Kennedy. Adams had pressed the Jackson case with those Washington delegates stuck to Stevenson. No sale. He now feels the delegation's failure to give Kennedy the last votes needed for nomination damaged, perhaps conclusively, Jackson's hopes. Jackson and his supporters were keenly disappointed when Kennedy named Johnson his running mate. Equally disappointed were backers of Symington and Minnesota's Orville Freeman. Kennedy's aide and biographer, Theodore Sorensen, says Johnson was always Kennedy's choice, "the next best man qualified to be president."[10] Johnson accepted and Kennedy handed Jackson the consolation, chairman of the Democratic National Committee.

Two decades later Magnuson was blunt about what took place in Los Angeles in the hectic days and hours after the presidential roll call. He told the *Post-Intelligencer*, "all this hullaballo about who would be vice president was just political business. Bobby [Kennedy] would go to a delegation and say 'you work for Jack and we'll put senator so and so on the ticket.' All the time they were going to ask Lyndon. [House Speaker] Sam Rayburn objected at first. He didn't like to break up the Texas team—him as Speaker, Lyndon as Majority Leader. Finally he agreed." In an oral history for the Johnson Library in Austin, Texas, Magnuson said, "I don't know why he changed his mind, but Kennedy would not have won without Johnson on the ticket. After the election, he [Johnson] would come around and grumble [about the job as vice president]. I'd say 'you asked for it and we [Rayburn and Maggie] told you not to do it.' It might have been [Johnson's concern over] his health. Being vice president is easier than being majority leader of the Senate."[11]

Significantly, Magnuson never sought a formal leadership role in the Senate and advised others to avoid it. In his judgment the real work of the legislator—the core of his influence—was in the committees drafting legislation and in the back rooms seeking the votes for passage.[12] He ran from any suggestion of "Magnuson for President."

Maggie threw all of his muscle behind the election of his young colleague, Jack Kennedy, in the cliff-hanger campaign against Republican Richard Nixon. With Irv Hoff and Kennedy's youngest brother, Ted, Maggie worked the western states. They had the matter of Kennedy's Catholic religion to overcome and the missile gap with which to play against Republicans. Jackson hit the campaign trail charging the Eisenhower-Nixon administration with being—sweet revenge!—soft on national security.[13] Nixon, said Jackson, was "naive" about the Soviet boss, Nikita Khrushchev.

A vile brew of religious hatred accompanied this campaign. The anti-Catholic, anti-Semitic publication *Common Sense* declared: "Kennedy is not loose from Rome. No man can be a Roman Catholic and an American at the same time." Besides, *Common Sense* alleged Kennedy had a "Marxist record" and friendships with Jews.[14]

Late in the campaign Viola Hofer of Seattle wrote Magnuson, "It is ironic that you and Scoop, both professing to be Lutheran, should be working for a man like John Kennedy, doing everything in your power to elect a Roman Catholic. Kennedy is an arrogant, self-seeking, ruthless man from a ruthless family. If Kennedy is elected we will not live to see another Protestant elected president. What is to stop Bobby [brother Robert Kennedy] four years from now? God forgive you."[15]

Hoff, who kept Johnson aide Bobby Baker informed prior to the convention, fed Robert Kennedy advice on western issues in September: "more investments, less tight money, proper utilization of forests and public lands, a need for forest roads and airplane jobs. Push [hydroelectric] power and JFK's interest in public welfare." At the same time Hoff gave Magnuson his outlook for the November election: "The religious issue is boiling, but I must say in fairness John Kennedy has some inexplicable qualities bordering on magnetism. I think he is going to be real hard to beat." By the narrowest of margins, Hoff was correct.

A few weeks later Hoff resigned as Magnuson's administrative assistant to become the top lobbyist for U.S. sugar cane refiners. Maggie accepted the resignation with "greatest regret" and declared him "one of the ablest men ever to serve on Capitol Hill." Magnuson wasn't prone to overstatement. It was a loss for the senator and western Democrats. Fred Lordon, an assistant to Washington State Attorney General Smith Troy with close ties to Dave Beck's Teamsters, joined Magnuson as Hoff's replacement.

Otherwise, it was a smashing year for Democrats, easy to overlook the arrest of Representative Don Magnuson for drunk driving and the subsequent publicity. Jessie Robertson had to reply to several constituent letters confusing Don with Warren: "Don is no relation to Senator Magnuson and his behavior has been a source of embarrassment." One of these letter writers, Earl Vines, apologized for the confusion. Nevertheless, John Stender, the Republican congressional candidate, complained that Don Magnuson was "trading on Senator Magnuson's name."[16] Representative Magnuson won this election, but left Warren Magnuson with a spot of trouble.

A few days after the election, Maynard Rundgren wrote a letter to Maggie, his old high school chum, recalling their days running up and down the halls of Moorhead High School, dodging the wrath of the dreaded "Miss Dredge," a disciplinarian. He wanted to know what Magnuson thought of the president-elect.

"I believe the new president will be a good one," judged Magnuson who could from personal knowledge compare Kennedy with Roosevelt, Truman, and Eisenhower.[17] Indeed, President Kennedy would inspire a new generation of postwar Americans. He was a sharp break from the past, a World War II combat veteran with movie star looks, extraordinary personal charm, and acute intelligence. He would, as promised, "get the country moving again" toward better health, civil rights, and an accelerated economy. He had a beautiful wife who could speak French, adorable children, and adoring friends among the elite of the nation's academic, literary, and journalism institutions. He liked the middle-brow music from a Lerner and Loewe musical about a never-never land, *Camelot*. This became the sobriquet for his abbreviated administration. He was slain by an assassin or assassins. In a subtle way the nation has never recovered. It was too hard to get our hopes up about our government after the murder of Camelot.

Kennedy spent the day before his inauguration at the family home in Palm Beach, Florida, with his father, wife, children, and Senator Warren Magnuson. As Magnuson told it years later, they swam in the Atlantic, chatted, and had dinner. Caroline Kennedy rode piggyback on Maggie, the high school quarterback. At the president-elect's urging, Magnuson stayed overnight with the family in Palm Beach and flew back with him next day to Washington. The senator was greeted by a mixed chorus of radio, television, and newspaper reporters asking variations on the question: What had he discussed with Kennedy on the inauguration eve? Maggie insisted then and decades later it had been nothing of significance, chatter about "cabbages and kings." He said Jackie Kennedy spent much of the time fixing her hair.[18]

Whatever passed between the senator and the president-elect, it is certain Kennedy wanted a strong man at his side, one with an expert touch on legislation and its makers, in the prelude to his presidency. The question, this being so, is why Maggie instead of Senator Richard Russell of Georgia, or Senator Robert Kerr of Oklahoma, or perhaps a half-dozen others with power in the Senate? He needed someone he liked, as well as trusted, and with whom he shared a common political philosophy. Kerr didn't drink; Russell was taciturn and southern. Maggie fit the bill, a steady prop for the start of a new adventure.

Maggie divided his colleagues into "show horses," who liked the glamour of their office much as they disdained its work, and the "work horses," committee chairmen like himself who did the job but avoided the publicity. Kennedy? "Sure he was a show horse," said Magnuson:

> He was away from the Senate more than any other member I can recall. It was a stepping stone to the White House. He was a smart, alert, humane fellow. He knew people. He was susceptible [sympathetic] to people with problems. He had this facade of looking like the elite. But he wasn't. It was a facade like those lace-curtain Irish. He had plans. Lyndon carried out those plans after Kennedy was killed—the poverty programs, the civil rights programs, the

Great Society. Kennedy was strong for civil rights. He would have passed that legislation had he lived. I was already at work on the public accommodations [Title II] section of the civil rights bill. Of course, Lyndon did bring in some southern support Jack would not have got—but Jack wouldn't have been elected President without Lyndon on the ticket.

Those who knew the "show horse," a man of insatiable intellectual curiosity, are sure he spent some of the hours prior to his inauguration gleaning information from the mind of the most productive "work horse" of his era.

Harry Brand wrote a gushing letter about the Kennedy inauguration, the eloquence of the new president, the poetry of Robert Frost, and suggested Magnuson submit legislation making inauguration day a national holiday "for the celebration of democracy." Maggie replied to "Washington Jefferson Jackson Lincoln Roosevelt Brand" that he would do so—and that he hoped the Republican boss of 20th Century-Fox wouldn't toss his pal off the studio lot.[19] In fact, Maggie blossomed again with Jack Kennedy in the White House. He was not an admirer of President Eisenhower, whom he would later characterize as a "caretaker of the status quo." Eisenhower, said Magnuson, "told the colonel to tell the sergeant to tell the private and that was that. He didn't send up any legislation." That is a harsh characterization of the father of the interstate highway system and the keeper of the peace for two terms.

But soon after Kennedy succeeded Eisenhower, a funny thing happened to Maggie one day at the races at Belmont. Magnuson had a run of losers. Out of cash, he spotted ex-President Eisenhower with his pal George Allen. As he explained later, "since they were the only ones I knew I made a small loan, $200. It was really embarrassing to ask them, but you know how it is to be a bum at Belmont."[20]

Come slow horses on Long Island, or tightly contested presidential elections, Maggie never neglected the needs back home. These were special in the first years of the 1960s. Seattle aimed to show itself to the world at the Century 21 world's fair opening April 21, 1962. Labor pledged a no-strike agreement, the city fathers were working overtime on structures and tenants, and Magnuson had to get $10 million from the federal treasury. It would not come easy.

Across the mountains at a bend in the Columbia River at Hanford, where federal scientists and workers manufactured plutonium for nuclear weapons, Sam Volpentest and the Chamber of Commerce were struggling over ways to keep the new urban area alive.[21] The means they sought were Magnuson.

John L. Scott, a most active fair maker, would later tell Magnuson, "We know you are the chief architect of the Pacific Science Center building, the finest thing we have seen in America."[22] Perhaps, but only after initial reluctance. Jim Faber, the fair publicist, was told absolutely "no" when he came to Maggie seeking funds for the building. Money was never appropriated for such civic improvements. Faber spent a day in the Library of Congress and returned to Magnuson with a long list of such appropriations, demolishing the senator's objection. "You sonofabitch," said Maggie to Faber.[23]

Working from Magnuson's Senate office, Faber arranged a dinner for fifteen of the nation's leading scientists at the Shoreham in March 1958. Magnuson made his pitch on the need to explain science to schoolkids and laymen. As Edward Carlson, the Seattle-based board chairman of Westin Hotels and United Airlines, was later to write, that night "the spark was lit. . . . Magnuson assumed the role of quarterback [of the fair]—leadership he was to maintain until the fair closed."[24] Getting the federal grant for Seattle's fair, Maggie was more like a line-busting fullback. To crack through opposition on the Appropriations Committee, the senator attached his modest $10 million onto the mammoth, $5 billion Mutual Security appropriation and then waited for a favorable committee attendance. Cleared of Senate appropriations, the fair funding hit a roadblock from Representative John Rooney of New York, a careful fiscal watchdog. The $10 million appeared doomed by the Brooklyn budget cutter until Magnuson reminded Rooney of another world's fair scheduled for 1964, this one in New York. The full measure passsed a Senate-House conference committee and became law. Its fruit, the Pacific Science Center, designed by Minoru Yamasaki, a Seattle native, is a white jewel of delicate arches reflected in shallow pools. Magnuson consulted with Robert Sarnoff, chairman of RCA, and with Massachusetts Institute of Technology Dean John Buchard on the scientific exhibit. Henry Broderick, the city's leading commercial real estate dealer, said that without the federal funds gathered by Magnuson the fair would have been a disaster.[25]

Maggie also attended sympathetically to Port Commissioner John Haydon's complaint that the fair bosses had "dumped Miller, McKay, Hoeck and Hartung—the most creative and talented ad agency on the coast," the firm behind Jackson-Magnuson political campaigns. "For the life of me," Maggie wrote his Republican friend, "I can't understand why they were dumped. I'm very disappointed." Gerry Hoeck later explained they were replaced by a firm with a surer touch on the pockets of Republican businessmen.[26]

Sam Volpentest got to know Maggie back in 1932 when the young lawyer went courting votes in Seattle's Italian Club. A slight, spry entrepreneur, Volpentest moved to Richland to run a tavern, and watched the Tri-Cities—Richland, Kennewick, Pasco—boom off the desert with Hanford's plutonium factory, then begin to wither as demand for the nuclear weapons' material slacked. He went to work raising money for Magnuson in 1956 when he decided, "We had to have government connections to survive and Maggie was chairman of Commerce Committee. We came to realize how powerful he was." Sam and the local chamber of commerce also came to realize that Richland had the look of a hastily built construction camp—one easy to come, easy to go. Sam, the chamber president, reasoned that a federal building several stories high would give Hanford an image of permanence.

"I called Maggie," said Volpentest. "He said, 'Sam, it takes fifteen years to get a federal building authorized and appropriated.' I said we can't wait fifteen years. We might not last that long. Two weeks later Maggie called and said, 'Hanford is at the top of the list for a federal building. Missoula doesn't want one.' Something had happened—Richland went to the top of the list. I don't know how. I didn't ask how. I told all this to the local Atomic Energy Commission director and he wanted to know where I got such a wild idea. Two days later he learned the project was authorized. The building was dedicated in 1964—the first in the Tri-Cities to need an elevator."[27]

It was a fine time for Magnuson: Jack Kennedy as president, the Tri-Cities made permanent, Seattle at the brink of its emergence as America's next great city. Truckers and shippers made Maggie Transportation Man of the Year in 1961. On the Senate floor he maneuvered the passage of a subsidy for U.S. shipbuilders. Less successful was a voting rights bill pushed by Senate liberals. It failed by twenty-four votes. Senator Paul Douglas, Democrat from Illinois, wrote Magnuson: "History will vindicate us. It took courage to stand fast in the face of Republican and Southern opposition. This is a long fight. From the bottom of my heart, thanks for your courage and insight."[28] Douglas was correct: there was more of this legislation to come.

"A shower has stopped haying and given me time to mention a few things on my mind," wrote John Goldmark from his ranch above the Okanogan Valley. Goldmark, the brilliant chairman of the Ways and Means Committee in the state House of Representatives, had a minor beef about Maggie's Seattle office. Magnuson replied with apologies and added, "I wish a shower would halt haying here for a while till we get even. We're swamped."[29]

He did get away, and in grand style, for the running of the Kentucky Derby that year, two private Chesapeake & Ohio Pullman cars for a party that included Jermaine, the Joe Drumhellers, Norman Winston, Leo Weisfield, and Dan Martin. They left Washington, D.C., on Friday and returned Monday. Transportation's Man of the Year got the accommodations for cost, $117.32 per person. Carry Back won the horse race.

CHAPTER 21

Triumph, Cuba, and Trouble

I f, as the Bible says, the Lord gives and the Lord takes, in 1961, Jack Kennedy's first year as president, the Almighty was mostly giving to Senator Warren Magnuson. Kennedy had a dreadful baptism of fire, the failed invasion of Cuba organized by the CIA and manned by exiles from the island bossed by Fidel Castro, a Soviet dependent and a threat to U.S. hegemony in the Western Hemisphere. It happened early in the year. On November 16, 1961, there was a great party in Seattle honoring Magnuson's silver anniversary as a member of Congress. The *Post-Intelligencer* called it the largest political affair of its kind in the history of the state—a statement that would hold for at least another thirty-four years.

Bill Edris's Olympic Hotel ballroom overflowed with 3,000 people paying $100 a plate. And what people. Much as it honored Maggie, it was a celebration of the state's business and trade union establishment with all of its major players present, except the Teamsters' Dave Beck. Pursued by Attorney General Robert Kennedy's Justice Department, Beck was on his way to the federal prison on McNeil Island south of Tacoma to start a two and a half year term for selling a Teamster Cadillac for $1,900 and pocketing the money. There were Republicans and Democrats at the affair. Party lines dissolved around Maggie, tribute to the largesse he gathered in Washington and sent home to the state. His Senate colleagues, Ed Muskie, Gale McGee, Jennings Randolph, and Bob Bartlett, came from the Capitol. They all told "Maggie stories," none more enduring and technically incorrect than one told by another Capitol guest, President John Kennedy:

"He [Magnuson] speaks on the Senate floor so quietly that few can hear him. He looks down at his desk . . . he comes into the Senate late in the afternoon . . . he is hesitant about interrupting other senators. When he rises up to speak most other senators have left. He sends a message up to the chair and everyone says 'what was it?' and Maggie says 'it's nothing important.' And Grand Coulee Dam is built!" Ironically, Grand Coulee is the only dam on the Columbia River system that can't be attributed to the legislative skill of Magnuson. More improbable, none of these works bears his name. But Kennedy, a superb dramatist, got his message across with only a bit of factual license. Maggie was the stealth dam builder.

'When Maggie went to Congress," Kennedy continued, "half the state was sagebrush and wasteland. The Columbia River ran unharnessed to the sea. There was no atomic energy plant at Hanford, no aluminum plants, no upriver navigation. Today there are millions of acres of new fertile farmland, 50,000 men at work in aluminum mills. The great waters have been harnessed."[1]

(The President created a commotion later that evening by slipping past his Secret Service guards and walking down the Olympic Hotel stairs from his room to Magnuson's suite. "May I come in?" he gently requested. He did and stayed for a nightcap that was abruptly interrupted by frantic Secret Servicemen who did not bother to knock on Maggie's door in search of their keep.)[2]

"Maggie can get more money with less commotion than any other senator," said Wyoming's McGee. "He is the most effective senator we have."

Magnuson replied to these tributes by saying, "My mother used to tell me not to talk with food in my mouth. Right now I've got my heart in my mouth."

Cuba, for the time being, was forgotten.

Time followed this extraordinary party with a profile, November 24, 1961, "In the Kitchen with Maggie." The magazine ran a list of his achievements in Congress, overlooking or not having space to report his works for health science, oceanography, and transportation. "In the cave of winds that is the U.S. Senate," said *Time*, "Magnuson speaks seldom, putters about the aisles with an unlit cigar clenched between his teeth . . . says 'if you've got the votes you don't need the speech.' " The article re-told a story of Maggie's days as "the Senate's Gay Blade": "When Georgia's venerable Senator Walter George chided him for missing a late night vote, Maggie replied, 'Senator, I knew you would take care of my interests and you didn't need my vote. To tell the truth I had an engagement in the late afternoon with a very beautiful woman. We had a cocktail, maybe two. Then we went to dinner at the Shoreham. It was a lovely dinner. The girl had a little wine—she was beautiful in the candlelight. Then—well, senator, you wouldn't have wanted me to be rude and abandon her would you?' Said courtly Walter George: 'Warren, I just never would have forgiven myself or you if you had abandoned that young lady.' " *Time* also noted, in its extravagant style, that there were fewer candlelight dinners these days, for "Maggie, 59, a sleepy-eyed, pot-raking, poker player likes to spend an evening with Cutty Sark and cards."[3]

Nothing before or since that memorable evening of tall tales and careless facts and its journalistic aftermath so enhanced the Maggie legend. He loomed in Seattle and elsewhere as a kind of legislative John Wayne, laconic but always able to corral votes needed to help the good guys.

Maggie, not President Kennedy, was the main attraction at this unusual celebration, noted the *Portland Oregonian*. By way of explanation, the *Oregonian* reported that Washington State got $1 billion in military-industrial payrolls in 1960 while Oregon got $65 million, "credit due in large part to the political shrewdness of Magnuson and his junior colleague Scoop Jackson. They work behind the scenes for money for dams and Century 21 [Seattle World's Fair]. They perform for Washington like Sir Francis Drake for Queen Elizabeth. Wayne Morse? He talks a great deal." Morse was Oregon's loquacious, acerbic senator. Drake looted Spanish shipping on behalf of Elizabeth; not as proper as Maggie getting the votes for federal appropriations, the envy of the *Oregonian*. Magnuson's reelection in 1962, the newspaper concluded, "is a sure thing."

It was not. It was nearly disastrous, prompting a great awakening by the senator and his staff and a sharp change in his legislative goals. That lapse of political judgment by the Portland newspaper was repeated elsewhere. Magnuson was regarded as unbeatable by all the newspapers, politicians, hangers-on, and even sophisticated opinion polls. The great silver anniversary party not only dulled the judgment of his peers. It lulled Magnuson and his supporters into a dangerously false sense of security.

"You never looked so good [politically]," wrote his former law partner, Bruce Bartley, late in the summer of 1962.[4] In June of that year Charles Parker of Central Surveys, an Iowa public opinion polling firm, wrote Fred Lordon the results of their just completed survey: "Results are very satisfactory to you. One Republican precinct committeeman said it wouldn't take a campaign fund of more than $10 to reelect Magnuson this year—and that's about the way it looks." The state is 57 percent Democratic, said Parker, "but even among Republicans he has a good reputation." The survey showed Maggie's greatest assets are "things he has done for the state. The issue of medical care for older people is strong." The poll did note a few blemishes on the senator's image: there was some confusion between Warren and Don Magnuson ("he was in a car wreck when he was drunk," said one poll respondent), and some concern about his lifestyle (he had a "personal life not as impeccable as it could be," said another). In sum, it looked like 1956 all over again. The survey showed little change in the public's opinion of Magnuson from the previous six years when he carried every county in the state, save tiny San Juan.[5]

What the poll didn't show was the personal attraction of Maggie's November opponent, the Reverend Richard Christensen, handsome, spellbinding as a speaker, and utterly unbounded in what he would attribute to the incumbent senator. An anonymous legman for Drew Pearson gave his boss this description of the Republican: "Dick Christensen, 32, a Lutheran minister who took a broken down church to a $250,000 church with 2,000 members. Republicans think he is a valuable property, but they are scared of him. They won't let him become state party chairman. He is simply sensational on a speaking platform. He has his own organization, 'Women on the Warpath.' " Another memo to Pearson, this one from his assistant Jack Anderson, called Don Magnuson "an albatross around Senator Magnuson's neck."[6]

"It was a bolt out of the blue," said Dan Evans of the Christensen movement. Evans, a three-term governor (1964–76) responsible for the state's pace-setting environmental protection laws, spent that summer of 1962 working to elect a Republican majority in the state legislature. "We kept running into 'Women on the Warpath,' but we had different goals — they were strictly interested in dumping Magnuson and electing Christensen."[7]

Magnuson missed Irv Hoff, mastermind of the brilliant 1956 campaign. Fred Lordon had replaced Hoff and he remained complacent about the opposition until after the September primary election, when Maggie attracted 569 fewer votes than Christensen. A few weeks later, in early October, Lordon would send a distress call to Hoff to come back and work on the campaign. It was almost too late and unnecessarily so. Late in August, when signs of trouble should have been apparent, Lordon wrote Magnuson, "I have not found anyone who feels your campaign is not going well and your standing is very high."[8] It was as if the campaign manager remained bedazzled by the great silver anniversary celebration. He did note that Christensen was extremely busy and that "he has had some TV coverage aimed at housewives."

"Everybody underestimated Christensen," said Featherstone Reid. They also overestimated Magnuson in that off-year election, despite troubling signs. The senator's campaign crowds were scanty, his personal looks an unhappy contrast with the movie star figure he cut as a naval officer twenty years earlier. He was overweight. Joe Forkner, a former funeral director in Seattle's University District, urged him early in 1962 to go on a fat free, tasteless diet, for the sake of his health, if not his reelection. His puffy visage appeared on billboards that said "Warren G. Magnuson Keeps Our State Moving," and some said the billboard was a campaign negative. Maggie looked like the caricature of the overstuffed, overindulged, pork-barreling politician. Christensen looked like a young Magnuson.

Even worse, Hoff would say much later, overconfidence led to a campaign that essentially copied Magnuson's 1956 reelection strategy. "They were talking about Magnuson's work in building dams, roads, and irrigation projects while people were worried about having an atomic bomb drop on them," said Hoff. "The critical issues were international, not local. We had to get away from roads and dams and make national defense our theme."

"The bolt out of the blue" carried more than the election hopes of the Reverend Christensen. He became a magnet for religious fundamentalists and bitter right-wingers, political currents which would always run against Evans, a GOP liberal. Early in his first term Evans told members of the John Birch Society, chief vehicle of this intolerant movement, to get out of the Republican Party, but he was never totally successful in his civil purge. By the mid-1990s, the "Rs squared"—the religious right—was a dominant force in the party of Eisenhower and Evans, despite the collapse of communism as a threat to international order and as a prop for right-wing extremists. The new religious right campaigned on a restoration of "family values," a major theme in the 1962 Christensen campaign against the bachelor Magnuson.

Anti-Communist paranoia, muscled with several powerful economic interests, gave Christensen's campaign a virulent emotional push. Washington Water Power, the intractable opponent of publicly owned power, sponsored anti-Communist films that helped feed the paranoia. William Fritz, sometime lobbyist for Boeing, provided a movie showing "Communist Encirclement, 1961." Fritz was a prime backer of Bill Stinson, the GOP congressional candidate running against the politically damaged Don Magnuson. Fritz staged meetings under the name of the "Lake Hills School of anti-Communism."[9] Something called "The Constitution Party" passed out literature from the pen of the Reverend Billy James Hargis, an Oklahoma evangelist who preached against communism using his own interpretation of the Gospels. These handouts said: "Satan is not asleep. How else to explain the fantastic success of mankind's enemies—Nazis, Fascists, and, most vicious, Communists?"

Prior to the September primary election, the astute Kathleen Prince, writing from Oroville in the Okanogan Valley, told Maggie of meetings "infested with John Birchers. It's a frightening thing to see—friendships and families are broken. There's character assassination. The main instigators are Ashley Holden and Don Caron. Holden is centering his shots at John and Sally Goldmark. . . . They [Caron and Holden] announce they will show that Magnuson belongs to many Communist fronts. They are trying to take control of the state Republican Party. Sally admitted to being a Communist Party member in the 1930s, but inactive since those days. She is a good loyal citizen, but you know what a smear artist can do."[10]

Holden, once the *Spokane Spokesman-Review*'s premier editorial critic of public power, had moved to Okanogan County as editor of the *Tonasket Tribune*, the organ with which he would attack state representative Goldmark. It cost Goldmark, an eastern intellectual and war hero turned Okanogan rancher, his seat in the state legislature. He sued for libel and won in the county court. Not all of this irrational fear was confined to the ranchers and orchardists of the remote central Washington valley. Captain Eddie Rickenbacker, the World War I air ace and boss of Eastern Airlines, wrote his Commerce Committee friend, "Dear Warren, Communists encircle us on three sides led by Khrushchev and Mao Tse tung. Our leaders are afraid to stand up. We need a rebirth of patriotism."[11] E. T. Raymond, a Boeing engineer, wrote Magnuson decrying President Kennedy's reluctance to "unleash" Chiang Kai-shek from Taiwan to invade Red China.[12] Small wonder that for once Magnuson did bend on the China issue. He backed a bill sponsored by Representative Tom Pelly, Republican from Washington, to cut off trade with Communists. The *Seattle Times* quoted Magnuson, "I've worked hard to open trade with China, but it is no use. They won't cooperate. They fail to give a ray of hope that we can trade peacefully or effectively." He said he would sponsor a Senate version, if Pelly's measure passed the House.

"I can't stress enough the difficulty we're having with the right wing," Jack Dean of Spokane told Magnuson. "Christensen has these hard core fanatics. The problem will continue. Scoop will face it in two years. I told Scoop, frankly, I don't know the answer to the problem."[13]

Christensen bestirred the alienated, "mad as hell and not going to take it any longer" voters with extravagant attacks on Magnuson and a slick campaign gimmick. While his "Women on the Warpath" raised campaign funds from cake and cookie sales, he debated with an empty chair—Magnuson—in his television ads. To the chair and the TV camera he said the nation's problems are "economic decay, political decay, social decay." He said: "Freedom is losing in China, Bulgaria, Cuba and North Korea. . . . When government does something for us, it takes something from us." Magnuson, he alleged, was responsible for the Texas swindler Billie Sol Estes, "our humiliation in Cuba," the loss of 65,000 timber jobs, and the placement of 135,000 people on welfare.[14] In his set campaign speech Christensen asked, "How does the incumbent compare with Lincoln, Jefferson, Andrew Jackson, Teddy Roosevelt, Woodrow Wilson, Eisenhower, Senator Taft or Goldwater?"[15] Barry Goldwater did come to the state to aid the Republican campaign. Ex-President Eisenhower stayed away.

A few days before the election, the reverend ran an ad implying Magnuson was a Communist collaborator, and he said Magnuson supported creation of a U.S. Arms Control Agency which would place the Army, Navy, and Air Force under the control of an assistant to the United Nations Security Council "who is always a communist." The source of these claims is as uncertain as Christensen's prospects as a significant influence inside the U.S. Senate. At one point Christensen said Magnuson was against the FBI. When word reached him in Washington, the senator was stunned. "I just had dinner last night with J. Edgar Hoover," he responded to an aide.[16] Maggie lamented to a friend, Brewster Denny, the woes of running against a man of the cloth who invented so many falsehoods. "I've run against all kinds of people in my time, but this is the first time against a preacher—especially one so loose with the truth," said Maggie, not smiling. "I know you wouldn't call me a religious person, but when the roll is called up yonder, and I'm standing next to that sonofabitch, they'll call my name first."[17]

There was work for Magnuson in Washington, where his aide Jerry Grinstein watched the reelection campaign with increasing anxiety. At hand was the critical decision on satellite communications, the next great leap ahead in radio-television-telephone. American Telephone and Telegraph (AT&T), whose balloon satellite "Echo" had made a spectacular debut, coveted the bulk, if not all, of the satellite business. Magnuson loomed as a "rock in the road" to their success. Accordingly, Walter Straley, the sophisticated, civic-minded head of Pacific Northwest Bell, AT&T's Northwest tentacle, was dispatched to remove the rock and secure for his firm operation of the satellite. Maggie favored COMSAT—a joint public-private satellite operation. Drew Pearson was a spur.

"You have such a fine record combatting monopoly, I know you'll want to give the [AT&T] proposal careful scrutiny," Pearson wrote Magnuson. "It's highly doubtful we want to give this to one company, AT&T, which has a bad record for monopoly and rooking the public." Straley, who began his communications career with radio station WHO in Des Moines, Iowa, alongside fellow announcer-salesman Ronald Reagan, got acquainted with Magnuson and made his pitch. The rock didn't budge from COMSAT, but the two men became close friends and mutual admirers for the rest of their lives.[18] Straley, a Republican turned Democrat, could laugh at Maggie's summming up of Reagan, the ex–Warner Brothers movie star: "Our greatest acting President."

Maggie's campaign dragged onward and downward, lulled by poll results and the happy talk of camp followers. "Lackluster" is the description offered by Grinstein, "very controlled. They ducked a lot of forums because they were always concerned that Christensen would show up and try to debate."[19] There was a devastating photo of a Maggie rally that showed 750 of the faithful, lost in the expanse of Spokane's civic auditorium. Inadvertently, Magnuson was playing to his negative image of a do-little, self-indulgent feeder at the public trough. Worse, his chairmanship of the business-oriented Commerce Committee was contributing to that image. The consumer crusader Ralph Nader would later observe that Maggie was viewed on Capitol Hill as an "agent for business and commercial interests"—a keeper of the status quo rather than an agent for change.[20] He got 569 fewer votes in the September primary than Christensen. Maggie's campaign needed a booster shot.

With unusual fanfare, the newspapers announced President Kennedy would come to Seattle October 21 for closing ceremonies at the Seattle World's Fair. This would be about two weeks before the November election. Christensen cried "politics." Magnuson denied it. But Kennedy never got closer than Chicago, where he abruptly reversed the flight of Air Force One and returned to Washington.

His press office said Kennedy suffered a cold en route to Seattle. In fact, he received photos that confirmed the presence of Soviet missiles in Cuba, 90 miles south of Florida. The president had to act at once. The Cuban missile crisis would last seven days and, so far as is commonly known, the planet has never come closer to thermonuclear war.

On October 28, while citizens of the world awaited a resolution or radioactive destruction, Kennedy met with Ed Wenk and Jerome Wiesner, the science advisers, in the Oval Office. At stake was Magnuson's proposal that national science grants be parceled to separate universities, rather than in individual fellowships—Maggie's way of spreading the money around the nation instead of channeling it to the elite institutions. As Wenk recalled, the discussion was businesslike, calm, and suddenly interrupted. Kennedy left the room. They waited until he returned, still calm, and asked that their discussion continue. They all agreed to distribute the education funds through grants to universities and colleges. Only when they left the office did Wenk learn the good news: Kennedy had been called from their talks to learn that Premier Khrushchev had ordered vessels bearing more missiles to Cuba to come about and return to the Soviet Union. The crisis had passed.[21]

Before that turning point, Magnuson flew to San Francisco to join other western members of Congress for a briefing on the missile crisis by Secretary of State Dean Rusk. Gerry Hoeck described the briefing as troubling and confusing for most of the congressmen. Maggie's sophistication did not extend deeply into Caribbean politics or geography, despite the fact that he had made two strictly private, unofficial trips to the gaming tables of Havana's Hotel Nacional in late 1958 and early 1959. On returning from San Francisco to Seattle the senator went straight to a live television interview at KING. Grinstein said he'd had too much to drink. On television he merely looked befuddled. It was not a good showing. Nevertheless, the newspapers forecast an election rout for the senator.

He won by 45,161 votes, a demoralizing margin of victory for the most successful and powerful politician in the state's history. Lordon's postmortem placed the blame on a smear campaign by Christensen and a billboard picture that gave the senator a dissolute image, plus deliberate efforts to confuse Warren with Don Magnuson. Lordon told Irv Hoff that Murray Chotiner, the top GOP hit man, coached Christensen that he couldn't beat Magnuson except through use of "smears, whispers and false rumors."[22]

A better insight comes from the vote in rural Grant County, a stretch of tumbleweeds and meager dryland farming until federal dams and irrigation projects, created with money extracted by Magnuson from the national treasury, made the semiarid plains bloom and its farmers, once dirt poor or bankrupt, rich. Formerly a Democratic stronghold, Maggie lost the county 54 percent to 45 percent in 1962. "It was an example of how much Maggie did for Grant County and how little its people appreciated the fact," said Harvey Vernier of Moses Lake, the senator's county campaign chairman. "But, again, somehow Maggie wasn't relating too well to the farmers. It's a problem that happens to any person who stays back in Washington for too long." Mabel Thompson, the daughter of Frank Bell, and Maggie's lifelong friend, still shakes her head at that 1962 vote. She says: "It goes to show. When farmers get two nickels to rub together they vote Republican."[23]

Magnuson was whistling past a graveyard when he told a friend "very few people remember whether Whirlaway won the Kentucky Derby by one length or by ten—he won!" In fact, he was depressed and suffering a loss of self-confidence, said Grinstein. As for himself, the aide said he was relieved. Magnuson slipped so badly in the campaign he feared a loss to the reverend. Two years later Christensen ran for the Republican nomination for governor, as the favorite to win in the early speculation.

"No," said Magnuson when told of Christensen's next campaign. "The people will send a preacher to Washington, but they won't send one to Olympia."[24] He lost the Republican primary election to Dan Evans and returned to duties as a minister. Magnuson took a long vacation before returning, chastened, to Washington, D.C. The local political experts, also chastened by his near loss, would never have foreseen that Magnuson was beginning the most productive years of his legislative career.

CHAPTER 22

Bumblebees

J erry Grinstein thought he saw the 1962 election slipping away from his senator, Warren Magnuson, chairman of the Commerce Committee. Late in that campaign he began to think of ways the senator could be revitalized, if in fact he pulled through to win another term. He got the idea of legislation to protect consumers when he read a *New Yorker* article, not, as might be expected, from the extensive public opinion polling done earlier in the year for the candidate.[1] "Consumer protection" did not appear as an issue in the surveys.

Changes had to be made. If the most influential legislator in the state's history, the man who made possible the Columbia and Snake River dams, the nation's medical research, the appropriations and federal influence for Boeing and Bremerton, could nearly be defeated by Dick Christensen's "bolt from the blue" and "Women on the Warpath," there had to be a profound defect in the man's image and actions. This cried for a major correction. Magnuson was simply too good for the state and the nation to lose.

A recent graduate of Yale University and Harvard Law School, Grinstein came to Magnuson as the son of the senator's physician, Dr. Alex Grinstein, and a family friend of Longacres' Joe Gottstein. Democratic politics in the state of Washington came as naturally to Grinstein as his analytical brilliance and humor. Before broaching his idea with the barely reelected, somewhat despondent Magnuson, Grinstein discussed the possibility of consumer protection as the vehicle for Maggie's political rehabilitation with Irv Hoff, Mac MacGowan, and Tom Foley, the young aide to Scoop Jackson. Hoff and MacGowan knew the senator's ways and instincts intimately. Foley had unusual political foresight. He helped buck up Magnuson after the election by reminding the senator that he was "captain of the team"—leader of the state's congressional delegation. Foley, MacGowan, and Hoff agreed if Magnuson was to continue as a public official, everything had to be changed, including his staff and the theme and direction of his office. They liked the prospect of consumer protection as an issue but were aware that unless Maggie felt comfortable with this new idea, it would not work. They put it to the senator.

At the time it must have seemed improbable to Magnuson's colleagues and to lobbyists, the professional sellers of influence, that a select member of the Senate establishment, a "senator's senator," one of four senators who could set a national policy, according to Tom Korologos, a top lobbyist of that period,[2] would step out in front of an issue bound to attract the wrath of the nation's business and industrial powers. Maggie was a player, not a bomb thrower; a romantic, perhaps, but not a social engineer. He was old shoe, a buddy to the business lobby. Consumer protection was nouveau politics. It would discomfort, if not alienate, his conservative backers in Seattle's business establishment. But it was exactly the issue needed to keep Magnuson apace with political changes of the 1960s. The senator, still shocked by the narrow margin of his reelection, did not take long in coming to the same conclusion.

"Maggie liked the idea," said Grinstein. "He said, 'It sounds good to me.' " Maggie had made a practice of grocery shopping, comparing the price and quantity of various packaged items. He had noticed glaring discrepancies. Consumer protection was a means of helping the average citizen, another promotion of the public interest. This would not be the making of a "new" Magnuson. It would be a revival of the Maggie of the 1933 state legislature and the 1937 Congress, a change in the Senator Magnuson of the 1950s. And, as Ralph Nader later noted, "When Maggie changed, the Senate changed."

Their direction settled, Grinstein reckoned they needed the brains and drive of young staffers to turn the ideas into legislation. The upshot was an arrangement between Grinstein and Professor Ralph Johnson of the University of Washington Law School, a leading expert on water rights and Indian rights, for the posting of a top graduate each year to Maggie's staff. The selection was done by committee and strictly nonpartisan. "Don't ask and don't tell" was Grinstein's rule about party politics. "Johnson sent us the best and the brightest, and a good staff tends to replicate itself," said Grinstein, who would later become chief executive office of Western Airlines and, still later, the Burlington Northern Railroad.

Legislation in our democratic bodies at state capitols and Washington, D.C., is compared so frequently to the making of sausage—"nice to eat but you wouldn't want to see it made"—the simile has become a cliché. Like most clichés, it is true. The committees of the legislative bodies take ideas from the executive, the special interests, and, infrequently, nonprofit interests, and meld them together to form a law. More likely than not, it is a law to protect some facet of the status quo, such as a "fair marketing" bill to fix the price of gasoline or beer. The higher sounding the title of a measure, the more likely it serves a pernicious interest. The Commerce Committee prior to 1962 was such a sausage maker, a processing plant for measures supported by the executive and the business lobbies, two branches usually in concert if the White House is Republican.

What Grinstein did was to connect bright, idealistic staffers, mostly from Washington State and the University of Washington Law School, with the legislative genius of Magnuson. The vehicle was the Commerce Committee. The combination produced an explosion of public interest legislation in the 1960s and 1970s. The committee became an initiator, a perpetrator, of legislation instead of a processor; it became active, no longer acquiescing to outside forces.

There is no accounting for the amazingly productive final two decades of Magnuson's public service without the contribution of the new staffers, the "Bumblebees." In nearly all cases their devotion to "the boss" and their shared sense of purpose went beyond the normal bonding inspired by common goals. They had a love of a sort usually found only among soldiers and occasionally mountaineer teams—never mind the disparity in the hazards between these endeavors. But it wasn't necessarily love at first sight.

The name Maggie eventually gave these staffers, Bumblebees, came from, of all people, John Ehrlichman, President Nixon's domestic adviser, but, before that, a Seattle attorney with an outspoken dislike of Magnuson's lifestyle and political policies. Ehrlichman said Washington was full of young staffers buzzing like bumblebees around the honey of power. Maggie laughed at the notion, liked it, and applied it affectionately to his multiplying staff. Mike Pertschuk now regards the appellation as a "gentle control mechanism," a reminder of who was the elected representative of the people—the one who held the power—and who were the supporters hired on to help.[3]

Most of them came from the UW Law School, via Professor Johnson: Stan Barer, Tom Allison, Norm Maleng, Sharon Nelson, Lynn Sutcliffe, Sue Crystal, Hayes Elder. Others were from the state of Washington: Eric Redman, Harley Dirks, Norm Dicks, Ed Sheets, Manny Rouvelas. Exceptions were Ed Merlis and Pertschuk, eastern bred and educated, the latter a classmate of Grinstein's at Yale. Grinstein hired Pertschuk from the staff of Senator Maurine Neuberger, Democrat from Oregon, to take the lead role in developing and passing consumer protection bills. He would be the key staffer in Maggie's legislative battle for the protection of the American consumer, a surrogate for the average citizens whose political leverage rarely extends beyond their votes on election day. As brilliant and dedicated as Grinstein, Pertschuk would not fail.

In the "dance of legislation"—the title of a superb account by Eric Redman of the passage of the National Health Services Act—Maggie, the master choreographer, directed this corps of young committee staffers in their handling of the accelerated business of the Commerce and Appropriations committees. Their dances would change American society and the way it conducts its business.

"When you worked with Senator Magnuson you never had to worry," said Brock Adams, who, as a leading member of the House Commerce Committee, and later as President Jimmy Carter's secretary of transportation. "You didn't worry because he had the best staff on the hill. Maggie knew how to delegate. They knew how to work."[4]

The big change did not begin agreeably. There was a "battle for Magnuson's soul," as Pertschuk put it, behind this radical switch in legislative direction; a struggle personified in the clash between Grinstein and Pertschuk, young activists of the Commerce Committee, and Fred Lordon, a devout Maggie loyalist of the old school, his close connection to Dave Beck's Teamsters. They personified the conflict between activism and the status quo. It was personally harrowing, especially for Pertschuk, but the outcome was never much in question once Magnuson accepted Grinstein's idea of an activist committee targeting consumer protection. There was also the specter of a close call with disaster in the 1962 election. His influence waning, Lordon was moved from the offices in Maggie's Alley in the Old Senate Office Building to the Dirksen Building a block away. Eventually he resigned, displaced by the Bumblebees.

This was at the core of Magnuson's survival. Asked in a 1971 television interview how he kept the pace of the Senate's fast dance, Maggie answered, "I keep young people around me and I read everything I can."[5] The Bumblebees were young and continuously invigorated. They were also inspired.

As Tom Allison and Jerry Grinstein later explained, they had a mindset that "from Magnuson's office you could go out and fix things that were broken in society, and if it didn't work, you could come back and try again." Theirs, and Magnuson's, was an attitude almost lost in the political climate of Washington, D.C., near the end of the century.

Allison: "There was no sense of limits with respect to the use of government as a tool to accomplish good. There was also the realization that it had to reflect well on Magnuson. You didn't want to embarrass him."

Grinstein: "Moreover, there was an obligation to do it [good]. It was a pleasure to go to work every day. There was loyalty to Magnuson—a tremendous bond. You understood you couldn't embarrass him and you had a sense of the limits of his power."[6]

Maggie was generous to his young staff in the use of that power, excessively generous said some critics who shunned the corridors of the Old Senate Office Building to watch events from the press galleries of the House and Senate and the watering holes, the Monocle and Carroll Arms, a few blocks away. What they noticed, especially in the senator's later years, was the contrast between Magnuson shuffling along the Capitol aisles, cigar clenched in his teeth, and the light-footed Ed Sheets or Manny Rouvelas at his side. It gave a distorted, unflattering, impression of the senator.

Magnuson's subcommittee on Appropriations handled the independent federal agencies, Health and Education. Its staffer, Harley Dirks, an eastern Washington farm boy with the brain of a Wall Street accountant, was virtually a senator unto himself—or so it appeared to lobbyists attracted by the millions of dollars of federal funds assigned by the subcommittees. Stan Barer would clerk a social revolution, the public accommodations section of the 1964 Civil Rights Act, to its passage. Norm Dicks, Allison, Rouvelas, and Sheets were the staffers behind the national policy on railroads, highways, airlines, shipping, and Puget Sound. At times they appeared to be instigators as well as managers. If so, it was an illusion Magnuson did not mind at all.

"Maggie sought to get the job done, not to raise a high profile," said Al Swift, the former aide to Representative Lloyd Meeds of Everett, and later himself the seven-term representative from Washington's Second District.[7]

With the power that he delegated, Maggie got the profound loyalty of his staff. His only rule: Don't screw up. "Once you had his confidence, he would delegate—if he accepted your idea," remembers Sheets. "Then he'd say, 'go ahead. Let me know if I need to call someone.' He did not need a lot of briefing. By 1977 Senator John McClellan, the Arkansas Democrat, was sick. Magnuson became de facto chairman of the Appropriations Committee, while continuing as chairman of its Health and Education subcommittee. Under a third hat he was a member of the Senate Democratic Policy Committee. That is an enormous work load, yet we never felt overwhelmed. What made this work—and what made us work—is that we were looking out for the public interest. You knew that if it was in the public interest Magnuson would support it. When I think of the public interest I think of Ralph Nader, Mike Pertschuk, and Warren Magnuson."[8]

The straw boss of this corps de legislative ballet, Jerry Grinstein, says much the same. No liberal legislator in this century, perhaps in the nation's history, sponsored and passed as much legislation as Magnuson, much of it in the aggressive final seventeen years of his forty-eight-year legislative career. Yet Grinstein says only once did he ever feel swamped, this in 1964 during a forgotten national railroad strike and the historic Senate debate on civil rights.

"Magnuson was not a manager—that was not a part of his exceptional life," said Grinstein. "His talent was in bringing his judgment and convictions to play." And so, of course, was his talent in bringing his Senate colleagues to play.

"I had no trouble explaining my case to other senators," Maggie once said in a televised interview. "I didn't have any feuds. It was never a matter of wheeling and dealing. When you are through with an issue you don't hold a grudge. There's always another day. If you play it that way, they [colleagues] respect you. You must be courteous. After all, you're among people who have to live together ten months out of the year. But, so many hold grudges."

Once he advised a reporter new to the Capitol, "Never hold a grudge." The absence of vindictiveness is a rare human trait. Perhaps it is the reason Senator Eugene McCarthy, Democrat from Minnesota, told the same newsman, "Maggie is the most loved man in the Senate."[9] This was an obvious source of his persuasive power.

Management of this legislative enterprise followed lines laid out in the budgets of the committees and their subcommittees. The budget, in essence, was the planning document. Grinstein says he worked closely with his counterpart, Jerry Kinney, the minority counsel with whom he had no great philosophical differences. But control of the Commerce Committee remained central; that is, with Magnuson, the chairman. To an outside observer, strolling down Maggie's Alley, visiting acquaintances on both sides of the corridor, the enterprise looked informal, seamless. The critical element was Magnuson's willingness to delegate, and having the young men and women around him to whom his power could be entrusted.

Mike Pertschuk, who brought Nader into an alliance with Magnuson, led the consumer protection battles as chief counsel to the Commerce Committee. This was a measure of Magnuson's trust in the British-born easterner. But that trust was slow in coming. Initially, says Pertschuk, "I was scared of Maggie. He was very gruff and identified with the Senate's old guard establishment. For a while he thought, or pretended, I was on the staff of Gale McGee's subcommittee. Gradually we came to know each other."

Magnuson could appreciate Pertschuk's brilliance, wit, and his fight for the public interest. It is not far-fetched to imagine the childless senator seeing Pertschuk and the Bumblebees as part of his family; projections of what he believed best about himself.

But it was the "gruff" Maggie best known to those unfamiliar with his power block on the first floor of the Old Senate Office Building—the "SOB"—the gruff and drinking Maggie. His lifelong delight in strong drink generated Capitol speculation about his state of sobriety. Staffers knew better. It is the close witness of Irv Hoff and Mike Pertschuk that they never saw the senator's work impaired by liquor. The best explanation for his tolerance of alcohol comes from Featherstone Reid: "Amazing genes." Grinstein attributes Maggie's gruff facade to a lifelong lack of self-confidence; a sense of inferiority he could never overcome. Others could see his manner as armor against impossible demands. Magnuson frequently explained himself as a legislative artist of the possible: "You fight for those things that are possible, but there are many things that you just have to accept, like it or not."

In pursuit of the possible, Maggie worked long days, frequently culminated in the early evening with "The Children's Hour," a meeting with the Bumblebees and an occasional outsider, to discuss outstanding business of the day, or work to be done on the morrow. But he did not reflect on old glories. His eye was on what's to be done, not what had been done.

"Oh, he was a fine speaker," said Mabel Thompson of Ephrata, Washington, Maggie's friend from their days at the University of Washington until his death. "But he never told people exactly what he was doing; that is he never did any bragging. He never told enough about what he was doing for his own political good. My father [Frank Bell] would get after Maggie about this. He'd insist, 'you must tell the people your accomplishments.'"[10]

Until he became chairman of the Federal Trade Commission in 1977, Mike Pertschuk began each work day by meeting with Magnuson. "I'd have a list of matters for work that day. He had to say okay before we could go ahead. It was very informal," said Pertschuk. Maggie, as noted by everyone with whom he dealt, was a very fast study as well as a very seasoned legislator.

Most of the business on Pertschuk's list dealt with consumer protection, potential acts of the Congress to protect average citizens from shady door-to-door salesmen, phoney-baloney product warranties, killer automobiles with defective tires, carcinogen-laden cigarette smoke (Maggie chewed on a cigar thoughout the hearings on the measure to label cigarettes as dangerous to one's health), misleading product labels, and combustible fabrics.

As Grinstein had anticipated, consumer protection—"corporate accountability" is Nader's other name for this legislation—became the cause of a new political generation. With Magnuson as its architect, the movement produced legislation that reduced public costs, saved untold lives, and possibly saved the career of Warren Magnuson. Consumer protection had not surfaced as an issue in the elaborate polls taken for Magnuson in 1962, despite a surprisingly positive reaction to Jack Kennedy's 1960 campaign speech on the issue. But Grinstein had tapped a political lode that amounted to campaign gold.

Its elements of success were mixed. There was the sine qua non of a powerful and sympathetic senator in need of an image overhaul and aiming for high goals with a bright, idealistic staff. Supporting Magnuson were liberal senators elected in 1952 and 1958—Phil Hart of Michigan and Frank Moss of Utah being most conspicuous—and a new breed of journalists, children of the Depression, wars, and—unlike their predecessors—college educated. These were journalists and senators eager to correct the excesses of a corporate culture that placed profits above public safety and was unwilling to correct an imbalance between the two.

The supporting senators included Estes Kefauver, Gaylord Nelson, Maurine Neuberger, Henry Jackson, Gale McGee, Paul Douglas, Hart, and Moss. National reporters most notable in their coverage of consumer legislation were Drew Pearson, the columnist, and his successors, Jack Anderson and Les Whitten, Pat Sloyan of United Press International and Hearst Newspapers, Hearst's Harry Kelly, and Morton Mintz of the *Washington Post*.

What they lacked in well-paid, high-powered lobbyists, the consumer protectionists offset with Ralph Nader and his cadre of young, idealistic investigators. Nader's Raiders were unpaid, in some cases unskilled, but ever-enthusiastic in exposing flaws of America's marketplace and keeping the press abreast of their work. There came also the occasional lone-wolf lobbyist, unpaid save for the compensation that comes with doing good works. The shining example is Dr. Abe Bergman, an irrepressible Seattle pediatrician, who pushed Magnuson and the Bumblebees to pass the "flammable fabrics act" over the objections of the cotton lobby and encouraged him to help create the National Health Service Corps, which sent medical doctors into the nation's hinterlands where health care is sparse. Bergman is the model of what one man can do with Congress, given a senator like Magnuson and a staff like the Bumblebees—and do it with brains and determination, instead of bourbon and campaign contributions.

Bergman did it with persistence and, for a medical doctor, an unusual ability to articulate problems and solutions. In the case of flammable fabrics, it was a matter of forcing manufacturers to fireproof their garments. But without his friends, Grinstein and Pertschuk, and the good senator Magnuson, there would have been no law on fabrics.

As Pertschuk later explained it, there came in the 1960s and early 1970s "a rare, if not unique, concurrence of economic and political conditions" that allowed passage of these regulatory reforms. The regulatory poles would reverse with the Republican victory in the 1994 election, but at that time in the 1960s there seemed to be no limit on what government could do to improve the American quality of life. Indeed, among politicians there was even competition to do so. Pretschuk sums it up: "Much of the political energy behind many of the consumer initiatives was reinforced, if not generated, by competition for credit as progenitor of consumer laws." Competitors included President Lyndon Johnson, who found his "Grinstein" in the equally brilliant Joe Califano. Magnuson, however, won this do-good competition. By 1968, five years after Grinstein began the restructuring of the Commerce Committee staff, nine major pieces of consumer protection legislation bore the name Magnuson.

These bills created a National Commission on Hazardous Products to protect consumers from faulty X-ray machines, television sets, power tools, and commonplace household conveniences; a Natural Gas Pipeline Safety Act gave the new Department of Transportation the power to regulate gas pipeline construction and maintenance; the Door to Door Sales Act, a major irritant to magazine publishers, gave consumers twenty-four hours to back away from flim-flam sales deals; the cigarette acts made tobacco companies label their product as hazardous to health and list the tar and nicotine content (Magnuson estimated 300,000 persons died prematurely each year from the effects of cigarette smoke); two separate bills mandated full disclosure on terms of credit and equal frankness on warranty terms; and an Auto Safety Law created the National Traffic Safety Agency to promulgate safe car design. This was in addition to the flammable fabrics act, and, most controversial, the Fair Packaging and Labeling Act to standardize packaging and, as Maggie put it, "to root out misleading and confusing packaging practices."[11]

"Warren Magnuson has done more to protect housewives from shoddy materials and false purchases than any other senator in recent history," wrote Drew Pearson in a 1967 year-end column devoted to citizens who had improved the quality of American life.

In the midst of his fight for consumer protection, Magnuson put his name and muscle behind two other measures that resonate into the twenty-first century and one of great symbolic importance. He fathered the Educational Television Act, provided it with 75 percent federal funding for equipment. Nonprofit public television would be run by a fifteen-member commission. President Johnson named Maggie's old friend and political and business associate, Saul Haas, to the initial commission after Haas sold KIRO-TV to the Mormon Church in 1964.

Maggie backed Majority Leader Mike Mansfield's resolution to draw down U.S. armed forces in Europe, troops placed there in the early 1950s when it appeared the Soviets would invade the West. That risk was not so great in 1967, if in fact it existed at all. But the resolution came to naught. The bill to allow eighteen-year-olds the right to vote came almost by accident. Mansfield ran into Maggie at the end of a session and offered him a ride to the Shoreham. En route they discussed the issue. Magnuson had tried and failed to push such voting rights through the 1933 state legislature. They agreed it was wrong that youth could fight in Vietnam but not be allowed to vote. They also agreed to change the law by statute rather than constitutional amendment. Norm Dicks drafted the measure, Maggie and Mansfield pushed it through Congress, and the Supreme Court, on a 5 to 4 vote, ruled it constitutional for eighteen-year-olds to vote in federal elections.[12] For Magnuson, these were super-sideshows to the main event: conflict over corporate accountability.

The fight over consumer protection legislation was not the equivalent of Notre Dame—Maggie and the Bumblebees—versus St. Joseph's Female Academy. The opposition lineup featured the National Association of Manufacturers, the auto industry, tobacco interests, and textile lobbies. Certain magazine publishers, wary of an adverse impact on door-to-door salesmen held accountable for their sales pitch, even raised the somewhat faded specter of "communism" in their fight with consumer advocates. But tactically, they were caught flat-footed by Maggie's change of direction, a late-blooming return to his populist ways of the 1930s; his shift away from business as usual.[13]

"What the business lobby had seen in Magnuson was a Northwest progressive, mellowing like other senators and playing ball with the interests, while taking care of constituents," said Nader. "They weren't prepared for the change in Maggie. He was not a flaming crusader, but he would go on to become the greatest legislative consumer advocate of the century. He would tell the lobby, 'Let's be fair.' They'd have to listen."[14]

Magnuson was scrupulous in allowing the business lobby to present its case for killing or amending the bills. Given a status quo of car wrecks, blown tires, addictive cigarettes, and kids fried in flammable fabrics, most of the fight took place behind the committee's closed doors, generally beyond the reach of the mainline press. Business didn't want regulation, and pointed out that it would be expensive. Magnuson argued that in the long run it would make them more money; better products would widen their markets. On the issue of cigarette smoking, he once said, "It's easy to quit drinking, but it's damned hard to kick the cigarette habit . . . I don't like to see young people fooled into the habit [of cigarettes]."[15] The cigarette lobby rolled out their impressive medical cannons to shoot down the cigarette warning label. In essence each said there's "no proof" tobacco smoke leads to cancer or heart disease. Senator Thruston Morton of tobacco-growing Kentucky suggested excessive booze and coffee consumption might be the real culprit; an odd defense, given Kentucky's excellent bourbon produce. Dr. Duane Carr of the University of Tennessee Medical School reminded the committee, "Lung cancer is also found in those who do not smoke." Dr. William Crissy, a professor of marketing at Michigan State University, took a different tack: "A warning label on cigarettes is at odds with the traditional and accepted role of advertising in our economy."[16] He must have drawn attention to the question of how much can the buyer beware in the face of advertising as pervasive as that promoting cigarettes. But each advocate got to speak.

"Magnuson had taught us well that the denial of the opportunity to testify invariably created a diversionary issue for a business group," said Pertschuk. "No matter how much delay ensued (and often that was the very motive of the request to testify, made at the eleventh hour), the committee leadership supporting legislation was always in a more commanding moral posture having afforded opponents their full day in court."[17]

The chairman listened, and then, literally or figuratively, he lowered the gavel. Television executives, pals of Magnuson's, protesting the bill banning cigarette ads on their stations were told, "Moss has a hold of that one—not much I can do." Frank Moss, a Utah Democrat, and a former Securities and Exchange Commission attorney, was one of those pivotal liberals elected in 1958.

When he commenced hearings on Senator Phil Hart's bill on fair packaging and labeling in April 1965, Magnuson said, "Once again the committee is engaged in its historic role as an arbiter of fair commercial practice." The bill mandated the Federal Trade Commission and the Food and Drug Administration to require that the net quantity of contents be stated on the package of the product. Business reacted immediately: undue government interference. Esther Peterson, the president's assistant for consumer affairs, said that, on the contrary, the bill would be good for business. It would level the playing field between the honest and shady manufacturers. For her efforts, industry lobbyists quietly spread the word from Washington to Seattle that Ms. Peterson was a pinko.

Whoa, said Senator Morton, with this bill "the government wants to start running the grocery store." Tom Baker, general manager of the soda pop trade association, said the bill was "needless and unduly restrictive," that it curtailed "the right of a businessman to exercise his own judgment in marketing his wares." The Chamber of Commerce said the bill would hike production costs and restrict the variety of choices. The National Association of Manufactuers said business had already demonstrated its respect for the American consumer, and Lee Bickmore, president of the National Biscuit Company, labeled the proposal "extremely dangerous."[18]

These opposition pitches to the Commerce Committee hearings were relatively muted compared with the hardball played when Magnuson closed the committee doors—a candor gap the chairman exploited to the advantage of the legislation.

With what Pertschuk admits is "perverse fondness," he recalls a summons to the chairman's office during closed committee action on the fair packaging and labeling act. A coalition of food manufacturers, led by Procter and Gamble's ace lobbyist, Bryce Harlow, opposed the measure. When Pertschuk arrived, Maggie was seated at his desk, cigar between his teeth. So was Drew Pearson. "Tell Drew what happened in executive session," said Magnuson. Pertschuk reported the action:

Told that potato chips were packaged in sixty different weights and sizes under a pound, making it impossible for a housewife to choose the bag with the most chips at the lowest price, Senator Ross Bass of Tennessee, a favorite of the food lobby, snorted: "Any woman who feeds her children potato chips isn't worth protecting." A few days later Bass was an item in Pearson's column "Washington Merry Go Round," along with news that the food lobby was desperately seeking to kill or water down the fair packaging bill.

Committee members, especially Bass, were infuriated at the leak and, at their next closed meeting, demanded the chairman investigate. Maggie solemnly asked committee staffers if any had talked with Pearson. Pertschuk remained silent. Maggie acted innocent. He cleared his throat and returned to the agenda. Within an hour the packaging and labeling bill went "do pass" from Commerce Committee. Enacted into law, it remains the reason for all that fine print on food labels detailing the fats, cholesterol, calories, and carbohydrates contained in the product.

Committee members pointed the finger of suspicion at Joan Claybrook, a young Capitol staffer affiliated with the Commerce Committee, for the Pearson leak. Maggie, ungallantly perhaps, did not try to dissuade them. Later he credited the food industry with a "roaring pitched battle" against the packaging and labeling act—behind closed doors, of course.[19]

"Those bills were really tough," said former Senator Moss years later. "There was great outside pressure in opposition, but we stood our ground and eventually got the legislation. Maggie had a lot of friends among the business people, but he stood by these bills. He was not demonstrative, didn't make a lot of fuss. He just went ahead—and got things done."[20]

"Maggie was delightful to deal with," recalled his ally Ralph Nader. "He wasn't the kind of guy to squeal and squirm over things, like some senators who wince and say, 'Oh if I do this it will anger that interest.' He just did things. He was courteous, brief, humorous, laconic, always observing people—but sometimes it was hard to figure what he was saying."[21] Nader's young raiders did much of the legwork and research on the consumer legislation, and his own image as an incorruptible consumer advocate gave extra push to Maggie's bills.

One of the persistent Magnuson myths of the Kennedy-Johnson era had it that the powerful senator was held captive by a rogue staff, which ran roughshod over industry to churn out the consumer protection measures. Some lobbyists fell for it. Accordingly, a few old hands got one of their profession, Irv Hoff, lobbyist for sugar refiners, to call on Maggie and inform him of their fears that zealous staffers were going overboard passing consumer protection legislation—ah, perhaps without the senator's knowledge.

Maggie, as Hoff recalled, listened, curled the corners of his lips in a funny little smile, and then spun out minute details of the committee's pending legislation and the actions of his staff. "You know I know what these young guys are doing," said Maggie. "They've got spirit and energy. They are doing what I want them to do." Hoff was not really surprised, and he properly reported the meeting and Magnuson's response to Pertschuk. After hearing reports of the exchange, industry lobbyists realized the futility of an end run around the staff with appeals to the chairman.[22] Regardless, this particular village myth helped Magnuson preserve his image as a Senate "good guy," the bad stuff coming from radical kids in his employ.

The chairman did give them great leeway, but if staffers proposed an idea he didn't like, or more likely, an idea whose time in Magnuson's judgment had not yet come, he would slam the door. There were limits to their free rein.

During the oil crisis of 1973, Pertschuk proposed a federal oil and gas corporation to contest control of this utterly critical commodity, then, as now, in the boardrooms of private corporations. He took the idea to

Magnuson, who, said Pertschuk, "wasn't comfortable with it." When Pertschuk persisted, Maggie got blunt: "He said he didn't like the idea and it wasn't going anywhere." Furthermore, the chairman suggested, "You guys ought to go back to Cuba."

A more serious breach of the limits occurred when Lynn Sutcliffe, one of Professor Johnson's prodigies, flew back to Ohio to investigate a local group sponsoring newspaper advertisements in favor of deregulating natural gas prices. They appeared to be funded by the natural gas industry. Legislation was pending before the Commerce Committee related to natural gas. When Ohio senators learned of the impromptu probe, they howled to Maggie that Sutcliffe was attempting to abridge free speech. Maggie reacted with some fury, refusing to authorize trips by members of his staff. For a time they were temporarily grounded.

Grinstein kept an eye toward the 1968 election, even as he hired new staff and steered Commerce Committee consumer protection activities. In 1964 he returned to his home state to manage Lyndon Johnson's campaign for president and to renew his knowledge of local politics. He was laying the groundwork for what would be a triumphant reelection campaign for Maggie in 1968. By that time they had easily arrived at a campaign slogan, one that was simple, accurate, and to the point: "Maggie Keeps the Big Boys Honest." With the consumer protection legislation, he had done so in spades.

CHAPTER 23

Civil Rights: The Whole Load
of Hay Falls on Maggie

June 1963: the commencement of a career for Stan Barer, just graduated from the University of Washington Law School and bound for the staff of Senator Warren Magnuson; the start of a hot summer of racial strife for the nation.[1] Barer—the first of Professor Ralph Johnson's star pupils to be propelled from the law school to Maggie's employ—was on his way to "the other Washington" while the country boiled with demonstrations against racial discrimination. A counterprotest, the bombing of a church in Birmingham, Alabama, killed four black children. Walter Lippmann, a leading national columnist and one not given to overstatement, said, "a revolutionary condition exists." Barer, the high-spirited son of a Russian immigrant turned Walla Walla businessman, had no inkling that his destiny and the black revolution would quickly become intertwined.

President Kennedy, with a crisis in Saigon as well as in Birmingham, had to address the domestic turmoil, like it or not. Six years before, when he had first sought southern support for his presidential bid, Kennedy spent two hours quizzing a newsman who had just returned from covering the racial integration of Little Rock's Central High School. That crisis required deployment of the 101st Airborne Division to keep the peace. In a private conversation at Love Field, Dallas, Texas, Kennedy sought details about Arkansas Governor Orval Faubus and his staff and talked generally about the looming crisis of race. As a liberal intellectual, the Massachusetts senator indicated strong support of the black protests against discrimination, and the need to redress the moral wrong of segregation. As a working politician, aiming for the White House, he knew the price to be paid in southern support if those sentiments were widely known.[2] He might hope that such redress would not have to come on his watch. By June 1963, after the Birmingham bombing, he ran out of that hope.

The president's response to this turmoil was a seven-part (seven titles) civil rights bill: In Title I a sixth-grade education would be evidence of literacy, making the adult citizen eligible to vote in federal elections.

Title II, public accommodations, would desegregate hotels, restaurants, theaters, and other facilities open to the public. Title III would empower the attorney general to sue segregated schools. Title IV would create a community service to assist local governments in desegregation disputes. Title V would extend the life of the Civil Rights Commission. Title VI would allow the federal government to withhold funds in response to racial discrimination. And Title VII would create a commission on equal employment opportunity.

Eighty-two years had elapsed before the Congress even addressed the heart of the civil rights issue. The tepid 1957 legislation, an unenforceable voting rights law, paled in comparison to Kennedy's proposed package. To pass this 1963 watershed bill, a twentieth-century bill of civil rights, Kennedy needed sixty-seven votes in the Senate, the two-thirds required under Senate rules to shut off debate (cloture) to end a filibuster certain to come from senators of the South. Senator Mike Mansfield of Montana, the Democratic majority leader, told the president on June 18 that to get those votes he would need "complete cooperation and good faith" with respect to Senator Everett Dirksen of Illinois, the Republican minority leader. Without Republican votes there would be no approved legislation. Two days later Mansfield informed Kennedy that he had met with Dirksen and reached agreement on all of the bill, except Title II, public accommodations. Dirksen told Mansfield he could not sponsor such a radical change in the way of life for many Americans, not all of them southerners.[3]

Once, in 1949, Magnuson had to write a letter of apology to Representative Adam Clayton Powell of New York, whose wife, the beautiful, multitalented entertainer Hazel Scott, was denied service at a Pasco, Washington, cafeteria. "We do not serve colored," the owner told Scott, who subsequently sued Harry Utz of Pasco for $50,000 over the insult— this in the liberal Northwest.[4] If he needed further evidence, the Scott incident had shown Maggie that racial discrimination was a fact of life for much of the nation.

Dirksen's intransigence on Title II left Kennedy with a dilemma. He solved it by separating Title II from the rest of the bill, which was destined for Judiciary and Education committees, and giving it to Senator Magnuson, chairman of the Commerce Committee. Then on June 11, 1963, the President announced to a national TV audience his legislation:

"If any American, because his skin is dark, cannot eat lunch in a restaurant open to the public, if he cannot send his kids to the best schools, vote for public officials . . . then who among us would be content to have the color of his skin and stand in his place?"

Alabama Governor George Wallace replied via television to the president's message: "You're going to have to bring back the troops from Berlin if you pass that law."

The most perceptive commentary came from columnist William S. White, a Texan with liberal instincts, a veteran and shrewd observer of the U.S. Senate. He wrote a piece titled "The Hayload Falls on Maggie." "This solid, uncomplaining, Scandinavian-American," wrote White, is assigned conflicting duties: On the one hand he must pass Title II, "the most controversial part of Kennedy's omnibus civil rights package"; on the other, as chairman of the Democratic senatorial campaign committee, "it is his urgent duty to reelect Democratic senators." The discharge of his presidential assignment, Title II, is "anything but helpful to the discharge of his other senatorial duty."

White nailed the essence of the conflict borne by Title II. It was a clash between the rights of all citizens not to be discriminated against because of their color and the rights of property ownership. His own feelings: "[The Senate] is most unlikely to accept the proposition that the refusal of a private business or lodging house to serve all comers, however unethical this might be, is actually to be made a federal offense. The concern, here, of course, is for the maintenance of the centuries old rights of property."

The columnist, a self-proclaimed skeptic of the motives of politicians, concluded he had "no doubt Magnuson is truly for the civil rights package, public accommodations and all. Equally, there is no question that Sen. Magnuson is no less devoted to his mission of electing Democrats. All this explains why when his fellow senators say the whole load of hay has fallen on Maggie, they utter the painful, but total truth."[5]

Stan Barer, who would share that load of hay along with Jerry Grinstein, arrived in Magnuson's office in August the day before Dr. Martin Luther King's speech to the multitudes of black and white demonstrators on the great landscape in front of the Washington Monument. "I have a dream," intoned King, alluding to the end of racial discrimination. Barer understood the sermon and the need for legislation to end legalized segregation. A few weeks later Grinstein, Commerce Committee's chief counsel and a master tactician, assigned Barer as the clerk for Title II. The new staffer would spend the next six months carrying his share of the load, satisfied, if not exhilarated, by the challenge. He was helping Magnuson make American history.

Barer came to this task with preliminary conditioning. The idea of attacking discrimination in public places under the Commerce Clause of the U.S. Constitution had been discussed by University of Washington law professor Robert Fletcher. The Commerce Clause gives Congress the power to "regulate commerce with foreign nations, and among the several states and with the Indian tribes." It has been interpreted to allow the Congress to override state laws. An attack on segregation through the Commerce Clause was, to say the least, unique. It would be a flanking attack that avoided earlier rulings of the U.S. Supreme Court that had upheld state laws permitting segregation under the Fourteenth Amendment.

In the aftermath of the Civil War, slaves, the foundation of the South's pre-1865 economy, were freed but remained segregated initially by custom and soon thereafter under state laws aimed at maintaining white supremacy. These laws were an American legal innovation. They ensured political and economic control by whites in those late Confederate states and reinforced the South's ideal of white superiority over blacks. In large measure they invalidated the outcome of our Civil War. They legalized white supremacy, a component as critical to defining southern populists as public power was to populists of the Northwest. Populists of both regions railed against Wall Street and pernicious eastern financial interests. But southern populists, the most notable being J. K. Vardaman and Theodore Bilbo, both of Mississippi, were shouting white supremacists. The Ku Klux Klan, white-robed, horse-mounted terrorists, put iron into the segregation laws. The Klan murdered blacks for asserting their equal rights, intimidating whites with their trademark, the burning cross. In 1877 the federal government, under President Rutherford B. Hayes, withdrew its troops and retreated from a commitment to equal rights in the South. So did the U.S. Supreme Court.

In October 1895, the nation's high court upheld the law of the great state of Louisiana calling for separate accommodations for "colored" and whites on railroads. This was the case of Homer A. Plessy, "a colored man of seven-eighths Caucasian blood, one-eighth African blood," against John Ferguson, a district court judge in New Orleans. The state charged Plessy violated the law when he sat in the white section of a train going from New Orleans to Covington, Louisiana. He was arrested, fined $25, and jailed twenty days for "race mixing." Plessy appealed to higher courts. Louisiana's state attorneys argued that such separation did not deprive a colored person of his rights under the Constitution, but was instead a reasonable exercise of state power.

The highest court agreed. A majority decided that "the owner of an inn, a public conveyance or a place of amusement refusing accommodations to colored people" isn't imposing slavery or servitude. In fact, the majority ruled that "separation laws do not necessarily imply inferiority of either race to the other." *Plessy v. Ferguson* imbedded the "separate but equal" concept in American society for nearly seven decades. Forgotten was the remarkable dissent from this decision by Justice John Marshall Harlan of Kentucky, who argued that the Louisiana railroad should be regarded the same as a Louisiana highway from which no one was barred regardless of skin color. He noted that the Thirteenth Amendment prevented "the imposition of burdens or disabilities that constitute the badges of slavery"; that the Fourteenth Amendment said, "No state shall make or enforce any law which shall abridge the privileges or immunities of citizens."

"In my opinion," concluded the justice from Kentucky, "This judgement will in time prove to be quite as pernicious and divisive as Dred Scott."[6] The Dred Scott decision by the Supreme Court in 1857 was taken to mean that the court upheld the right of states to have laws allowing slavery. Our Civil War followed three years later.

Ultimately, Title II would continue the undoing of the "separate but equal" denigration of black citizens which had begun with the Supreme Court's 1954 decision in *Brown v. Board of Education*. That decision, theoretically, put an end to segregated common schools.

Magnuson and the Commerce Committee would not directly address *Plessy v. Ferguson*, but, instead, an 1883 decision by which the high court struck down the public accommodations section of the Civil Rights Act of 1875. This decision cemented the right of states to have laws allowing property owners to discriminate on the basis of race. The court's 1883 decision did specifically what *Plessy v. Ferguson* allowed indirectly. It was a pillar of states' rights based on the court's interpretation of the Constitution.[7]

It takes a stretch of the imagination to visualize the Republican Congress of the mid-1990s setting out to correct a social injustice through an assault on private property rights, no matter how indirect. On the contrary, the balance between property rights and human rights tilted in favor of the former in 1995. In 1963, however, there was the proper mix of legislative talent, moral outrage, and political courage—all stimulated by the whiff of insurrection—to change American society. But how to do it; where to find the legal key that would unlock those Supreme Court decisions made under the Constitution's Thirteenth and Fourteenth Amendments.

"Bob Fletcher taught us that segregated facilities create a burden on commerce," said Barer. "Blacks had the right to travel, but for what, if they couldn't go to the toilet—whites only—a restaurant—ditto—or a motel—ditto again—that would accommodate them. The Justice

Department under Attorney General Robert Kennedy was aware of the Commerce Clause theory and bought it. Burke Marshall and Nicholas Katzenbach, assistant attorneys general, and Grinstein were the drivers behind it."

The key player, or, as Charles Ferris, the Senate secretary, put it, "the capstone on the arches that bridged the parties," was Maggie. Ferris, the ebullient general counsel to the taciturn Majority Leader Mansfield, described the Magnuson of Title II as a pragmatic senator, "not a social engineer, or a romantic, a guy who didn't need the ego feed of publicity." What President Kennedy saw in the Commerce Committee chairman was a Northwest populist, an irrepressible egalitarian who nevertheless had close ties to Senators John Stennis, Richard Russell, Harry Byrd, and Walter George, southerners who would fight Title II to the end in order to preserve the southern way of life—as well as their own careers. Maggie could pull together thirty senators of differing political slants.[8] He was intuitive, nonjudgmental, and, as Barer said, "Everybody liked him—he wasn't threatening."

In sum, Maggie was big enough to carry the whole load of hay. It fell on July 1, 1963, in Room 318 of the Old Senate Office Building.

"We begin deliberations on the most important and sensitive bill that has been referred to the committee in many years," Magnuson opened. "The eyes of the nation and the world are on us—with conflicting opinions—and I am painfully aware of the too long deferred responsibility that we confront."

Barer clerked the hearings. Attorney General Robert Kennedy was the lead witness on behalf of Title II. There was graphic testimony of the perils of public accommodations for a black person traveling the Interstate highway from New York to Miami; how to satisfy the need for rest at night and how to eat and relieve oneself during the day. What this testimony said was that segregated facilities amounted to an obstruction to the nation's commerce which the Congress needed to remove. Magnuson kept matter-of-fact order in committee. Everybody had a chance to talk. It was deliberate and slow, as befitting a potentially major change in American society.

Most press attention went to the bill's opponents, starting with Strom Thurmond, the Commerce Committee member from South Carolina: "Mr. Attorney General, I want to say that I don't think your bill will pass Congress [because] it deprives states and the people of certain powers." The power to discriminate based on race, replied Robert Kennedy. Their argument over the Constitution lasted hours. Senator John Pastore, the Rhode Island Democrat, openly complained that Thurmond was being allowed to talk too long. Barer would later question how badly the Kennedy brothers, eyeing the 1964 presidential election, wanted Title II.[9] There was reason to wonder. Robert E. Thompson, writing in the *Los Angeles Times* on the day the hearings commenced, reported "real concern in the White House over the sharp decline in President Kennedy's popularity as a result of his civil rights leadership." Regardless, Magnuson plowed ahead.

Governor Ross Barnett of Mississippi and George Wallace, the latter a self-described "loyal American and a loyal Southerner who has never belonged to any subversive organization," lowered the arguments against Title II from the Constitution to the Red scare. Barnett, once described as "bone dumb," gave a vivid image of the national doom the measure posed:

> This is a critical time in our history. . . . groups are agitating, breaking the peace, provoking violence in an effort to blackmail Congress into passing this law in direct violation of the Constitution. It is part of a pattern of Communist activity around the world. Cuba, Laos, Berlin, Vietnam, Haiti [*sic*] are the same as Jackson, Birmingham, Cambridge [Maryland] and Philadelphia. It's the same old Communist offensive . . . the divide, disrupt and conquer technique. Passage of this bill will provoke more violence, not just in the South but in all areas of the nation—part of the Communist plot for the overthrow of our nation. . . . [P]assage of the bill will put hundreds of thousands of white businessmen into the streets. . . . [T]he purpose of government is to protect the individual and to see that no one interferes with private property. . . . [T]his socialistic measure allows government to dictate property rights. It is a threat to the safety and stablity of the nation—it usurps property rights. It will reap a bloody harvest. May God have mercy on your souls.

Magnuson let Barnett express himself fully. Governor Wallace went a step beyond the Red scare by arguing, "Leaders of the federal government have misused Negroes for selfish political reasons" and "each day we see our own government going to ridiculous extremes to appease a minority bloc of voters. . . . [A] minority is threatening to intimidate Congress with tactics approved by sponsors of S. 1732 [Title II]."

"Stop right here," Magnuson interrupted. "This committee is sitting to soberly and seriously consider legislation and we are not going to be intimidated by anyone."

"Mr. Chairman," replied Wallace, "Of course this governor doesn't try to intimidate anybody, but I really believe what I have just said . . ."

Maggie intercepted Wallace again: "As Dr. Johnson once said, you could be right. We don't know. We are here to consider a piece of legislation and [*voice rising*] no one will coerce a decision."[10]

After these encounters between the chairman and the southern governors, Maurice Rosenblatt, Maggie's old friend from the American League for a Free Palestine, wrote, "Dear Warren, you certainly did a splendid job interrogating [Barnett and Wallace]. . . . it shows there is still some honest indignation left in our public leaders. This is the 'old' Magnuson which proves that you are still the 'young Magnuson.' Writing fan letters to Senators is something I never do, but I thought you should know how much satisfaction you gave to many of your friends."[11]

With an eye on the promise of convention commerce, the Atlanta Mayor, Ivan Allen, gave a sober testimony, saying he preferred a local solution to the segregation problem, but admitting that it was a problem and that Title II might have to be passed "as a last resort." Allen was a pivotal witness.

Before the committee went behind closed doors to begin "mark-up," the process of amending legislation, John Kennedy was shot and killed in Dallas. This was November 22, 1963, shortly after he had flown into Love Field. Certainly one newsman would associate his murder in Dallas with his legislation to bring civil rights to black citizens.

"I was in the Capitol cafeteria when word came, about 11:30 A.M.," said Barer. "I rushed to Magnuson's office. The door was open. I went inside. The senator was by himself, seated at his desk, tears running down his face. I said, 'Senator, I'm very sorry.' He said, 'It's so sad.' That was all. He just sat there crying, terribly hurt. I left the office."

The assassination did not mute critics of Kennedy's civil rights proposals. Senator Robert Byrd, the West Virginia Democrat and Senate majority leader to be, wrote the new president, Lyndon Johnson, on December 7, 1963: "The civil rights legislation impinges upon the civil and constitutional rights of white people." He said that his position on civil rights would be in accord with Senator Russell's. Byrd seemed to plead with Johnson to back off: "Remember, I was with you when the going was rough in West Virginia"—an apparent reference to West Virginia's 1980 presidential primary election, won (some said bought) by Jack Kennedy.[12]

Johnson would not back off from the civil rights measures. On the contrary. As holder of the veto, he had a critical role to play both in promoting their passage through Congress and in seeing them adopted into law. Sad to say, public reaction to Kennedy's death, an aftermath of guilt, also aided the act to passage. Jerry Grinstein doesn't think Title II would have been accepted otherwise.

While the remarkable Grinstein pushed Title II's passage, Fred Lordon warned Magnuson that the legislation would damage the senator's political career. Featherstone Reid says Magnuson answered, "Fred, if I have to be defeated on an issue, what better issue to go down on?"

"Yes, we were fearful, politically threatened," said Frank Moss, the senator from Utah. "And eventually, it may have helped defeat me. Maggie was always calm, never short tempered like many of our colleagues. But he never caved under. The surprising thing is that he kept his friends among the Southern senators—except that he would listen to them and give them small favors."[13] Moss, the liberal stalwart, would lose his seat to the conservative Republican, Orrin Hatch, in 1976.

"Mark-up" in Commerce Committee began before the end of the year and continued until February of the New Year, 1964. Nearly all of the action took place off camera, out of the hearing of reporters. Barer recalls Senator Norris Cotton, a New Hampshire Republican, as most supportive of the measure; Phil Hart, a Michigan Democrat, was "very aggressive." Ralph Yarborough, the Texas Democrat and longtime feuding rival of Lyndon Johnson—President Kennedy had gone to Texas in an attempt to end their feud when he met his fate—had to be turned around. Strom Thurmond, the unreconstructed South Carolina Republican, was a "gentleman." His attempts to amend and cripple Title II were heard and rejected by the committee majority. When all of the amendments were heard, Magnuson announced an executive committee meeting to accept or reject Title II. He had no question the measure would pass—if the committee had a quorum.

The proposed law made it a federal offense to bar persons, on the basis of race or religion, from restaurants, hotels, theaters, and even barbershops if these were part of a public facility such as a hotel or bus station. Haircuts were a particularly sticky issue in committee deliberations, but barbershops stayed in the bill.

On the day designated by Magnuson for a final vote, television cameras and newsmen gathered at the committee doorway on the fifth floor of the new Senate Office Building. Members began arriving, along with tension. Suddenly, the doorway exploded in a wild fury of flailing arms and legs. Strom Thurmond, furious at the prospect of a southern senator favoring Title II, perhaps attempting to prevent a quorum, had thrown Ralph Yarborough to the floor, wrestled the Texan until he got a chokehold on the man's throat. "You're not going through that door," Thurmond shouted. One witness says he thought Thurmond was about to choke the life out of Yarborough. Someone shouted to Maggie, "They're killing each other!" The chairman came outside, observed the pandemonium for a few seconds, then commanded, "Now fellows—break it up."[14]

They complied, and went inside the room for final committee action on Title II.

The committee report, drafted by the clerk, Stan Barer, went to the heart of the controversy, the rights of property owners: "Does the owner of private property devoted to use as a public establishment enjoy a property right to refuse to deal with any member of the public because of that member's race, religion or national origin?" English common law said "no." Common law held that innkeepers must accept any guest who comes along, as long as that person could pay the bill and was not a "public nusiance." And further, the report argued: "The denial of a right to discriminate or segregate by race or religion would not weaken the attributes of private property that make it an effective means of obtaining individual freedom." In fact, the report concluded, ordinary zoning laws place a greater restriction on private property, since they tell the owner what kind of a business he may—or may not—establish on his zoned property.

Over Thurmond's relinquished chokehold, Title II emerged "do pass" from Commerce Committee, and on to the Senate floor. This was in February 1964, the first round in a fight that wouldn't end for another four months. Proponents, led by Senator Hubert Humphrey on the Senate floor and behind the scenes by President Johnson, needed to win over the votes of at least twelve more uncommitted senators in order to beat a southern filibuster.

"Nothing speaks louder to Western and Southern senators than wheat and cotton," Mike Manatos, the ubiquitous White House congressional liaison, told Majority Leader Mansfield. He urged Mansfield to stall such legislation—wheat and cotton subsidies speaking loudest—until completion of action on the civil rights bill. The delay "would be a fine inducement to counteract the filibuster."[15]

In May, a memo to the president from Interior Secretary Stewart Udall said, "your gambit in cloture [votes to halt a filibuster] with Hayden is very persuasive. . . . he will carry the other [Arizona] vote with him and two from Nevada."

What the president had done to persuade crusty Carl Hayden, the ancient Arizona Democrat, to vote for cloture was revealed in a White House memo signed by Manatos: "Our arrangement with Carl Hayden on the Central Arizona [irrigation] Project is contingent on promise of a cloture vote by Hayden on civil rights."

Johnson conducted the senatorial squeeze with a special sense of urgency, a warning from Professor Eric Goldman, a Princeton historian on the White House staff, that they needed to pass the legislation in order to "head off violence." The professor also urged Johnson to call a meeting with black leaders "to help establish their authority" and keep the lid on racial protests.

Television, emerging full-voiced as the dominant medium of public communication, amplified to the rest of the nation the Senate's struggle over civil rights. The White House and Charlie Ferris made sure it stayed focused on the four-month-long drama. Ferris says the prolonged debate, which did not end until mid-June, was a blessing disguised as pain. It educated the nation by giving people time to ponder the consequences of the most significant social legislation in one hundred years.[16]

"Television was very important," says Ferris, a Bostonian of blue-collar Irish descent, once labeled by the *Washington Post* as the "101st senator." "Through daily television coverage—Roger Mudd of CBS on the Capitol steps—people knew that the Senate was deliberating on the social order of the country. The Southerners [senators] were very frustrated. Trade unions, churches, the League of Women Voters all lobbied for the legislation at the local level—that's where we had to go to get those extra twelve votes."

Early in the debate, Ferris recalls, there was a feeling among Democratic leaders that Title II, the heart of this legislative package, might have to be watered down in order to overcome the filibuster. But Maggie and the leadership decided, finally, "No. We'll go for broke." Title II would stand as it left Maggie's committee, and in the three-month debate the committee chairman was at his magnificent best. A dramatist might say that all his life—his uncertain origins, his Northwest populist ideology, his caring for the underdog, and over-thirty years as a premier legislator—reached a climax with his arguments for the rights of all citizens. But to say so is to slight his earlier achievements, the Columbia River dams, medical research, consumer protection, and the accomplishments yet to come.

Maggie was already a great senator when he commenced his four and a half hour speech on the floor of the Senate on behalf of Title II, public accommodations for all citizens, not whites only. Barer was at his side.

"The senator wanted to make the record as clear as possible," said Barer. "He delivered every word of the speech—the usual practice is to make a few remarks and place the written speech in the Congressional Record. Then he answered questions. The questions were very detailed, sometimes hostile. What amazed me is how much he knew; he had mastered the subject."

Once he faltered on a question and turned to his clerk, Barer, for an answer. "I had to remind him that clerks could be seen, but by no means heard on the Senate floor," said Barer. "He said 'yes,' looked up and gave a detailed answer to the question himself. He had absolute mastery of Title II."

The filibuster through the late spring placed a dreadful workload on Magnuson and his staff. He had to maintain the vital business of his Commerce and Appropriations committees. He was one of forty liberal senators assigned to hold the Senate floor while they found the sixty-seventh vote to break the filibuster. Each of the forty senators was assigned a time to hold the floor—a hardship for all of them. Nearly all, on occasion, asked to be excused from the extra duty. "Not Maggie," said Barer. "He never missed a single assignment."

On June 10, 1964, the debate ended. The Senate invoked cloture with a vote to spare. President Johnson said, "It demonstrates that the national will will manifest itself in Congressional action. One year ago President Kennedy said, 'A great change is at hand—our task is to make that revolution peaceful and constructive for all.' The Senate action is a major contribution toward that national responsibility." He signed the Civil Rights Act into law a few weeks later.

Among the papers from the ever-sensitive Johnson White House is a memo on foreign reaction to the law: "Non-communist countries universally acclaimed it, the Soviets played it down." A clipping of an editorial from the *Norfolk Virginian-Pilot* said: "If not the will of the land, the Civil Rights Act is the will of the majority. The South is particularly obligated to itself as well as to the nation to accept it in good grace."[17]

It was still not yet done. Title II, bearing the enormous question of private property rights, had to pass the test of the U.S. Supreme Court. The plaintiff would be one Lester Maddox, an unreconstructed segregationist and Georgia governor-to-be. The "Heart of Atlanta" suit, so named for the Atlanta motel which wanted no black guests, was argued October 5, 1964. It would take its place in American legal history alongside *Plessy v. Ferguson* and *Brown v. Board of Education*. By an odd twist of urban transportation, at least two of the justices would come to the case unusually well briefed. Evan Schwab, clerk for Justice Douglas, and Alan Dershowitz, clerk for Justice Arthur Goldberg, carpooled to and from the Capitol with Stan Barer during the winter and summer of congressional action on Title II. They had more than sufficient time to discuss its details in the Washington, D.C., commuter traffic. On December 14 the court upheld the law and, in effect, ordered "Heart of Atlanta" to accept black guests.[18]

Stan Barer went home to Seattle, and was for a few weeks unemployed. Idled, he went to the King County law library to peruse the court's decision in "Heart of Atlanta." When he reached Justice Douglas's opinion he realized that he was reading, verbatim and in quotation marks, the report of the Commerce Committee, the one he had written for Maggie. He had never felt so good about anything in his professional life.

And Maggie? Did he regard Title II as the capstone of his career? "It was his greatest achievement," said Jerry Grinstein, his invaluable associate. "But he never dwelt on past accomplishments. It was always 'let's get on with something else.'" Senate southerners continued to remain best of friends with Magnuson and, instead, aimed their bad feelings about Title II at Senator John Pastore, the majority whip. It was a matter of style. Pastore was feisty and aggressive in his manner on the Commerce Committee, a contrast with the easygoing chairman.

Magnuson, his staff, and the Senate had surely done the Lord's work with Title II, assuming that the Lord is at least a bit of a democrat. Separate public facilities, backed by force of law, told black Americans you can't eat in my restaurant, use my toilet, drink from my water fountain, or sleep in my hotel; these are for "whites only." By implication, these laws reinforced a bogus idea of white supremacy and black inferiority, a terrible psychological burden for both, but especially for blacks. It haunted American society three decades later.

Maggie corrected the law in the Senate. Alas, the Lord has not worked so swiftly to repair damaged hearts and minds.

CHAPTER 24

The Sixties

Two themes dominant in twentieth-century American politics collided in the 1960s with tragic consequences. Our dark obsession with communism led John Kennedy and Lyndon Johnson into the bloody morass of a war in Vietnam. The bright hope of government as a tool to improve the lot of ordinary Americans, a hope sprung from the Great Depression, led President Johnson to the creation of the Great Society. The tragedy was Johnson's inability to sustain both the war in Southeast Asia and his ambitious domestic programs. The Great Society would ultimately become another casualty of the Vietnam War, along with 58,000 U.S. troops.

The Wise Men—respected presidential advisers—in Washington, D.C., Dean Rusk, Robert McNamara, Paul Nitze, Dean Acheson, and, so far as we know, John Kennedy, viewed Communist North Vietnam's attempt to reunite with South Vietnam, via military conquest, as an extension of aggression from Beijing and Moscow. They were rational men and at least nominal Democrats. President Eisenhower had overruled his generals and Vice President Nixon and, but for the stationing of a few military advisers, stayed clear of Indochina as the French colonial empire collapsed. The president did not see Vietnam as a vital national interest. But, then, his Republican Party had never been charged with being "soft on communism" or being the "party of treason."

Kennedy placed U.S. military advisers in predominantly Buddhist South Vietnam to prop up an unpopular Catholic regime. (The North and South had been divided at Geneva in 1954 as a means of ending, temporarily, civil war.) Those advisers became Johnson's somber legacy. Perhaps the Texan's personality, the needs of an overeager ego, kept him stuck in the quagmire. His deference to the Ivy League Wise Men helped keep this graduate of Southwest Texas State Teachers College glued to the anti-Communist commitment in Vietnam even as it ripped the nation asunder.

The legacy became Johnson's war shortly after August 3, 1964, the middle of a presidential election campaign, when three patrol torpedo boats, presumably North Vietnamese, possibly phantoms, allegedly attacked the USS *Maddox*, a destroyer, in the Tonkin Gulf off Vietnam.

An aroused Johnson requested and received from the Senate a resolution authorizing his use of armed force "to defend freedom in Southeast Asia," a stunning blank check for the conduct of war. Two senators voted against it, Wayne Morse of Oregon and Ernest Gruening of Alaska.[1]

The November election was a landslide. Johnson swamped Senator Barry Goldwater, the hawkish Republican nominee. Democats emerged from the election with 68 senators compared to 32 Republicans; 295 Democratic House members, compared to 140 Republicans. Washington State sent Scoop Jackson back to the Senate along with four new Democratic congressmen, including Brock Adams, a future secretary of transportation, and Tom Foley, a future Speaker of the House. But there was a deviation in the pattern: the state elected Dan Evans, a civil engineer, state legislator, and a Republican, as its new governor. Evans would push through virtually all of the state's landmark environmental protection laws, create a brace of new state parks, a new system of community colleges, and run a three-term administration virtually free of scandal. He was as cool toward the Vietnam War as he was hot for the environmental legislation which he rightly conceived as a means of leaving a historic mark on the Pacific Northwest.

Evans remembers the 1965 National Governors Conference in Washington, D.C., where the president had Secretary of State Dean Rusk, Defense Secretary Robert McNamara, and five other cabinet officers urge support for the Vietnam War. McNamara, who would later declare the war a tragic mistake, said they needed only another 50,000 troops to win. Johnson, says Evans, was nervous: "He couldn't sit still. He was like a caged lion." There were subsequent meetings between the president, his officials, and the governors in 1966 and 1967. At the latter, Johnson and McNamara said, "With 500,000 troops we can get the job done." In the next session, February 1968, Evans says: "they had charts showing 36 different ways to end the war. It was a bizarre kind of briefing. I said to [Iowa Governor] Bob Ray, 'They don't know what to do next!' And it was the same people briefing us all three years. They still didn't know what to do."[2]

Warren Magnuson, a major congressional lieutenant in Johnson's war of domestic uplift, the Great Society, was troubled but initially supportive of the war. Difficult for him to be otherwise, given his friendship with Johnson and his extraordinary working partnership with Henry Jackson, now chairman of the Senate Interior Committee and a hawk's hawk who, like Rusk, believed that Vietnam was the result of China's historic urge for suzerainty over Southeast Asia. Calling for an American force of a half million men in Vietnam, Jackson could foresee China tumbling countries like dominoes from Saigon to India and Japan, given a U.S. withdrawal or a "humiliating compromise" peace.[3] Three decades later the Rusk-Jackson China theory was turned on its head: In giving diplomatic recognition to Communist Vietnam, the Clinton administration would argue that it could serve as a bulwark against a potential threat from China.

At first Magnuson subscribed to the domino theory. Early in 1963 he wrote a skeptical constituent, "The war being fought there is not our war. Our country is providing military and economic assistance in order to help Vietnam preserve its independence." He said "the State Department feels . . . that the Vietnamese people have amply demonstrated their courage and that with their determination and our assistance victory in Vietnam will eventually come. If Vietnam were lost all of Southeast Asia would be threatened."[4] That, of course, was the State Department's official position.

Two years later Maggie was still firm, but not so effusive. He said we had to keep our commitment until "a final settlement can be negotiated." As for "extremists," mostly young people protesting against the prospect of being drafted into the fight, Magnuson said, "I do not agree with these individuals nor do I agree with how they demonstrate their disapproval. However, the right of opposition is an inherent right in our country and it is important to all Americans, right or wrong." If he wobbled on what to do about Vietnam, Maggie remained steadfast in this belief of the right to dissent.

The best indication of Magnuson's feelings came after he went to Brock Adams, complaining that the congressman was "giving Scoop a bad time on Vietnam." Adams broke away from the hard party line early in 1966, calling for more civilian aid to South Vietnam and less military support. Jackson disliked this breach of delegation prowar solidarity. But as soon as Maggie delivered his remonstrance, he paused. Then he told Adams, "I suppose it is a case of us big white men against little brown men in black pajamas."[5] Despite Jackson's attitude toward Adams's deviation, Magnuson may have privately cheered.

An apparent draft of a speech, handwritten and undated, revealed Magnuson's mixed feelings: "We're engaged in an agonizing and messy business. . . . I do not profess to know all the answers. I think our course is basically sound. No use arguing about how we got there. We are there. We are at war. Our boys are being killed. Our moral and material fibre is being strained. Our concern for the future of a free world is great . . . cannot allow peace at any price. The only way I know for us to win a war is to unite the nation. . . . Concerned about violence, riots, draft [card]

burners, lack of respect for law and order—[It's] not my America. . . .
[The] last thing we want is a federal police . . . we have the right to dissent.
We have the greatest country in the world—big, powerful and complex.
Sometimes so much that the answers seem to be more complicated than
the problems."[6]

"Actually, Maggie never talked much about Vietnam," said Adams.
"Vietnam was Scoop's area." And Jackson was adamant; no mixed feelings. Early in 1967, when support for the war frayed under protest
demonstrations and intellectual critiques, Jackson took to the Senate
floor to assert that "Hanoi is hoping for a political victory in the United
States in 1968" and "one power [China] threatens to gain political hegemony—it affects our national interest."[7] The Soviets, warned Jackson,
are "making giant strides in space and in military and economic growth.
Moscow supports the Vietnam War. Without our stand in Vietnam,
Communism in Indonesia would be boosted. . . . I have no confidence
in Chinese benevolence in Asia." Jackson concluded: "Ultimately we'll
win. Our bombs are persuasive."[8]

Much as Maggie valued his partnership with Jackson, he would stay
the course on Vietnam because of his friendship with Johnson. By the
end of 1966 his incoming mail indicated a deep disaffection with the
war. His stock reply to constituents: " . . . I conclude the president is
right in his commitment to the people of South Vietnam. . . . We are not
imperialists but opponents of real and deadly Communism. . . . The war
will end when Communists are convinced they can't win by prolonging
the fighting."

Maggie met privately with the president during these war years. Little
of what they exchanged was recorded, save a comment by Magnuson
that Johnson would like to end the war—if only he knew how. A note
from White House aide Jack Valenti to Maggie in February 1965 hints of
the importance of these talks: "It was mighty good seeing you last night.
I hope you feel as I do that these small meetings with the President are of
great value to all. . . . let me know if there's anything I can do for you."[9]

As a matter of fact, yes, Maggie did have a request. He and Jackson
went to the White House to urge Johnson to "review" Defense Secretary McNamara's decision to cancel the DYNASOAR aircraft project slated
for construction by Boeing. Maggie said "all hell is breaking loose in
the state" over the pending loss of 4,000 jobs in an area "already depressed." One outraged constituent had written Maggie that cancellation
of DYNASOAR was a sign "we are apparently engaged in suicidal unilateral
disarmament." Scoop offered a deal: no complaints about the loss of
DYNASOAR if McNamara closes naval yards in Boston and Philadelphia. Ap-

parently such closures would offset Boeing's employment loss with ship-yard jobs in Bremerton. Nothing came of this ploy.[10] DYNASOAR crashed and was soon forgotten as Boeing rolled out a new fleet of commercial aircraft.

But nothing reveals the disarray over the war better than a report by Mike Manatos, Johnson's congressional liaison, on a White House political strategy meeting January 9, 1967. Participants were the president, Vice President Hubert Humphrey, and Democratic Senators William Fulbright of Arkansas, Allen Ellender of Louisiana, George Smathers of Florida, Stuart Symington of Missouri, John Pastore of Rhode Island, Daniel Inouye of Hawaii, and Magnuson. Manatos's report:

> Fulbright, Chairman of Foreign Relations Committee: The first priority is "the liquidation of the war in Vietnam—the war poisons everything else."
>
> President Johnson: "I agree." When Fulbright replies that Secretary of State Rusk demands North Vietnam surrender before the war can end, Johnson answers, "That's not Rusk's position—but I'll talk with him."
>
> Ellender, Chairman of Agriculture Committee: "Most people in the South are with us but don't understand why it's taking too long to win the war."
>
> Smathers, a ranking member of both Finance and Judiciary committees: Our greatest trouble in Vietnam is caused by "dissident voices here which encourage our enemies to resist."
>
> Symington: "Air power is not being allowed to do its job on military targets."
>
> Inouye: "Are we getting our money's worth in billions of dollars of bombs on Viet Nam?"
>
> Pastore [most perplexing of all these Democratic leaders]: "I'm disturbed by the pressure from responsible people to escalate the war." The killing of civilians has shaken the American people like nothing since the atomic bombing of Nagasaki. Yet . . . "If third party—United Nations—negotiations don't work, the President should use his Sunday punch."
>
> Magnuson: "Everybody in the Northwest gives solid support to the national leadership concerning the Vietnam War, but let's quit nit-picking and get it over with."[11]

The Vice President, Manatos noted, "passed." And "pass" he would continue to do on the Vietnam War until October 1968, when it was too late to turn the corner away from Johnson and toward election as president.

Thus the White House and the Senate Democratic Policy Committee scattered in opinion from abject withdrawal to Pastore's apparent suggestion of nuclear bombing. They were utterly indecisive, danger-ously unaware of the tenacity with which a people defends its native terrain—thereby providing an accurate reflection of American opinion.

In an aside, Manatos noted Johnson's anxiety about passage of the current civil rights legislative package that was working its way through

Magnuson's Senate Commerce Committee. The memo doesn't record a response by Maggie.

Magnuson had stretched reality when he spoke of solid war support in the Northwest. Brock Adams had already deviated, albeit slightly, from the White House line. Governor Dan Evans was gathering second thoughts. Young men were quietly voting with their feet by drifting up to the Canadian border near Blaine and Lynden and going, in many cases permanently, to the other side. Paul Coughlin, chief deputy to King County Prosecutor Magnuson, wrote to his old friend, reminding him of their good times together in the early 1930s and thanking him "for my career." Then he urged Maggie to "divert Johnson from what seems to me to be a truly reckless course he is pursuing in Vietnam." Once upon a time, said Coughlin, he accepted the "theory." But no longer: "We had no commitment [to South Vietnam]. To him, "talk of preserving a democracy has a hollow sound. . . . [T]here's no government [in South Vietnam] except a small corrupt group of soldiers allied with greedy landowners" and "thousands of our young men are being killed. . . . [T]he image of the United States as a fair and humane country is being destroyed."[12]

Across the hall from Maggie's office on the first floor of the Old Senate Office Building, Mike Pertschuk got up his courage to add his protest to the storm of dissent gathering around the nation. He crossed the way to Room 127. Maggie was at his desk. "I had to tell him that I would sign an antiwar statement being circulated among staffers on Capitol Hill," said Pertschuk years later. "I thought that when I told him my intentions Magnuson would have every right to be angry. But, to my surprise, he wasn't. Instead, his reaction was to justify support for the war. He was defensive, not angry." In fact, as the staff came to realize, while Magnuson could not bring himself to break with Johnson, he could not begrudge Pertschuk (or Adams) their opposition to Johnson's conduct of the war.[13]

These years between 1963 and 1968 were extraordinarily busy for Magnuson. He was dealing with civil rights and consumer protection measures, and was too shrewd not to understand that the Great Society legislation coming down from Lyndon Johnson's superenergized White House was becoming, as Fulbright put it, "poisoned" by Vietnam. The pace forced Magnuson to skip mentally in a matter of seconds from one subject or problem to another. The Vietnam War created an internal conflict between his own doubts and his personal loyalty to Johnson. Stan Barer says the senator's pattern was to become quiet when troubled. "He'd let the problem roll around in his head until there came a decision to do something," said Barer.[14] The decision to do something about

Vietnam would not come until 1968 when Johnson decided against another term as president.

In the midst of this volcanic legislative activity, rumors began to float about Magnuson's possible appointment to the U.S. Supreme Court. Some cheered. "If Lyndon puts it in the form of a motion, I would second it," Seafirst Bank's Lawrence Arnold wrote Maggie.[15] But not Philip Bailey, the waspish owner-editor of the Seattle *Argus*. Bailey, a political maverick with a genius IQ, was the grandson of a Confederate soldier turned southern California rancher. A graduate of the University of California, Bailey came to Seattle, where he made a fortune as a paint manufacturer. A restless sophisticate, he turned his energy to work as chairman of Washington's Citizens for Stevenson in the 1952 presidential campaign and purchased the venerable *Argus*. This impressed Irv Hoff, if not Warren Magnuson. Hoff said Bailey would make an ideal state Democratic chairman, but the job would have to be handed to him. He wouldn't work for it through the normal process of backslapping and handshaking with party officials. Apparently, Magnuson turned thumbs down on Bailey for state chairman, and possibly refused to anoint him for Democratic national committeeman. Phil Bailey would not forgive the senator.[16]

In early 1956, Bailey's *Argus* lashed Magnuson for "neglecting to build the party organization. Instead, he has his own personal organization." That was a fair critique and would also apply to Henry Jackson. Bailey continued the sniping after the 1964 election, characterizing "Great Society" programs as "the coddling and wrapping of people in cotton batting." By this time, Magnuson had taken, with considerable talent, to oil painting. Carol Parker Cahill, his longtime friend, said that once, while they were at an exhibition in Paris, Magnuson turned to her from a painting by Pablo Picasso and declared, "if I worked at it, I could paint better than that." When the senator had an exhibition of his own pictures (at least one critic said they were better than average), Bailey retorted, "Three years ago he [Maggie] wouldn't have known Pablo Picasso from Grandma Moses." But now the politician was "jumping on another bandwagon—art." That judgment was spiteful nonsense. Painting became Magnuson's great relaxation. In his later years it was beginning to take the place of poker.

But nothing got Bailey's goat so much as rumors about Magnuson and the Supreme Court. He wrote: "I don't know whether to laugh or to cry. Maggie and Johnson are great friends in the never-never land, and cronies must be taken care of. . . . at least the appointment would get him [Maggie] out of the state."

And in a later *Argus* edition, Bailey raged at greater length under a headline: "Magnuson at the Peak of His Power—No Model for the Young Generation." He wrote that Magnuson epitomized "everything that is wrong with American politics" and had managed "to keep his feet [*sic*] in the political trough by shifting with the times, serving the needs of the state's tycoons and receiving their campaign money." He said that Magnuson had no true political philosophy: "he believes voters are boobs. His only concern is to get reelected, a con man who flim flams voters. Magnuson has never really been socially accepted by any substantial people in the community . . . at home he spends his time at the Olympic Hotel with his cronies. And what cronies! It's doubtful he ever read a serious book." The editorial went on to say that, like Johnson, Magnuson used taxpayers' money "to cure all ills and insure reelection. The murky miasmic fog generated by Magnuson and his ilk that clouds the political landscape may yet be blown away to allow a brighter, cleaner, day."[17]

By "serving the needs of the state's tycoons" Bailey probably recalled Magnuson and Jackson's successful effort to allocate part of the federal forest in Grays Harbor County for exclusive—that is, noncompetitive—sales to the Simpson Timber Company owned by William Reed and his family. The idea was to keep Simpson's mills in the county in continuous operation, thus saving the small towns McCleary and Shelton and scores of jobs. Its effect meant an immense windfall of profits for the Reed family. One estimate placed those profits, and the attendant loss to the U.S. Treasury, in the millions of dollars. The U.S. Forest Service would never again make such a deal. The Republican William Reed became a staunch financial supporter of the Magnuson and Jackson campaigns.[18]

Otherwise, Bailey's judgment of Magnuson was flawed and insensitive to facts. Parts were toned down or cut from the editorial by the editor's attorney. Nevertheless, the piece reflected a slice of Seattle establishment sentiment about Maggie, the interloper orphan from Minnesota who battled against private utilities, whose stock establishment members held, and for labor unions, who would strike against business for better wages and conditions. Bailey ran a journalistically stimulating sheet of news and opinion, the likes of which are nearly impossible to find in the 1990s. But he was remiss in failing to report Maggie's work for civil rights, consumer protection, and public health. Such was his loathing.

Ironically, given this editorial vitriol, there's no evidence Magnuson was ever considered for the U.S. Supreme Court despite his obvious liberal qualifications—a former prosecutor, a master legislator, a humane public official, and devout follower of the Bill of Rights. On the contrary. President Johnson's press secretary, George Christian, said he never heard the rumors. George Reedy, one of Christian's predecessors, sounded astounded when asked about the reports.

"I can't imagine President Johnson offering Magnuson a seat on the Supreme Court, or, for that matter, Magnuson accepting it," said Reedy, now a professor at Marquette University. With Bailey's stinging commentary in mind, Reedy was asked why this was unimaginable. "Because on the Supreme Court Magnuson would only have one vote," he said. "In the Senate he had a majority. If a bill could be passed he would pass it. Magnuson had the personality of a riverboat gambler—he was sharp, quick. If Maggie was for it [a bill] you assumed it would pass. Of course, he got everything in Washington, D.C., not nailed down and sent it back to Washington state. No, Magnuson was needed by Johnson in the Senate."[19]

There was great affection between the two politicians. Recovering in Austin, Texas, from a heart attack in the fall of 1955, Johnson wrote, "Dear Maggie, how about coming to see me? It would help both of us." And a few days later: "Dear Maggie, awakened at 6 A.M. this morning thinking of my good friend Warren Magnuson. I read your recent letter again with a feeling of warm affection. . . . I couldn't tell you how much it meant to me. . . . [M]y feelings represent a deep gratitude for all you have done for me over the years, including the top-notch performance as chairman of the [Senate Democratic] Campaign Committee last session. It may be hard to get Maggie up in the morning, but awake or asleep, he is still one of the finest men I know. I'm sure proud to have you as a friend."[20]

Jerry Grinstein says the personal styles of the two friends complemented each other in the passage of legislation: "Johnson used force to get his way. Magnuson engendered trust among his colleagues." At times Johnson would use his towering physical presence to intimidate colleagues. Maggie treated everybody alike—as if they were the only other people on the planet who mattered.[21]

Magnuson, said George Christian, always called his friend, the president, "Lyndon." Johnson was equally fond of Jermaine Peralta, by 1964 Magnuson's constant companion. The president joshed Maggie about Jermaine. "If you don't marry her, I might just do it myself," was the remark heard more than once by Christian.[22] Irv Hoff recalls Johnson telling Magnuson, "You'd be the biggest fool in the world if you don't marry her—and Johnson could be very persuasive." A single working woman with a young daughter to raise, Peralta initially put off Maggie's marriage proposal. But he persisted and Jermaine said yes. They wed October 5, 1964, in the Shoreham suite of Bernard Bralove, one of Maggie's successful businessmen friends. As Magnuson's best man, President Johnson bore the wedding ring. At the critical moment, the president fumbled and dropped the ring. Later he said, "I was never so nervous in my life except the day Bird and I married." "Bird"—Mrs. Johnson—escorted Jermaine. A select guest list included Dr. Frank Stanton of CBS, Bill Edris, Senators Harry Byrd, Richard Russell, and Alaska's E. L. Bartlett. It was a warm occasion that preceded the Democrats' great victory in November.[23]

"I guess he gave up his harem to marry me," Jermaine commented much later. Theirs was not a congressional marriage of the sort that leaves the wife at home minding children or club work while the husband leads a separate life in the business of Capitol Hill. Instead, Magnuson consulted each day with Jermaine and gave her authority to keep an eye on his Senate staff. Her influence on his private and professional life thus became enormous. He adored her.

Johnson defeated Senator Barry Goldwater, the hawkish Republican nominee, one month after Maggie's wedding; it was a presidential election landslide that added momentum to his legislative proposals. From the outset of his term, January 1965, Johnson insisted that Congress make haste with Great Society programs, beginning with Medicare, a national health program for citizens over sixty-five.[24] He knew those Democratic majorities would wane in the next "off-year" election. There's no indication, however, that the president anticipated the rising tide of protest against the war.

What Johnson proposed was legislation for a "Great Society, laws to end discrimination, fight poverty, to provide medical care for older citizens and education for the young; to clean the air and water from decades of pollution, to preserve lands for recreation and to protect the beauty of the continent; to bring art, theater and music to every corner of the nation and to protect consumers in the marketplace."[25]

Such was the stuff of the greatest outpouring of legislation at least since the New Deal, in Johnson's words "an extension of the Bill of Rights; a broadened concept of freedom." The inspiration, Magnuson suggested in an oral history for the Johnson Library in Austin, Texas, came from their experiences in the Great Depression: "All of us are creatures of our times. We needed to do something, no matter what it was called"—whether it be a New Deal or a Great Society. Magnuson believed as strongly in the Great Society as Johnson did; they both held the conviction that government could make life better for Americans.[26] Was it political opportunism? Perhaps. Was it what Magnuson and Johnson, as a result of their experiences, felt imperative? Absolutely. Good policy and good politics are not always exclusive of each other.

The president's chief domestic aide, Joe Califano—"Joe Cauliflower" in Magnusonese—summed it up years later when most Americans had forgotten about the "Great Society" except as something Republicans sought to repeal: "Did we legislate too much? Perhaps. Did we stub our toes? Of course. . . . often we didn't recognize that government couldn't do it all, but our excesses were based on our hope in government and fueled by the frustration of seeing so much poverty and ignorance and illness amidst such wealth."[27]

The Johnson-Magnuson combine passed the civil rights package in 1964, and then the president swung in behind Maggie on consumer protection. "Lyndon didn't quite understand what I was trying to do," Magnuson said in his oral history. "But he said, all right if you think it's all right. He told people [congressmen] to vote for it; that the leadership wanted it." Califano pushed the president, citing the Fair Packaging and Labeling Act as one of the most important of that busy year, "one that benefits every housewife in America."[28]

But Johnson had his own wish list submitted to Maggie for action. The president asked the chairman of the Appropriations Subcommittee for $40 million for rent supplements, $400 million for Model Cities, the urban renewal program, and another $20 million for urban research. The Great Society would not be the cheap society. One of the Johnson proposals pushed by Magnuson, creation of a small-tax division inside the U.S. Tax Court, attracted a warm editorial of approval from Phil Bailey's *Argus*. Otherwise, this small break for minor taxpayers was overlooked.

Magnuson never let his interest stray from local concerns during this avalanche of national legislation. Boeing had begun the push for federal funding for a prototype of the Supersonic Transport aircraft (SST). To get it off the ground, the Seattle airplane manufacturer needed congressional approval for loans from the federal treasury, which the company aimed to repay once the airplane climbed out of the red into corporate profits. The proposed aircraft was expected to cost $1.14 billion, fly 1,750 mph and carry 300 passengers.

A memo from Mike Manatos to Johnson alleged, "Maggie is playing games with the model cities bill. He is parcelling out [model cities] projects and wants his due [votes] in SST funds. He sees no problem in this either."[29] The fight over these SST funds was long, hard, and complex. It would end in defeat for Magnuson, despite his sleight of hand with urban renewal monies, the most publicized defeat of his legislative career, one of only three defeats of much significance. When Magnuson took a bill to the Senate floor he went to win.

Califano advised the president late in 1965 that Magnuson had to be neutralized, if not converted, in order to create a new cabinet office, the Department of Transportation (DOT). "It's important that we get Magnuson's agreement to keep an open mind before any interest [particularly trucking interests] gets to him and gets a commitment to oppose the DOT," said Califano, aware of Maggie's close ties to the Teamsters and truckers. A few days later Califano told Johnson that Maggie was "disturbed about budget cuts in Northwest power project funds—quite disturbed. I told him you would welcome his advice and that you would call him about the cuts."

Johnson, or, more likely, a member of his staff, wrote to Magnuson: "Our tangled transportation policies must be reformed . . . to a fast, safe, economical system." The president also said there was a need to deregulate the industry to create "more freedom for competition." The two men usually communicated face to face.

Maggie got his money for Northwest water projects and Johnson got Maggie's wholehearted support for creation of a DOT. Whether this was coincidence or quid pro quo, no one can say. But two public interests, one national, the other regional, had been served. Califano informed the president that Magnuson wanted to introduce the DOT measure and that he would urge Senators McClellan and Karl Mundt, majority and minority leaders of the Appropriations Committee, to move with haste on the DOT.[30]

The Maggie-Lyndon connection was so close and so obvious to their aides that Mike Manatos could write a White House memo regarding an unspecified Magnuson request, "I don't know if there is any merit in this but I'm sure the President would want to do it for Maggie."[31]

Manatos sent the president a memo of an off-the-record meeting in Magnuson's Senate hideaway office with Al Barkan, the AFL-CIO's top lobbyist, a volatile insider with bulldozer clout among Democrats. Barkan allowed Democrats weren't doing enough for labor and taunted them with the question, "Is Dirksen [the GOP minority leader] running the Senate?" Senator Jennings Randolph of West Virginia said Democrats should "come out fighting" for repeal of section 14-B of the Taft-Hartley labor act. This was the section allowing the separate states to approve "right to work" laws—laws disallowing exclusively union shops. Claiborne Pell of Rhode Island cautioned that 14-B "is not like the civil rights issue which aroused the nation," for "the man in the street is not concerned with 14-B." Magnuson pleaded for secrecy. He did not want Mike Mansfield, the majority leader, to think that a rump group was being organized to challenge the elected leadership. Magnuson urged that they push Mansfield to act more aggressively on labor issues. According to Manatos, Magnuson concluded the meeting by noting that debate on Vietnam was hurting the president and his programs by having "50 senators suggesting 50 solutions" to the war.[32]

That was, indeed, the rub. Costs were rising. While Sargent Shriver, director of the Office of Economic Opportunity, would thank Magnuson for his "strong support" on behalf of antipoverty funds, Maggie would have to tell *Tri-Cities Herald* publisher Glenn Lee to forget about a particle accelerator for the Hanford Reservation: "There's no money as long as there is Vietnam."[33]

The rising tide of antiwar protest had begun to physically constrict the president. In early winter, 1968, Johnson and entourage made an orderly, but very hasty, retreat from rear doors of the main auditorium at the University of Texas to avoid a howling crowd of students at the front of the building. The Tet offensive by Communist forces in 1968 brought fighting to the U.S. embassy compound in Saigon and the haplessness of the situation to living rooms across the nation. Johnson had to decide whether to commit another 100,000 U.S. troops or quit the fight. While making up his mind, he made a series of abrupt flights into guarded sanctuaries across the country.

Newsmen on the White House beat were on short notice of takeoff from Andrews Air Force base, with no word of their destination until after their craft took flight. Each takeoff came with the assumption that the president was headed to Saigon. The actual destinations were otherwise: the Lockheed aircraft plant near Marietta, Georgia, for rollout of the C5-A transport; the space flight control center in Houston, Texas; a late-night stop at a Beaumont, Texas, motel where the Texas State Democratic Central Committee was gathered and where Johnson alleged that "Ho Chi Minh was never elected to nothing in his life." Finally, Air Force One landed at the Strategic Air Command Base in Puerto Rico. The general public was excluded from each of these stops, although the president appeared to be making reelection campaign speeches. Or so the press reported. How else to make sense of these apparently random destinations?

On the last of these flights—the return to Washington, D.C.—pool reporters flying with the president on Air Force One confronted him with opinion polls showing a precipitous decline in support for the war. With some heat, Johnson denied their validity. The *Chicago Tribune* correspondent, Dan Young, tried to change the subject: "Mr. President, now that you're running for reelection . . ." He never completed the sentence. Red-faced and restless, Johnson nearly ejected from his seat, leaning across the cabin's small table into Young's face: "Who said I was running for President? . . . I never told anybody I was running for President."[34]

This was late February 1968. A few weeks later, March 16, Stan Barer entered Magnuson's office, closed the door, and handed him a statement that welcomed Senator Robert Kennedy into the race for the Democratic presidential nomination. "He read it, put it down on his desk," Barer recalled. "It lay there for a while. He let the idea of the statement stew. Finally, I said, 'Senator, we've got to say something.' He was very upset, trying to avoid the matter, shuffling papers on his desk. After a few minutes of suspense he looked up and said, 'I just wish I didn't have to say it.' We released Magnuson's statement to the press. Later that day he went to the White House and told the President we had to get out of Vietnam. When he returned to his office he told me, 'Poor Lyndon. He wants to get out of this as much as anybody else. But he didn't know how.' "[35]

In a newspaper interview seven years later, Magnuson said Johnson "never calculated on the terrible thing of Vietnam. It got to where nobody was thinking of anything else. One year before he made his decision [to negotiate with Vietnam] I tried to tell him to get out. I told him privately 'why don't we simply pass a resolution declaring victory and get out?' Later [Senator George] Aiken said the same thing publicly. But he [Johnson] was getting bad advice from his military."[36]

On March 31, 1968, two weeks after Kennedy joined the race, Johnson startled the country by announcing that he would not seek reelection. Instead, he would initiate "unconditional negotiations" with Vietnamese Communists to end the war.

But it would not end for another five years, despite those negotiations in Paris. There remained the rending of the nation over Vietnam, the assassinations of Dr. Martin Luther King and Senator Robert Kennedy, and a riotous Democratic National Convention in Chicago that virtually ceded the 1968 presidential election to Republican Richard Nixon. Hubert Humphrey, the Democrat nominee, "passed" on the question of Vietnam until mid-October. He had remained a shade too steadfast to his boss.

The Great Society, the great social dreams of Lyndon Johnson and Warren Magnuson, was too expensive to coexist with the even more expensive war in Vietnam. The programs they produced survived, but under increasing Republican attack, and they have never thrived, except with the public majority.

The great loss, however, was the dream—the Johnson-Magnuson notion that government could improve the lot of ordinary citizens, given the political will and a modest redistribution of the nation's wealth. After Vietnam came the shock wave of cynicism, and a sharp decline in trust in government and its leaders. By the 1990s the term "Great Society" was almost derisive.

CHAPTER 25

Revival

C ame the election of 1968, a year of turmoil over Vietnam that overshadowed a flood of progressive social legislation from Congress, and Senator Warren Magnuson had his political reelection theme: "Maggie Keeps the Big Boys Honest." The election would not be a reprise—or worse—of his near defeat in 1962, much credit to Jerry Grinstein, who had replaced Fred Lordon as Maggie's administrative assistant three years earlier.

Nobody wanted Vietnam on a bumper sticker that year, unless it was to say: "Get Out!" Vietnam turned the 1968 Democratic National Convention in Chicago into a street brawl with tear gas, bashed heads, and fractured Democrats; a fight between Chicago police and antiwar protestors and between the antiwar delegates of Eugene McCarthy and the nominally prowar forces of President Johnson and his anointed presidential candidate, Vice President Hubert Humphrey.

Chicago was a blown-up replication of a state Democratic Convention showdown earlier that summer in Tacoma, Washington, where an anguished Magnuson tried to make sense of the conflict and to remain loyal to President Johnson: "We're engaged in an agonizing and messy business. . . . I don't know all the answers but I pray and work for peace." He said, "Our course is basically sound . . no use arguing about how we got there. We are there. We are at war. Our boys are being killed [and] our moral and material fiber is being strained . . but we cannot allow peace at any price. . . . [T]he only way I know to win a war is for us to unite the nation. . . . I'm concerned about violence, riots and draft-card burners, but the last thing we would want is a federal police as in the Soviet Union and Nazi Germany. . . . we have the right to dissent."[1]

They were fully exercising that right of dissent in Tacoma while Maggie tried to walk the narrow line between war and peace in a convention hall overcharged with emotion. When it ended, one newspaper lead paragraph summed up: "The McCarthy crusade met the Humphrey machine in Tacoma yesterday and the winner was Richard Nixon." The same could have been said of the convention in Chicago. Democrats were fatally divided entering the campaign against Nixon, the rebounding Republican presidential nominee.

In more conventional Democratic gatherings, Maggie would have reminded audiences of the need for a third powerhouse at Grand Coulee Dam and a nuclear power plant at Hanford, and warned them of the nefarious plot by California, Arizona, and New Mexico politicians to siphon water from the Columbia River via a great western ditch to irrigate the orchards and farms of the Southwest. In fact it would take the full power of Scoop Jackson, chairman of the Interior Committee, and Magnuson, to prevent the mammoth water diversion. They did this through legislation cutting off Corps of Engineers funds for any Columbia River diversion study.

But, given Grinstein's strategy, this would not be Maggie's pork-as-usual, look-what-I've-done-for-you, campaign. The flurry of consumer protection laws pushed by the senator and publicized by one of the slickest (and truest) advertising campaigns warded off several Republican potential challengers. Governor Dan Evans would run, successfully, for reelection. Jim Owens, the popular, which is to say, winning, football coach of the University of Washington, stayed with the gridiron.

Instead, the GOP candidate for senator was state representative Jack Metcalf, forty, a high school teacher and commercial fisherman from Mukilteo. Metcalf might have been conceived as Magnuson turned upsidedown: tall, angular, and somber in appearance, he came from a Northwest nativist political atmosphere that favored the pro-Hitler Silver Shirts in the 1930s rather than the Communist-Party-lining Washington Commonwealth Federation. In 1963 Metcalf introduced to the state legislature the Liberty Lobby Amendment which proposed to eliminate twelve federal agencies created by the New Deal, including the Securities and Exchange Commission, the Veterans Administration, and the Bonneville Power Administration, the Northwest agency responsible for distribution of the region's cut-rate electric power.[2] This notion was a triumph of ideological conviction over practical politics and no one else in the legislature gave it serious attention. If Magnuson had a legislative majority virtually every time he took a bill to the chambers, Metcalf rarely had more than one vote—his own; a decent man, but not one given to liquor, poker, oil painting, or backslapping. Later he would become a congressman from Washington's Second District, but in 1968 Metcalf had less appeal among mainstream Republicans than Magnuson. His base support came from the party's right-wing fringe, a distinct minority in the heyday of the liberal Dan Evans.

With money raised by the conservative direct mail maestro, Richard Vigurie, Metcalf pitched his campaign to the right-wing choir: "Magnuson has done much to promote trade with Communist countries [quite true]; the senator [unlike Henry Jackson] supported the 1963 atmospheric nuclear test ban treaty with the Soviets"; and, sin of sins, Magnuson proposed legislation to control the distribution and use of handguns in June 1968.

Magnuson's campaign actually began in Manhattan at the advertising studio of George Lois, where Grinstein and Mike Pertschuk helped translate the new consumer protection laws into a series of television commercials. "Maggie Keeps the Big Boys Honest" by forcing them to make fireproof fabrics, safe cars, and safe natural gas pipelines; provide honest packaging and labeling on their products; and place a health warning on cigarettes.

"They were brilliant ads," says Pertschuk. "We brought them back to Washington to Maggie's apartment at the Shoreham to show them. Maggie greeted us in his bathrobe, then watched the ads. When all of them had been shown he was asked for his reaction. He thought for a minute, mumbled something, then said, 'Well, it's okay—but what about NOAA?' "[3]

Several years after Dr. Ed Wenk came to advise the Senate on science, Magnuson had, indeed, pulled together research on the atmosphere and the oceans into one federal agency, the National Oceanic and Atmospheric Administration, an act that helped him win the reelection endorsement of John M. Haydon, otherwise a GOP stalwart, and publisher of the *Marine Digest* in Seattle.[4]

"For his contribution to marine science, Maggie deserves the title 'Senator for Oceanography,' " Haydon editorialized. Maggie's college chum and sometime Republican Speaker of the state House of Representatives, R. Mort Frayn, joined Haydon in a newspaper advertisement proclaiming their support of Magnuson's reelection. A few Republicans howled at the breach in party ranks. Haydon and Frayn laughed. Maggie was above partisanship.

Long before the television advertising campaign began, Grinstein worked to close a gap that had developed between Magnuson and his constituents across Washington State. Maggie had grown all too cozy with Manhattan towers, Palm Springs swimming pools, and Hollywood night spots, to the neglect of places like Aberdeen, Bellingham, Omak, and Walla Walla. After 1962, the senator began visiting the hometowns of his home folks, an essential part of the Magnuson revival. Results were sometimes mixed.

Tom Foley, the Fifth District congressman and the Northwest's expert on farm price supports, set up a meeting between Maggie and wheat farmers in Walla Walla, the senator's first visit to southeastern Washington in over five years. He had a rapt audience, already warmed by Foley's tour de force on current federal farm policy—and he nearly blew it. "We don't get home much anymore 'cause Congress is now full time," said Magnuson clearing his throat in excuse of his long absence. "But I'm back here now 'cause it's 'Publican day week—a recess in honor of President Lincoln."[5] Grinstein could only twist in discomfort at the admission of a continental disconnect, but Maggie, with Foley's help, did carry the county on election day.

Magnuson's consumer protection campaign strategy helped divert attention from his support of President Johnson's war policy. But Maggie didn't duck the Vietnam issue—in his word "Veet-nam"—and did not stint in his advocacy of the Great Society programs. Campaigning in the state in the summer of 1968, he told audiences: "There's still a gap in our society between abundance and poverty and a growing concern about our role in Vietnam. I share it. We must decide on the limits of our power."

The "war on poverty" was a Marshall Plan to rebuild cities, said Magnuson, and to help put down "Negro insurrection in the ghettoes." He would quote from Jack Kennedy: "Those who make peaceful revolution impossible make violent revolution inevitable."

Campaigning that fall, Maggie took a step away from the administration line on Vietnam by calling for a bombing halt. He told the *Spokane Spokesman-Review*, "The war must be rapidly de-Americanized. South Vietnam troops must take the burden of combat. We must force immediate, total, land reform. Future U.S. policy should focus on political, social, economic and institutional development. We have relied too long on military solutions which haven't produced the results we seek."[6] So saying, Maggie assumed a position on Vietnam close to the one taken by Brock Adams two years earlier, one which caused Scoop Jackson great displeasure.

Maggie was running for reelection that year with a hot state economy, one still based on cheap electric power from dams boosted, if not created, by Senator Magnuson. At the end of 1967, civilian employment was up by 50,000 workers; unemployment was at 4 percent; personal income had increased 10 percent from the previous year. A report, prepared for Pacific Northwest Bell, noted federal funds for oceanographic research at the University of Washington, and new investments at the Hanford Reservation valued at $43 million. The economic news was a de facto campaign plug for the status quo—federal largesse routed home by Senator Magnuson. Call it pork, but it made for pleasant living.

In a stunning rebound from his near upset in 1962, Magnuson defeated the hapless Metcalf, a Republican candidate abandoned by Republican moderates by a margin of two to one. Otherwise, it was not so good for Democrats, whose candidate for governor, John J. O'Connell, lost to the incumbent Republican, Dan Evans.

Afterward, George Lois outdid himself, slapping his own back. His ads were good but hardly decisive, as he would have readers of his memoir *George Be Careful* (Saturday Review Press, 1972) believe. Maggie, wrote Lois, was "a sure loser" against "young trim Jack Metcalf" in 1968, so discouraged he appealed to President Johnson for a job. Even the "press was stacked against him." In fact, Metcalf posed so little threat only part of the Lois ads were aired on television—no need for the balance. Far from being against Magnuson, the state press regarded the race as a walk for the incumbent. The news reporting concentrated on races for the White House and the statehouse. The most notable story of the Senate race came after Mort Frayn and John Haydon, pillars of the Republican establishment, came out in favor of Maggie's reelection. Warren appealing to Lyndon for a job? Outlandish. The Senate was Magnuson's job, the whole of his ambition. Even more outlandish is the idea that Lois, or anyone else, would be aware of private talk between the two close friends, Magnuson and Johnson. Lois's ads were good because they were true. As such they helped divert attention from Magnuson's support of Johnson on the war in Vietnam—a help, not a tiebreaker.

Richard Nixon's election in a close vote over Hubert Humphrey did not hamper the pace of legislation generated by Magnuson through the Commerce Committee, although the president's veto would bring a halt to some funds appropriated through his Appropriations Subcommittee. Grinstein is blunt about the White House change: "Nixon was symbolically wrong, but as a practical matter there wasn't great change. We [the Commerce Committee] routinely disregarded what the administration sent down and created our own laws." John Ehrlichman, the new president's domestic adviser, cannot recall a time when the White House butted heads with Maggie's legislative juggernaut. "We were centrists. The House and Senate were Democratic," said Ehrlichman. "We spent our time building coalitions on issues. We liked to make friends with committee chairmen."[7]

Maggie's staff, if not the senator himself, thought of themselves as a government in exile, keeping faith with the public interest in the face of an opposition administration, one possibly intent on the destruction of thirty-six years of Democratic social reforms. But on the contrary. Preference for hiring racial minorities on federal projects came from Richard Nixon, not Lyndon Johnson. So did the creation of the Environmental Protection Agency. It's Richard Nixon's signature on Scoop Jackson's legislative monument, the National Environmental Protection Act. Still, the idea of Nixon terrorized liberals, and the president would not bring an end to the Vietnam war for another five years. Maggie and the Bumblebees proceeded, undaunted, with public interest business as usual.

In 1972 they rolled out of Commerce Committee measures to cut the level of air pollution emitted by autos, a measure originated by the Environment Committee and to provide minimum standards for the honesty of warranties covering consumer products. Other measures updated the 1966 auto safety bill and allowed the secretary of transportation to set standards for railroad safety.

But it was not straight sailing.

Magnuson and Senator Ed Muskie's 1970 clean waters bill required a full cleansing of sewage and industrial wastes from waterways by 1976, and prohibited waste dumping in waters where fish and wildlife were endangered. The White House stepped in before its final passage. Ehrlichman said the measure was "two times over the budget. It carried an appropriation so great there was literally no way the money could be spent. There weren't enough contractors to do the work. We had 12 members of the House and Senate down to the White House to explain our case. We said we would veto the bill. They passed it anyway. We vetoed it."

Maggie had no more luck with a hefty appropriation for the benefit of health, education, and welfare from his Appropriations Subcommittee. Ehrlichman, riding high as Seattle's "Man of the Year" and, some said, a potential rival to Magnuson in the 1974 election for the Senate, made much of the senator's profligacy in an address to Washington State delegates to the 1972 Republican National Convention in Miami Beach. Nixon had vetoed the appropriation.

And Magnuson? "He's no credit to the state in fiscal responsibility," Ehrlichman told the delegates. "Maggie seems to have round heels when it comes to every request for money. When Maggie sends over these expensive bills, the President will veto them—and Congress won't be able to override [the veto]."[8]

From his first major piece of congressional legislation, establishment of the National Cancer Institute in 1937, an act he shared with Senator Homer Bone, Maggie wanted the federal purse tied to medical research. A cynic could say this was as safe as favoring motherhood. (Some have.)

But the happy result eclipses Maggie's motivation, whether it was base politics or noble altruism. "In essence Magnuson sponsored all the funding for medical research in the nation through the National Institutes of Health [NIH]," said Jerry Roschwalb, the top Washington lobbyist for colleges and universities. "The NIH is the work of a lot of people, to be sure, but it needed a leader to make it work. Maggie was that leader. Of course, he always took care of the University of Washington."[9] Unlike any of the Columbia River dams, the university's medical school bears his name. The Warren G. Magnuson Health Sciences Center sprawls over ten acres of a former golf course at the south end of the university along Portage Bay.

"I can't explain how Maggie understood the importance of basic medical research," says Dr. Jack Lein, a vice president of the medical school and liaison to Magnuson's Washington, D.C. "There was something intuitive about him. He just understood. Every medical school, not just UW, benefited from Magnuson." But Lein does admit to having had an advantage: "We'd have meetings in Maggie's office, get tipped off where the federal money was going. Sometimes he'd make a telephone call—most of what you see around here [UW] came as a result of Maggie's influence. I'd say we need something and eventually it would materialize." As of 1995, the university was the second largest recipient of federal grants among U.S. universities. Johns Hopkins University, with its strategic think tanks, is the top recipient.[10]

Maggie's man on the Appropriations Subcommittee, the Mike Pertschuk of federal funding for health, education, and welfare, was Harley Dirks of Othello, a stoplight in a road across eastern Washington. Once, campaigning through the Othello hinterland, Maggie spied a cornfield and asked an aide his estimate of its yield per acre. "Oh, about a 100 bushels per acre," the aide guessed. "Not bushels," snapped Maggie. "How many barrels?"[11] Dirks kept the liquor store and shoe store—"shoes and booze"—in Othello before going to the other Washington to work for Maggie. He was the face of the committee most seen by lobbyists like Jerry Roschwalb. Like Pertschuk, Dirks was a power unto himself, subject only to Magnuson. If Harley said "yes" to a request for federal funds, they were nearly certain to be included in the federal budget—subject to a final nod from Magnuson and absent a veto by Nixon.

Bill First, administrative aide to Tom Foley in the congressman's first term, remembers going to Harley beseeching the clerk to allow Foley to talk to Magnuson about several million dollars for an eastern Washington dam project. Dirks remained silent while First, a stranger to the subcommittee's operations, pleaded. "How much?" Dirks finally asked. First gave him the estimated cost. "It's in the budget," said Dirks. "What about the meeting for Foley?" asked First. "It's in the budget," Dirks repeated.[12] And so it was; a fiscal affair settled in a short talk between two congressional aides.

"Once we screwed up the NIH budget and came up $30 million short," remembered Roschwalb. "We went to Harley and asked that the money be restored. He was furious. He screamed at us. We had to stand in his presence and take it. But when the budget came out, the $30 million had been restored. It was Maggie. He knew what was needed. He fooled a lot of people who thought of him as lazy and a drunk. But nobody ever out-foxed him because he knew the details."

"Lyndon Johnson," says Roschwalb, "was a charlatan who would sell the city of Seattle if he could get something else. Magnuson was influential because he stood for something. His power came from the way he worked with other senators. Harley Dirks once told me 'I've known people raised in foster homes and they turn out to be sonsofbitches. Maggie never knew his real parents and it taught him to care for people. His job was to get power to do good for people.' "

The record shows he cared for nothing as much as for the social services—health, education, medical research. At another time, when Dirks balked at a $4 billion budget request for NIH, Roschwalb talked him into allowing a hearing. Maggie presided and the witnesses, strategically selected by Roschwalb, spent their time answering the senator's questions about one of his pet projects, WAMI (the medical training center for Washington, Alaska, Montana, and Idaho at—where else?—the University of Washington). "Maggie had a wonderful time," said Roschwalb. "Harley was ready to kill me. But Maggie had a way of letting people down graciously. He admitted Harley was right. They were sorely pressed for money—there was still a war in Vietnam—but he didn't know of anything that did more good for people than medical research.

"We got our budget request."

Dirks, the skillful storekeeper from Othello, remained an invisible power on the federal budget until an excess of impatience got the best of his judgment. Frustrated at arranging a subcommittee quorum, Harley took statements from members and lobbyists and put them together in a faux commitee report just as if the subcommittee had met and done its official business. This was published by the government printer. It worked until a Washington columnist discovered the cut-and-paste committee meeting and reported it. As a result of the ensuing notoriety, Magnuson fired Dirks, who returned to shoes and booze in Othello and died a few years later from a lingering illness.

Maggie's great and good lifelong friend, Bill Stern—a "blustering, warm and true friend" said Norman Winston—died in 1964. Afterward, Magnuson became a director of Stern's Dakota National Bank in Fargo. Stern had requested this. But Magnuson resigned the position early in 1972 and explained why in a letter to the bank president, A. M. Eriksmoen: "Now I'm too busy to make the meetings in Fargo. . . . Also I'd be very unhappy if there was any reflection on the integrity of a fine old institution because of a U.S. senator's being on its board. I've been meticulously careful with regard to banking legislation. . . . I intend to keep it that way."[13]

This sensitivity about a possible conflict of interest, almost unthinkable in the 1930s and 1940s when a congressman's private business was of limited concern to his constituents, reflected the change in public attitudes. Citizens had a new and acute awareness and curiosity about a public official's private interests. Common Cause, a national organization devoted to this new concern, was an immediate success. In Washington State a citizens initiative would require full disclosure of public officials' financial interests as well as the sources of their election campaign funds. By resigning from the bank board, Magnuson, as usual, was keeping up with the times—a constituent concern for conflict of interest.

Maggie's constituents were also aroused and angered by the bright lights of Soviet fishing trawlers off the Washington coast. The livelihood of coastal towns dependent on fishing was at risk. Hank Soike, the Grays Harbor port commissioner, got the point across to Magnuson when he took the senator to the end of a jetty at Westport, a fishing community on the coast. There Magnuson observed what appeared to be another night city at sea—the bright lights of Soviet trawlers somewhere between the coastline and the horizon. Maggie looked stunned at the sight. Reading his mood, Jerry Grinstein drafted and released a statement expressing the senator's concern and determination to get rid of the Russians.[14] The matter quickly shifted from Westport, Washington, to the Oval Office of the White House.

Joe Califano informed President Johnson on June 2, 1966, that Magnuson reported "a tremendous furor over the Soviet fleet. That commercial and sports fishermen in Washington were up in arms. The State Department isn't moving fast enough—he wants your personal attention. I'll call [Secretary of State] Rusk and ask that he contact the Soviet embassy and Sen. Magnuson."[15]

But the issue and the Russians lingered. While Maggie worked the White House, the Russians worked the coastline for fish for the markets of Leningrad and Moscow. Accordingly, the senator drafted a bill banning foreign fishing boats from working within 200 miles of our Pacific coastline, determined to do with law—and the U.S. Coast Guard—what imperfect diplomacy had failed to accomplish. In so doing, he was patient—he wouldn't get the 200-mile limit measure past Congress until 1970.

"Toward the end of this fight for a 200-mile limit, Maggie pulled out a roll call every day, counting votes," says Norm Dicks, the former Husky football linebacker who would soon replace Stan Barer as Magnuson's administrative assistant. "He didn't bring the bill up until he had the votes for passage. How did he know when to act? Maggie had the best political instincts of anyone I know. He just had a great feeling for how people would react."[16] When the proper time came, he moved the bill. A 200-mile limit endures to this day.

The senator had less success with his bid to rebuild the U.S. Merchant Marine. "He had a feel for the importance of the sea," said Manny Rouvelas, Maggie's maritime aide in 1969, himself the son of a Greek seaman who stayed ashore in Seattle and, with Magnuson's help, became a U.S. citizen. The senator wanted to spend $2 billion to build 300 new merchant vessels and sail them under U.S. flags with U.S. crews holding U.S. union cards. He would never forget his early election debts to the Marine Firemen's union and the Sailors' Union of the Pacific.

"Those ships and those union members were articles of faith with Maggie," said Rouvelas. "In the last analysis his heart was with the unions. He wanted American shipping to be split 50–50 between U.S. and foreign bottoms." Alas, Maggie could never make that wish come true. Far less than 300 vessels were launched.[17] Foreign vessels flying flags of convenience, paying seamen wages far below American union scale, would dominate traffic into U.S. ports. By the mid-1990s, U.S. maritime union membership had dropped to a fraction of its numbers in 1950. The Sailors' two-story hall on the corner of Seattle's First Avenue and Wall Street bore a "for sale" sign. The Firemen's hall a block below on Western Avenue, a modern brick structure built to withstand bombs and armed assault, had long since been sold to an electronics firm. American seamen had become the first casualties of the global marketplace. The world was changing, and even if he had been around, Maggie would have been at a loss to help the seafarers.

The Commerce Committee kept churning out laws to protect consumers and spare their money. A "bumper bill" required cars made after 1974 to have bumpers built to withstand 10 mph collisions without sustaining damage to the vehicle. The idea was to save at least $8 million a year in superficial car damage. Maggie's consumer protection act of 1970 opened the way for class action (group) lawsuits for damages sustained from defective products.

Dr. Abe Bergman's inspiration, the National Health Service Corps, became law January 2, 1971. In lieu of military service, medical doctors could serve in urban ghettos or remote rural areas for two years. The pilot project had a $10 million appropriation. Almost unnoticed by the urban world at large, the program continues, a medical godsend for out-of-the-way places of America. Maggie also pushed a bill to provide dental care at federal expense for half a million elementary school students from low income families.

More pressing on the senator was an abrupt nosedive by Boeing in 1969 and the attendant panic in the western Washington economy. ("When Boeing sneezes Seattle has the flu.") The aircraft company's employment dropped from a peak of 148,672 in 1968 to about 54,000 three years later. The causes were mixed: the end of Pentagon orders for B-52 bombers and C-135 transports; sluggish airline growth as Nixon cooled inflation; a heavy investment in the 747 airliner with returns yet to come; loss of federal money for the SST; and a general corporate cleansing of a bloated payroll.[18] Seattle had not witnessed its like since the Great Depression; the "Boeing recession" left middle-aged professional men, engineers, and managers, many with advanced college degrees, on the street unemployed for the first time in their lives. The sight was painful to observe and responsible for the only poignant billboard ever erected: "Will the Last Person Out of Seattle Please Turn Off the Lights?" Although many had forgotten or taken it for granted, the Boeing recession was mitigated by unemployment insurance and Social Security—legacies of an earlier Magnuson era.

Maggie was swamped with calls for help. One project, which he promoted at Boeing's urging, would have placed a giant solar panel in space to collect sun rays and transmit the electric energy back to earth. As the senator graphically (if unscientifically) described the project to a newsman, the solar panel, built by Boeing, of course, would be like a Grand Coulee in the sky, taking enough energy from the sun to electrify most of the state. But how to get the energy back to earth? "Well," he answered, chewing the end of his perpetual unlit cigar, brow wrinkled in deep thought. "It would be just like hanging a long light-cord down from a high ceiling in your house."[19] The Grand Coulee from outer space with its long light-cord never got off the ground.

But another Boeing inspiration, the airport-airways development bill to upgrade the nation's aviation system, passed out of Commerce Committee and through Congress and into law with President Nixon's signature in May 1970. At least indirectly, it helped ease Seattle's recession while adding greatly to the protection of the consumers of airline tickets.

An even more down-to-earth scheme to ease the recession's pain was an extension of unemployment benefits for laid-off workers. There was such a bill, but it was locked in the House by its dominant Ways and Means Committee chairman, Wilbur Mills, and it would not budge until Maggie came across the Capitol to the House chambers and negotiated directly with Mills. The demand was nearly unprecedented, but Maggie, accompanied by Norm Dicks, made the symbolic journey.

When these two exceptionally powerful legislators met, Magnuson, to Dicks's horror, greeted Mills as "Orville," instead of his real name, Wilbur. Dicks thought the day—the bill—was lost because of Maggie's gaffe. It was not. Mills released the bill from Ways and Means and laid-off workers in Seattle got an extra measure of money to hold them over until the next job. After the measure passed, Dicks, as tactfully as is possible for a Husky linebacker, asked the senator about the apparent insult to Mills. Magnuson laughed. "Orville" became an old joke between the two legislators, a badge of their familiarity.[20]

There were "thousands of starving" people in Seattle during this recession, Magnuson told the Senate late in 1971 as he demanded Nixon's agriculture secretary release surplus food for the needy. In this speech he noted news stories that said citizens of Japan were sending food packages to their transpacific neighbors in Seattle. "Why must citizens of the richest nation in the world have their survival depending on mercy shipments of rice and canned goods from another nation?" asked Maggie. The Agriculture Department relented and released surplus food stocks.

"These were gut issues for Magnuson," said Dicks. "Unemployment compensation, food for the needy, and resolving the boxcar shortage."

A shortage of railroad boxcars at one time in the mid-1960s had farmers and businesses along the U.S. northern tier in a horrific logjam, unable to move the wheat harvested from our Great Plains and already overflowing grain elevators along the railroad right-of-way. Telephone calls from Magnuson to the chairman of the Interstate Commerce Commission (ICC) urging the dispatch of boxcars to ease the distress had no effect. Wheat began to rot on the ground. Magnuson called an informal fact-finding hearing with the ICC chairman, and representatives of the railroads, farmers, and farm towns. Al Swift, a future congressman from Bellingham, Washington, who was at that time administrative aide to Representative Lloyd Meeds, described the meeting as "chaos—everybody talking at once. Total disorder. Scoop Jackson got so mad he walked out of the hearing. There were rumbles about Maggie being drunk and senile. In fact, he knew exactly what he was doing—he was letting everybody blow off steam, clear their chests. And then he would settle the issue."

The problem was endemic: Instead of building new boxcars, the railroad lines were borrowing rolling stock from each other. It saved money, but the borrowers frequently held on to the lender's boxcars for extended periods. Thus a surplus in one region could cause a boxcar shortage elsewhere.

"It seems to me the chairman has a problem," Swift quotes Magnuson as having said at the conclusion of the chaotic hearing: "It's a case of the sheets being too short for the bed. Boxcars are short in the north because they are held somewhere else. Now if I issued an exclusionary order [mandating the immediate dispatch of cars to the northern tier] that would take days. But I'll see what else I can do." What he did, says Swift, was to call the White House—Johnson was still inside—which, in turn, issued a strongly worded suggestion the next day for the ICC to speed the return of boxcars to the northern tier. The crisis ended.

Years later, Al Swift reflected on the boxcar episode: "What it showed me was how Magnuson could get his way, solve an acute problem, without embarrassing or humiliating anybody. He made no fuss. He just quietly used his power to get what he wanted when he wanted it."[21] It also illustrated the senator's mode of operation: taking an action with a significant impact on the lives of citizens, but doing it outside the glare of TV cameras and next-day headlines. Like most of his even more significant consumer protection legislation, it happened almost without publicity. What these actions had in significance for average citizens, they sorely lacked in glamour.

Magnuson's 1965 bill requiring tobacco companies to label cigarettes as dangerous to health was an exception to the limited publicity mode. It got plenty of attention, but Maggie still wasn't satisfied with the results. He noted in an unpublished statement that since that act the tobacco industry had offset the warning by increasing its advertising budgets by 50 percent and that half of teenaged Americans smoked cigarettes—the cause of 300,000 premature deaths each year. What followed in 1970 was a measure requiring tobacco firms to label cigarettes with their tar and nicotine content and banning cigarette advertisements on television.

Magnuson's proposed legislation for the 1971 congressional session had a twist. Along with health and education measures, the senior senator joined Henry Jackson, chairman of the Energy Committee, in proposing bills to protect the environment.

Maggie sought $10 million for cancer research, $13 million for children's dental care, and $20 million for food programs for the needy. An oil spill off Cherry Point in northern Puget Sound triggered his concern with saving the Sound—a concern that would eventually lead him into a rare open conflict with another public official. Maggie's initial bill in 1971 imposed tough new standards on construction and operation of oil tankers, and a vessel traffic control system for Puget Sound and approaches to it through the Strait of Juan de Fuca.[22] His friendship brought along support from Senator Russell Long, Louisiana's good buddy to the oil industry. This legislation created the nation's first vessel traffic control system.[23]

"Maggie likened Puget Sound to a big bathtub," said Featherstone Reid. "If a major oil spill occurred in the Sound it would leave a giant black ring around the shoreline—one difficult or impossible to remove. He was determined that this would never happen."

More than any one person, Magnuson is responsible for sparing Puget Sound from such a catastrophe, and for that reason Reid believes the preservation of Puget Sound was Magnuson's greatest accomplishment as a public official. There are certainly others who feel the same, but they would not have included the late Governor Dixy Lee Ray, who had succeeded Dan Evans, but who cared less than the Republican or Maggie for the safety of the environment.

CHAPTER 26

"Scoop and Maggie"

F or three decades in the middle of the twentieth century it was the most improbable, yet formidable, political partnership in the U.S. Senate, perhaps all the more improbable because the senators came from the same state. Instead of rivalry there was friendship and cooperation. "Scoop and Maggie": The two proper nouns, nicknames, became melded almost as one to their joint constituents, as in "Scoop and Maggie" beat the Southwest in its attempt to steal our Columbia River water; Scoop and Maggie got us a third powerhouse at Grand Coulee, and now they'll get us the SST.

To most of these constituents, the personalities, as well as the nicknames of Senators Henry M. Jackson and Warren G. Magnuson, merged. Indeed, there were symbolic and real similarities between the two politicians. Both were Americans of fresh Scandinavian descent, Democrats, liberals (at least on domestic policies), and creatures of Northwest populism—egalitarian, firm believers in common schools and public power, and skeptical of political power overly concentrated on either the left or the right. Both were committed to care of the home folks and to "bringing home the bacon." But their differences in manner and lifestyle were greater than these similarities. And their spheres of influence in Congress were as different as their personalities—Scoop for the Pentagon and national defense, Maggie for health and human services.

If Maggie liked women, liquor, fast horses, and late-night poker, Jackson liked to go to movies, read the financial pages, and watch the late news on television. Scoop was, in the old-fashioned word, "square." He was so wedded to the Protestant ethos of hard work, fair play, straight shooting, and upward striving that even those who disagreed with his ardent support of the Vietnam War and a virtually unlimited Pentagon budget held him in respect and perhaps even with a grudging admiration.

A scientist would call the Jackson-Magnuson relationship symbiotic; they were political creatures who, in a sense, fed off each other. Magnuson was invaluable to Jackson in the Congress, perhaps even nudging him into the Senate over the more cerebral Hugh B. Mitchell. Jackson was equally helpful to Magnuson come election time. They played to separate sides of the voter psyche: Maggie, the earthy, carousing, good guy to have a drink with; Scoop, the sober, up-at-daybreak, home-in-the-evening citizen. Both were gentlemen of a most practical bent, so whatever the gap in their lifestyles they ignored it in favor of the benefits of working together.

But there were more fundamental differences between the two senators. They had opposite world views: Maggie saw the world and its inhabitants in shades of gray; Jackson seemed to see only black and white. Maggie was forgiving. He told Drew Pearson he could never be a judge because he couldn't deliver a sentence. Instead, he would tell the defendant "go forth and sin no more."[1] Jackson appeared never to forgive a slight; never mind an insult. Magnuson, as Al Swift noted, allowed himself to be underestimated—one of the tools of his political craft. From network television interview to private party, Scoop liked to be the center of attention.

Irv Hoff, a great friend and observer of both of these remarkable legislators, notes the difference in the way they acquired knowledge. "Scoop had to study, to read everything about a subject and get all the facts before he reached a decision," said Hoff, looking back several decades. "Magnuson never did much research. He reached decisions from his gut—his intuition." That is not a casual distinction. The Italian philosopher and statesman Benedetto Croce defined knowlege as coming either from intellect or from intuition, the latter a mingling of concepts with imagination and perceptions. Croce also noted that even though his colleagues in academia gave it short shrift, intuitive knowledge could stand on its own apart from abstract data accumulated through study.[2] Croce could have used Magnuson as a prime exhibit for his thesis.

"Here's another difference," said Charles Hodde, a close friend of both men, and a former Speaker of the Washington State House of Representatives. "When you went back to Washington, D.C., to visit with them Scoop would greet you and say, 'All right, Charlie, here's what we've got to do and here's how you're going to do it.' And he'd tick off the business. Go down the hall to Maggie's office and he'd greet you and say, 'Charlie what's going on out there? And what can I do for you?' It was quite a difference in approach."[3]

"They were rarely together and didn't travel in the same circles," says Gerry Johnson, one of Magnuson's last administrative assistants. (In Seattle, while Maggie held court in his suite at the Olympic Hotel, Jackson had membership in the citadel of the state's business, finance, and social establishment, the University Club. Not coincidentally its membership was mostly Republican; Philip Bailey of the *Argus* perhaps its most liberal member.) "They had different routines in the Capitol:

Scoop worked out in the Senate gym, Maggie worked the cloakroom. But Scoop was constantly haranguing us [Magnuson's staff] about Maggie's political problems at home: 'Maggie is in terrible shape—you've got to do something about it.' He worried about it. Their relationship was so finely honed, each knew his role and they worked easily together." By the time Johnson arrived in Washington, D.C., in 1974 to handle Maggie's mail, Magnuson and Jackson had worked together for thirty years.[4]

Jackson came to Congress as an overachiever. An admiring colleague, Senator Bill Bradley of New Jersey, has marveled at Scoop's preparation for Senate debate—intense personal lobbying and the drafting of a "battle book" in which potential questions were anticipated, understood, and answered. The book was a staff task and Jackson, like Maggie, won and kept the undying loyalty of his Senate employees. As a member of the House he picked up the cause of the Columbia Valley Authority, or "Communism on the Columbia" as it had been called when sponsored by Senator Hugh Mitchell. But his bill never got through the House Interior Committee and the curtain dropped on the CVA in 1949. A twenty-nine-year-old bachelor, Jackson served briefly in the U.S. Army during World War II, never smelling cordite. He returned to the House when President Roosevelt permitted members to waive military service and keep their congressional seats. From the start of his political career until its finish, Jackson was a ceaseless campaigner. Never mind the opposition—generally weak—he treated each race as a mortal threat to his career. After his election to the Senate in 1952, he won reelections by lopsided margins. Along with Maggie, Scoop took care of the home folks, but he bridled at the pejorative "the senator from Boeing" and should have, since the label better fit Maggie. But Magnuson attracted less attention and animosity.

What separated Jackson from Magnuson and sent their Senate careers in different directions was the junior senator's appointment in 1959 to the Government Operations subcommittee on national policy. Scoop made the most of this investigation into the machinery of national security. He was already a cold warrior who thought of himself as "Churchillian," that is, acutely aware of the lesson of Munich—appeasement doesn't work. In his critical biography, Peter Ognibene reports that the subcommittee investigation gave Jackson an unsurpassed insight into the workings of the Pentagon and State Department; the people and subagencies "which can initiate, revise, or obstruct national policy." This knowledge was a critical source of Jackson's influence as a ranking member—but not chairman—of the Armed Services Committee.[5] In 1962, Jackson became chairman of the Interior Committee and later chaired its successor, the Energy Committee, a post as critical to the power and water needs of the Northwest as Armed Services was important to the Pentagon.

"They worked different sides of the street," said Tom Foley of Spokane, a friend of both senators who served in the House of Representatives as chairman of the Agriculture Committee, majority whip, and Speaker until 1995. "They didn't spend much time together, nor was there much contact between their staffs. But they established a tradition of a delegation working together for the state."

Maggie presided over meetings of the state delegation, usually held in his office in the Russell (Old) Senate Office Building just down the hallway from Jackson's office. As Foley and other members have described these sessions, Maggie created the climate for cooperation, but Scoop would be the driver, saying: " 'Maggie, shouldn't we do this?' And name the project. Scoop acted like a schoolteacher. Maggie would chew his cigar, mumble and respond, 'Yeah, that's right. We should.' The delegation would respond accordingly."[6] And what a superb delegation, if the criteria are intellect, civility, sophistication, and legislative know-how. At the peak of the Scoop and Maggie power, it included, but not all at the same time, Representatives Lloyd Meeds, Al Swift, Floyd Hicks, Brock Adams, Tom Foley, Julia Butler Hansen, Norm Dicks, Mike Lowry, and Joel Pritchard, the lone Republican. They worked together under Scoop and Maggie's leadership. As Swift later described the relationship between the senators and the congressmen: "We respected Scoop. We loved Maggie."

"I think Scoop sometimes despaired of Maggie," said Adams, who would eventually succeed to Magnuson's seat in the Senate. And so he did. Once in late October 1970, Jackson, accompanied by two reporters, took his campaign for reelection to Clarkston in southeastern Washington for a partisan speech in the local Grange Hall. Maggie was to make the introduction. The Jackson party greeted the senior senator at a private home where he had dined and consumed more than a few drinks. Magnuson drank much liquor, but very rarely showed its effects. This evening was one of the exceptions. He was deeply in his cups and obviously affected. Scoop looked peeved at the first sight of his comrade.

"Pour these boys a drink," Maggie commanded his host. The reporters imbibed. Jackson abstained.

"Maggie, time to go," commanded Jackson, who lacked the will or authority to suggest that Magnuson stay behind. Despite his obvious impairment, and Scoop's bad case of nerves, Maggie made it up the Grange Hall platform, rose to his feet and delivered a hell-fire Democratic speech, assailing "'Publicans and their Wall Street bosses" with such clarity and brio that the audience stamped their feet and cheered. Then he sat down. Scoop looked distressed enough to die. He jabbed Maggie in the ribs, whispered into his ear.

"Oh, yeah," said Magnuson, back on his feet. "I want to introduce my good friend, your once and future senator and friend, Scoop Jackson." Jackson did not utter a word of disapproval for Maggie's lapse of rectitude during the long flight back over the Cascades, mountains whose moonlit upper reaches had turned white from a late autumn snowfall. Instead, he reminisced about early days in the Senate. He had long ago accommodated himself to Maggie's manner.[7]

Apart from friendship, as Tom Foley noted, Jackson was aware that "Maggie had great power in the Senate." Maggie's help was worth the occasional frustration; he was the legislator with influence on both sides of the aisle and, until the coming of Richard Nixon, in the White House; a Senate "whale" in the words of Lyndon Johnson—in contrast to the rank and file, the "minnows." In his memoir, *A Political Education*, Harry McPherson, President Johnson's counsel, describes Jackson as "something of a loner, not a Senate power like Magnuson. He was consistently reasonable; this and his youthful appearance denied him weight in the Senate."[8]

But Jackson gained "weight" with the departure of Johnson and the arrival of Nixon in the White House. The newly elected president offered Jackson the appointment of secretary of defense. Jackson declined but became one of the president's most favored Democrats—if not *the* most favored. Magnuson's White House influence declined; Jackson's soared. "Nixon certainly felt closer to Scoop than to Magnuson," said John Ehrlichman, Nixon's domestic adviser from Seattle. "If we had anything to do with the Northwest, we went through Jackson."[9]

The war in Vietnam created a major strain between the hawkish Jackson and the ambivalent Maggie. As long as Johnson was in the White House, the strain wasn't serious. Maggie stayed the course with Lyndon and relations with Scoop remained stable. But Maggie was too circumspect and too aware of his own limitations in geopolitics to share Jackson's zeal in the Southeast Asian warfare—zeal which initially was built on his vision of Red China as a Communist empire with unharnessed expansionist goals. In a new version of the old "yellow peril" theory, cleaned up for delivery to the World Affairs Council of Philadelphia in 1966, Jackson warned that unless North Vietnam was checked in its drive on South Vietnam "the spread of Chinese domination could threaten even securely based nations such as Japan" and thence east. He seemed obsessed with "Mao's Red China." In a speech prepared for the Senate floor, Jackson argued against a withdrawal of U.S. troops from Vietnam. To do so, he said, would "open the door to a vast extension of Chinese influence in Asia. . . . To know Mao's Red China is to fear its expanionist ambitions."[10] There was contrary evidence at that time which suggested China, a nation in social and economic turmoil from its disastrous Great Leap Forward, was trying to make peace, not war, along its Asian borders. There was greater evidence of a fatal split between the Soviet Union and China, the Communist superpower "monolith." Yet for Jackson, Red China, not North Vietnam, was the real enemy. This was a gross misreading of Chinese intentions in 1966, and one with profound consequences for the nation. Finally, in the late 1960s, by which time the evidence of a split in the Communist monolith was overwhelming, Jackson backed away from the notion of China as the "real enemy." Jackson wasn't alone in his protracted misreading of Chinese-Soviet relations. Stimson Bullitt says his Yale classmate, James Jesus Angleton, chief of CIA counterintelligence, told him that the apparent hostility between the Communist powers was a deception by the Kremlin to propagate communism and to unmask its heretics.[11]

But Jackson didn't back off from his support of the Vietnam War, which would expand into Cambodia under President Nixon, despite the peace talks in Paris initiated by President Johnson. Maggie began to shift away from support of the war as the political clamor against it reached a crescendo. The left-liberal wing of the state Democratic Party turned against the war with a fury frequently expressed in harsh protest.

The most eloquent and reasoned statement against the war came in 1966 from Stimson Bullitt in a television editorial on KING-TV, the station owned by his family and managed by himself. Bullitt, a Purple Heart veteran of World War II, said, "We must acknowledge a fact repulsive to American ideals: Our intense warfare fails to enable construction of a just and stable society in Viet Nam" and "it disrupts the society, tends to degrade and corrupt large elements of it and makes ever more enemies by war's inevitable mistakes. . . . Our destructive course now spirals downward. The more we claw the place into a plowed field populated by refugees, prostitutes and hostile guerrillas, the less we can achieve at helping them build the kind of society we would like."[12] Scoop remained steadfast, and six years later at the 1972 Democratic State Convention he lashed out at the "kooks" and "extremists" protesting the war—many of them present before him in the convention hall. They would support Senator George McGovern, not Henry Jackson, for the Democratic presidential nomination.

Under these circumstances, tension between Scoop and Maggie was inevitable, but there was no open breach until Nixon proposed an antiballistic missile system (ABM) to protect our Minuteman missile silos from a preemptive nuclear strike by the Soviets. Jackson more than liked the idea of this new weapon. He became floor manager for its passage in the Senate.[13]

When Jackson took an issue, it became a question of right and wrong—not nuts and bolts—especially if the issue involved national security. The ABM, a pocket version of the even more extravagant Star Wars proposal which would follow, was designed to shelter U.S. intercontinental missiles so we could retaliate should the Soviets shoot first. It became a critical question in the cold war theology of the late 1960s: could the nation survive a Soviet first strike without an ABM system? The theoretical debate carried religious intensity, like the question of the Nicene Creed posed to early Christians. Maggie was not a believer.

Debate raged all summer in 1969. Jackson, using a Pentagon hypothesis, argued that some time soon the Soviets would develop multiple nuclear warheads for their long-range missiles which could, somewhere down the road to Armageddon, attack and destroy 95 percent of U.S. Minuteman missiles. He and Nixon wanted to deploy four ABM sites around missile silos on the Great Plains. Scoop argued his case forcefully with colleagues and newspaper editorial boards. When questioned to a standstill by one of the latter, the senator would close by saying, "If you had the information that I have" and repeat the necessity for the ABM. The ABM was right. Skeptics were wrong. But Maggie wasn't sold. The senior senator faced a quandary.

"Maggie didn't want to hurt Scoop, but he didn't want to vote with the Hatfields and McGoverns [pro-peace senators who, in Magnuson's view, carried little weight with their colleagues]," explained Stan Barer, who had just replaced Jerry Grinstein as Maggie's administrative assistant. "But he was opposed to the ABM."

Given Magnuson's Senate tonnage, an early announcement of his opposition to the ABM would likely have killed its passage, a blow to the prestige of his colleague from Washington State. So instead of speaking out, Maggie remained silent. This was driving Jackson's overeager assistant, Richard Perle, to distraction. Scoop never lobbied Maggie on the ABM. Perle, a hawkish "neo-conservative" not much trusted by newsmen or his staff colleagues down the hall in Maggie's alley, couldn't restrain himself. He approached Barer and Norm Dicks of Maggie's staff.

"Perle said the vote [for an ABM] was down to five senators," said Barer:

He asked to speak with Senator Magnuson on the issue. Now it is presumptuous of a staffer to make such a request and it is rare. I said I'd think about it. Dicks and I came up with an idea—a scam. We told Perle he could speak with the senator—Maggie had mumbled an okay. We also set up Perle by telling him that Magnuson wants to let the Soviets think we've got a real big ABM system, not just a mere four sites. So he wants to dig big holes all over the country and fill them with fake ABMs, a Potemkin ABM system. The Russians will never know the difference and will be deterred from a first strike launch. Perle fell for it. He went to Magnuson's office, closed the door and began to argue against a fake ABM system. Finally Magnuson brought the meeting to a close by asking Perle, "What in the hell are you talking about?"

A little later Maggie raised the subject of his meeting with Perle: "I don't know what's wrong with that guy. I couldn't understand a thing he said about the ABM." Perle nearly had a heart attack when he learned he had been tricked. Scoop laughed. But on the real issue, Maggie kept his silence. He didn't want to cost Scoop votes.

Barer's fellow trickster, Norm Dicks, says Maggie's position on the ABM was generally known—and shared—by his staff, but they all kept quiet: "Maggie just didn't want to hurt Scoop. They needed each other. Scoop needed Maggie in the Senate. Scoop was indispensable to Maggie in elections."

Magnuson broke his silence on the Senate floor on the day of the decisive ABM vote when he delivered a speech written in his own careful hand—his writings were never as careless as his everyday talk would have suggested—on yellow legal paper. He said he opposed deployment of the ABM as "too high a price to pay for the illusion of defense without its substance—there are better ways to spend our money. . . . Some say failure to deploy the ABMs will undermine the President's prestige in the arms control talks. . . . [T]he Soviets will negotiate arms control when it serves their political interest to do so—regardless of whether we deploy the ABM."[14]

In private talks, with Ancil Payne and others, Magnuson put it even more simply: "The ABM will cost a lot of money and you'll never know whether the thing will work until it is too late." And he told a shaggy-dog story about two cockney drunks in a subway shelter during the Nazi bombing of London: " 'I say, isn't that the bloody Archbishop of Canterbury standing over there,' says one. The other says, 'I'll go see.' He does. The man tells him to bug off. 'Well,' says the first drunk, 'was that the Archbishop of Canterbury?' 'He bloody didn't say,' said the other. 'Well now,' replied the first drunk, 'we'll never know.' " The trouble with the ABM, Maggie told Payne, is that "we'll never know."[15] To Maggie, the ABM was a matter of nuts and bolts and dollars and cents. He clearly favored arms control over weapons development with uncertain prospects.

Jackson won the ABM battle by defeating a killer amendment on a 50-50 tie. There is controversy about the vote cast by Senator Clinton Anderson of New Mexico, a Senate "whale" according to Lyndon Johnson and somewhat of a mentor for Senator Jackson. The night before the final vote, Anderson's office issued a press release saying he would vote against the ABM, thus voting for the killer amendment. But when he was called by the Senate president to vote, Anderson, ailing, mumbled something unintelligible. Jackson rushed to his side, placed an arm around his shoulder, and, when the New Mexican was asked to repeat his vote, Jackson said, "Anderson votes no" (on the amendment that would have killed ABM deployment). After he left the floor, Anderson was asked why he had switched his position on the ABM. He couldn't answer. His staff felt that he had been humiliated.[16]

Jackson's ABM victory was substantially washed away when Nixon and Soviet boss Leonid Brezhnev subsequently signed a treaty limiting each side to two ABM sites, only one of which could defend U.S. Minuteman missiles. Outraged, the senator himself later became a constant critic of U.S. attempts at arms control and of our arms control negotiators.

Magnuson and Jackson differed increasingly on the cold war issues of weapons, arms control, and Pentagon budgets. This was not without some political calculation. With an eye on the 1974 election, Maggie leaned toward the doves and away from Scoop. So, too, did a majority of the activist Democrats in Washington State. This marginal cleavage, never publicized, created additional tension between the two men. Jackson, a candidate for reelection to the Senate in 1970 against an attractive but outgunned Republican opponent, had been rebuked by the party's state convention, which adopted a "peace now" platform calling for an end to the Vietnam War no later than June 30, 1971. As political writer Mike Layton wrote for the *Argus*, the convention action "no doubt will endear Jackson to the Republican fat cats and Silent Majority, but it was an embarrassment Jackson sought to avoid."[17] Magnuson's ringing endorsement of Jackson was a sharp disappointment to the convention majority which favored Spokane attorney Carl Maxey for the Democratic senatorial nomination in the state's September primary election. Maxey lost to Jackson and so did the Republican nominee in the general election, Charles Elicker, an outstanding state senator with a remarkable resemblance to Teddy Roosevelt.

If there was no open break between the two senators, there was increasing sniping at Magnuson on the editorial page of the *Seattle Times*. As Magnuson repeatedly voted to whack the Pentagon budget and put the money into health, education, and welfare, it became a *Times* editorial staple to suggest that he defer to Jackson, his better on "national security" issues. A 1969 editorial critical of Maggie's position concluded, "If he [Magnuson] prevails, the Russians [*sic*] will have scored a critical victory even before [arms control] negotiations have begun." Jackson had a way with newspaper editorial boards and it would be naive not to think that he or his office influenced such criticism. Another sample, from an August 1973 edition, says that Magnuson's proposed reduction in arms spending is "myopic, favoring the left Congressional clique. . . . [This] position is fashionable, yet Sen. Jackson does not echo Magnuson's illusions. . . . Jackson is far more qualified to espouse the correct national [defense] policies."[18]

Those polite manifestations of the Scoop and Maggie tension could have been fueled by Magnuson's outspoken attacks on budgets proposed by Nixon. Maggie told the *Seattle Post-Intelligencer* of February 25, 1973, that Nixon had cut $7 billion from social programs while adding $5.5 billion to the Pentagon treasury. "We're not spending enough on health programs—I'd like to see another $5 million for Children's Orthopedic Hospital [in Seattle]. He said, "cutting defense spending won't cost us in national security" for "we could cut from six divisions to two or three divisions [in Europe] and still have security. We can't police the whole world. If they [Europeans] can't take care of themselves after 27 years, they'll never be able to."

This reduction in U.S. Forces in NATO, proposed by Magnuson, was consistent with the amendment offered by Senator Mike Mansfield. Both were consonant with what we now know was an unrealistic threat to Western Europe from the Soviet Union by the mid-1970s. The Communist superpower was a nation falling apart. Yet our NATO expenses, reaching up to $200 billion a year, continued until the end of the 1980s, when even the CIA came to realize the threat was gone along with the Berlin Wall.

Jackson surely despaired of such talk by Magnuson. And Maggie? Once, in the midst of the tension, in a private conversation with a newsman, Magnuson mused, "The problem with Scoop is that he thinks war with the Russians is inevitable."[19] The quote appeared in print, source unnamed. Magnuson's observation seemed neither incorrect, given Jackson's consistently hawkish positions, nor unflattering. But Jackson was furious, demanding the reporter name his source (the reporter refused) and calling the quote an instance of "yellow journalism." It was a lop-sided reaction. Yet Jackson may have recalled Maggie's admonition to constituents at the start of the cold war: those who believe war with the Soviets is inevitable are in fact promoting the apocalypse. If so, Scoop could have guessed the source. But this tension never reached a breaking point.

"My intuition," says Tom Foley, "is that Maggie's shift in his positions on Vietnam and arms spending made him more acceptable to an [anti-war] element of the state Democratic Party, the anti-Jackson faction. But Magnuson had to follow his instincts. Why was there never an open break? My intuition says that while it got to be like a bad marriage, it was more convenient for the two senators to stay together than to break up."[20]

In fact, the Magnuson-Jackson partnership worked in harmony for most of their tenure, a tribute to forbearance and good sense—and a contrast to relations between many other senators from the same state. A most conspicuous example was the open hostility between the senators from neighboring Idaho, Frank Church, Democrat, and Jim McClure, Republican. They kept a running feud on the Senate floor and McClure felt too vindicated to disguise his delight in the defeat of Church in 1980. In the last analysis, for all of their differences, Scoop and Maggie respected and admired each other as much as they needed one another's rare assets.

But apart from taking care of the home state, Magnuson and Jackson rarely worked as a team when tackling a regionally transcendent issue. They stuck to their different sides of the street—Magnuson dealing with civil rights and appropriations, and Jackson with national security—usually voting alike and helping each other with advice. Their one major power play as a team came in 1970 on behalf of federal funding for a commercial Supersonic Transport (SST), and, irony of ironies, it was a legislative failure. Aside from Hells Canyon high dam, and his fight for "no fault" auto insurance, this was the only major battle ever lost by Magnuson on the Senate floor. Insurance lobbyists whipped "no fault." Ultimately, the SST became a debate over the nation's priorities. Boeing was the other apparent loser.

A lesser paradox: According to Norm Dicks, Magnuson's chief aide in the full-scale fight for federal loans to develop the SST, "The senator was never really hot about the airplane. He would say, 'If it's so good why don't market forces pay for it?' "[21] But fight he did, trading votes, shuf-fling the appropriations agenda, and using Model Cities appropriations to lever SST support. Scoop threw all of his considerable weight behind the fight, including his longtime top assistant, John Salter, who had returned to Seattle to become a Boeing lobbyist.

The genesis of this struggle over national priorities appears to be a handwritten note dated "Feb. 17 or 18" written to Magnuson by Lowell Mickelwait, a Boeing vice president, while airborne between Seattle and the East Coast. Mickelwait requested an urgent meeting on a "matter of considerable importance." The executive apologized for his shaky handwriting and blamed it on the "DC-8 which is noisy and vibrating." (The DC-8 is a Douglas aircraft.)[22]

A year later Boeing won the design competition over Lockheed and Douglas for a contract to construct the faster-than-sound aircraft, a rival to the European Concorde and what others, including Jackson, claimed was a forthcoming Soviet SST. Indeed, the Soviets did launch an SST only to witness its failure as a commercial carrier. To build an American supersonic flying machine Boeing needed massive federal loans for research and development of a prototype. The idea was to repay the government loans once the craft turned a profit.

Apart from home folks in Seattle and aviation buffs around the nation, the SST didn't attract much attention until the matter of federal loans passed through the House, where Representative Brock Adams carried the heavy load, and hit the Senate. The showdown came in December 1970 as Congress began to anticipate the Christmas holidays. Scoop and Maggie, each in his own persuasive fashion, had done their work for the SST out front and behind the scenes. But so had Senator William Proxmire, the Wisconsin Democrat, normally regarded by such as Warren Magnuson and Lyndon Johnson as a Senate "minnow." On this issue he would turn killer whale.

At stake was a $290 million appropriation for development of an 1,800-mph prototype craft, a sum tucked inside the $7 billion appropriation for the Department of Transportation. Maggie handled the DOT funding inside the Commerce Committee. Dicks made certain the committee hearing starred Treasury Secretary John Connally, AFL-CIO President George Meany, and DOT Secretary John Volpe, all favoring funds for the SST, as did President Nixon.

Behind the scenes Magnuson won the vote of Senator John Stennis, the Mississippi Democrat and chair of the Armed Services Committee, by voting for an amendment to the health, education, and welfare budget that put a crimp in mandatory busing of school students. Scoop and Maggie got the votes of the West Virginia senators, Robert Byrd and Jennings Randolph, by promising their votes to Byrd in his contest against Senator Ted Kennedy for majority whip. Later, when Byrd won the contest and Kennedy became aware of the "secret" ballot, the younger brother of Robert and John Kennedy told a newsman that he would forgive Maggie, but that he could never forgive Jackson "after all that my brothers did for him."[23]

Their pursuit of SST votes led Senator Walter Mondale of Minnesota to describe for Dr. Abe Bergman the contrasting styles of Maggie and Scoop: Magnuson, he said, never directly asks for a vote for fear of embarrassing a colleague; Scoop warns that if he doesn't get the senator's vote there'll be fewer national parks in his home state.[24]

But the day, December 3, 1970, belonged to Proxmire, who bestirred environmentalists into a frenzy of protests, handouts, and news conferences with wildly exaggerated claims widely seen on the nightly network news. In addition to labeling the SST a "boondoggle" and a distortion of national priorities, Proxmire's forces claimed the fast airplane would deplete world oil reserves and the ozone layer of the atmosphere, and that its sonic boom would devastate sea-life as it passed overhead on transoceanic flights. This prompted H. W. Whittington, Boeing manager of the SST program, to comment, "The kindest thing I can say about what I've heard is that I sure don't understand it." Senator Barry Goldwater put it less delicately. He called the environmentalists' assertions "lies."[25]

The vote to reject SST funding was 52 to 41, a clear victory for SST opponents, who included Senator Clinton Anderson, Jackson's erstwhile mentor. Scoop was most upset. He said, "The Senate bugged out on the nation's scientific effort, turned its back on 30,000 workers building the SST," and predicted American airline passengers would soon be flying faster than sound on aircraft bearing the Red Star of the Soviet Union.[26]

For the record, Magnuson called the vote a serious blow to U.S. air superiority. Privately, he indulged in a rare bit of name-calling: "I just hope that pissant Proxmire doesn't get credit for the vote."[27] Taking the vote with a casual shrug of his shoulders, John Salter seemed almost indifferent: "Bill Allen [Boeing president] didn't really want it anyway."[28] Was Salter, the ever-slick operator, kidding?

No. The final irony, given the enormous struggle by Scoop and Maggie for its passage, is that Salter had it right. The vote may have saved the Boeing Company from financial disaster. Engineers had wind tunnel difficulties with the SST airframe, never really solving the question of where to locate the craft's engines given its "swing-wing" design. Economists were seriously in doubt about how soon the plane could make a profit, given the high cost of jet fuel and low interest of airline passengers. By putting the SST aside, Boeing forged ahead with the slower but enormously profitable 747, 737, 757, and 767 aircraft, and thus, prospered.[29]

On the strength of his stature as national security hawk, and with the backing of organized labor and American Jews, many of the latter dedicated to unequivocal, no-questions-asked U.S. support of Israel—neo-conservatives like Richard Perle and *Commentary* editor Norman Podhoretz—Jackson made two runs for the Democratic presidential nomination, the first in 1972 and again in 1976. Magnuson gave Jackson his full backing in these efforts, both of which failed when votes were counted at the party's national conventions in Miami Beach and New York City. Magnuson did so at some risk to his support from the young antiwar activists in the state Democratic Party—no small peril, given Maggie's decision to seek reelection in 1974. Brock Adams, who aimed to make the Senate race if Magnuson didn't, got the news during the 1972 National Convention in Miami Beach, where Maggie was staying at a plush home owned by Senator George Smathers. Stan Barer told Adams, sorry, Maggie will run again.[30] Adams would have to wait until 1986, when he won the seat that had been held by Magnuson for six terms.

Jackson's strike for the 1976 presidential nomination went well in the Massachusetts and New York primary elections, then fell apart in Florida and Pennsylvania, where Governor Jimmy Carter of Georgia showed his great strength. Maggie helped, but privately expressed his skepticism about Scoop's effort. Abe Bergman quotes Maggie as saying, "Do you know it cost Scoop $10 for every vote he got in Pennsylvania?" Bergman says he asked Magnuson if he pointed out this fact to Senator Jackson. "He looked at me as if I were crazy," said Bergman. "He said, 'Of course not. If Scoop is crazy enough to run for President I'm going to help him all I can.'"[31]

The ultimate paradox of this great political partnership came when Henry Jackson, the embodiment of clean living, Presbyterian morality—he converted from his family's Lutheran faith—and good health, died in 1983, preceding the hard-living Magnuson to the grave by six years. There was the equivalent of a state funeral in Everett for its favorite son, with Vice President Bush and Chief Justice Burger among the Washington, D.C., contingent of several dozen dignitaries. Senator Ted Kennedy, his bitterness forgotten, gave an eloquent eulogy, but the most moving farewell came from Magnuson, who hobbled to the front of the Presbyterian Church and let his voice boom while his eyes wept:

"Scoop used to drop by my office pretty near every morning. He'd say 'Who's in trouble today? Who can we help? And we'd get together and work it out the best way we knew how. . . . He was a humane compassionate man."[32]

CHAPTER 27

The Prime of Public Interest

I t is unlikely that any congressional office, including those of the leadership since the time of Sam Rayburn, has ever been so productive of legislation with such scope and impact as that of Senator Warren Magnuson in the 1970s, the last decade of a political career commenced nearly half a century earlier.

Maggie was no longer the robust figure of a physically powerful man, given to working all day and playing all night. He was aging and showed it. There were the first signs of a disease, diabetes, which would plague him the rest of his life. His social life centered around Jermaine, their circle of close friends, and the customary early evening functions that attend Capitol Hill. But he still worked all day. He would not quit or slack—"retire on the job" as some politicians wearied of their occupation have done. Instead, the work of the Commerce Committee, which he chaired, and the Appropriations Committee, which he would come to chair, accelerated.

From this last burst of populist/Democratic legislation, the nation's railroads were reorganized, Seattle was revitalized, Puget Sound was spared the threat of supertankers and the Sound's marine mammal inhabitants—whales, seals, and porpoises—were spared extinction, and the obsolete structure of Northwest power production was reorganized with an emphasis on saving energy rather than burning it.

Magnuson was the "Senator's Senator, the man I admire more than any other man in the Senate," said his Commerce Committee colleague, Senator Norris Cotton, a conservative Republican from New Hampshire. A "Senator's Senator" was the label given one who, "if he can't help you, he makes you look good losing." Maggie was taking the lead on issues critical to the nation as well as the state. He no longer invited criticism as a shrewd politician merely staying abreast of his constituency. In tribute for his leadership in medical research, Magnuson received the Lasker Award, the "Nobel Prize of health" on October 20, 1973. There was a banquet at the Olympic Hotel with Dr. Michael DeBakey, the renowned surgeon, and Washington Governor Dan Evans as keynote speakers. Evans said: "No one in America has worked more vigorously to promote the health of Americans."[1] Nevertheless, the governor at this time was pushing a liberal Republican candidate for the Senate in the 1974 elections. Maggie would understand. Mutual respect was not a barrier to partisan politics.

In 1973, in the midst of this extraordinary legislative productivity, Magnuson went to China—still "Red China" in normal American parlance—leading the first congressional delegation through the door formally opened by President Nixon one year earlier. And Nixon, the old Commie hunter, would be forced to resign the presidency for his role in obstructing justice by trying to cover up the burglary of Democratic National Committee headquarters in the capital's Watergate Hotel.

Maggie made the China trip against the wishes of President Nixon and at the insistence of Chou En-lai, the elegant, English-speaking foreign minister. Chou was the Chinese leader subordinate only to Mao Tse-tung, the state's founding father. It was the trip of a lifetime for Maggie and Jermaine, a major step toward formal relations and trade between the United States and China, relations frozen in ideological ice for twenty-four years. The trip also brought to light the most inexplicable twist in Magnuson's career.

"Magnuson was delighted when Nixon and Henry Kissinger went to China to open the door," said Stan Barer, the administrative assistant. "But Nixon didn't want Maggie to go to China in 1973. After Chou insisted—we had already been in touch with the Chinese through their embassy in Ottawa—Nixon backed down. Magnuson got a briefing from Nixon in San Clemente, California, before leaving. Nixon said to tell the Chinese we were prepared to resume bombing North Vietnam."[2]

As a congressman, Magnuson had been responsible for repeal of the "Chinese exclusion act," the law banning immigration to America from China. Jermaine Magnuson says Warren always felt that Chinese immigrants became excellent American citizens, smart and productive. From the outset of the cold war, through the Joe McCarthy era, to Nixon's China breakout in 1972, Maggie argued for trade and normalized relations with the Chinese. He did this at no small risk to his political career. Even in Seattle, the seaport with most to gain from Chinese trade, hostility to "Red China" persisted into the 1970s. Magnuson was not intimidated. He kept a foot in the door to China by providing a measure of political cover to those scholars and internationalists brave enough to call the U.S. China policy self-defeating. None such, incidentally, were left in our thoroughly purged State Department. By opening the China door, Nixon relieved the acute pressure on Maggie's foot.

Writing to Chou En-lai (Zhou Enlai) in June 1973, Magnuson said, "My longstanding interest in a Sino-American exchange stems from my position on Commerce Committee and as a senator from a state bordering on the Pacific ocean." His letter stressed the need for trade, and informed Chou that his committee would entertain the matter of a most-favored-nation trading status for China. Significantly, the letter did not mention any previous visit by Magnuson to China.[3]

While in China in July 1973, Magnuson met with Chou, Ch'iao Kuan-hua (Qiao Guanhua), the vice foreign minister, and Li Chiang (Li Qiang), vice minister of trade. He attended the first Fourth of July celebration held in Beijing in twenty-four years, one hosted by U.S. Ambassador David Bruce at the American embassy. In his room at the Hotel Beijing, Maggie scribbled these notes, apparently for his use in conversations with Chou: "Chou: China can no longer be an island in the world—needs our technological help—potential for hydro power—no private cars, no dogs, no meat—important for China to participate in detente with U.S." On July 6 he and Chou talked for two hours in the Great Hall of the People, much of the time discussing the U.S. bombing of Cambodia. This was Nixon's attempt to interdict North Vietnam's supply line to Communist forces in the south; a military decision with catastrophic political and human consequences to Cambodia.

When he returned to the United States, after a stop in Guam where he witnessed B-52s taking flight for Cambodian bomb runs, Magnuson issued a newsletter that began:

> When I stepped off an Air Force jet in Shanghai, I couldn't help thinking one overwhelming thought: how times have changed. They had changed drastically in Shanghai. I had been there many years earlier as a young man, and Shanghai then was everything that was vivid—an oriental city of intrigue and dangers. It was here the term "Shanghaied" was coined and for good reason. . . . [Y]ou couldn't walk the streets safely in daytime then. Now it is safe. Jermaine and I walked everywhere. . . . [T]he streets of Shanghai were impressive, especially to one like me who had seen it so radically different just a generation earlier.[4]

And Jermaine Magnuson told of going to the Cathay Hotel, "where Warren lived in 1923—he told me stories of when he lived there." Jermaine said Magnuson directed their taxi to the old hotel. Jack Doughty, the tough, ever-skeptical editor of the *Seattle Post-Intelligencer*, was born in China and served there with the U.S. Office of Strategic Service (OSS) behind Japanese lines in World War II. Doughty said Maggie told him of the night spots and racetrack in Shanghai in such detail as only a visitor could have known. To others, Magnuson said he had shipped from Seattle on an American Mail Lines freighter as an engine room wiper, then stayed ashore in Shanghai as a company clerk. Here the puzzle begins.

Magnuson's transcripts from Moorhead High School, the University of North Dakota, North Dakota State University, and the University of Washington indicate he had no time in the midst of this schooling for a round-trip sea voyage to Shanghai, given the speed of vintage steamships, much less time to work ashore. More puzzling is the report of Carol Parker Cahill, who began a fifteen-year relationship with Magnuson in 1934 on her arrival in Seattle from a singing engagement at a Shanghai hotel. Mrs. Cahill was astonished to hear of Magnuson's claim he had been in China before 1973: "He never said a word to me about that." His valued aide for two decades, Irv Hoff, said that he had never heard of a trip to China by Maggie until 1973. The report surprised him.

A search of the National Archives in College Park, Maryland, for seaman's papers issued in the years between 1918 and 1941 and for records of certificates issued to lifeboatmen and seamen in that same period did not yield any record or reference to a Warren Magnuson (or Magnussen).[6] Records of Magnuson's application in 1936 for a Naval Reserve commission show that he reported his only sea experience had been on small boats on Puget Sound. Records of the American Mail Line business in Shanghai were seized by Chinese Communists in 1949 and untraceable through American Mail's subsequent owner, American President Lines.

Thus, the story of his adventurous voyage to China in 1923 told by Magnuson, a level-headed, temperamentally stable pragmatist, a man by all accounts totally ungiven to fantasy—unlike, say, President Ronald Reagan, who appeared to confuse movie roles with reality—is unsubstantiated by any official record.

It is remotely possible that he could have made such a journey covertly, possibly on assignment to check out the new Chinese regime for one of his friends in the White House, Harry Truman or Lyndon Johnson, and then stayed quiet about it until Nixon opened the Chinese door. He was greeted with exceptional warmth by Chou En-lai in 1973. Records of the CIA and FBI that might shed light on the matter are not available. But aide Stan Barer's theory of such a possible covert trip is the only plausible explanation for Maggie's tale of Shanghai prior to 1973.

So it remains a mystery; a tale vastly overshadowed by Magnuson's career-long effort to scrape away the cold war blinders and make peace and business with the one billion people on the far side of the Pacific from Seattle. "Magnuson was ecstatic when we got the Chinese Overseas Shipping Company to establish routes to Seattle—it was the fulfillment of his goal," said Barer who completed these negotiations, and subsequently, as a private citizen, profited from the Chinese connection. Considering the political risk that it carried, there are some who would argue that this contribution to the nation's peace and prosperity was Maggie's greatest achievement—and not all of them are on Washington State waterfronts across which $6.5 billion of the China trade flowed in 1994.

"The senator wasn't cautious about 'politics' even though he frequently [excepting 1956] had only marginal election victories," observed Gerry Johnson, Magnuson's administrative assistant for most of the 1970s.[7]

Maggie hadn't decided whether to face another election when, in 1970, he turned his power to the effort to save Seattle's Pike Place Market. So whether this was a political plus or minus is moot. In so doing, he bucked most of Seattle's downtown business establishment and, again, showed the exceptional range of his interests and power.

"The Market" is now established as Seattle's answer to San Francisco's Fisherman's Wharf. It is a lively, heterogeneous piece of the city's relatively short history, much favored by tourists as well as the city's urban and suburban dwellers. To think of Seattle now without the market is to think of Philadelphia without the Liberty Bell, yet in the late 1960s it came within a narrow plebiscite, and Warren Magnuson's congressional clout, of falling to developers' wrecking balls. The deacons of the city's downtown, mostly Republican but, for business reasons, usually helpful to Maggie, wanted the property overlooking Elliott Bay and the city's waterfront demolished for smart shops and condominiums. Maggie, however, had a personal interest. He liked to shop at the market, where fishermen and farmers brought their produce fresh from salt water and the earth. He liked to banter with the fishmongers and vegetable hawkers, savor the aroma of sea air mixed with the odor of fish, fruit, and flowers, and talk with constituents, themselves a social mix of colors and class—club women from Bellevue or Capitol Hill, bums up from Skid Road, bargain shoppers from Chinatown.

The citywide plebiscite led by architect Victor Steinbrueck stopped the market's execution. Magnuson gave the market a new life, putting aside money from the Housing and Urban Development (HUD) appropriation for its badly needed rehabilitation. "It was expensive," admits Gerry Johnson, who figures at least $20 million was routed from HUD funds into the market. One chunk, $10 million, came from the "urgent needs program" which was under a subcommittee chaired by Senator William Proxmire, the Wisconsin Democrat and victor in the SST battle with Scoop and Maggie. Though Proxmire was not one of Maggie's favored colleagues, he was sympathetic to the $10 million request. He was also amused. "That's some kind of a market you've got out there," Proxmire remarked after signing off on the generous appropriation. It was and so remains. Ironically, the market is a critical factor in the vitality of downtown Seattle business.

Maggie wasn't finished reshaping the Seattle landscape. When the Navy declared its Sand Point Naval Air Station surplus property, the senator skipped the normal process whereby federal property is disposed for other uses. Instead, he passed a law giving the land on Lake Washington's northwest shore to the City of Seattle—provided the city plow Sand Point's runways back under the earth. There was a furor over this from Seattle aviation buffs, a determined group led by a pilot, Pete Bement, who became a fixture in letters-to-the-editor columns and a frequent visitor to newspaper editorial offices. The pilots wanted the runways for their light aircraft. Another plebiscite, in 1974, settled the issue in favor of people over airplanes and the city named the area Magnuson Park.

On the other side of the Cascade Mountains, Spokane, the eastern Washington mini-metropolis built on silver, wheat, privately owned water power, and rock-hard Republicanism, set out to attract a world's fair for 1974. Some Seattleites laughed. Senator William Fulbright, the Arkansas Democrat, balked. The formidable chairman of the Senate Foreign Relations Committee, a man at odds with Senator Henry Jackson over the Vietnam War, wasn't going to give his committee's blessing for a Spokane world's fair. Without committee approval, Spokane's fair was a dead issue.

"Fulbright wasn't going to give Washington state anything," said Norm Dicks, Magnuson's former administrative assistant, now the Democratic congressman from Tacoma. "So Maggie went to Fulbright and requested a hearing on the authorization of Spokane for a world's fair. Fulbright relented. The authorization bill came out of his committee and on to the Senate floor. It carried a $3 million appropriation to get the fair started and passed 67 to 19. During floor debate Fulbright called it 'the nation's second greatest urban renewal project—after Seattle.' We were almost embarrassed, however. Tom Foley got it out of the House after we had already sent out a press release announcing Congressional support."[8]

President Nixon dedicated the opening of the fair on a beautiful May day in 1974, dropping for the happy crowd of state dignitaries and hometown folk a pitch-perfect Freudian slip. He introduced Dan Evans as "Governor Evidence." Evidence of White House involvement in the Watergate burglary and subsequent cover-up was mounting, apparently a presidential preoccupation. By the time the scandal of the century reached a climax in early November, Nixon had resigned the White House to Vice President Gerald Ford. President Ford taped a message for the closing ceremonies of a fair that had generated $300 million in downtown improvements to Spokane, anchored by a handsome park in the city's downtown core. Fulbright had been snide, but not inaccurate.

The Commerce Committee, meanwhile, had another consumer protection issue on the table, a bill to set standards for warranties on consumer products—another struggle with business-as-usual practices. Stiffest resistance came from the automakers, General Motors, Ford, and Chrysler, whose lobbyists argued that the warranty standards infringed on the principles of free enterprise and would raise the price of their product. They lost. "We rolled over them," recalls Tom Allison, the committee counsel. As a result, new autos come not only with a warranty but with a sticker listing price, mileage performance, and extra equipment, thus providing car buyers with a fair idea of what they are getting for their money. The limited warranty forced Detroit to build a better product, a boost, in the long run, in their sales battle with imports from Japan and Germany. But why another battle with big business? Allison explained: "We were always looking for a way to solve problems. This law would solve a problem with product quality. The beauty of our jobs with Magnuson was that we at least thought we were doing good."[9]

But there would be no further opportunity for good or ill unless Magnuson ran and won the 1974 election. To wise-guy political consultants and quite a few Republicans, the aging senator looked vulnerable—given the right kind of opponent. Magnuson's decision to run came more than two years before the election. During the 1972 Democratic National Convention in Miami Beach, Magnuson called Representative Brock Adams to the senator's convention quarters at the home of Senator George Smathers. Stan Barer told Adams, a certain Democratic candidate for the Senate seat in the absence of Maggie, that there would be no vacancy. Magnuson would seek reelection.[10] Whatever his disappointment, Adams would not challenge Maggie, a man he admired and a liberal like himself.

Senator George McGovern, the South Dakota "dove," easily won the Democratic presidential nomination, snuffing a bid by his opposite on the Vietnam War issue, Henry Jackson. This convention was the first to reflect ethnic and gender diversity mandated by the new party rules. Not so coincidental, it also was dominated by the party's antiwar activists. With Jackson on the sidelines and the Watergate scandal approaching, Maggie got behind McGovern's candidacy. Stan Barer figured Magnuson would need all the help available from party foot soldiers. Accordingly, Barer became McGovern's state coordinator; Magnuson, the McGovern state chairman. Barer was counting on a tough campaign. Jerry Grinstein

figured there were potential Republican candidates eager to accommodate those expectations.

The race for Maggie's seat began in 1973 with informed speculation
that John Ehrlichman, the former Seattle land use attorney, would leave
his office one floor below President Nixon's desk in the White House
and come home to make the run for the Senate. His alleged role in the
Watergate scandal had yet to surface. Whether or not Ehrlichman ever
became serious about the Senate race, Magnuson's staff were serious in
their concern about his candidacy. Seattle's "Man of the Year" in 1973,
an honor bestowed by the city's real estate interests, sounded like a
candidate when he addressed Washington State delegates to the 1972
Republican National Convention, also in Miami Beach.

After chiding the national news media for paying too much attention
to "war protestors," Ehrlichman switched to a local matter: Magnuson,
who is "no credit to his state in fiscal responsibility—Maggie seems to
have round heels when it comes to every request for money." If he was
not considering a Senate race, it was a highly unusual speech for a member of the White House staff dealing, like it or not, with the chairman of
Senate Appropriations. He noted Nixon's veto of Magnuson's budget for
health, education, and welfare and promised the Republican delegates
that "when Maggie sends over expensive bills, the President will veto
and Congress won't overrule."[11]

Ehrlichman took a dim view of Capitol Hill after coming to Washington with Nixon in 1969. He saw it as the prophet saw Sodom: a
place of sloth, venality, duplicity, and, alas, power. He writes: "There is,
I discovered, the Congress of the civics books—perhaps to some extent
the figment of college professors' imaginations—and there is the real
Congress." The real Congress, according to Ehrlichman, was another
world from the industrious White House, where staff worked long hours
and, quite often, Sundays as well. He was scornful of House minority
leader (and later president) Gerald Ford as a legislator slow to grasp
substantive information given him by the White House, and distrusting
of Senate Minority Leader Hugh Scott, whom he described as devious.[12]
Small wonder that Christian Scientist Ehrlichman, like Presbyterian Governor Arthur Langlie before him, would look askance at the lifestyle and
legislative manner of Warren Magnuson.

A year after the GOP national convention, Magnuson was questioned
about Ehrlichman's possible candidacy: "If he made the race, he'd have
plenty of money. He'd just go to the [White House] safe and pull it out."
By this time, June 1973, stories about Nixon's 1972 reelection campaign
funds, collected from ask-no-questions sources and stashed around the

nation, were a daily newspaper staple with play comparable to the O. J. Simpson trial two decades later. Magnuson was asked if he felt President Nixon should be impeached.

"I've given no thought to an impeachment," the senator answered. "I'm too busy." He did note the visit of Soviet boss Leonid Brezhnev with Nixon in Washington, D.C.: "Times have changed. The other stuff [Nixon's strident anticommunism] is inoperative, as they now say. I think the people of the world want peace." In the fall of that year, Maggie said the Watergate drama "has taken the place of soap opera."[13]

Whatever its impact as TV entertainment, Watergate had altered the balance of power between the Nixon-Ehrlichman White House and Maggie's Congress. The former was so distracted by the scandal that Magnuson's hand in Commerce and Appropriations was greatly strengthened. Congress and Maggie were also boosted by Nixon's frequent, and constitutionally questionable, impoundments of congressional appropriations. Maggie was particularly incensed by the president's blocking of funds for health, education, and welfare. There was no effort to redress the loss; Nixon simply didn't want the money spent. An aroused Congress steamrolled over the Watergate stricken White House with a law forbidding the executive to impound monies appropriated by Congress.

From the standpoint of liberal staffers on Capitol Hill, Watergate provided an unexpected dividend. Tom Allison explained: "It allowed us to make policy and even to have a hand in naming those who would implement those policies."[14]

By the summer of 1973, the "soap opera" growing ever more a public attraction, Ehrlichman had faded as an election threat to Magnuson or anyone else. Dismissed by Nixon from the White House, Ehrlichman would be indicted in September in connection with the break-in at the office of Daniel Ellsberg's Los Angeles psychiatrist. Ellsberg, a former Marine officer, had been the source of the "Pentagon Papers" critical of the war in Vietnam. This indictment did not lessen Jerry Grinstein's fears for Magnuson's reelection.

A more formidable threat, one that gave Grinstein nightmares, came from a charismatic, politically savvy professor of political science at the University of Washington. David Kirk Hart was thirty-five years old, liberal, Republican, a veteran of California politics and political business, and a cofounder of the respected Los Angeles polling firm, DMI. He had turned down a position in Governor Ronald Reagan's cabinet to teach in Seattle, where he quickly became engaged with the state's "Evans Republicans," eventually a member of the governor's kitchen cabinet, and the bright hope of his party's liberal faction.

Evans was concerned, rightly as it has developed, about a loss of liberal-moderate hold on the state GOP to its well-funded right-wing faction. A decade earlier Evans had earned national attention, and much local favor among Democrats, by telling members of the semisecret John Birch Society to get out of his party. Presumably most Birchers had done so, but the influence of Ronald Reagan conservatives was fast rising. Evans wanted Kirk Hart to run against Magnuson to check the threat of his party's right wing. Hart was willing, but, having seen candidates rise and fall under a massive campaign debt, he wanted $100,000 up front before taking leave of the university to make the race. If Grinstein was nervous about the prospect of the professor as opposition, Hart was quite certain: "Magnuson could have been whipped in 1974."

The climax to this race was premature by nearly one year. It came at a meeting in a downtown Seattle bank among Professor Hart, Governor Evans, Attorney General Slade Gorton, Fred Baker, the veteran GOP strategist and fund-raiser, Ken Fisher of Fisher Mills and KOMO-Television, and Norton Clapp and George Weyerhaeuser, the principal owners and operators of the Weyerhaeuser timber colossus. In 1973, when this combination of enlightened civic and political leaders decided to speak (and put up the money), the state began to move.

"Dan urged me to run for the sake of the party," said Hart twenty years later, recalling the meeting as if it had happened the day before. "Fred Baker was very supportive. What impressed me most was the tone of the meeting. There was nothing negative said about Magnuson. Gummie [C. Montgomery] Johnson [Evans's handpicked state GOP chairman] liked to go for the groin. Not these men. When they spoke of Maggie there was the sense of a great man. There was a clear understanding that it would not be a negative campaign."

But there was not to be any Hart-Magnuson campaign. The $100,000 up-front money was not forthcoming. "Evans warned that if I didn't make the race the party would shift to the hard right," said Hart. "But George Weyerhaeuser said, in effect, 'not this year. Business isn't good and we need Magnuson too badly in the Senate. He has too much clout and we need him. Anything you want after 1974 is fine.' Without the money and with a wife and children to support, I decided against the race."[15]

Afterward, Hart says he was offered the fund-raising services of Richard Vigurie, the direct mail angel of the party's most conservative wing, and the source of Jack Metcalf's campaign money in 1968. But Vigurie wanted "certain stands on issues as a condition of his aid. I said to hell with it," Hart recalled. He remained at the University of Washington, winning several awards for his teaching and coauthoring *Organizational America*, one of the most insightful, if pessimistic, critiques of American society in the past three decades.

Would Hart have defeated Magnuson in the November election? As the senator says in his tale of the two cockney drunks and the archbishop of Canterbury, "Now we'll never know."

It was, however, the year of Richard Nixon's disgrace; a tough one for any Republican candidate, even one as attractive and smart as Kirk Hart. But creeping into the mainstream of state politics were questions about Magnuson's health—questions that would not be truly resolved for another year. The senator looked vulnerable, slow of speech, no longer quick in movement—in fact, as he came to know, already in the early stages of diabetes.[16] Tales of his taste for strong drink were clichés in both Washingtons. But looks were deceiving, perhaps wishful thinking by Republicans. In reality Magnuson was in the prime of his power to work for the public interest and ready to make the most of it.

The 1974 election to the U.S. Senate in Washington State was a television rerun, Magnuson against Jack Metcalf, the state legislator. Maggie had the established funding sources; Metcalf had Vigurie's strings-attached direct mail solicitations.[17] The result was much the same as in 1968—Magnuson by a margin of three to two.

"All we needed was just one break," lamented Jack Metcalf as he conceded the loss. "Just one debate before a college group." That judgment is doubtful, given Maggie's broad support, but there is no questioning Jack Metcalf's perseverance. He would keep trying and in 1992, nearly two decades later, won election to Congress from Washington's Second District.

"We didn't do too badly, did we?" said Maggie with a wink and a smile to an aide on election night. For the record he said: "This is not a celebration, it's a response to responsibilities that we Democrats now have." Then he talked about controlling oil prices and expanding public works. It was a good night for the veteran politician, his last successful campaign.

CHAPTER 28

The Great Dictator

I n the mid-1970s, at the peak of his power, Warren Magnuson's zeal
to save the waters and creatures of Puget Sound, a romantic notion
with extraordinary environmental consequences, brought him into
open conflict with another elected state official. For Maggie this was
unprecedented. Accommodation and compromise, not conflict, were the
senator's lifelong mode of conduct.

The "senator's senator," the legislative maestro who battled southern
senators over the monumental 1964 civil rights measures without alien-
ating their friendship; the "soft hearted" man, as described by the *Wall
Street Journal* in a flattering portrait of the legislative father of consumer
protection,[1] collided head-on with Washington State's new governor,
Dixy Lee Ray. It was the political equivalent of the *Exxon Valdez* crashing
into a reef—one-sided as a contest, yet dramatic to behold.

The conflict had aquatic origins: the development of oil wells on
Alaska's north shore and the exploitation of Puget Sound's native orcas
(killer whales) for entertainment. Alaska oil, tied by law to U.S. refineries,
was shipped by vessels in excess of 125,000 dead weight tons—supertankers—through the Strait of Juan de Fuca, up Rosario Strait to refineries
at Cherry Point and March Point in northern Puget Sound.

The matter of the whales came first. With great fanfare, several orcas
had been trapped and sold to aquariums in the 1960s. The black and
white mammals loomed as a major media attraction. In April 1974,
Magnuson asked the NOAA administrator, Dr. Robert White, to declare
Puget Sound an orca sanctuary and to refuse further permits for their
capture or killing. Maggie told White he wanted protection for the orcas
from their "only real enemies—men who attack them for profit." White
complied with the request from NOAA's legislative creator.

Two years later when Ted Griffin, a whales-for-profit entrepreneur,
rounded up a pod of the sea creatures for potential sale, U.S. District Judge
Morell Sharpe halted their removal from Puget Sound with a temporary
restraining order. Magnuson and his staff made haste to block the transfer
for keeps. If the speed of legislation is normally described as glacial, the
speed with which Maggie and staff drafted and passed through Congress

the Marine Mammals Protection Act could be likened to the flood tide rushing up Rosario Strait.

"We worked at breakneck speed on the act for two days," said Gerry Johnson, administrative assistant to the senator. "Still, it wasn't fast enough. Time was running out on the restraining order. I so informed the senator. He said 'Get me Mo [Judge Sharpe] on the telephone.' I was surprised and told Magnuson 'you can't interfere with a federal judge.' But he insisted. I got Judge Sharpe and Magnuson told him, 'I've got this little bill on marine mammals but I need just a few more days to work it out.' When he hung up, Magnuson said, 'He's going to extend the order.' We passed the bill through Congress a few days later."[2]

Two decades later, evidence of a legislative success abounds. Not only have seals, sea lions, and orcas survived. These remote kin of man, land creatures who went to the sea in eons past, now thrive in abundance in waters from Olympia, in south Puget Sound, north into Canada. Thanks to Magnuson and federal law, the sea creatures displaced supertankers on Puget Sound. This did not happen, however, without a bitter fight.

Pressure for supertankers came from the need to move oil from the North Slope to northern Puget Sound; the larger the vessel the cheaper the refined oil, but the greater the risk to Puget Sound and its shoreline. These aircraft-carrier sized ships are slow to start, slower to stop, and cranky to turn. Given frequent fog and currents running over four knots, the passage up Rosario Strait between Blakely, Orcas, and Cypress Islands—at one point between reefs it narrows to a mile—is treacherous. It can be uncomfortable for a small pleasure craft. Possible damage to property and fisheries from a major oil spill in these waters borders on the incalculable. Nevertheless, the oilmen found a champion in Dixy Lee Ray.

A former associate professor of zoology at the University of Washington with a popular science program on the Public Broadcasting channel, and director of the Pacific Science Center, Ray made her run for governor in 1976 in the aftermath of the Watergate scandal. Like Governor Jimmy Carter, the Democratic candidate for president that year, Ray benefited from an image as an outsider, a "nonpolitical" candidate innocent of the messy business of democratic governance. She got an extra boost in fallout from a legislative scandal in Olympia, payoffs by garbage businessmen to Democratic leaders. The "outsider" image was for real, not the creation of a press agent. Ray was truly "nonpolitical" if this means innocent of the urge to compromise and deal. She was outspoken to a fault, quick to judge, and totally unfamiliar with the ways of Olympia. Built square and stout and given to short hair and knee socks, Ray had a faith in science rivaling that of Job's faith in the Lord, although perhaps not so sorely tested. Science could part the waters, remove the stain of an oil spill, and turn nuclear waste from dangerous to benign.

Consumer advocate Ralph Nader labeled Ray, a categorical proponent of nuclear energy, "Ms. Plutonium." But as such she fit the bill of John Ehrlichman, President Nixon's domestic adviser, and perhaps that of Senator Henry Jackson, for appointment to the Atomic Energy Commission. It was not a happy fit and did not last for long. Even less happy was her subsequent stint as an assistant secretary of state under Henry Kissinger. Ray's main congressional supporter, Representative Mike McCormack, said her troubles on the AEC stemmed from Ehrlichman: She said "to hell with it" when the White House adviser said he would tell her what to do. The problem with Kissinger was that he refused to communicate with his assistant. When Ray requested a meeting with the secretary of state to determine his policy on the laws of the seas, another assistant told her "if you want to know his policy, read his speeches."[3] That broke it with the great and imperious global strategist. She quit Kissinger to come home and run for governor.

Despite a remarkable lack of political sophistication—she did not know the difference between the federal Environmental Protection Agency and the state Department of Ecology—and a temperament better suited to pedagogy than political discourse, with an incendiary temper to boot, Ray won the Democratic primary against a divided opposition and the general election over Republican John Spellman. She had critical campaign help from Arco and Texaco, the oil refinery operators in northern Puget Sound; from the nuclear industry, which she also championed; and from Senator Jackson, who would privately assure skeptics Ray was capable of performing the task of governor.

Magnuson, possibly in deference to his valued colleague Jackson, kept a public silence. When boosting her appointment to the AEC, Magnuson had described Ray to the Joint Committee on Atomic Energy as "an extremely able educator, highly effective community leader and a fine human being." Privately, however, he seemed to contradict this undue flattery. A decade earlier the senator had quietly blocked Ray's appointment to a federal Commission on Science, Engineering and Resources. An unsigned White House memo, dated August 25, 1966, said simply "Senator Magnuson is highly negative on Dixy Lee Ray's candidacy."[4] In Lyndon Johnson's White House that was enough said.

As a governor, Ray made enemies as easily as Magnuson made friends. She kept a running feud with the press, exasperated legislators, and bucked a strong tide of public sentiment running in favor of preserving the environment. Her four-year performance was cited by statehouse professionals as evidence that state government could run itself through its established bureaucracy with or without a steady hand in the governor's office. She is also criticized for having spent a $350 million state surplus, accumulated from inflation, instead of saving it for harder times. The upshot was a lower bond rating on loans needed from Wall Street and a massive fiscal headache for her eventual successor, John Spellman. The scandal of the Washington Public Power Supply System (WPPSS), builder of nuclear power plants, began to unfold in the last half of her administration. It would culminate in the biggest default of bonds in the history of public finance. Yet she remained a four-square advocate of nuclear power. In gratitude for her support of supertankers on Puget Sound, Arco placed her at the wheel of a tanker as it steamed up Rosario Strait. She beamed like a Cascade Mountain snow bum with a new pair of skis as photographers snapped away. The picture endured, forever fixing Ray with supertankers.

There was a new hand on the wheel of the ship of state back in Washington, D.C., and a new chairman of the Senate Appropriations Committee. Jimmy Carter clobbered Henry Jackson in the Florida and Pennsylvania primaries and went on to defeat Gerald Ford, heir to the Nixon misfortune, to win the White House. In retrospect, Magnuson and his staff had easier dealings with Nixon, and his congressional lobbyists, than with the Carter camp even though Democrat Carter would name Representative Brock Adams to his cabinet as secretary of transportation. But it did little to smooth his congressional relations.

"The White House was not very cooperative with Magnuson," said Duayne Trecker, the senator's press aide at that time. "In fact they were almost paranoid about all those damned Democrats on Capitol Hill."

"President Carter had this fault," said Magnuson a year after his (and Carter's) defeat in 1980. "He would allow people around the White House—amateurs—to think of some idea that would require legislation. They'd go down to the basement, type up something and send it to Congress—just like that. Then [congressional lobbyist Frank] Moore would bring it over and sometimes Carter would change his mind. After a while nobody paid any attention to Moore. But Carter was a very nice man. He has a tremendous sense of humor that never came though the media or in his speeches. A very nice man."[5] Maggie's aides lamented the lack of experience in the Carter staff and the fact that partisanship—a Democratic senator dealing with a Democratic president—inhibited a devil-may-care attitude toward the White House. It had been otherwise with Nixon.

The Democratic senator, now starting his fourth decade in Congress, was still moving up. The death of Senator John McClellan, an Arkansas Democrat, opened up the chairmanship of the full Appropriations Committee. Seniority still counted over most everything else in the Senate power lineup. But it was a move Magnuson was somewhat loath to make, since it meant relinquishing control of the Commerce Committee. He could reason that by holding to the Commerce chair, he could still have his way with appropriations as chair of its Independent Offices Subcommittee. In the end Maggie switched. Tom Allison had to be summoned home from a strictly unauthorized, unofficial, off-limits trip to Cuba to become counsel to the Appropriations Committee.

Maggie certainly had his way with appropriations. There was a $1 billion example in May 1980 when a cubic mile of ice and rock exploded off Mount St. Helens, a formerly extinct volcano in the southern Cascades, carrying darkness and a fine white dust over much of eastern Washington, and felling thousands of board feet of timber. Magnuson went to Senator Daniel Inouye, the Hawaii Democrat, a ranking member of Appropriations, and said "I've had a volcano go off in my state." Inouye replied, "Maggie, I've got them going off in my state all the time." Magnuson retorted: "Danny, your time will come." He walked away with $1 billion in emergency relief funds.[6]

Senator Jackson's way with the military persuaded the Navy to locate its new base for the mammoth Trident submarine at Bangor, inside Puget Sound's Hood Canal. It was generally viewed as a coup for the state and by Kitsap County real estate dealers as a bonanza. But it left Maggie the task of supplying federal funds for the new roads, sewers, water, and garbage facilities serving the multimillion-dollar project—funds out of the reach of Kitsap County officials. One local politician, state senator C. W. "Red" Beck, could not conceal his envy at Bangor's acquisition of such a mighty federal plum. Beck told a reporter, straight-faced, "I got to get me one of those Trident bases for Gig Harbor." Reminded that the entrance to Gig Harbor, a fishing port turned tourist attraction on the Sound opposite Tacoma, was so shallow and narrow that it would barely allow passage of a purse seiner, Beck answered, "Aw, that's no problem—the Corps [of Engineers] will take care of it."[7] Bangor remains the only West Coast haven for U.S. submarines that carry multiple warhead nuclear missiles, the heart of the nation's strategic defense.

Maggie's muscle on behalf of the home folks did not end with Mount St. Helens and new highways to Bangor. A more blatant example of such help came after he was badgered by Seattle Mayor Wes Uhlman and the Seattle Port Commission, particularly Commissioner Merle Adlum, for federal money to construct a new bridge from the Seattle mainland across the Duwamish River to West Seattle. The port wanted a super high-rise structure to accommodate its vision of extending its cargo docks up the Duwamish. West Seattle real estate dealers had sweeter dreams of a new sales boom, given a new six-lane bridge that did not have to break open and halt traffic for passing ships. They added to the clamor.

Staffers dubbed it the Parade of Lists, an annual lineup of requests presented, usually in January, to Magnuson, for purely local projects. For several years Adlum led the parade, pleading for a new high-level bridge—one that would allow passage up the Duwamish for the world's largest blue-water vessels. It got to be a nuisance and Maggie wanted to be shed of it, but, as Gerry Johnson noted, "there was no way we could do it; no federal program for new bridges."

As it happened, Magnuson and Johnson were in Seattle on June 10, 1978, when Captain Rolf Neslund, at eighty the oldest pilot working on Puget Sound, steered the freighter *Chavez* into the old West Seattle Bridge while attempting passage up the Duwamish. It knocked out half of the structure linking West Seattle, a peninsula between the Duwamish and Puget Sound, and downtown Seattle.

"It was a Sunday morning and we were on our way back to Washington," Johnson recalled. "Maggie got up in his suite at the Olympic Hotel chipper, hopping about and beaming. I was puzzled. He had already heard the news about the *Chavez*. He greeted me: 'This is the best thing that could happen—the wreck is a hazard to navigation. Now we can pay for a new bridge from the federal bridge replacement fund.' We needed $100 million—the total sum of the fund. Brock [Adams, President Carter's secretary of transportation] balked but we rolled over him. We vacuumed the bridge replacement fund to build a new West Seattle bridge."

It came mired in scandal. Three officials, including the city engineer, the state Democratic National Committeeman, and Robert Perry, the untitled boss of the state House of Representatives, were indicted and convicted in connection with kickbacks from bridge contractors. At one point Magnuson warned Mayor Uhlman to clean things up or he would turn the bridge construction over to the Army Corps of Engineers. Thanks mainly to Adlum's nagging, the new bridge was constructed to allow passage of the highest mast conceivable for a ship at that time; higher than has ever been remotely needed. The Port subsequently dropped plans for development of the upper Duwamish. As one former Port official now admits, the bridge should have been built more modestly.[8] It remains, however, a dream come true to West Seattle real estate dealers and gives some credence to George Reedy's otherwise exaggerated observation that Maggie took everything not nailed down in Washington, D.C., and sent it to Washington State.

In the macabre aftermath of the West Seattle bridge scandal, and reconstruction, its catalyst, Rolf Neslund, disappeared from his home on San Juan Island in 1982. His wife, Ruth, professed ignorance of his where-abouts. In fact, parts of the pilot were found by investigators beneath the kitchen floor of his home. Mrs. Neslund was charged and convicted with having placed them there after murdering her husband. She was sentenced to twenty years in the state prison in 1986.

For all of their constituent concerns—and its impact on the federal purse—it took the skill and clout of two Northwest legislators to solve what may have been the most pressing national economic issue of the 1970s. This attended the collapse of the Penn-Central and seven other northeastern and midwestern railroads, arteries and veins of the American economy. Magnuson handled the convoluted and complex package of legislation in the Senate. Brock Adams, then the Democratic congress-man from Seattle's Seventh District, carried the load in the House. Work on the three railroad recovery and regulatory reform measures took eight years, 1972 to 1980. Adams regards it as his greatest achievement in a distinguished legislative career. There are scholars who call it the most important legislation of the 1970s.

"We didn't go looking for this issue," said Adams. "It came looking for us. The railroads couldn't meet their payrolls. Their creditors were demanding a dollar back for a dollar invested, but the railroad stock was practically worthless. It was an economic catastrophe that threatened, at least those regions, with depression."

Despite its importance, Magnuson left the detail work on these mea-sures to his staff in the Senate—Tom Allison, Lynn Sutcliffe, and Linda Morgan—and to Adams, still a member of the House. This was in contrast with his deeper involvement in the public accommodations section of the civil rights bill, consumer protection, and his unsuccessful fight on Hells Canyon. Embroiled in Watergate, the Nixon administration wanted a "market solution" to the crisis, which, given the low market value of the railroads, amounted to no solution at all. The trouble, as railroad execu-tives told Congress, was that bidders for the rails were scant and cheap; the creditors, many. But Claude Brinegar, the secretary of transportation, was adamant: no "government bailout."

"We had to bypass Brinegar and the administration," said Allison. So doing, the Congress kicked in $2.1 billion for recovery, streamlined the system by allowing the railroads to cut excess tracks and service, created Conrail (the new northeastern freight carrier) and Amtrak (the passenger carrier), and allowed deregulation. The latter speeded up track abandonment, removed rate regulation, eased mergers, and left the re-shaped railroads sufficiently flexible to compete with trucks and barges for transportation business. Conrail has been such a success as a rail-road much of the money invested by the federal government has been returned.

One key to passage of this complex legislation, says Allison, was to lay the bills before the legislative bodies, accompanied by a book detailing the state by state impact of the collapse of northeastern and midwestern rail service. An independent agency, the U.S. Railway Association, was created as a vehicle for going around the Department of Transportation. The agency drafted a plan for track abandonments, mergers, and a myriad of lesser changes. The bill with funding then went before the Congress. Votes were taken strictly on the basis of passage or defeat—no mister-amendment-in-between. Thus there was none of the floor action of the kind that nibbled to death President Clinton's health care legislation in the 1990s.[9]

For all of its importance, the Great Railroad Rescue, performed by Magnuson and Adams, got less home-state attention than the collapse and reconstruction of the West Seattle Bridge and the subsequent reorder-ing of the Northwest electric power structure. The latter was born of a purported demand for new sources of energy. Don Hodel, the Bonneville Power Administration (BPA) administrator, warned of power "blackouts" unless the region got behind twenty new power projects, the first five being nuclear plants under way or on the drawing boards of the Wash-ington Public Power Supply System. His warning echoed those of Jackson, chairman of the Senate Energy Committee, which had jurisdiction over the BPA. Hodel's idea, urged by the private power utilities and the alu-minum manufacturers, was to meld the expensive nuclear power with the cheap hydropower distributed by the BPA. This would save the private utilities money by relieving them of the increasingly costly construction of nuclear plants. The initial bill gave the BPA authority to decide how much new electric power was needed and where plants might be built. But it was no sale in the House after environmentalists and public power advocates unmasked the measure as a de facto subsidy for WPPSS's nukes. At the time, 1977, there were only rumors of WPPSS's construction prob-lems and little public means of checking the BPA/private utility claims of imminent energy blackouts. Nevertheless, the measure was too lopsided in favor of private utilities and aluminum plants for acceptance in the House.

With Congress nearing its August recess in 1978, Jackson, his aides, and lobbyists or friends of the aluminum companies, private utilities, and the BPA went back to work on Jackson's kitchen table on a revised bill. This one, known for its birthplace as the Kitchen Table bill, gave nominal attention to conservation as an energy resource and to a body outside the BPA for advising on the need for new power resources. Seattle City Light and most Public Utility Districts (PUDs) were absent from the kitchen table when the bill got written. Time running out, Jackson wanted to move the bill quickly through Congress. To do so, he needed Magnuson as a cosponsor.

Initially passive—energy was Scoop's territory, not Maggie's—Magnuson backed away from the Kitchen Table bill after a torrent of calls from Seattle City Light, environmentalists, and PUDs who wanted a bill paying more attention to power resource planning with an emphasis on conservation and alternative energy sources. Jackson's bill, said Dan Leahy of Wenatchee, allows the "BPA to subsidize private power." Maggie refused to sign on Scoop's measure and, for several days while the clock moved Congress toward recess, avoided confrontation with his seatmate from Washington State.

"Maggie got cold feet after the telephone started ringing," said Gerry Johnson. "Scoop couldn't find him. It turned out to be the most pressure I ever felt in the senator's office. Scoop came to the office. When told Maggie wasn't in, he said, 'Well, let's go find him.' We found him in the Capitol at a leadership meeting. Scoop burst into the room, a serious breach of protocol. The other senators were offended—Jackson was not part of the leadership. Magnuson sent him away: 'See you later after I read the bill. . . . I just want to read the bill.' Jackson was furious. When Scoop got angry his neck turned red. On this day his neck was red. Since time was running out, he demanded that I sign the bill for Magnuson. I couldn't do that. Without Magnuson's signature, the bill failed. Afterward in his office Maggie got Scoop on the telephone—I could hear from a few feet away Jackson shouting at him. Maggie answered: 'Simmer down, Scoop. simmer down. It will all work out.' Then he slammed down the telephone. I was speechless at the scene. Maggie calmly turned to me, 'Scoop will be all right, he'll be all right. I never take any of that stuff personally.' "

Argument over the power bill dragged on into 1980. The upshot was participation in an act by all of the Northwest power interests, working through Northwest Democratic representatives Mike Lowry and Jim Weaver as well as Magnuson. With Lowry, later Washington governor, and Weaver pushing hardest, the act created a breakthrough model for rational regional energy development with an emphasis on conservation and alternative resources instead of on more fossil fuel or nuclear power plants. The Northwest Power Planning Council, representing Washington, Montana, Idaho, and Oregon, was charged with assessing energy needs.[10] This was a critical departure from estimates submitted by utilities which did, on occasion, amount to wish lists. One of its early assessments showed the BPA threat of blackouts to be crudely exaggerated.[11] Indeed, after a clumsy and skewered start, the Northwest power act turned into the region's most significant energy innovation since the building of Grand Coulee.

A conference committee, composed of members from the Senate and the House, settled the final details of the Northwest power act, as similar conferences settled virtually every other piece of major legislation. Magnuson was a grand master of the conference committee. Once, near the end of his congressional career and at the end of a long day's conference, he went with an aide, Tom Keefe, to one of his three offices in the Capitol Building, obscure places designated only for the most powerful members. Keefe, a young attorney from Seattle, remembers what happened.

"Pour me three fingers of vodka in this tumbler and put in four ice cubes," Keefe recalls the senator instructing. He followed the orders and handed Maggie the glass. "Maggie took a drink and said with feeling, 'You know—I really love this.' I looked at the glass and nodded. He sort of snapped back, 'Not this [vodka]! I mean the conference committees. This is where the institution works. This is where you deal. This is where you can do things for your state. I love this.' "

None of this local, regional, and national business of the 1970s emerging from House-Senate conferences—the new bridge to West Seattle, the reconstitution of American railroads, and Northwest power—distracted Magnuson's eye from the health of Puget Sound. The Sound became an increasing concern. It may have had to do with his purchase of a home on Wing Point, the eastern tip of Bainbridge Island. It certainly had to do with his love of the water and its creatures: fish, mammals, and seabirds. Puget Sound was a personal not a political issue with Magnuson, his former aides emphasize. However, it was a personal issue consonant with an overwhelming majority of his Puget Sound constituents. The threat of oil spills from new supertankers, especially after the wreck of the *Torrey Canyon* just off the English coast in March 1967, raised the level of the senator's concern. Maggie began to press the Coast Guard for new safety standards. When Coast Guard brass balked, the senator attracted their attention by holding up all promotions to admiral. This professional stimulation led to a new marine traffic control system on the Sound, new construction standards for vessels, and a mandate for the Coast Guard to monitor the loading and unloading of oil and chemicals at Puget Sound ports. It was a big leap forward, but still not enough to ensure the safety of the Sound from catastrophe, a tanker oil spill.

The oil issue became critical when Governor Ray climbed down from the bridge of the Arco tanker alongside Cherry Point, apparently determined to amend the Coastal Zone Management Act to allow an oil port at Cherry Point—an open door into Puget Sound for supertankers of over 125 DWT. It was too much for Maggie.

In response, Magnuson issued a statement saying "Washington state has little to gain from oil transshipment, but much to lose." Besides, he noted, "far too little has been said about financing any pipeline. . . . I would hope they are not thinking of federal financing." Then he backed his words with action.

"We had good intelligence in NOAA," said Ed Sheets, the Magnuson aide on maritime matters and later the executive director of the Northwest Power Planning Council. "We knew the moves taking place. Magnuson thought the combination of an oil port and the pipeline put the Sound at too great a risk. He had no confidence in technology saving Puget Sound from an oil spill. The problem loomed suddenly. The question was what to do."[12]

As it happened, in 1977, Maggie's Marine Mammals Protection Act, passed by Congress a year earlier, came up again for reauthorization. Ed Sheets realized the routine reauthorization measure was a vehicle Maggie could use to place a ban on supertanker traffic east of Port Angeles, Washington, a mill town on the Strait of Juan de Fuca opposite Victoria, British Columbia. There wouldn't be a hitch getting such an amendment through the Senate, although Senator Jackson was cool to the idea. Maggie's aides asked Majority Leader Robert Byrd to place the amendment on the "consent calendar," where routine bills are almost always approved without questions or debate.

"No problem," Byrd told staffer Ed Merlis, who with Gerry Johnson reported the action to Magnuson. Johnson now says this may have been an instance of the staff getting a bit ahead of the senator on a major policy issue. But Magnuson immediately approved of the staff maneuver and understood that the real problem came in the House where Representative Robert Bauman, a conservative Maryland Republican, kept watch on the consent calendar. Bauman did so if only to pick out bills potentially useful as leverage for his ideological causes. One of these was opposition to the use of federal money for abortions. "No deals," instructed Magnuson, referring to the potential of a Bauman shakedown. No deals meant the trick to fast passage of the supertanker ban was a run around, rather than through, Bauman. The key became Bauman's fellow Republican conservative: Jack Cunningham, Brock Adams's one-term successor, from Seattle. The key to Cunningham was Joel Pritchard, a liberal Republican also from Seattle. Maggie's men asked Pritchard to ask Cunningham to ask Bauman to lay off the consent calendar when the amendment to the Marine Mammals Act reached the House floor. Pritchard complied and Cunningham appealed to Bauman.[13] To the delight of most in the Washington delegation, Cunningham succeeded in getting Bauman to allow the amendment to pass. "Jack Cunningham is the secret hero of the tanker ban," said Gerry Johnson.

Passage of the amendment effectively banned supertanker traffic east of Port Angeles by forbidding construction of new oil ports. No oil ports at Cherry Point, no supertankers. Ed Sheets, the staffer who drafted the amendment and kept Magnuson briefed on its progress, said years later, "Out of deference to Jackson, Maggie didn't go all the way in banning oil ports, and, thus, supertankers, from Washington waters inside Cape Flattery." Nevertheless, fixing the oil port (supertanker) limit at Port Angeles killed the proposed oil pipeline from Cherry Point to the Midwest.

News of the oil port–tanker ban ignited an explosion of favorable comment from Puget Sound media and an explosion of temper from Governor Ray. The press hailed Maggie as a savior of the Sound. Ray promptly declared the senator a "dictator." Maggie replied softly that he had merely decided to "resolve this issue." Privately, he delighted in Dixy's appellation: "She called me a dictator," he noted more than once to members of his staff, his mouth curling into a familiar smile that indicated pleasure. Indeed, apart from sparing Puget Sound from a heightened threat of catastrophe, the flash amendment to the Marine Mammals Act showed that the senior senator could micromanage a major regional issue. For a change, it was out front, instead of in the back rooms; a highly visible example of Magnuson's legislative craft.

Except for one stiff, uncomfortable, and unsuccessful session in Magnuson's Washington, D.C., office, Governor Ray and Senator Magnuson did not speak with each other until a year later when he went to Olympia for an address to the Rotary Club. The time had come for a courtesy call on the governor who had labeled him a "dictator." Privately, Maggie called Ray "Madame Zonga" after a famous tattooed lady on Seattle's salty First Avenue. The meeting was polite. She offered no apologies. He said nothing about rumors of his ill health and Ray's search for political favors. The governor was said to have offered Magnuson's Senate seat to several Democrats, should it become prematurely vacant, in exchange for their political support. The connection was ugly, if not a breach of the state's bribery laws.

The rumors, later verified, would culminate in Ray's political devastation. She could not win the Democratic Party nomination for a second term.

"We never doubted the reports," said Johnson, Maggie's chief aide. One of the rumors made print. Richard Larsen of the *Seattle Times* wrote that Ray offered Maggie's Senate seat to state Senate Majority Leader Gordon Walgren in exchange for his campaign support—and Ray confirmed the story. The governor, apparently losing count, also offered the seat to two other Democrats.

"Dixy was new in this business; she was such a novice," says Mike McCormack, who, in 1979, was the congressman from Washington's Fourth District and Ray's best friend in Washington, D.C. He confirms the unpublished report that the governor did "volunteer" to appoint him to Magnuson's seat, "if the political considerations were realistic." McCormack recalls, "I didn't ask [for the appointment] and there was no quid pro quo. She was so new in this business she made a lot of mistakes. . . . She may have talked to a lot of people about this [appointment]."[14]

An emissary, C. Montgomery "Gummie" Johnson, the former GOP state chairman turned manager for Ray's reelection campaign in 1980, did talk to his old friend Brock Adams about the possibility of a prematurely vacant Senate seat. Adams, who had resigned as secretary of transportation over a conflict with the Carter White House, said Johnson indicated "I would get first consideration for the seat" if anything happened to Magnuson. Johnson's aim was to sign on Adams as at least the nominal chairman of Ray's reelection campaign. To the utter dismay of his liberal backers, Adams did so. The reason, he said many years later, was because of "friendship with Gummie," a classmate in the late 1940s at the University of Washington. Otherwise, Adams insists, "there was no deal—although they were peddling it [a possible Senate appointment] around."[15]

According to his aides, Maggie made no fuss over this unseemly matter and said nothing to them until June 14, 1980, at the Democratic State Convention in Hoquiam, Washington, the town adjacent to Aberdeen where, forty-four years earlier, Magnuson held the Democratic Party together in a back-room compromise with Communists over Initiative

119, the proposal for a socialized state economy. On this day in 1980 there would be no compromise.

"Maggie didn't talk about it, but we knew that Dixy's offer to barter his seat grated on him," said Tom Keefe, a Washington, D.C., staffer who came home in December 1979 to run Magnuson's reelection campaign. He drove the senator from Seattle to Hoquiam. "When we got to the city limits he turned to me and said, 'She [Ray] doesn't have much support down here at the convention, does she?' I said I thought not. He repeated, 'She doesn't have much support down here.' "[16]

The senator opened his keynote speech with a Democratic litany of jobs accomplished and jobs to be done. He told a new generation of Democrats about the fisticuffs and fire hoses that marked the knock-down, drag-out 1936 party convention in Aberdeen. It was vintage Maggie and everyone was pleased, including Governor Ray, who sat behind him on the platform of the high school auditorium, smiling. Her smile began to wilt and delegates began to squirm when Maggie paused, smiled, and started: "This state is not going to be a dumping ground for nuclear waste and there are not going to be any supertankers on Puget Sound. . . . Little monkeys in trees have thrown coconuts at me from time to time—I've even been called a dictator!" A wild cheered interrupted. "Yeah," Magnuson began again. Ray's face went red. She turned to talk to Scoop Jackson, seated beside her and himself looking uncomfortable. "Now, one more thing. While I've been back in Washington working on problems of the state and nation, I hear that some have been bartering my job. Well, I want to tell the governor and any other governor there ain't gonna be any vacancy in the U.S. Senate!"[17]

"It was a total surprise," said Tom Keefe. The governor appeared stunned. "Why is he doing this to me?" she asked Jackson.

The hall shook as delegates, stacked in favor of Ray's Democratic primary opponent, Jim McDermott, came out of their seats in a wave of emotion that had more in common with human joy than a conventional demonstration. Suddenly, Ray bolted from the platform—from repudiation by the convention—away from the tumult through a backdoor to a waiting car. As she raced, Ray was heard to say, "I don't have to stand for this." The convention eventually got on with lesser business. Delegates had just celebrated a political death and none would stand to express regret or sadness.

"Dixy was crushed by Maggie—deeply crushed," said Louis Guzzo, a former editor of the *Post-Intelligencer*, the Henry Higgins to this unfortunate Eliza Doolittle. Guzzo had brought her back from Washington, D.C., and engineered her run for governor in 1976. "She was deeply hurt; she had relied on Maggie," said Guzzo. "She didn't understand why he had done this to her."[18]

So far as his aides recall, Magnuson never again discussed the affair in Hoquiam. He was not a callous man, not at all given to incidental political road-kill. But he was old and seasoned and knew what he had to do—and when to do it. What he couldn't know was that Hoquiam was his last great show on the state's political stage.

CHAPTER 29

A Time to Go

arly in 1975, after his reelection to a sixth term in the Senate, Warren Magnuson submitted to the urgings of Dr. Jack Lein and aide Jerry Grinstein and checked into the University of Washington Medical School for a detailed physical examination. Scoop Jackson had always fretted over Maggie—in Irv Hoff's description, "like a mother hen over a chick"—exhorting him to better health habits and more exercise. Maggie's lone concession was an exercise bicycle. It was not overused. After seventy years of hard living, the senior senator was already half joking to staffers, "If I had known I was going to live this long, I'd have taken better care of myself." Dr. Lein thought him to be ailing. But from what specific cause?

The diagnosis, delivered by Dr. David Dale, Magnuson's physician and dean of the medical school that would come to bear the senator's name, was diabetes. Dale's first prescribed remedy: Magnuson was to cease the consumption of liquor. The senator's response was categorical: "Okay, I will." That's asking too much, thought Lein, the school's ebullient vice president and its liaison to the federal funds lavished on it through Magnuson. Lein darkened at the prospect of Maggie without a handy vodka bottle. So he pulled a medical improvisation. Into a cabinet alongside Maggie's bed, Lein bootlegged a bottle of vodka—just in case the patient's withdrawal from alcohol resulted in unbearable nervous tremors. Nothing of the sort happened and to Lein's astonishment the vodka bottle was untouched, its seal intact. Maggie kept his word. He quit drinking temporarily and, when he resumed, it was with moderation.

"For a man of his age, Magnuson was in pretty good shape," said Dr. Dale later. "There were no apparent effects from alcohol. His kidneys, brain, heart, lungs, and digestive tract were in good shape. His manner in the hospital was that of a guest, not a bigshot. I urged him to take care of himself and he said that he would. He seemed to trust me. The irony is that Magnuson was a man so concerned about the health of a nation, yet neglectful of his own health."[1]

The health question weighed heavily on the senator's decision about a campaign for reelection to a seventh term in 1980, and, as it turned out, on the result of that election. Diabetes hampered Magnuson's mobility.

He moved slowly, talked slowly. But it had little effect on the legislative master's "kitchenwork." As he came to say in oblique response to reports that he was slowing, "The meeting doesn't start until I get there." The meetings would include those of the Democratic leadership and the full Appropriations Committee, which he chaired. By the late 1970s, Magnuson's institutional power in Congress, hard to imagine in the 1990s given the subsequent devaluation of seniority, was almost unparalleled. In addition to committee chevrons, Maggie was president pro tempore of the Senate, a largely ceremonial office, but one that placed him fourth in line of succession to the White House. Being President of the Senate was the peak of Warren's ambition, said Jermaine Magnuson.

Going into this office as a new staffer fresh out of law school impressed Tom Keefe as "like going into the control room of the *Nautilus* submarine—there were so many levers of power." Magnuson enjoyed this power. Keefe recalls Senator Wendell Ford, a Kentucky Democrat who coveted one of Maggie's three hideaway offices inside the Capitol Building. These were in addition to the bank of offices along Maggie's Alley in the Old Senate Office Building across from the Capitol grounds.

Ford asked Keefe to request that Maggie relinquish one of the Capitol offices. Keefe complied, but Magnuson said, "No, I don't want to give up the office." Says Keefe: "I supposed that it was a sign of his prestige." If so, it was an uncharacteristic show of power by Maggie.[2]

As the man with his hand on the ultimate lever, Magnuson was bothered by an ailing foot, caused by diabetes, but busy as ever. Apart from his roles in reorganizing American railroads, steering supertankers around Puget Sound, and crafting a new electric power structure for the Northwest, there were measures to spare the environment from toxic substances and to keep alive the failing Milwaukee Railroad, the last vestige of a competitive rail line across the northern tier states. The latter effort, and the railroad, failed.

Some Senate observers, not very careful, thought Maggie himself was failing. Shades of Carl Vinson and Carl Hayden, his legislative mentors and peers, and Mort Frayn, his old college buddy, an unsuccessful candidate for mayor of Seattle in 1969, Magnuson had lapsed into the habit of mumbling or slurring—it was hard to tell which—his speech. It got to be a regular pattern as he presided over the all-important Appropriations Committee meetings.

"It was an act," said Terry Lierman, the young staffer who replaced a Capitol Hill legend, Harley Dirks, as chief clerk of Appropriations. "And it worked. Committee members would start to think, 'Aw, hell, let's give ole Maggie what he wanted.' Afterwards we would go back to his office to talk and there would be a senator as lucid and articulate as anyone on Capitol Hill—no mumbling or slurring. He had been playing dumb."[3]

It's possible that Frayn, a highly successful Seattle businessman and a onetime Speaker of the state's House of Representatives, learned the trick of dumbing down from Maggie, rather than the reverse. Regardless, to advance their ends both pals could make short of their intellect. It was not an act that played well on television, but by no measure were the rumpled veterans, Mort and Maggie, made for the new medium.

Maggie was made for the business of legislation. Early in the administration of President Carter, he moved separate environmental measures creating a "super fund" for the clean-up of toxic substances and raising the level of liability for owners and operators of vessels spilling oil.

But nothing loomed larger to Magnuson in the final years of the Carter administration than the budget conflict between guns and people; between the Pentagon and human health, education, and welfare. It played out before Magnuson's Appropriations Committee. The conflict weighed on Magnuson when he made an address on the fortieth anniversary of the National Cancer Institute. Along with its parent organization, the National Institutes of Health, NCI was Maggie's "pride and joy."

"I can't take credit for having the idea of establishing a National Cancer Institute," he said. "The idea had been around Congress for at least ten years . . . but it was not universally supported and it was not popular among some members of the health profession. . . . We charged the surgeon general with a new mission: to investigate the cause, diagnosis and treatment of cancer; to assist and foster similar research activities by other public and private agencies. The first [appropriations] bill gave NCI $700,000 for operations, $750,000 for construction. In 1978 funding totaled $183 million. More than 1.5 million Americans are alive and cured of cancer, one in three victims is saved."[4]

Maggie's preference for medical research and better education brought him to swords' points with John Stennis, the Mississippi Democrat who chaired the Armed Services Committee and who preferred the bulk of the national defense budget for U.S. forces in Europe, despite a greatly diminished threat from the Soviet Union. The two Senate powers had what one aide described as "angry words" during one encounter overheard in the Senate cloakroom; a flash of temper that flared, then subsided within a few minutes. The tension continued.

"Magnuson could see the short term benefits from defense industries, but in the long run he thought the money should be spent on 'people programs' so he consistently tried to shift money for weapons into money for schools," says Terry Lierman. "Usually he succeeded. He just couldn't understand why others wouldn't let go of the Pentagon funds—I think it genuinely baffled him."

Perhaps equally baffling, given the tension between Magnuson and the Armed Services Committee, was the calm with which Scoop Jackson, a leading advocate of military spending, reacted to Maggie's budget shifts. According to Lierman, the best witness excluding the two senators, Jackson said nothing. But neither did Magnuson block military projects sought by Jackson, chief of these being funds for the Trident submarine base at Bangor, Washington.[5]

"There were zero conversations with Jackson or his staff on appropriations, except for several education and welfare programs Jackson was most interested in," said Lierman, years later. "I've always wondered about it." Jackson may have left criticism to *Seattle Times* editorial writers, who charged the senator with undermining national security by taking from the Pentagon to give to the poor. The matter of such budget shifts is now moot. With the passing of Magnuson, the Senate built a wall around defense requests, forbidding shifts from the Pentagon budget to the domestic budget without a two-thirds vote of the entire body.

Back in Magnuson's office along Maggie's Alley, there were other levers to pull. In 1980 an old dream came true: Congress approved most-favored-nation trading status for (Red) China. Maggie made another speech: "For 25 years I've urged the resumption of non-strategic trade with China. We simply could not go on ignoring nearly one-third of the world's population. . . . [T]rade and cultural exchanges reduce tensions and lead the way to expanded peaceful relations."[6] In this instance, they also led to expanded benefits to the great Northwest port, Seattle. Puget Sound's business interests dropped their hostility to trade with a Communist nation and embraced the change with enthusiasm.

Joe Gottstein's son-in-law, Morrie Alhadeff, heir and boss of Longacres race track, wanted a national compact between the racetracks and off-track betting operations, such as pioneered in New York. Maggie came through. When Peter Von Reichbauer, a young state legislator and sports buff from Washington State, asked for national regulation of football and basketball agents, Maggie, the old horse player, said, "What about jockeys' agents? Better take this back to the drawing board."[7]

There was some office turmoil behind this great and humble business, "considerable boat-rocking" in Keefe's description. Magnuson staffers were squabbling among themselves over committee assignments. Those having their way were ones most favored by Jermaine Magnuson, a wife increasingly protective of her husband. The senator gave Mrs. Magnuson free rein over office personnel and kept himself clear of the dissension. Mrs. Magnuson favored those staffers who favored another reelection campaign.

The trouble reached its climax in January 1979, when Tom Allison and Gerry Johnson, the top aides, resigned. Johnson cited what amounted to irreconcilable differences with Mrs. Magnuson over office management. Allison wished to be relieved of assignment to the Appropriations Committee. Asked for comment, Magnuson said, "You know how these staff things are—they are like a ladies' aid society." As for Jermaine's role, the senator said, "A good wife cares about your office."[8]

Johnson returned to a private law practice in Seattle. Within a few months Allison became general counsel to the department of transportation under the new secretary, Neil Goldschmidt, the Portland mayor who replaced Brock Adams. Adams had resigned the cabinet post over irreconcilable differences with the Carter administration. When Johnson told Magnuson of his decision to quit, the senator—very unhappy—replied, "If I had been younger, this wouldn't have happened." Johnson took this to mean that there would not have been any controversy stemming from a younger Magnuson's decision to seek reelection.

That controversy was the prime source of boat-rocking along Maggie's Alley. Inside the staff, it became a litmus test, with the naysayers falling from Mrs. Magnuson's grace. But there were few public naysayers.

Maggie's power and his 120-person staff were not inducements for retirement. The Senate's seniority system, still intact and bestowing power with longevity, reinforced the urge to seek reelection. But Magnuson's health was less than vigorous; good enough for Senate work, said Johnson, but maybe not for a long election campaign.

When Dr. Dale was questioned about Magnuson's fitness, he said, "Maggie has stayed in pretty stable health. In the past several years, he has been quite well."[9] But the senator had diabetes and a sore foot that would not heal.

An opinion poll taken in the state by Peter Hart showed significant weaknesses, leading Johnson, Allison, Jerry Grinstein, Stan Barer, and Norm Dicks to regard Maggie's run for a seventh term as, at best, a decided risk. Allison and Johnson took the next step by advising Magnuson not to run. "He didn't deserve a miserable, ugly campaign that might end with a loss," said Johnson. "He deserved to go out in a blaze of glory. We so told him."

"A lot of people privately said he shouldn't run," recalls Tom Keefe, one of these being Dave Sweeney, a top Teamster lobbyist on Capitol Hill, a native of Washington State, and a close friend of Brock Adams.

Sweeney was worried about the loss of the Senate seat. Keefe says Sweeney asked what it would take to make Magnuson forgo the race. "I told Dave someone has to go to his office and tell him firsthand not to run," said Keefe. "But nothing happened."

Actually, someone oustide the staff had already addressed the issue firsthand. In 1979, Irv Hoff, the trusted former aide, went to Magnuson for a private conversation. This came after the departure of Johnson, Allison, and press aide Paul Boyd. He said: "I know this may come under the heading of none of my business, but we've been together too long not to talk. You look more feeble than you are—but age will be a big factor in the race. Why not announce a year in advance of the election that you will not run? Go home, rest on your laurels." Magnuson said he would think about it.

Hoff came back two months later and asked Maggie for his decision. "Maggie said, 'The staff and other people think I owe it to the state to run again,'" Hoff remembered. "I said, 'Don't rely on advice from your staff. Their aims are not the same as yours. You are at the height of your powers. You have nothing left to prove.'" It was too late for such persuasions. "The boss loved his job, loved his work," says Hoff, the ex-cowboy, still fit and lean in his mid-eighties. "And maybe he got to thinking the country and his constituents needed him. He had decided to run again. It was the only big mistake Maggie ever made."[10]

In the last analysis Magnuson felt that the prospect of losing the election was not as bad as walking away from the office without a fight. "He couldn't imagine himself not being a senator," said Gerry Johnson. Why did he seek reelection? asked Washington newsman Steve Forrester. "It's what I like and what I can do and what I know," said Maggie.

Duayne Trecker, the former radio-television newsman hired to help Maggie enter the electronic age, didn't like the prospects for a seventh term: "I had mixed feelings about the greatest boss I ever had. I told him that if I had my druthers I'd say you should hang it up and bask in the glory. He said, 'Well thank you for your opinion, but I'm not going to take your advice.' I replied: 'In that case, I'm on your team.'"[11]

For that matter, so were Johnson, Allison, Grinstein, Barer, and Dicks. But as all of these once and present aides noted, Magnuson looked frail, regardless of his real condition. It would show in his carefully controlled public appearances and even in news photos. Nevertheless, the campaign was on. Tom Keefe returned to Seattle in late 1979 to help run the show. Trecker would soon follow. The start was inauspicious. As late as February 1980 there was no campaign budget, and, ultimately, insufficient campaign funds. Maggie would have to take out a $200,000 loan on his own account. Jermaine Magnuson apparently laid some blame on Grinstein for the shortfall and the subsequent election result. She would not be forgiving.

The state's able attorney general, Slade Gorton, at that time an "Evans Republican" in the party's moderate-conservative dichotomy, won the GOP primary and made the most of Magnuson's age and slow movements in the campaign that followed. If Arthur Langlie ran a moral crusade against Maggie, whom he regarded as a "total crook," Gorton steered clear of such aspersions. Instead his theme: "Maggie is a good man who has done good works, but it is time for him to go."

If Toni Seven was forgotten—another face on Hollywood's cutting room floor—a few, including Governor Ray's adviser Louis Guzzo, remembered Magnuson's more recent connection with dubious legislation on behalf of El Paso Natural Gas and attributed the worst to the senator. This was a paradox, a trap of misconceptions.

"You didn't have to be a genius to figure out what Magnuson wanted," says Terry Lierman. "If it benefited the people, okay. If it served some special interest—look out." El Paso was a prime example of the latter. The gas company wanted legislation to overturn a Supreme Court decision divesting it of the Pacific Northwest pipeline.

To gain its way, El Paso spent $12.6 million over a four-year period for lawyers, lobbyists, and public relations firms. Among the lawyers hired to engineer public consent for this special legislation were Albert Rosellini, the former Washington governor, and Clark Clifford, the Washington, D.C., gray eminence. Much of the PR money focused on Washington State. Eventually Magnuson relented and signed onto the bill.

"There was tremendous pressure on him—on Congress," said Mike Pertschuk, Commerce Committee staff director at that time. "Maggie wasn't at all comfortable with the idea. He didn't want to do anything, but after the committee held a hearing on the bill, he was trapped."

Another irony in this affair is that Pertschuk instigated the committee hearing. An investigation by Hearst Newspapers related that witnesses, alleged to be independent, had their scripts prepared by attorneys under contract to El Paso. The newspaper reports effectively killed the bill. But they never revealed that a prime source of information had been Pertschuk himself, Maggie's chief aide on the legislation.

Did Magnuson conspire with Pertschuk to leak information damaging to the El Paso bill? "No," said Pertschuk years later. "He never said anything at all to me about it except to remark, 'You guys [staffers] have more games going than they do in Las Vegas.'" But neither did he fire or reprimand his aide, as the El Paso lobbyists might have urged. Clearly,

Magnuson was not displeased with the game played by his aide. All the senator had gotten from the measure was trouble.[12]

Whatever damage the El Paso trouble may have caused in the 1980 campaign was minimal compared with the impression left by Magnuson's physical condition, and the state of the nation under the Carter administration.

Democrats were hobbled by the "Three I's"—inflation, high interest rates, and Iran (the fundamentalist Islamic nation holding a score of U.S. embassy employees hostage in Teheran)—all of them accountable to the Carter administration. Carter himself faced an election challenge from former actor and California governor Ronald Reagan, a consummate charmer who made Americans feel good. And, deserved or not, Magnuson shared the blame for at least two of the Three I's. It was hard to blame him for the rise of the Ayatollah Khomeini and the holding of American hostages.

"I'm not saying Maggie hasn't done some good for the state," Slade Gorton told *Time* magazine. "He has. I'm saying he has now become part of the problem of inflation and I'm part of the solution."

Newspaper editorials struck similar chords. The ever hostile *Seattle Times* called Maggie "the candidate of nostalgia; highly expensive nostalgia." The private power advocate, *Spokane Spokesman-Review*, noted that it had been forty-four years since Magnuson went to Congress: "Those years and the problems of those years are gone. Magnuson needs to go too."

The *Centralia Chronicle* held Magnuson accountable for "all the wasteful deficit spending" that had resulted in high income taxes, inflation, recession, "and all the other economic maladies." The *Chronicle* left all the others to the public imagination.

Compared with the Reagan years to come, deficits run up by Carter and the Congress were relatively insignificant—$57.9 billion in 1980 compared with $155.1 billion at the end of Reagan's two terms; credit for this increase due to the shoot-the-moon spending of the Pentagon.[13] In fairness to soldiers, pressure for this spending came as much from the weapons industries as from purported strategic realities. A decade later it became clear that the Kremlin's threat to Western civilization was not so great as the spiritual and economic decay inside its own borders. The rationalization for this military spending is that it helped bring down the Soviet empire; a dubious proposition that ignores its cost to domestic welfare. The shrinkage of the American middle class and the growth of a cancerous urban underclass parallel the excessive investment in weapons and NATO and attendant budget deficits which turned the United States into a debtor nation.

Maggie's real fiscal sin, in the view of Republicans and hawks, had less to do with deficits than with his efforts to shunt the flow of federal money from useless weapons, and outrageously priced military toilet seats, and into health and education.

Those realities, however, never intruded on the GOP campaign issue. In fact it would also become apparent that failure of the administration and Congress to control the economy eroded the Democrats' base of blue-collar support. Wages pushed workers into high tax brackets while inflation left them with less power to purchase goods. Postwar prosperity had elevated the material expectations of Americans to a level virtually unimaginable in 1932, the year of Maggie's first legislative election.

This provided a gloomy economic background to Maggie's run for another term. Bad enough. But worse, Gorton looked young and peppy; Maggie looked old and slow. That, in essence, was the campaign. Pictures, in the maturing electronic age, were nearly everything. "Maggie's record was there," said Tom Keefe. "The problem was to connect with the people." The New York advertising whiz David Sawyer was hired and Magnuson said later he made a mistake: "I let them take me out of character."

There was a critical lapse of stage managing, in Trecker's judgment, when Air Force One arrived in Portland, Oregon, bearing Senator Magnuson and the commitment of $1 billion in federal funds for the relief of communities stricken by fallout from the eruption of Mount St. Helens. With television cameras focused, Maggie stumbled as he tried, unaided, to walk down the aircraft's steps to the runway. The ailing foot failed him. The TV footage, carefully used by the Republican campaign, was politically crippling. It showed an old, frail man.

"Magnuson should never have been allowed to come down those steps, in front of television cameras, without help," said Trecker, who met him on the ground. "The staff hadn't been consulted about this trip. That image of the senator moved a lot of votes."

The senator rested daily, but his foot pained him and helped betray his age. Norm Schut, the former aide to Arthur Langlie, recalled a campaign reception where Maggie stood shaking hands. When his turn came, Schut complained of a bad cold: "I should be home in bed but I had to come and wish you well." Magnuson replied, "We both should be home in bed."

Magnuson's campaign leadership proved an uncomfortable mix: the young Tom Keefe and the seasoned businessman turned government functionary, Aubrey Davis. "Davis was trying to run it like a small business while I was trying to run a rock concert to attract young people," said Keefe. "There were also money problems, as in, not enough."

Scoop Jackson campaigned furiously—his only known campaign tempo—for his friend Maggie. In Keefe's fond memory, Jackson was "the hardest working guy in show business." But Jimmy Carter didn't help, looking like an errant lad, not the president of the United States, in debates with his intellectual inferior, Reagan. "There you go again," retorted the affable showman, blunting Carter's thrusts. Keefe watched this on television and winced.

Nevertheless, polls looked favorable for Maggie up until the day before the election. The senator thought he had a shot. In one of the national campaign's inexplicable twists, President Carter showed up with Scoop and Maggie the night before the election in a hangar at Seattle's Boeing Field, a continent away from his home in Plains, Georgia, and the White House. It was an exuberant rally for Democrats, one of their best of the year. It masked a bitter truth.

"It's all over," Jackson confided to a newsman over the din of cheering Democrats. "I saw his poll this afternoon. Carter is finished—too much inflation and Iran."[14]

Actually, it was much worse for Democrats. Gorton defeated Magnuson by 70,000 votes. Democratic senators Frank Church, Birch Bayh, Gaylord Nelson, John Culver, John Durkin, Robert Morgan, Herman Talmadge, and George McGovern, the 1972 presidential candidate, lost. So did Representatives Al Ullman of Oregon, the House Ways and Means chairman, and Washington's Mike McCormack. Ronald Reagan was elected president. He carried all but five states and the District of Columbia. He even carried Washington State. The traditional Democratic coalition of labor, minorities, liberals, and the South had dissolved under Reagan's sunny manner.

"It was like a plane crash," noted Rick Redman, the Seattle attorney and former Magnuson aide. "Everyone killed regardless of merit."[15] It had been thirty-four years since the last Republican tidal wave swamped Democrats in Congress and statehouses. In 1946 the wave signaled a quest for a new postwar order. In 1980 it was apparent that the administration and Congress hadn't met the new American expectations.

A younger Democratic candidate, Brock Adams or Norm Dicks, might have fared as badly as Magnuson, given the election's landslide proportions. But this was scant consolation on election night in Seattle at Maggie's campaign headquarters, a onetime Pontiac auto showroom on Fifth Avenue near the *Post-Intelligencer*. Tears fell. Magnuson was as composed as anyone in the showroom: "There is a time to come and a time to go and I guess after forty-eight years they decided to turn me out to pasture."

A few minutes later, in a backroom with staffers and a few old friends, someone asked the old legislator how he felt. Maggie looked up at former Senator Hugh Mitchell, a friend and ally from the 1930s, and said, "Mitch, you're the only other person in this room who knows what it feels like."[16]

Magnuson had not spared himself to rest on his laurels, and in the end, when it was time to go, it hurt.

CHAPTER 30

Coming Home: The Green Light

T he Seattle to which Warren Magnuson returned after the 1980 election was changing faster than the congressional institution he had left behind. Far removed from the semi-isolated port with an economy based on fish and timber, the city he had discovered in 1925, Seattle now stretched up above Elliott Bay in an architectural imitation of Manhattan. Slick eastern magazines touted the town as "America's most livable city" and its population began to explode with emigrants from the structural decay and uncivility of New York City and Los Angeles, as well as from the political storms of Southeast Asia. This was a migration trend that would accelerate as the twentieth century rushed to a close.

Waterfront piers along Alaskan Way, where the city's tall buildings meet Puget Sound, still gave refuge to four-masted sailing schooners when the young Magnuson discovered Seattle. These ships were gone by the end of his political career, displaced by restaurants and shops for T-shirts and other tourist attractions. Sailing schooners and 10,000-ton freighters had become relics, like the longshoreman's hook. The port now accommodated 100,000-ton container vessels on the massive docks south of the city's downtown. Replacing longshoremen's hooks there were towering multimillion-dollar cranes. Some of these ships came from the People's Republic of China, Seattle's newest trading partner. Nothing was more pleasing to Maggie. It was hard to remember when the suggestion of trade with "Red China" was regarded as only a cut below treason.

Fish and timber had long shared the city's economic base with the Boeing Company, credit due to Magnuson's intervention with President Truman when it appeared the company would shift its military production to Kansas. Now Boeing had a giant industrial counterpart for the twenty-first century, Microsoft, creation of a young local genius in mathematics, and the leading manufacturer of computer software. The processing of coffee, a tropical farm commodity, gave Seattle a new set of millionaires and a new image in postindustrial America. The nation's tastes had softened from bourbon to latté, and Americans consumed Starbucks coffee by the barrel.

Less conspicuous was the shift in the state's political establishment, no longer concentrated among the squires of Seattle's University Club and Spokane's Spokane Club and the union chiefs in Seattle's Labor Temple and Teamsters' headquarters. Power had dispersed from the likes of the Bullitts, Fishers, Lawrence Arnold, D. K. McDonald, Norton Clapp, the AFL-CIO's Joe Davis, and Teamsters' Arnie Weinmeister to invisible corporate managers and their hired "political consultants." Many of the new managers came from the late surge of migration into the state. Davis, brilliant, innovative (prime mover behind the state's consumer protection laws), scrupulously honest, and one of the state's most influential citizens in the 1960s and 1970s, got nary a Seattle obituary notice when he died in 1995. The new crowd didn't look back.

Seattle's new political elite came from a postwar generation untouched by the material deprivations of the Great Depression in a city where soup lines were a bad memory. They faced no barriers of class, few of race. Seattle was as firmly egalitarian in 1980 as in 1880. They ate in new restaurants and smart cafés, tailored to feed a range of extravagant tastes, and read the *Weekly*, the city's alternative newspaper replacing the long-gone, blue-collar *Star*. The *Star* was meat and potatoes. The *Weekly* appealed to the tastes of the affluent with coverage of arts, restaurants, entertainment, and extensive "personal" advertisements for those seeking companionship. The city was lonelier, more impersonal, than it had been. It was a new crowd without much connection to the world of Warren Magnuson, perhaps even disdainful; a subtle factor in Maggie's replacement in Congress by the younger Slade Gorton, a jogger and political strategist, a critic of federal deficits, but not of the Pentagon budget. (Gorton would lose the seat in 1986 to Brock Adams, then return to the Senate in 1988 when he won the seat that Jackson had held for so long and that had been occupied by Dan Evans during the Reagan years.)

Reform, as it was called, had come to Congress where Magnuson worked for forty-four years, accumulating power from seniority as well as his personal skill. New rules watered seniority as the sole criterion for position by giving more authority to party caucuses to select committee chairmen. Laws and strictures forbade a member's conflict of interests. In the aftermath of the fight between President Nixon and the Congress over his refusal to spend appropriated monies—the word for this was "impoundments"—Congress established budget committees to set overall budgets and place limits on spending. This diluted the clout of the Appropriations Committee.

Overshadowing these changes in the way Congress does its business was the impact of television. If the electronic medium had helped the

Senate enact its civil rights legislation, it proved a greater boon to the body's "show horses"—good-looking, carefully groomed politicians with a gift for the bumper-sticker phrase. Maggie, a creature of radio and newspaper communications, may have departed Congress at the proper time. His style and manner was not the stuff of TV glamour and he surely suffered, as a result, in the 1980 election.

Maggie didn't come straight home to Seattle after his defeat. As Senate Appropriations chairman he had to go back to the Capitol for a marathon postelection session of Congress, one that dealt mainly with the federal budget. It did not end until 5 A.M. December 17, and Maggie described it as "one of the toughest sessions I ever had to deal with." Exhausted, seventy-five years old, he stopped in Palm Springs to rest at the desert home he had purchased from Bill Edris.[1] Tributes from his colleagues followed his wake, none more to the point than Scoop Jackson's: "Senator Magnuson did more to better the quality of life for his fellow human beings than any other U.S. senator. That's a mighty big statement and I do not make it lightly. . . . Maggie always knew there would be a tomorrow. In the Senate today's opponent may be tomorrow's ally. It's a simple thought, but one often lost among today's single issue, media-minded public figures." The source of his Senate power, said Jackson: "Friendship, trust and a willingness to help when there was seemingly nothing in it for him or his constituents. He knew there would be another day, another vote, another battle to be won or lost."[2]

"Maggie worked wonders for people," said Senator Ted Kennedy. "His legislation is the measure of Maggie's humanity and his greatness." Senator Inouye described the Appropriations Committee chairmen preceding Magnuson as "secretive and almost dictatorial." Maggie, said his younger friend from Hawaii, brought democracy to Appropriations, allowing members to share in the committee's responsibilities.

And Magnuson? In a departure from his normal shyness, he shared his own reflections on the institution and its participants in several talks with a newsman two months after his departure from Washington, D.C.[3] The talks at his home in Palm Springs were without rancor. The new president, Ronald Reagan—a show horse of show horses in Magnuson's political dichotomy—would work well with Congress, said Maggie, given his experience as governor of California—but only if he "moderated his views" and got realistic about the federal budget. (Reagan did neither, as Magnuson would soon observe.) Magnuson, however, came close to a rare lapse of foresight when he suggested "Ree-gin" (as Maggie pronounced it) and the conservatives wouldn't be able to overturn forty years of Democratic programs by slashing funds for Social Security, education, unemployment, and Medicare. He failed to measure the size of the conservative tide that would carry through the next decades, after having swept him from his Senate office.

"People wanted a change in November [1980]," said Magnuson, seated in a soft couch overlooking his swimming pool on a ridge above Palm Springs. "They expect Reagan to come out for change. That's why they voted for him. Sure, it affected my election. . . . You take a guy who comes home from work. He's got a good job. He's not mad at anything. He doesn't like inflation but he's not mad. He opens a bottle of beer and turns the tube on. He hadn't thought of being mad at anything but here's this guy on the tube saying that he ought to be—he's been stirred up. [pause] They'll get mad at Reagan and once you get mad you take it out on the political ins."

Had Magnuson ever become obsessed with the urge to run for the presidency or vice presidency? The answer to the question was already self-evident. He had not. Maggie had done more to shape the nation through his longevity and genius in Congress than most of the presidents (never mind vice presidents) of this century. He answered the question anyway:

"No. I was happy doing what I was doing, which was being a good senator. Besides in those [pre-TV] days I didn't figure I came from the right place. We in the Northwest didn't have any electoral votes and nobody paid attention to the state of Washington on the national scene until Scoop came along to run for the Democratic presidential nomination. . . . Scoop changed things."

The vice presidency?

"Well," said Maggie, before a puff on his cigar. "Truman mentioned it at the [Democratic National] convention in 1948 before he picked [Kentucky Senator] Alben Barkley, the majority leader. Truman really didn't say much except that he was looking around. He wanted Barkley but there was a question about whether Barkley would leave the Senate. If he didn't, Truman wanted me. I said to him, 'Let's see what happens.' Barkley took it and became vice president. Later Barkley told me it was the worst decision he ever made. He loved the Senate and should have stayed there."

Warren Magnuson loved the Senate and did stay there to put through legislation for medical research, consumer protection, civil rights, maritime safety, railroad reorganization; in sum to exceed in his last two decades his earlier efforts on behalf of the public interest. He would have failed at this had he become obsessed with the other end of Pennsylvania Avenue.

Warren and Jermaine were not long for Palm Springs. One evening before they left they went out to dinner in a Palm Springs restaurant with a piano bar. Maggie liked to sing. An inebriated customer wanted the piano player to run off an Alaskan period piece, "Those Squaws Along the Yukon." Nobody in the room, including Maggie, knew the tune, much less the words. But when the man played "I'll Be Seeing You," a poignant lyric from the 1940s, Magnuson joined in with a fine baritone. He knew every word and enjoyed the sound.

Gordon Culp, the Seattle attorney who with Howard MacGowan negotiated the U.S.-Canada power treaty, owned the house coveted by Magnuson on the west side of Seattle's Queen Anne Hill. The place had a commanding view of Elliott Bay and Puget Sound, and the Olympic Mountains, thirty miles, as the eagle flies, to the west. It was for sale. As for many Northwest citizens, the mountains and the water had come to dominate the spiritual side of Magnuson. But as Culp would explain, the house came with a catch.

"I told Maggie I couldn't sell it to him," said Culp. "It wasn't the price. It was the fact that the home across the street was that of Vance and Peggins Sutter. Peggins was Maggie's first wife. When I reported this to Maggie he said, 'Aw, dammit Gordy, that was fifty years ago.' I also told Jermaine, who said that 'if it didn't bother Peggins, it wouldn't bother me.' I talked to Peggins, who said it would make no difference that Warren and Jermaine lived across the street. Maggie and Jermaine bought the house."[4]

There among the trees and flowers of Queen Anne Hill, with its stunning view of sea and mountains to the west, Warren spent the last eight years of his life. Visitors came and went, some like Senators Mark Hatfield and Brock Adams for kindly advice, others school kids in awe at meeting a political hero. Old age had not dimmed Magnuson's uncanny attractiveness for small fry. Once during the 1984 presidential race between Reagan and Walter Mondale, a high school student accompanied her father for lunch with Warren and Jermaine and began to tease: "Dad thinks Reagan is the greatest—a dynamic friend of the people and articulate. He even likes his old movies." Maggie, smiling around the curled corners of his lips and knowing better, replied with a thoughtful appreciation of Mondale, the Minnesota senator who had once said of Magnuson, "He is scrupulously fair with federal funds; one half for Washington state, one half for the rest of the country." The kid went back to high school with a tale for her classmates, and perhaps offspring to come. She said she loved Senator Magnuson because he was like a kindly grandfather.

The state held a Warren Magnuson day in March 1981. There was a banquet and Maggie said he was overwhelmed—but not sufficiently submerged to stifle a comment: "Don't give in to the tyranny of single issue politics." At least one critic, Henry Gay, publisher of the *Shelton-Mason County Journal*, was underwhelmed. In a muted echo of the *Argus*'s late Philip Bailey, Gay wrote: "Maggie was a disaster as a legislator. The effect of his 44 years of irresponsible spending and backscratching is a nation in deep trouble. . . . Maggie needed public money to stay in office." But Maggie's venerable editorial nemesis, Ross Cunningham of the *Seattle Times*, said that contrary to his image, Maggie was a "fiscal conservative"—a friend of free enterprise.[5]

Magnuson went back to the hospital—"like being in prison," he later complained—in the summer of 1982. His foot, infected from diabetes and not healing, had to be amputated and replaced with an artificial foot. He called it "my Seattle foot." Hobbled and ailing with diabetes and old age, Maggie still made public appearances. There were annual gatherings with the Bumblebees and a few friends at Victor Rosellini's 410 restaurant every April 12 after his return. These were informal birthday parties. "I'm proof of what living a clean life can do for your longevity," he proclaimed at his eightieth birthday. In an aside, he told a friend, "the older I get the more liberal I get."

"You taught us habits of the heart," said Mike Pertschuk, forgoing a gag for a comment from the heart.

It was the happy fortune of Magnuson, and other senators of his era, to serve during a period of increasing personal income and, consequently, increasing federal revenues. They did not have to raise taxes, bane of the elected official. Maggie's fiscal sin, as Cunningham frequently noted, was to shift money from the Pentagon budget into health, education, and welfare, where he believed the national security would be better served. The federal deficits that so alarmed conservatives came after Magnuson's departure and under the aegis of the conservative poster-boy, Ronald Reagan, duly backed by Senator Gorton and ever pressing for more Pentagon dollars. From a liberal perspective it was a paradox and costly beyond calculation: As the Soviet threat diminished in the 1970s and 1980s, "defense" spending increased with the election of President Reagan in 1980. Maggie took notice.

"Americans are being misled about the balance of power," said Magnuson in an interview in mid-August 1982. "Reagan is wrong in raising the defense budget and cutting taxes. This is causing a whopping deficit. When I left Congress the Pentagon had $29 billion in unspent funds. Put more money in [the Pentagon] and you'll have awful scandals. They're building up a big offense. Who are we going to attack?"[6]

The scandals of a bloated Pentagon budget followed as predicted: guns that would not shoot straight, $7,600 coffeepots, $435 ball-peen hammers, a 50-mph bulldozer, and Star Wars, a budget-busting scheme to shoot Russian rockets from the sky as they rose from Soviet silos toward the United States. Only the ideologically committed argued that the Star Wars scheme would work, but these included President Reagan.

Maggie stayed reasonably active into the mid-1980s, serving on a citizens committee sponsored by the United Nations organization to study nuclear proliferation. He came to the aid of John Spellman when the former Republican governor and son of Maggie's college football coach, Bart Spellman, needed to retire a debt from his failed 1984 reelection campaign. He advised the state legislature to approve a flat rate income tax with its proceeds earmarked for common schools. When Scoop Jackson died in the late summer of 1983, a stricken Magnuson went to the Presbyterian Church in Everett to give a final oration. He had never dreamed that Jackson, a politician of exceedingly moderate indulgences, would die before he did.

These public appearances gradually lessened. Magnuson spent more time at his home overlooking Puget Sound, resting. Early in 1988 he wrote a brief will leaving all of his property to Jermaine. Maggie had not wound up out of office selling apples and feeding from a soup line as he once feared. The estate was considerable, worth well in excess of $2 million according to records filed in the King County Courthouse. The bulk of this was in stocks, bonds, and property, much of it based on his original investments in Northwest Airlines and KIRO radio and television.

Maggie's interest in politics and people never lagged during those last years. Neither did his keen intellect. But it became more difficult to move on his "Seattle foot." The planned gathering of the Bumblebees in April 1989 had to be put aside, and a few weeks later Maggie wasn't well enough to receive a friend bearing a biography of Edgar Snow, the first journalist to tell Americans about China's Communist revolution. His last conversations with Gerry Johnson, his former aide and now his attorney, were as lucid as ever. They dealt with his estate and the need to care for Jermaine.

True to the work of his life, Magnuson's last public act was to dictate testimony on behalf of the Puget Sound Tanker Safety Act of 1989, sponsored by Senator Adams. The bill mandated that new tankers be built with double hulls and was prompted by the catastrophic wreck of the *Exxon Valdez* in Alaska's Prince William Sound. The design would leave a large space between the vessel's outer hull and its oil tanks, a construction that would have prevented much of the damage to Prince William Sound. Maggie dictated his statement to Juanita Garrison, Jermaine's daughter:

"Puget Sound is not safe from the dangers of an oil spill. We must improve the construction and operation of large tankers that come into the Sound. . . . Senator Adams' bill would require comprehensive oil spill contingency plans and practice drills. This would mean that adequate, workable, plans would be in place in the event of an accident. . . . I want to thank Senator Adams for his leadership on this issue."

Just before the end, the nurse attending Magnuson at his home asked her patient, "Why did you work so hard and accomplish so much?" Magnuson answered, "I wanted to prove something to myself." He had once told Jermaine, "I feel at peace with you; I feel like I've been out in a rough sea and I've come home. I'm in a safe harbor with you." In his last days Jermaine would reassure him of the safe harbor.[7] He died May 20, 1989, of old age and congestive heart failure. He had reached the green light, the goal that eluded Jay Gatsby because his desire was selfish and petty. Warren, said Mabel Thompson, his friend from the Young Democrats in 1930 until his death fifty-nine years later, never changed. He was always a kind man, considerate of others, and most appreciative of Jermaine.

Gerry Johnson organized the grand funeral at St. Mark's Cathedral and joined with other Bumblebees, excepting Jerry Grinstein, as Maggie's pallbearers. Jermaine selected the pallbearers. Grinstein, the catalyst in Magnuson's revival after he almost lost the 1962 election, was hurt by the slight. But he made no fuss. He listened in agreement to the eulogies from Senators Brock Adams, Mark Hatfield, and Dan Inouye, and Representatives Tom Foley and Norm Dicks. They did not have to exaggerate and they voiced a common theme: Power did not corrupt Magnuson. He carried it with as much humility as skill.

Dorothy Bullitt, the widow of Scott Bullitt, made her final public appearance, sitting upright and alert in a pew alongside her granddaughter, Dorothy. A few years earlier she had her last meeting with Magnuson, who had been the attorney for the unemployment commission on which she had served in 1933. Mrs. Bullitt and Maggie sat side by side at a Rainier Club dinner and watched a KING-TV documentary on the senator's life. She said, "Maggie, so much time has gone by. I wish we were young enough to dance again." "Dorothy," he replied, touching her hand, "if I could dance with you, I would right now."[8]

At the last farewell in St. Mark's, the organ boomed and the choir sang "Eternal Father Strong to Save" and Martin Luther's "A Mighty Fortress Is Our God." Young Dorothy said her grandmother enjoyed all of the service, especially the music. Maggie would have preferred "I'll Be Seeing You."

"There are no second acts in American lives," wrote F. Scott Fitzgerald, perhaps considering his own life and that of his tragic creation, Gatsby.[9] But he did not know of Magnuson, whose life and work could be demarked by second and third acts and an epilogue—each succeeding passage of his career stronger than the one preceding. He kept getting better.

Much later, nearly a decade after the funeral orations, when they had all reflected, his former aides and accomplices were asked to cite the most significant legislation to emerge from Magnuson's sponsorship and work in the Congress. None was old enough to remember the young Washington State legislator's skill in the passage of the nation's first unemployment relief act. That was ancient history, swallowed by acts of the New Deal. But none hesitated with their answers.

"The dams," said Irv Hoff.

"Saving Puget Sound and reviving the marine mammals," said Featherstone Reid.

"Medical research embodied in the National Institutes of Health," said the college lobbyist, Jerry Roschwalb.

"Consumer protection," several of the younger aides insisted.

They could have mentioned his persistence in a hostile political environment in calling for recognition and trade with China.

Any one of these accomplishments would have been a fitting monument for a career. They helped shape the national quality of life and the economy of the Pacific Northwest. But his extraordinary effort—his genius—in passing the public accommodations section of the 1964 civil rights bill changed American society like nothing since Abraham Lincoln's Emancipation Proclamation.

And he had done it all with pleasure.

Notes

The Warren G. Magnuson Papers are part of the accessions of the Manuscripts and University Archives Division of the University of Washington Libraries, and they are organized according to accession numbers 3181–1, 2, 3, 4, and 5. Items from this collection are cited in the notes below by the appropriate accession number followed by the box and folder numbers (for example, 3181–2, 49/58).

Newspapers frequently cited in this book include the *Seattle Post-Intelligencer*, the *Seattle Times*, the *Seattle Star* (no longer published), the *New York Times*, and the *Fargo Forum*—all daily papers. The *Argus* was a weekly Seattle journal of politics, business, and the arts.

As a journalist of thirty-five years, one disciplined to do his own legwork, the author conducted all of the interviews, unless otherwise indicated. Notes and/or tapes are in his possession. Exceptions are the accounts of off-the-record talks with Senator John F. Kennedy on civil rights, Senator Edward Kennedy on the Senate struggle over the Boeing SST and the majority whip job, and Senators Warren Magnuson and Henry Jackson over the latter's apprehension about war with the Soviet Union. Off-the-record protocol and good journalistic manners prohibit taking notes. The scholar in search of specific items in the Warren G. Magnuson file at the Lyndon B. Johnson Library in Austin, Texas, will find expert, speedy, and kindly help from the abundant staff at that splendid institution.

Chapter 1   *Seattle, May 24, 1989*

1. *Memorial Services Held in the Congress of the United States, Together with Tributes Presented in Eulogy of Warren G. Magnuson, Late a Senator from Washington* (Washington, D.C.: Government Printing Office, 1991).

2. Ralph Nader, interview, Washington, D.C., December 12, 1995.

3. F. Scott Fitzgerald, *The Great Gatsby* (New York: Scribner's, 1925).

4. Warren G. Magnuson file, Lyndon B. Johnson Library, University of Texas, Austin.

5. Stimson Bullitt, *To Be a Politician*, rev. ed. (Seattle: Willows Press, 1994), pp. 3–6.

6. George W. Scott, "Arthur B. Langlie: Republican Governor in a Democratic Age" (Ph.D. diss., University of Washington, 1971), p. 441.

Chapter 2   *Fargo/Moorhead*

1. Interviews: Maude Elaine Knudtson, Gertrude Hansman, Oliver Sondrall, Ed Stern, and Frank Van Osdel, Fargo, North Dakota, and Moorhead, Minnesota,

April 14–25, 1994; Peggins Sutter, Seattle, May 10, 1994; Carol Parker Cahill, Ajijic, Mexico, April 10–12, 1994.

2. Warren G. Magnuson Papers, University of Washington Libraries, Accession 3181–1, box 10, folders 12 and 13 (hereafter abbreviated: Magnuson Papers, 3181–1, 10/12–13).

3. Magnuson Papers, 3181–2, 6/14, 6/16.

4. *Collected Works of Abraham Lincoln*, ed. Roy P. Basler, vol. 2 (New Brunswick: Rutgers University Press, 1953).

5. *Junkin v. Junkin*, divorce proceedings, 1937, Clay County Courthouse, Moorhead, Minnesota.

6. Warren G. Magnuson file, *Fargo Forum*, Fargo, North Dakota.

7. Warren G. Magnuson transcripts: North Dakota University (1923–24), North Dakota State University (1924–25), and University of Washington (1925–29).

Chapter 3   *Seattle, 1925*

1. Peggins Sutter, interview, May 10, 1994, Seattle.

2. Don Brazier, "History of the Washington State Legislature," Olympia, undated, work in progress.

3. Jorgen Dahlie, "Old World Paths in the New: Scandinavians Find a Familiar Home in Washington," in G. T. Edwards and Carlos A. Schwantes, eds., *Experiences in a Promised Land* (Seattle: University of Washington Press, 1986), pp. 100–103.

4. Guy Williams, conversation with author, Seattle (maybe a joke that tells a true story).

5. Charles LeWarne, *Utopias on Puget Sound* (Seattle: University of Washington Press, 1975), passim.

6. Thomas W. Riddle, "The Old Radicalism in America: John R. Rogers and the Populist Movement in Washington, 1891–1900" (Ph.D. diss., Washington State University, 1976), pp. 45–67, 286.

7. Terry Slatten, "Homer T. Bone, Public Power, and Washington State Progressive Politics in the Mid-1920's" (M.A. thesis, Western Washington University, 1980), pp. 84, 226, 234–35.

8. Shelby Scates, *Firstbank: The Story of Seattle-First National Bank* (Seattle, 1970), passim.

Chapter 4   *Mr. Smooth*

1. Magnuson Papers, 3181–1, 6/6 (box 6, folder 6).

2. University of Washington transcript.

3. Magnuson Papers, 3181–1, 10/14, 11/4.

4. Ibid., 10/9–12.

5. Peggins Sutter, interview.

6. Judge Charles Cone, interview, Wenatchee, Washington, August 9, 1994.

7. Warren G. Magnuson, interview, Palm Springs, California, January 10–15, 1981.

8. Delphine Haley, *Dorothy Stimson Bullitt* (Seattle: Sasquatch Books, 1995), p. 138.

9. Richard Fisch, "History of the Washington Democratic Party" (Ph.D. diss., University of Oregon, 1986), pp. 229–30, 235.

10. Magnuson Papers, 3181–1, 5/10; 6/8–9, 6/12.

Chapter 5   *Depression*

1. Magnuson Papers, 3181–1, 10/5, 10/9.

2. Terry Pettus, Seattle Public Library video interview.

3. Magnuson Papers, 3181–1, 6/6–7, and 6/23.

4. Ibid., 14/23.

5. Magnuson Papers, 3181–2, 4/15–18, 4/20.

6. Fayette Florent Krause, "Democratic Party Politics in the State of Washington during the New Deal: 1932–1940" (Ph.D. diss., University of Washington, 1971), pp. 20, 23, 39.

7. Magnuson Papers, 3181–1, 10/4.

8. Ibid., 1/5, 1/20, 1/23; 3/5.

9. *Journal, Washington State House of Representatives*, 1933 (Olympia: State Printing Office), pp. 6–7.

10. Charles Hodde, interview, Olympia, Washington, January 13, 1994.

11. Gordon R. Newell, *Rogues, Buffoons and Statesmen* (Seattle: Hangman Press, 1975), passim.

12. Hodde, interview.

13. Jean MacGowan and Ian MacGowan, interviews, Seattle, January 8 and February 8, 1994.

14. *Journal, Washington State House of Representatives*, 1933, pp. 196, 448, 945.

15. Haley, *Dorothy Stimson Bullitt*, pp. 165–66.

16. George Sundborg, *Hail Columbia: The Thirty-Year Struggle for Grand Coulee Dam* (New York: Macmillan, 1954), passim.

17. Magnuson Papers, 3181–1, 1/8.

18. Haley, Dorothy Stimson Bullitt, p. 167.

19. Ibid., p. 166.

20. Magnuson Papers, 3181–1, 5/15.

21. Ibid., 6/9–10, 6/18.

22. Ibid., 1/20.

23. Ibid., 6/9–10, 6/17.

24. Ibid., 6/10–11; 7/8.

Chapter 6   *Young Man in a Hurry*

1. Magnuson Papers, 3181–1, 5/12.

2. Northwest Airlines early connections: ibid., 4/8–10; 5/10–16.

3. Ibid., 5/10, 5/12–14, 5/16.

4. Scripps Newspapers, KIRO: ibid., 6/14, 6/20–21.

5. Ibid., 6/15.

6. Ibid., 6/22.

7. Albert Rosellini, interview, Seattle, January 17, 1994.

8. Magnuson Papers, 3181–1, 4/8–10.

9. Richard C. Berner, *Seattle, 1921–1940: From Boom to Bust* (Seattle: Charles Press, 1992), p. 351.

10. *Seattle Times,* November 10, 1936.

11. *Argus* (Seattle), June 16, 1934.

12. Magnuson Papers, 3181–1, 4/21–22.

13. Ibid., 4/8–10, 4/20.

14. Magnuson Papers, 3181–2, 4/15–18, 4/20.

15. Magnuson Papers, 3181–1, 4/20.

Chapter 7   *New Deal, New World, the "Soviet of Washington"*

1. A. J. P. Taylor, *The Origins of the Second World War* (New York: Atheneum, 1961), passim.

2. Fraser M. Ottanelli, *The Communist Party of the United States* (New Brunswick: Rutgers University Press, 1991), pp. 83, 105.

3. Select Committee on Subversive Activities, U.S. House of Representatives, "Guide to Subversive Organizations" (Washington, D.C.: Government Printing Office, March 1951).

4. Krause, "Democratic Party Politics in the State of Washington," p. 39.

5. Magnuson Papers, 3181–1, 10/6.

6. Ibid., 10/9.

7. Rosellini, interview.

8. *Argus* (Seattle), 1936.

9. Albert A. Acena, "The Washington Commonwealth Federation: Reform Politics and the Popular Front" (Ph.D. diss., University of Washington, 1975), pp. 126–27, 135.

10. *Bremerton Journal,* May 28, 1936.

11. *Tacoma News Tribune,* May 23, 1936.

12. *Seattle Star,* May 25, 1936.

13. Magnuson Papers, 3181–1, 5/8–9.

14. Ibid., 6/8.

15. *Seattle Star,* July 27, 1936; August 8, 1936.

16. On Zioncheck: *Argus,* February 1936, June 1936, August 1936, July 1936.

17. Magnuson Papers, 3181–1, 10/8–9.

Chapter 8   *Mr. Magnuson Goes to Washington*

1. *Time,* October 12, 1936.

2. William Davis, *The State of Washington 1936* (Seattle: Davis Publishing, 1936), preface.

3. Acena, "Washington Commonwealth Federation," p. 135.

4. *New Republic,* August 1, 1949.

5. *Argus* (Seattle), August 22, 1936.

6. Magnuson Papers, 3181–1, 4/20.

7. The 1936 campaign: ibid., 10.

8. *Seattle Star,* August 14, 1936.

9. *Seattle Times,* October 26, 1936.

10. Magnuson Papers, 3181–1, 10/12–14.

11. Ibid., 10/9.

12. Magnuson Papers, 3181–2, 37.

13. Magnuson Papers, 3181–1, 14/5.

14. Magnuson Papers, 3181–2, 37.

15. Magnuson Papers, 3181–1, 13/9.

16. Ibid., 5/12.

Chapter 9   *"Ensign" Magnuson*

1. Magnuson Papers, 3181–1, 6/16.

2. Alfred Steinberg, *Sam Rayburn: A Biography* (New York: Hawthorn Books, 1975), pp. 36, 114.

3. W. Featherstone Reid, interview, Seattle, March 20, 1995, and Oral History, UW Archives.

4. *Seattle Post-Intelligencer,* December 10, 1980.

5. *Seattle Times,* January 12, 1971.

6. Robert A. Caro, *The Years of Lyndon Johnson* (New York: Knopf, 1982), pp. 537–38, 554.

7. Magnuson Papers, 3181–1, 6/16.

8. Magnuson Papers, 3181–2, 1/18.

9. Ibid., 51/44.

10. Magnuson Papers, 3181–1, 5/10.

11. Magnuson Papers, 3181–2, 1/3.

12. Ibid., 1/11.

13. Ibid., 46/44.

14. Ibid., 46/21–22.

15. Ibid., 46/14.

16. Ibid., 1/3; 46/52.

17. Ian MacGowan, interview, Seattle, February 8, 1994.

18. Magnuson Papers, 3181–2, 46/14.

19. Ibid., 46/51.

20. *Seattle Star,* July 14, 1938.

21. Magnuson Papers, 3181–2, 46/14.

22. Ibid., 46/18–19.

23. Ibid.

Chapter 10   *Adonis from Congress*

1. Magnuson Papers, 3181–2, 46/51.

2. Ibid., 48/1–2, 48/24–35.

3. Ibid., 49/49–51; 51/30.

4. F. Scott Fitzgerald, *The Last Tycoon* (New York: Scribner's, 1941; Cambridge University Press, 1993), p. 11.

5. Mrs. Howard (Jean) MacGowan, interview, Seattle, February 12, 1994.

6. Carol Parker Cahill, interview, Ajijic, Mexico, April 12, 1994.

7. Magnuson Papers, 3181–2, 7/47–51.

8. Ibid., 47/38.

9. Mrs. Harry (Sybil) Brand, Los Angeles, April 15, 1994.

10. Magnuson Papers, 3181–2, 48/1–2.

11. Ibid., 47/33.

12. Ibid., 48/14–15.

13. Schenck: ibid., 51/15.

14. Scott Berg, interview, Los Angeles, April 15, 1994.

15. Carol Parker Cahill, interview.

16. Berg, interview.

17. Magnuson Papers, 3181–2, 47/38.

18. Ibid., 48/45.

19. Ibid., 48/2.

20. Ibid., 46/30.

21. Judge Charles Cone, interview, Wenatchee, August 10, 1994.

22. Magnuson Papers, 3181–2, 46/51.

23. Overton: ibid., 170/61; 46/51; 51/9.

24. Mrs. Herbert Kraushaar, interview, Alexandria, Louisiana, April 6, 1994.

25. Irv Hoff, interview, Hilton Head, South Carolina, June 4, 1994.

26. Ibid.

27. Maurice Rosenblatt, interview, Washington, D.C., November 2, 1995.

28. Hodde, interview, January 1994.

Chapter 11 *Horses, Flaxseed, and Dutiful Son*

1. Magnuson Papers, 3281–2, 49/13.

2. Ibid., 48/12.

3. Blaine Johnson, interview, Seattle, May 20, 1994.

4. Carol Parker Cahill, interview.

5. Eugene Corr, interview, Seattle, April 1, 1994.

6. Magnuson Papers, 3181–2, 49/27.

7. Ibid., 49/19.

8. Ibid., 49/14.

9. ADM: ibid., 48/24–32; 56/7–19.

10. Rosenblatt, interview.

11. Magnuson Papers, 3181–2, 47/45.

12. Ibid.

13. Ibid., 47/58.

14. Ibid., 47/31.

15. Ibid., 47/41; 48/52.

16. Ibid., 49/18.

Chapter 12 *Commander Magnuson*

1. Magnuson Papers, 3181–2, 46/58; Scates, Firstbank, p. 87.

2. Magnuson Papers, 3181–2, 48/34.

3. Ibid., 49/4.

4. Ibid., 5/3–4; 3/5.

5. Ibid., 47/47; 48/41–42.

6. Ottanelli, *Communist Party of the United States,* p. 205.

7. Magnuson Papers, 3181–2, 46/47.

8. Ibid., 52/13–15.

9. Ibid., 49/26.

10. Ibid., 48/40; 49/6.

11. Ibid., 44 (Al Cohn letters).

12. Ibid., 49/43.

13. *Seattle Post-Intelligencer,* June 6, 1976.

14. Magnuson Papers, 3181–2, 49/46–47.

15. Ibid., 49/18.

16. David S. Wyman, *Paper Walls: America and the Refugee Crisis, 1938–1941* (Amherst: University of Massachusetts Press, 1968; New York: Pantheon Books, 1985), passim.

17. Magnuson Papers, 3181–1, 49/17, 49/41, 49/42.

18. Anna Joachim, interview, Seattle, March 22, 1994.

19. Merle Miller, *Lyndon, an Oral Biography* (New York: Putnam, 1980), pp. 89–90.

20. Magnuson Papers, 3181–2, 49; 56/20.

21. Ibid., 49/5.

22. Ibid., 51/19–20.

23. Ibid., 53; 54; 55/16; 56; Jermaine Magnuson interview, Seattle, May 9, 1994.

24. Jermaine Magnuson, interview, Seattle, February 21, 1994.

25. Magnuson Papers, 3181–2, 49/58; 51/10.

26. Ibid., 51/24; 49/55; 47/59; 50/1; 52/5.

27. Ibid., 49/57–59.

28. Ibid., 52/5; 49/55, 49/57, 49/59, 49/46, 49/58.

Chapter 13   *War, Politics, and McGoozle*

1. Magnuson Papers, 3181–2, 50/13.

2. Mitsuo Fuchida and Masatake Okumija, *Midway: The Battle That Doomed Japan: The Japanese Navy's Story* (New York: Ballantine Books, 1958); introduction by Nobutake Kondo, admiral, Imperial Japanese Navy (ret.), p. 10.

3. Magnuson Papers, 3181–2, 51/7.

4. Ibid., 49/54.

5. Ibid., 49/59.

6. Ibid., 51.

7. Ibid., 49/62.

8. Ibid., 49/64.

9. Ibid., 50/19.

10. Ibid., 51/23.

11. Ibid., 51/14.

12. Ibid., 51/5–6.

13. Ibid., 51/20.

14. Ibid., 51/10.

15. Ibid., 51/14.

16. Ibid., 51/16–17.

17. Ibid., 51/18.

18. Ibid., 51/23.

19. Ibid.

20. Alan Bullock, *Hitler and Stalin: Parallel Lives* (New York: Knopf, 1992), p. 542.

21. John Maxwell Hamilton, *Edgar Snow* (Bloomington: Indiana University Press, 1988), pp. 53, 115, 155. Conversations with William Henry, veteran, USMC Special Commando Battalion ("Carlson's Raiders"), Sequim, Washington, and William Glueck, Lt. Col. USMC (ret.), Seattle.

22. Magnuson Papers, 3181–2, 51/31.

23. Ibid., 51/32–33.

24. Ibid., 51/61.

25. *Mother and Daughter: The Letters of Eleanor and Anna Roosevelt,* ed. Bernard Asbell (New York: Coward, McCann and Geoghegan, 1982), pp. 159–62.

26. Magnuson Papers, 3181–2, 51/63.

27. Ibid., 51/36.

28. Ibid., 54/33.

29. Ibid., 58/37.

Chapter 14   *Senator Magnuson*

1. David McCullough, *Truman* (New York: Simon and Schuster, 1992), pp. 339–42.

2. Rosenblatt, interview.

3. Magnuson Papers, 3181–2, 167/32.

4. Magnuson Papers, 3181–3, 40/23.

5. Ibid., 47/43.

6. Ibid., 40/28.

7. Ibid., 41/10–11.

8. Ibid., 41/10, 41/11, 41/44.

9. Ibid., 167/62.

10. Ibid., 41/16.

11. *Truman in the White House: The Diary of Even A. Ayers,* ed. Robert H. Ferrell (Columbia: University of Missouri Press, 1991), pp. 78–79.

12. Magnuson Papers, 3181–3, 167.

13. Irv Hoff, interview, Hilton Head, South Carolina, June 4, 1994.

14. Magnuson Papers, 3181–2, 51/62.

15. Magnuson Papers, 3181–3, 167/3.

16. Scates, *Firstbank,* p. 95.

17. Richard Kirkendall, "Politics of the Boeing Company," undated manuscript, pp. 1, 2.

18. On the B-52: Magnuson Papers, 3181–3, 171/27–28, 40/25, 44/4.

19. Ibid., 179/50.

20. Senator Hugh B. Mitchell, interview, Seattle, January 11, 1994; Irv Hoff, interview, June 4, 1994.

21. Magnuson Papers, 3181–3, 41/31.

22. Ibid., 41/32.

23. Ibid., 168/10–11.

24. Ibid., 167; 168.

25. Ibid., 167/71.

26. Irv Hoff, interview, Hilton Head, South Carolina, October 5, 1995.

27. Magnuson Papers, 3181–3, 167/16, 167/32.

28. Hutton, Madame Chiang: ibid., 167/9, 167/16, 167/28–31.

Chapter 15   *The "Pol's Pol," the Playboy's Playboy*

1. Interviews: Norm Schut, Ocean Shores, Washington, February 17, 1994; Gerry Hoeck, Seattle, December 10, 1993, and April 6, 1994; Ancil Payne, Seattle, January 5, 1994; Joe Miller, Seattle, June 6, 1995, and December 5, 1995.

2. Magnuson Papers, 3181–3, 168/30–33.

3. Ibid., 168/24.

4. Irv Hoff, interview, October 5, 1995.

5. Magnuson Papers, 3181–3, 167/71.

6. *Yakima Republic,* October 8, 1946.

7. McCullough, *Truman,* pp. 541, 583.

8. Ibid., pp. 561–62.

9. Magnuson Papers, 3181–3, 172/1.

10. Ibid., 171/36.

11. *UW Health Sciences Review,* November 1978.

12. Joe Miller, interview, Washington, D.C., December 21, 1994.

13. *Seattle Post-Intelligencer,* October 31 to November 3, 1948.

14. McCullough, *Truman,* p. 695.

15. Magnuson Papers, 3181–3, 170/56.

16. Joe Miller, unpublished memoir, 1994, Washington, D.C.

17. Magnuson Papers, 3181–3, 172/17.

18. Musak, Las Vegas, Toni Seven, racetracks: ibid., 170/65; 171; 172/38; Carol Parker Cahill, interview.

19. Austine McDonald, Walter Winchell, June Millarde (Toni Seven): Magnuson Papers, 3181–3, 172; Irv Hoff, interview, October 5, 1995.

20. Magnuson Papers, 3181–3, 172/34, 172/52.

21. White House Oval Office tapes: Warren G. Magnuson file, LBJ Library, University of Texas, Austin.

Chapter 16   *Cold War, Monkey Business*

1. Bullock, *Hitler and Stalin,* passim.

2. Vern Countryman, *Un-American Activities in the State of Washington: The Work of the Canwell Committee* (Ithaca: Cornell University Press, 1951), passim.

3. Magnuson Papers, 3181–3, 172/46, 172/49.

4. Mrs. William (Marge) Edris, interview, Seattle, May 19, 1994.

5. Magnuson Papers, 3181–2, 40; Hugh Mitchell, interview.

6. Neal Gabler, *Winchell: Gossip, Power and the Culture of Celebrity* (New York: Knopf, 1994), passim.

7. Magnuson Papers, 3181–3, 173.

8. Ibid., 172/28–31, 172/46, 172/49.

9. Ibid., 136/32, 136/36.

10. McCullough, *Truman,* pp. 552–53.

11. Magnuson Papers, 3181–3, 173/59.

12. Warren G. Magnuson, interview, January 12–14, 1981.

13. Irv Hoff, interview, October 5, 1995; Carol Parker Cahill, interview.

14. W. F. Reid, Oral History, UW Archives.

15. Richard H. Rovere, *Senator Joe McCarthy* (New York: Harcourt, Brace, 1959), passim.

16. Irv Hoff, interviews; Gerry Hoeck, interview, Seattle, December 12, 1994.

17. Hoeck, interview; Miller, interview, Seattle, 1994.

18. Scott, "Arthur B. Langlie," preface and p. 247.

19. Magnuson, interview, January 12–14, 1981.

Chapter 17   *Maggie, Scoop, and Overdrafts*

1. Magnuson Papers, 3181–3, 182/11–13.

2. Ibid., 182/21.

3. Ibid., 181/8–9, 181/28–30.

4. Ibid., 171; 173/53, 173/55.

5. Ancil Payne, interview.

6. *Seattle Times,* July 14, 1978.

7. Robert O'Brien to Irv Hoff, March 4, 1948, Magnuson Papers, 3181–3, 184 (O'Brien letters).

8. Magnuson Papers, 3181–3, 181/23.

9. Ibid., 46/26.

10. Magnuson, interview, January 12–14, 1981.

11. Magnuson Papers, 3181–3, 47/38, 47/40.

12. Ibid., 174/18.

13. Magnuson, interview.

14. Magnuson Papers, 3181–3, 172/1.

15. Ibid., 169/71–73.

16. Jack Lait and Lee Mortimer, *USA Confidential* (New York: Crown Publishers, 1952), pp. x, 114, 123, 125–27.

17. *Spokane Spokesman-Review,* files, March 9, 1950, July 7, 1951, and August 1, 1951.

18. Magnuson Papers, 3181–3, 188/12.

19. Ibid., 177/44.

20. Ibid., 172.

21. Interviews: Payne, Mitchell; Magnuson Papers, 3181–3, 175.

22. Interviews: Payne, Miller, Hoeck.

23. Scott, "Arthur B. Langlie," p. iv.

24. Dr. Abraham Bergman, "The Washington Senators," unpublished recollections, Seattle, 1994.

25. Magnuson Papers, 3181–3, 191/29.

26. Warren G. Magnuson, Oral History, LBJ Library, Austin, Texas.

Chapter 18   *The Sinner and the Saint*

1. Norm Schut, interview.

2. Scott, "Arthur B. Langlie," pp. 441–42, 438.

3. Magnuson Papers, 3181–3, 197/30.

4. Richard Neuberger, *Adventures in Politics* (New York: Oxford University
Press, 1954), p. 193.

5. Magnuson Papers, 3181–3, 194/30–31.

6. Henry M. Jackson Papers, University of Washington Libraries, 3560–3,
270/10.

7. Magnuson Papers, 3181–3, 197.

8. Ibid., 198/4.

9. Interviews: Hoeck, Miller, Payne, Hoff.

10. Judge Charles Cone, interview, August 9, 1994.

11. Magnuson Papers, 3181–3, 197/34, 197/36.

12. Scott, "Arthur B. Langlie," p. iv.

13. Harry "Kid" Matthews, interview, Everett, Washington, December 5,
1995; Magnuson Papers, 3181–3, 178/6; 175.

14. Magnuson Papers, 3181–3, 179/26, 179/34.

15. Hoff, interview.

16. Magnuson Papers, 3181–3, 178; 179.

Chapter 19   *American Prime Time*

1. Magnuson Papers, 3181–4, 50/26.

2. John L. Gaddis, *Strategies of Containment* (New York: Oxford University
Press, 1982), passim.

3. Dr. Edward Wenk, interview, Seattle, March 20, 1995.

4. Hearst Newspapers, June 1959.

5. Manny Rouvelas, interview, Washington, D.C., May 8, 1995.

6. Magnuson Papers, 3181–4, 51/17.

7. Ibid., 50/22, 50/27.

8. *New York Times,* March 3, 1956.

9. Magnuson Papers, 3181–4, 50/12.

10. Brock Adams, interview, Washington, D.C., May 7, 1995.

11. Magnuson Papers, 3181–4, 50/9.

12. Magnuson Papers, 3181–3, 40/28.

13. Adams, interview.

14. Magnuson Papers, 3181–4, 52/17–18.

15. Ibid., 50/12.

16. *Annual Obituaries, 1983* (Chicago: St. James Press, 1983), p. 226.

17. Magnuson Papers, 3181–4, 52/19.

18. Interviews: Jerry Grinstein, Seattle, April 5, 1995, June 2, 1995, and August 16, 1995; Mike Pertschuk, Washington, D.C., May 10, 1995.

19. Irv Hoff, interview, June 1994.

20. W. Featherstone Reid, interview, Seattle, March 20, 1995.

21. Hoff, interview.

22. *Reader's Digest,* July 1953.

23. Magnuson file, LBJ Library, Austin, Texas.

24. Paul Nagle, "Hells Canyon Dam," manuscript, University of Washington Libraries, Special Collections, pp. 82–83.

25. Harry McPherson, interview, Washington, D.C., May 10, 1995.

26. Magnuson Papers, 3181–4, 52/17–18, 52/21, 52/34.

27. Ibid.

28. Ancil Payne, interview.

29. Hoff, interview.

30. Gordon Culp, interview, Seattle, March 23, 1995; Magnuson Papers, 3181–4, 54/15.

Chapter 20   *Camelot and Comeback*

1. Magnuson Papers, 3181–4, 54/1.

2. Peter Grose, *Gentleman Spy: The Life of Allen Dulles* (Boston: Houghton Mifflin, 1994), passim.

3. Magnuson Papers, 3181–4, 52/38.

4. Interviews: Brock Adams, Joe Miller, Washington, D.C., 1995.

5. Hoff, interview.

6. Magnuson Papers, 3181–4, 54/23–24.

7. Tom Foley, former Speaker of the U.S. House of Representatives, interview, Washington, D.C., May 9, 1995.

8. Miller, *Lyndon, an Oral Biography,* p. 253.

9. John Salter, interview, *Argus,* August 1964.

10. Theodore C. Sorensen, *Kennedy* (New York: Bantam Books, 1966), p. 184.

11. *Post-Intelligencer,* February 8, 1981; Magnuson, Oral History, Warren G. Magnuson file, LBJ Library, Austin, Texas.

12. Representative Norm Dicks, interview, Washington, D.C., May 10, 1995.

13. Magnuson Papers, 3181–4, 188/9–11.

14. *Common Sense;* ibid., 188.

15. Magnuson Papers, 3181–4, 76/18.

16. Ibid., 54/22.

17. Ibid.

18. Warren G. Magnuson, interview, Palm Springs, January 1981.

19. Magnuson Files, 3181–4, 54/2–3.

20. Magnuson, interview, January 1981.

21. Sam Volpentest, interview, Richland, Washington, March 24, 1995.

22. Magnuson Papers, 3181–4, 57/42–48.

23. Gerry Hoeck, interview, Seattle, 1994.

24. Edward Carlson, *Recollections of a Lucky Fellow* (Seattle, 1989).

25. Magnuson Papers, 3181–4, 57/21–22.

26. Ibid., 54.

27. Volpentest, interview.

28. Magnuson Papers, 3181–4, 50/20–22.

29. Ibid., 55/19.

Chapter 21 *Triumph, Cuba, and Trouble*

1. Magnuson Papers, 3181–4, 188/29.

2. Jermaine Magnuson, interviews, Seattle, February 21 and May 6, 1994.

3. *Time,* November 24, 1961.

4. Magnuson Papers, 3181–4, 188/31.

5. Ibid., 189/23.

6. Warren G. Magnuson file, Drew Pearson Papers, LBJ Library, University of Texas, Austin.

7. Dan Evans, interview, Seattle, May 23, 1995.

8. Magnuson Papers, 3181–4, 250/7.

9. Ibid., 189/2, 189/5–11, 189/24.

10. Ibid., 57/38.

11. Ibid., 59/27.

12. Ibid., 188/30.

13. Ibid., 189/31–32; 190/1–2.

14. Ibid., 189/24; see Christensen 1962 Campaign.

15. Ben Wolfe and Jack Zeigler, *Candidate Christensen* (Seattle: Evergreen Press, 1963).

16. Tom Keefe, interview, Seattle, September 28, 1995.

17. Brewster Denny, interview, Seattle, September 12, 1995.

18. Walter Straley, interview, Seattle, March 21, 1995; Magnuson file, Pearson Papers, LBJ Library.

19. Grinstein, interview, June 2, 1995.

20. Ralph Nader, interview, Washington, D.C., December 12, 1995.

21. Wenk, interview.

22. Magnuson Papers, 3181–4, 189/30.

23. Interviews: Mabel Thompson, Ephrata, Washington, and Harvey Vernier, Moses Lake, Washington, September 7–8, 1995.

24. Ex-Representative Al Swift, interview, Washington, D.C., May 11, 1995.

Chapter 22 *Bumblebees*

1. Jerry Grinstein, interview, Seattle, June 2, 1995.

2. Hedrick Smith, *The Power Game: How Washington Works* (New York: Ballantine Books, 1988), p. 237.

3. Mike Pertschuk, interview, Washington, D.C., May 11, 1995.

4. Adams, interview.

5. Warren G. Magnuson, interview, KVOS-TV, Bellingham, Washington, October 1971 (tape available, Magnuson Papers, University of Washington Libraries).

6. Interviews: Tom Allison and Jerry Grinstein, Seattle, June 2, 1995.

7. Swift, interview.

8. Ed Sheets, interview, Olympia, Washington, April 26, 1995.

9. Warren G. Magnuson, interview, Palm Springs, January 8, 1981; Eugene McCarthy, interview, en route by air between St. Paul and Missoula, December 1971.

10. Mabel Thompson, interview.

11. Magnuson Papers, 3181–4, 256/22–23.

12. Dicks, interview.

13. Michael Pertschuk, *Revolt Against Regulation: The Rise and Pause of the Consumer Movement* (Berkeley: University of California Press, 1982), pp. 12, 36.

14. Nader, interview.

15. Nard Jones, *Seattle* (Garden City, N.Y.: Doubleday, 1972), p. 223.

16. U.S. Senate Commerce Committee Reports, 89th Cong., March 22, 1965, Hearings [cigarettes], vol. 880, 405–980.

17. Pertschuk, *Revolt,* p. 36.

18. U.S. Senate Commerce Committee Reports, 89th Cong., Hearings on S. 985 [fair labeling], vol. 888, 54–1280.

19. Pertschuk, interview.

20. Frank Moss, ex-senator from Utah, interview, Washington, D.C., November 24, 1995.

21. Nader, interview.

22. Hoff, interview.

Chapter 23   *Civil Rights: The Whole Load of Hay Falls on Maggie*

1. Stan Barer, interviews, Seattle, April 20, 1994, June 23, 1994, and March 3, 1995.

2. Senator John F. Kennedy, interview (Scates), International News Service, November 1957, Dallas, Texas.

3. Richard Reeves, *President Kennedy: Profile of Power* (New York: Simon and Schuster, 1993), p. 528.

4. Magnuson Papers, 3181–3, 44/26.

5. Reprint, Congressional Record, 1963, no. 696–353-89531.

6. *Plessy v. Ferguson,* U.S. Supreme Court decisions, 1895.

7. U.S. Supreme Court decisions, 1883, Civil Rights Act of 1875.

8. Charles Ferris, ex–U.S. Senate secretary, interview, Washington, D.C., May 11, 1995.

9. Barer, interview.

10. U.S. Senate Commerce Committee, 88th Cong., Hearings on S. 1732, parts 1 and 2, July-August 1963.

11. Magnuson Papers, 3181–3, 60/34.

12. Warren G. Magnuson, Civil Rights file, LBJ Library, University of Texas, Austin.

13. Moss, interview.

14. Interviews: Barer, Reid.

15. Magnuson, Civil Rights file, LBJ Library.

16. Ferris, interview.

17. Magnuson, Civil Rights file, LBJ Library.

18. Supreme Court decisions, 1964.

Chapter 24   *The Sixties*

1. *Seattle Post-Intelligencer,* August 3, 1964.

2. Dan Evans, interview, Seattle, May 23, 1995.

3. Jackson on Vietnam: Jackson Papers, 3560–4, 231/23, 231/24–25, 231/52; 3560–5, 232/28, 232/21, 232/38.

4. Magnuson Papers, 3181–4, 79/10.

5. Adams, interview.

6. Magnuson on Vietnam: Magnuson Papers, 3181–4, 191/12.

7. Ibid., 194/14.

8. Ibid., 179/47–49.

9. Magnuson file, LBJ Library.

10. Magnuson Papers, 3181–4, 186/11–12.

11. Magnuson file, LBJ Library.

12. Magnuson Papers, 3181–4, 67/16–17.

13. Pertschuk, interview.

14. Barer, interview.

15. Magnuson Papers, 3181–4, 62/23.

16. Hoff, interview.

17. Philip Bailey, "As I See It," Argus (Seattle), February 1956; February 19, 1965, August 20, 1965.

18. Carsten Lien, *Olympic Battleground: The Power Politics of Timber Preservation* (San Francisco: Sierra Club Books, 1991), p. 356.

19. George Reedy, interview, Marquette University, Milwaukee, Wisconsin, October 24, 1994.

20. Magnuson file, LBJ Library.

21. Grinstein, interview.

22. George Christian, interview, Austin, Texas, October 12, 1994.

23. Jermaine Magnuson, interview, February 21, 1994.

24. Miller, *Lyndon, an Oral Biography,* pp. 408–12.

25. Magnuson file, LBJ Library.

26. Magnuson, Oral History, LBJ Library.

27. The quotation from Califano is taken from a plaque on the wall at the LBJ Library, Austin, Texas.

28. Magnuson file, LBJ Library.

29. Ibid.

30. Ibid.

31. Ibid.

32. Magnuson Papers, 3181–4, 64/37.

33. Ibid., 64; 192.

34. Scates, Hearst Newspapers, February and March 1968.

35. Barer, interview.

36. *Seattle Post-Intelligencer,* August 8, 1975.

Chapter 25 *Revival*

1. Magnuson Papers, 3181–4, 192/14–16.
2. Ibid., 192/4.
3. Pertschuk, interview.
4. Edward Wenk, interview, Seattle, July 14, 1995.
5. Grinstein, interview, Seattle, June 2, 1995.
6. Magnuson Papers, 3181–5, 10.
7. John Ehrlichman, interview, Atlanta, Georgia, August 17, 1995.
8. *Seattle Post-Intelligencer,* August 24, 1972.
9. Jerry Roschwalb, interview, Washington, D.C., May 9, 1995.
10. Dr. Jack Lein, interview, Seattle, April 7, 1995.
11. Volpentest, interview.
12. Bill First, interview, Spokane, Washington, May 20, 1994.
13. Magnuson Papers, 3181–5, 58/17.
14. Lein, interview; Hank Soike, interview, Aberdeen, Washington, April 7, 1995.
15. Magnuson file, LBJ Library.
16. Dicks, interview.
17. Rouvelas, interview.
18. *Year by Year: 75 Years of Boeing History, 1916–1991* (Seattle: Boeing Historical Archives, 1991).
19. Warren G. Magnuson, interview, Washington, D.C., June 26, 1969.
20. Dicks, interview.
21. Swift, interview.
22. Magnuson Papers, 3181–5, 20.
23. Rouvelas, interview.

Chapter 26 *"Scoop and Maggie"*

1. Pearson Papers, LBJ Library.
2. Benedetto Croce, *Aesthetic as Science of Expression and General Linguistic,* 2d ed. (London: Macmillan, 1922), passim.
3. Interviews: Hoff, Hodde, Olympia, 1994.
4. Gerry Johnson, interviews, Seattle, July 25, 1995, and August 10, 1995.
5. Peter J. Ognibene, *Scoop: The Life and Politics of Henry M. Jackson* (New York: Stein and Day, 1975), p. 100.
6. Interviews: Foley, Swift, Adams.
7. Scates for *Seattle Post-Intelligencer,* October 1970.
8. Harry McPherson, *A Political Education* (Boston: Little, Brown, 1972), p. 39.
9. John Ehrlichman, interview, Atlanta, September 26, 1995.
10. Jackson Papers, University of Washington Libraries, 3560–5, 232/18, 232/21, 232/38.
11. Stimson Bullitt, *River Dark and Bright* (Seattle: Willows Press, 1995), p. 165.
12. Ibid., pp. 169–70.

13. Jackson Papers, 3560–4, see "ABM" folder 5. Interviews: Grinstein, Barer, Dicks.

14. Magnuson Papers, 3181–5, 151/19.

15. Ancil Payne, interview.

16. Ognibene, *Scoop,* pp. 108–9; John Finney, interview, Washington, D.C., May 11, 1995.

17. Mike Layton, *Argus,* July 1970.

18. *Seattle Times,* editorials, August 11, 1969, and August 22, 1973.

19. Magnuson, private conversation with author, Washington, D.C., November 1971.

20. Foley, interview, May 9, 1995.

21. Dicks, interview.

22. Magnuson Papers, 3181–5, 56/32, 56/37. The letter is otherwise undated but was probably written in 1967.

23. Dicks, interview, May 10, 1995; Senator Ted Kennedy, private conversation with author, December 1970.

24. Bergman, interview, Seattle, September 12, 1994.

25. *Seattle Post-Intelligencer,* December 18, 1970.

26. *Seattle Post-Intelligencer,* December 17, 1970.

27. Magnuson, private conversation with author.

28. Salter, comment to the author, Washington, D.C., December 5, 1970.

29. Interviews: H. W. Whittington and Clyde Lince (Boeing), Seattle, July 1994.

30. Barer, interview.

31. Bergman, interview, March 1994.

32. *Seattle Post-Intelligencer,* July 11, 1994.

Chapter 27   *The Prime of Public Interest*

1. *Seattle Times,* October 20 and 21, 1973.

2. Barer, interview.

3. Magnuson Papers, 3181–5, 60/36–38; 146.

4. Ibid.

5. Jermaine Magnuson, interview, 1994.

6. Letter from R. Michael McReynolds, Textual Reference Division, U.S. National Archives, College Park, Maryland. The letter is undated but refers to an inquiry of May 1995 from this writer.

7. Gerald Johnson, interview, Seattle, June 1995.

8. Dicks, interview.

9. Tom Allison, interviews, Seattle, July 27, 1995, and August 10, 1995.

10. Barer, interview.

11. *Seattle Post-Intelligencer,* August 24, 1972.

12. John Ehrlichman, *Witness to Power: The Nixon Years* (New York: Simon and Schuster, 1982), pp. 191, 197–98.

13. *Seattle Post-Intelligencer,* June 21, 1973.

14. Interviews: Allison, Johnson, Grinstein, Seattle, 1995.

15. David Kirkwood Hart, interview, Brigham Young University, Provo, Utah, July 29, 1995.

16. Dr. David Dale, interview, University of Washington Medical School, Seattle, October 12, 1995.

17. Representative Jack Metcalf, interview, Washington, D.C., August 2, 1995.

Chapter 28   *The Great Dictator*

1. *Wall Street Journal,* April 2, 1965.

2. Interviews: Allison, Johnson.

3. Mike McCormack, interview, Richland, Washington, September 12, 1995; Louis Guzzo, interview, Seattle, September 15, 1995.

4. Magnuson Papers, 3181–5, 253/42–43; 231. Magnuson file, LBJ Library.

5. Magnuson, interview, January 1981.

6. Interviews: Allison, Johnson, Seattle, September 15, 1995, October 20, 1995.

7. State Representative C. W. Beck, interview, Olympia, Washington, February 1977.

8. Dick Ford, interview, Seattle, July 27, 1995.

9. Interviews: Adams, Allison, Johnson.

10. Mark Riese, interview, Seattle, September 11, 1995.

11. Governor Mike Lowry Papers, University of Washington Libraries, 000-87-0003.

12. Ed Sheets, interview, Olympia, Washington, April 26, 1995.

13. Lieutenant Governor Joel Pritchard, interview, Olympia, January 20, 1994.

14. Mike McCormack, interview, September 12, 1995.

15. Adams, interview, September 13, 1995.

16. Tom Keefe, interview, Seattle, September 28, 1995.

17. *Seattle Post-Intelligencer,* June 15, 1980.

18. Guzzo, interview.

Chapter 29   *A Time to Go*

1. Interviews: Dr. Jack Lein and Dr. David Dale, University of Washington Medical School, October 12, 1995.

2. Tom Keefe, interview, Seattle, September 28, 1995.

3. Terry Lierman, interview, Washington, D.C., October 17, 1995.

4. Magnuson Papers, 3181–5, 234.

5. Lierman, interview.

6. Magnuson Papers, 3181–5, 235.

7. Keefe, interview.

8. *Seattle Post-Intelligencer,* January 14, 1979.

9. Dr. Dale, interview, Seattle, October 12, 1995.

10. Irv Hoff, interview, Hilton Head, South Carolina, October 6, 1995.

11. Duayne Trecker, interview, Bellingham, Washington, October 23, 1995.

12. *Seattle Post-Intelligencer,* November 1, 1971; Pertschuk, interview.

13. U.S. Treasury Department reports for FY 1980 and FY 1988.

14. Senator Jackson, private conversation with author.

15. *Seattle Post-Intelligencer,* November 6, 1980.

16. Keefe, interview.

Chapter 30   *Coming Home: The Green Light*

1. Interview, *Seattle Post-Intelligencer,* February 8, 1981.

2. Ibid.

3. Magnuson, interview, January 1981.

4. Culp, interview, Seattle, March 23, 1995.

5. *Seattle Times,* editorial page, September 3, 1977.

6. *Seattle Post-Intelligencer,* August 21, 1982.

7. Jermaine Magnuson, interview, November 30, 1993.

8. Haley, *Dorothy Stimson Bullitt,* pp. 320, 330.

9. Fitzgerald, *The Last Tycoon.*

Index

McGee, Gale, 192, 193, 202, 203, 219
McGovern, George, 273, 289, 318
McKeller, K. D., 138
McNamara, Robert, 239
McNary, Charles, 122, 124
McNary Dam, 185
McPherson, Harry, 186, 187, 272
Meeds, Lloyd, 216, 271
Meehan, Jack, 84
Merlis, Ed, 214, 304
Messick, Hank, 78
Metcalf, Jack, 255, 293
Meyers, Victor A., 45, 91, 164
Mickelwait, Lowell, 279
Microsoft, 320
Midway, 104
Millarde, June (Toni Seven), 80, 138, 139, 140, 144, 168, 171, 174, 188, 315
Miller, Joe, 136, 138, 152, 165, 173, 194
Miller, McKay, Hoeck and Hartung, 199
Mills, Wilbur, 5, 265
Minow, Newton, 156
Mintz, Morton, 219
Mitchell, Hugh B., 113, 124, 125, 130, 136, 145, 151, 155, 161, 163, 164, 165, 319
Mondale, Walter, 324
Morgan, Linda, 300
Morgan, Robert, 318
Morrison, Zelma, 193
Morse, Wayne, 204, 240
Morton, Thruston, 222, 223
Moss, Frank, 219, 222, 234
Mount St. Helens, 298
Mudd, Roger, 236
Mundt, Karl, 145
Municipal League News, 31
Music, Inc., 138
Muskie, Ed, 202
Mussolini, Benito, 50
Myers, Francis, 152

Nader, Ralph, 3, 209, 213, 224, 296
National Airlines, 180

National Association of Manufacturers, 223
National Environmental Protection Act, 259
National Institutes of Health, 135, 169, 260, 261
National Maritime Union, 146
National Oceanographic and Atmospheric Administration (NOAA), 179
National Security Resources Board, 162
Naval Affairs Committee, 66, 94
NBC, 192
Nelson, Gaylord, 219, 318
Nelson, Sharon, 214
Nelson, Stub, 174
Neslund, Rolf, 299
Neuberger, Maurine, 214, 219
Neuberger, Richard, 94, 169
Newell, Gordon, 34
Newgard, George R., 104
Newsweek, 101, 137
New Yorker, 212
New York Herald, 35
New York Herald Tribune, 59
New York Journal, 35
New York Mirror, 139, 161
New York Sun, 35
New York Times, 171, 179
Nicolai, Max, 102
Niedfelt, M. A., 80
Nimitz, Adm. Chester, 97, 100
Nitze, Paul, 239
Nixon, Richard, 86, 152, 171, 178, 183, 191, 288
Northern Pacific, 19
Northern Transcontinental Airways Association, 42
Northwest Airlines, 30, 41–44, 48, 87, 122, 123, 144, 155, 172–73, 326
Northwest News Company, 85, 173
Northwest Power Planning Council, 303

Oak Ridge, Tennessee, 117
O'Brien, John L., 5